Ulster political lives 1886–1921

Edited by James Quinn and Patrick Maume

Ulster political lives, 1886–1921

First published 2016
Royal Irish Academy, 19 Dawson Street, Dublin 2
www.ria.ie

Text, James Maguire and James Quinn (eds), *Dictionary of Irish Biography*, © Royal Irish
Academy 2009, published by Cambridge University Press, reproduced with permission

ISBN 978-1-908996-85-5

During the production process some photographs and illustrations have been retouched
for aesthetic purposes. Every effort has been made to trace the copyright holders of these
items and to ensure the accuracy of their captions. See Photo Credits.

British Library Cataloguing in Publication Data. A CIP catalogue record for this book is
available from the British Library.

Editor: Helena King
Design: Fidelma Slattery
Picture research: Anne Rosenbusch and Jeff Wilson
Index: Eileen O'Neill

Printed in Poland by Przedsiebiorstwo Uslugowo Produkcyjne INTROKAR Karina Luczak

This publication has received support from

An Roinn Ealaíon, Oidhreachta,
Gnóthaí Réigiúnacha, Tuaithe agus Gaeltachta
Department of Arts, Heritage,
Regional, Rural and Gaeltacht Affairs

ÉIRE 19·16 Clár Comórtha
IRELAND 20 Céad Bliain
Centenary
Programme

An Roinn Gnóthaí Eachtracha agus Trádála
Department of Foreign Affairs and Trade

Ulster political lives 1886–1921

Contents

Chronology

1870

19 May: Home rule movement launched by Isaac Butt in Dublin

1871

1 January: Gladstone's Irish Church Act, disestablishing the Church of Ireland, comes into effect

1877

28 August: Charles Stewart Parnell replaces Butt as president of the Home Rule Confederation of Great Britain

1879

21 October: Irish National Land League founded in Dublin

1881

22 August: Gladstone's Land Act grants fair rent, fixity of tenure and free sale to Irish tenant farmers

1883

26 January: Ulster Land Committee formed in Belfast to represent the province's tenant-right associations

1884

6 December: Representation of the People Act enfranchises small farmers and labourers, more than tripling the Irish electorate to 740,000

1885

1 May: Irish Loyal and Patriotic Union formed to defend the union with Great Britain

November–December: UK general election; the Liberals are the largest party but narrowly fail to win an overall majority; 85 Irish nationalist MPs hold the balance of power

17 December: Gladstone's conversion to home rule for Ireland revealed

1886

8 April: Gladstone introduces home rule bill in House of Commons

4–10 June: Riots in Belfast against home rule

8 June: Home rule bill defeated in Commons; opposed by 93 Liberals

July: UK general election; Conservatives and unionists win a majority; Salisbury becomes prime minister

1890

December: Irish parliamentary party splits into pro- and anti-Parnell factions

1891

6 October: Death of Parnell

1892

17 June: Ulster unionist convention in Botanic Gardens, Belfast, resolves to oppose home rule

July: UK general election; the Liberals are the largest party but need Irish nationalist support to form a government

1893

13 February: Gladstone introduces second home rule bill in Commons

21–22 April: Riots in Belfast against home rule

2 September: Home rule bill passes third reading in Commons

9 September: Home rule bill defeated by 419 to 41 votes in Lords

1894

3 March: Gladstone resigns

1895

July: UK general election; Conservatives and Liberal unionists form a government

1898

12 August: Local Government (Ireland) Act, provides for the creation of elected county and district councils

1899

11 October: Outbreak of Boer war (ends 31 May 1902)

1900

6 February: John Redmond elected leader of re-united Irish parliamentary party

1903

11 June: Independent Orange Order formed in Belfast

1904

2 December: Ulster unionist MPs form Ulster Unionist Council in Belfast

1905

8 March: Bulmer Hobson founds first Dungannon club in Belfast

1906

January: UK general election; Liberals win comfortable overall majority; Irish nationalists win 82 seats, Irish unionists 20

April: Ulster Liberal Association founded, with backing from W. J. Pirrie of Harland and Wolff

1907

6 May: Strike of dockers in Belfast begins a series of strikes organised by James Larkin of the National Union of Dock Labourers

5 September: Nationalist groups unite to form Sinn Féin under the leadership of Arthur Griffith

1908

1 August: Irish Universities Act replaces the Royal University with a National University based in Dublin and Queen's University of Belfast

1909

10 December: H. H. Asquith, the Liberal prime minister, promises 'self-government' for Ireland

1910

January: UK general election; the Liberals need the support of John Redmond's 70-strong Irish parliamentary party to govern

21 February: Sir Edward Carson elected leader of Irish unionists in Commons

December: Another UK general election; Liberals still the largest party with Irish parliamentary party holding the balance of power

1911

23 January: Ulster Women's Unionist Council formed

18 August: Parliament Act restricts House of Lords' veto to 2 years

21 August: Irish Women's Suffrage Federation founded

23 September: Massive unionist demonstration against home rule in Belfast addressed by Carson

1912

8 February: Winston Churchill and John Redmond address pro-home rule rally at Celtic Park in Belfast

9 April: At a unionist demonstration at Balmoral, near Belfast, Andrew Bonar Law, leader of the Conservative party, pledges the support of British unionists to resistance to home rule

11 April: Asquith introduces third home rule bill in Commons

28 September: Unionists throughout Ulster sign the Solemn League and Covenant to resist home rule

1913

16, 30 January: Third reading of home rule bill carried in Commons, but defeated in Lords

31 January: Ulster Volunteer Force founded

15 July: After passing in Commons, home rule bill again defeated in Lords

17 September: Ulster Unionist Council appoints 'provisional government', chaired by Carson, to come into effect if home rule bill becomes law

25 November: Irish Volunteers formed at meeting in Dublin, presided over by Eoin MacNeill

1914

20 March: 'Curragh mutiny'— Most officers of the 3rd Cavalry Brigade announce their unwillingness to enforce home rule on Ulster

24–25 April: UVF gun-running: large quantity of rifles landed at Larne, Co. Antrim, and Donaghadee and Bangor, Co. Down

25 May: Home rule bill passes through Commons for third time

23 June: Government introduces bill in Lords to provide for temporary exclusion from home rule for individual Ulster counties

28 June: Assassination of Archduke Franz Ferdinand and his wife by a Slav nationalist in Sarajevo, Bosnia

10 July: Ulster unionist provisional government meets in Belfast

21–4 July: Government, nationalists and unionists fail to reach agreement on the status of Ulster at Buckingham Palace conference

26 July: Rifles for Irish Volunteers landed at Howth

4 August: UK declares war on Germany after German invasion of Belgium

18 September: Suspensory Act suspends the introduction of home rule for the duration of the war

1915

25 May: Carson joins Asquith's coalition cabinet as attorney general, but Redmond refuses to take office

1916

24 April: Irish Volunteers and Irish Citizen Army mount insurrection in Dublin; they surrender on 30 April

3–12 May: Executions of insurgent commanders

12 June: Ulster Unionist Council agrees to implementation of home rule, with 6 Ulster counties temporarily excluded

1 July: Somme offensive begins; 36th (Ulster) Division suffers heavy casualties

20 July: Public meeting in Derry leads to formation of Anti-Partition League (later Irish Nation League)

24 July: Redmond repudiates government's partition proposals

1917

25 July: Irish Convention meets in Dublin; opposed by Sinn Féin and Ulster unionists

1918

6 February: Parliamentary franchise given to all men over 21 and most women over 30

11 November: Great War ends

14–28 December: UK General election won by Conservatives; Sinn Féin wins 73 of 105 Irish seats, Ulster unionists win 26

1919

21 January: First meeting of Dáil Éireann at Mansion House, Dublin, declares Ireland's independence; Irish Volunteer attack on RIC at Soloheadbeg, Co. Tipperary, kills two policemen and begins the war of independence

1920

20 March: Ulster Unionist Council accepts Government of Ireland Bill, which provides for two subordinate Irish parliaments: one for six Ulster counties, the other for the remainder of the country

23 December: Government of Ireland Act passed

1921

4 February: Carson resigns as leader of Ulster unionists and is replaced by Sir James Craig

24 May: Northern Ireland general election; unionists win 40 seats, nationalists 6 and Sinn Féin 6

22 June: George V opens Northern Ireland parliament in Belfast

9 July: Truce ends Irish war of independence

9–15 July: Over 20 killed in serious disturbances in Belfast

6 December: Anglo–Irish treaty signed by British government and Sinn Féin delegates in London; border between Irish Free State and Northern Ireland to be settled by a Boundary Commission

1922

14 January: Irish Free State provisional government elected by pro-treaty representatives

21 January: Michael Collins meets Craig and agrees to end boycott against northern businesses

12–15 February: 27 killed in gun battles between IRA and opposing forces in Belfast

31 May: RUC established

28 June: Free State troops attack anti-treaty forces in Four Courts, beginning the civil war

6 December: Formal establishment of Irish Free State with W. T. Cosgrave as president of the executive council

7 December: Both houses of Northern Ireland parliament agree to opt out of Irish Free State

1923

24 May: Éamon de Valera orders anti-treatyites to cease armed operations, ending the civil war

6 November: First meeting of the Boundary Commission in London

1925

3 December: UK, Northern Ireland and Free State governments agree to revoke powers of Boundary Commission; existing border to be maintained

1931

11 December: Statute of Westminster grants constitutional independence to Commonwealth dominions

1939

3 September: Britain and France declare war on Germany; de Valera announces his government's intention to remain neutral

1945

14 November: Irish Anti-Partition League formed in Dungannon, Co. Tyrone

1946

19 February: National Insurance Act applies British welfare legislation to Northern Ireland

1949

18 April: Ireland declares itself a republic and leaves the Commonwealth

1956

12 December: IRA begins its 'border campaign', which lasts until 1962

1965

14 January: Taoiseach Seán Lemass and Prime Minister of Northern Ireland, Terence O'Neill, meet in Belfast, leading to improved co-operation between the two governments

1968

October: Civil rights demonstrations in Belfast and Derry

22 November: Terence O'Neill announces proposals for reform

1969

28 April: O'Neill resigns as prime minster after growing demonstrations and violence

July-August: Sectarian clashes and rioting in Belfast and Derry; British troops on the streets

1971

9 August: Reintroduction of internment without trial in Northern Ireland

1972

24 March: British government suspends Northern Ireland parliament and introduces direct rule from Westminster

Introduction

The crooked road to partition

Any introduction to Ulster politics in the period covered by this collection must skirt several pitfalls. One may be called Ulster nationalism: the assumption that partition was more or less inevitable and that the pre-partition era can be treated with minimal reference to events in the rest of Ireland, as if the Northern Ireland state existed decades before its formal creation. Another is the presentation of Ulster politics simply in terms of two communities; the fact that the Catholic/nationalist versus Protestant/unionist division predominated should not obscure the existence of other groups and mindsets seeking to reshape Ulster society, and the need to analyse the triumph of some agendas over others, rather than simply taking that triumph for granted. A third pitfall is the tendency for supporters of one viewpoint to assume that its opponents were self-evidently delusional and need not be taken seriously. No analysis should avoid the flaws, blindnesses and self-seeking involved in certain political viewpoints and agendas, but these must be faced rather than invoking sophistries or citing exceptional cases to evade central issues.

This introduction tries to contextualise Ulster politics in the period 1885–1925, first by sketching major themes of the region's nineteenth-century political development, then discussing how these tensions worked themselves out between Gladstone's conversion to home rule in 1885 and the abandonment of the Boundary Commission in 1925. The Ulster in question is not the six-county 'Ulster' created as Northern Ireland in 1920, but the nine-county province. Carson's Ulster Volunteers were a nine-county force, and the retreat to six counties after 1916 was regarded by Cavan, Monaghan and Donegal unionists and by their six-county sympathisers as a bitter betrayal of the Ulster Covenant.

Two cities

The interpretation of nineteenth-century Ulster history as the pre-history of partition is not necessarily fallacious. Evidence can be cited in its favour: as early as 1833, the British whig litterateur Thomas Macaulay argued that every argument in favour of Repeal could justify an Ulster parliament, which he assumed would be based in Derry. This assumption rested on the historic memory of the siege city, whose resistance Macaulay himself celebrated for a wider British readership with an enthusiasm that led to the saying that describing the siege of Derry after Macaulay was like describing the siege of Troy after Homer, and which led Orangemen to cite Macaulay (excising Macaulay's criticism of the unseemly and provocative manner in which they celebrated these triumphs).

Even as Macaulay spoke, however, the growing industrial city on the Lagan outpaced Derry, with the overspill of shipbuilding and engineering from the Clyde adding to an older-established textile industry resembling the mills of Lancashire. Around these, and their financial, commercial and professional spin-offs, rose the imposing spectacle of Victorian Belfast with its nexus of world-class firms (and its slums and ghettoes, which philanthropists and controversialists publicised). At the same time, the migration of Catholic labourers from east Tyrone and south Ulster, and of Presbyterians from Antrim and Down, created the settlement patterns that shaped the city's sectarian divisions for the next two centuries, with Catholic settlements to the north and east of the city centre, and particularly along the great artery of the Falls Road in the west, surrounded by Protestant districts, with boundaries blurring in times of peace and reasserted sharply during riots. The Ulster question was not reducible to Belfast, but the burgeoning industrial city lay at its centre, with its web of satellite factory towns in east Ulster and its growing net of transport links (which some hoped might be finalised by a tunnel under the North Channel to Scotland) tying it to the political and economic modernity of empire in an 'Irish Sea triangle' with Glasgow and Liverpool.

The fact that Presbyterians predominated in Antrim and Down, and were increasingly conspicuous in Belfast, while Scottish Presbyterian identity was at its highest point of cultural prestige and the Scots role in industry and empire was seen as vindicating the Anglo-Scots union of 1707, contributed to this sense of Ulster as Imperial Province and the Ulsterman as distinctly Presbyterian. In 1921, when discussing the negotiations for the Anglo-Irish treaty with the editor of the *Scotsman*, the former Conservative leader Andrew Bonar Law (born in Canada of Coleraine parents) explained why he would if necessary challenge Lloyd George's government for the sake of Ulster unionists, but not for southern unionists. He recalled how in his earlier career as a Glasgow businessman he frequently visited Ulster and it seemed to him that the people in Belfast resembled Glaswegians more than the people of Edinburgh did (Glasgow of course had a large Irish-Catholic minority), whereas Dublin felt like a foreign country.

The symbolism of Derry also shifted during the nineteenth century, as Protestant in-migration from west Tyrone, the Laggan district of East Donegal and eastern Londonderry was outweighed by the Catholic influx from Donegal and Tyrone, its political weight increasing as formal Catholic disability became harder to defend. The commercial district and walled Anglican cathedral city, still Protestant-dominated, defied a new siege from an army of the dispossessed in the Bogside. The Catholic institutional assertion of a rival claim to the heritage of St Colmcille in the construction of St Eugene's cathedral and prominent educational institutions was matched by the new Apprentice Boys' Hall, and by the erection of Governor Walker's statue in defiance of the Bogside during the last struggles over Catholic emancipation. For much of the nineteenth century a third narrative, of predominantly Presbyterian liberalism trying to recruit Catholic support in a common struggle against Anglican privilege, was represented by such figures as the tenant-right editor of the *Derry Standard*, James MacKnight.

With the electoral rise of Parnellism in the 1880s and the formation of a unionist alliance, independent liberalism largely disappeared as a political factor in Derry. Continued unionist political dominance was only secured, on a fine balance, by the residual weight of property in an electoral system still short of complete manhood suffrage, and by divisions within nationalism between local clericalist practitioners of quiescent brokerage politics (usually backed by the Catholic bishop) and advocates of

3

affiliation to a strong, island-wide, nationalist movement whose political leverage might overbear unionist power and deliver the political kingdom. (Nationalists might have gained control of Derry Corporation in 1899 and retained the parliamentary seat after 1900 but for the refusal of the national Dillonite faction to co-operate with Healyite Derry MPs.) The fact that the two principal unionists to represent the city seat in this period were a lawyer who became a judge through his political activities and the future third duke of Abercorn (whose mansion at Baronscourt was the centre of similar knife-edge battles for the north Tyrone seat) reinforced the nationalist image of unionism as an ancient regime secured by corruption of apostate liberals—if Derry with west and south Ulster, rather than Belfast and East Ulster, were seen as its microcosm. The Scots-Ulster ancestry some unionists claimed in West Ulster derived from the Scottish borderers familiar to Edwardian schoolboys through Sir Walter Scott, as well as from the Presbyterian reformers.

The crisis of the *ancien régime*

The nationalist view of Ulster unionism as simply an extension of the *ancien régime*, and of rank-and-file unionists as dupes of an exploitative elite was exaggerated, but not invented out of whole cloth. It is important to remember the high visibility in the nineteenth century of a Church of Ireland Ulster, centred on the ecclesiastical metropolis of Armagh (whose passing-over for the Queen's College in favour of Presbyterian Belfast had a certain symbolic resonance) and the great houses of Fermanagh (the most Church of Ireland county, where Presbyterians are less numerous than Methodists), whose social network extended into neighbouring counties to encompass the Saundersons and Farnhams of Cavan and the Maddens of Monaghan.

The novelist Shan Bullock (1865–1935) whose father was steward on the Crom Castle estate of the Earls of Erne on the Fermanagh–Cavan boundary, captures many of the paradoxes of this milieu: the Ernes are presented both as the natural leaders of their Protestant tenants in a deeply divided society (they even maintained an unofficial yeomanry corps, long after the yeomanry had been officially disbanded, which can be seen as linking older plantation paramilitary structures to the later Ulster Volunteer Force and B-Specials) and as utterly exotic and remote from Protestant small farmers who had more in common with the Catholic neighbours with whom they lived in suspicious co-existence. Cavan was 'th'inimy's country' yet the principal market town was Belturbet, just over the Cavan boundary. The everyday co-operation of Protestant and Catholic in rural Ulster led some observers to argue that there was no real division between them, yet Bullock, like Rosemary Harris (whose *Prejudice and tolerance in Ulster*, based on research in Aughnacloy in South Tyrone in the 1950s, is the classic academic study of this phenomenon) knew that this co-operation was structured by hidden rules, and that under certain conditions the communities could be pulled apart with horrific violence, as was to happen in 1914–23.

The fate of the Saunderson family, who left Castle Saunderson in Co. Cavan after unsuccessfully trying to persuade the Ulster Unionist Council in 1916 to stand by the three-county unionists, the raids conducted by Monaghan IRA men into Fermanagh during the war of independence under the direction of Eoin O'Duffy, and the mobilisation of Protestant self-defence vigilantes in the county under the leadership of Basil Brooke illustrate the cost in this particular border region of the form eventually taken by partition.

For most of the nineteenth century Ulster conservatism was led by a network of gentry families across south Ulster, from Donegal to south Down, feeling increasingly under siege from nationalism and liberalism. This elite drew on the residual military structures of the Ulster Plantation, with the Orange Order as a focus for socialisation and paramilitary self-assertion and official law-enforcement and administration blurring into these structures. During the nineteenth century the social, military and patronage structures of the Plantation were rolled up along their edges like a scroll, not merely by the mobilisation of the Catholic population but by tensions between Protestant-paternalist 'moral economy' and the demands made by marketisation, new standards of social and political respectability, the partial marginalisation of political Protestantism and the growth of professional administration at the expense of older local and aristocratic structures.

Orangeism was officially suppressed in the 1820s and 1830s but survived at local level and later regenerated. Its history was marked by a recurring sense that 'official' toryism and aristocratic Orangeism—centred as much in Dublin as in Ulster—did not genuinely hold Protestant principles as understood by plebeian Orangemen, but exploited them as stepping-stones to maintain their own positions and obtain well-paid official positions for relatives and protégés. As the land issue became more prominent, independent Conservative candidates (often small landlords), stood against official candidates in Ulster, appealing to a combination of tenant-right activism and Orangeism. Edward Saunderson, the first leader of Ulster unionism as a (relatively) autonomous party, began as a Palmerstonian liberal MP for his native Cavan and critic of the Orange Order. After losing his seat he reinvented himself as an Orange conservative during the land war of the early 1880s. He asserted his claim to leadership by displacing a law officer of the (conservative) Dublin Castle administration as candidate for North Armagh in 1885, appealing to grassroots fears that Ulster conservatives were regarded as expendable by the official leadership.

William Johnston of Ballykilbeg, the small Co. Down landowner who set himself up as the political embodiment of Orangeism and political Protestantism—going to prison for defying legislation against party processions and winning a Belfast seat from an official Conservative in the 1868 election—reflected a more intensive form of such discontent. One reason for the lasting popularity of Johnston among rank-and-file Orangemen was their awareness that he identified with them to the point of going to jail himself; the official leadership wanted nothing to do with them when they got in trouble. Johnston's career also marks the difficulty of creating a lasting organisation on such a basis; after his spending on political Protestantism brought insolvency, he was bought off by Disraeli's government with a civil service job. Although Johnston returned to parliament from 1885 until his death in 1902 as mascot of an Orangeism 'respectabilised' as a means of mobilisation against the nationalist threat, he was no longer an independent political force. The next major Orange-populist revolt, which produced the Independent Orange Order under Lindsay Crawford and T. H. Sloan from 1902, denounced Johnston as having betrayed the principles he set out to establish.

The Liberal challenge

From the 1860s, with expansion of the franchise under the second reform act, tory dominance in Ulster was challenged by liberal appeals to tenant farmers, to Presbyterian resentment at the association of conservatism with landed power and the Church of Ireland. Liberalism in the southern provinces in this era was badly organised, often represented at parliamentary level by landlords, placehunters and carpetbaggers, and had little sense of a separate identity from conservative nationalism. Thus, it was easily swallowed by it at times of political mobilisation (though radical nationalists thought the assimilation worked both ways). Liberalism in the north had a stronger sense of identity and a genuine popular base. It had older roots in Belfast among a Presbyterian mercantile elite, who found expression in the *Northern Whig* newspaper from the 1820s and tried unsuccessfully to take control of the borough after the 1832 reform act. Most Ulster boroughs had similar oppositional liberal groups opposed to the dominant local interest. The fall of a Belfast seat to a Liberal in 1868 (through a secret pact with Johnston) was seen as a major breakthrough, but subsequent liberal gains in 1874 and 1880 were predominantly in the counties; it was strongest in north Antrim and east Down.

The failure of Ulster liberalism to secure what many regarded as an inevitable triumph derived from a number of factors. Presbyterians and businessmen did not necessarily see themselves in Cobdenite terms as warring against Anglican feudalism; major business dynasties assimilated with the landed and professional classes; sections of Presbyterianism were attracted to a pan-Protestant alliance against the perceived Catholic threat; liberals relied on Catholic voters but rarely recruited Catholic candidates, and most Ulster Catholics defected to nationalism once this became a serious political alternative; the 1884 reform act enfranchised Orange and Catholic labourers and smallholders to outweigh middle-class liberalism. Indeed, in some instances up to 1885, nationalists and conservatives formed a tacit alliance to undercut liberalism. When liberalism split in 1885–6, Ulster liberal unionists were very much junior partners, though their ideological and organisational contribution should not be underestimated. The Belfast businessman

Thomas Sinclair, who eventually drafted the Ulster Covenant, was a leading organiser and publicist of the campaigns against home rule. *Northern Whig* editor Thomas MacKnight, former associate of Gladstone and consistent enemy of Disraeli, in his history-memoir *Ulster as it is* (1896) opposed the Gladstonian claim that home rule was the logical culmination of the liberal tradition of Irish reform with the rejoinder that liberal reforms were made possible by the union with Britain, and without the union reform would have triggered anew the extreme violence of 1798, whose potential recurrence was signalled by the irruption of sectarian riots in Belfast. Well into the twentieth century, MacKnight's book remained a resource for those seeking more liberal forms of unionism.

Other forms of political activism grew out of the liberal milieu. The women's suffrage movement developed as an extension of the philanthropic and educational activities of predominantly Protestant upper and middle-class women, linked to a wider British milieu of liberal evangelical social reformism. The major late-Victorian Belfast suffragist, Isabella Tod, became a prominent figure on liberal unionist platforms during the Gladstonian conflict. William Johnston included support for women's suffrage among his radical positions (possibly calculating that women, being more religious, would be more reliable Protestant voters). In the Edwardian period, while the women's movement developed a stronger nationalist-radical presence, Mary Galway's organisation of the notoriously hard-worked and low-paid textile workers bridged the gap between women's activism and another political movement that grew out of the mid-Victorian liberal political coalition.

The extension of the franchise in 1885 produced in Belfast (as elsewhere in the United Kingdom) working-class 'Lib-Lab' candidates backed by the trade union movement and seeking direct labour representation in parliament. Although the labour movement was rapidly caught up in the nationalist–unionist division, the north shared the growth of mass trade unionism throughout Britain from the late 1880s, and extension of the local franchise in the 1890s led to the re-establishment of an independent labour party on Belfast Corporation under William Walker. Walker briefly posed a serious political challenge to Belfast unionism and contributed to the early Edwardian crisis of the unionist support coalition (see below), while the 1907 dock strike (part of a wave of similar strikes around Britain) saw the emergence of the Liverpool-Irish James Larkin (whose family came from Rostrevor in South Down, where Larkin himself mistakenly claimed he had been born) as a tribune capable of uniting Catholic and Protestant workers. These gains were short-lived: Walker's consistent support for the union with Britain, and willingness to support sectarian Protestant measures on the grounds that Protestantism was synonymous with liberty, undermined the tactical balancing-act whereby he sought nationalist and Catholic support, and the revival of home rule as a defining political issue completed his marginalisation. Sectarian divisions bridged by the dock strike re-emerged as Larkin departed for Dublin and the creation of a specifically Irish-based union. Meanwhile, the resurgent forces of unionism developed their own 'unionist labour' political wing, and during the sectarian outbreaks of 1913–22 'rotten Prods'—mainly labour sympathisers—were targeted with nationalists.

Ulster invaded?

For much of the nineteenth century, nationalist activity in Ulster, from John Lawless's 1828 attempt to agitate for Catholic emancipation in Co. Monaghan against armed Orange opposition, to Tim Healy's Parnellite candidacy in the 1883 Monaghan by-election, was described as an 'invasion of Ulster'. This was challenged both by reminders of the large Catholic presence in Ulster and by invocations of earlier Ulster Protestant nationalists, notably the Ulster United Irishmen of the 1790s—in turn reinvented by liberal unionist descendants as frustrated reformers—and John Mitchel, probably the most influential Ulster nationalist of the nineteenth century, regularly celebrated as a role-model for Ulster Protestants by such *fin de siècle* activists as Bulmer Hobson and Eoin MacNeill. There were instances of Covenanters (Reformed Presbyterians disatisfied with the government for not upholding the seventeenth-century Scottish covenants) being recruited by the IRB in the 1860s, as some had been recruited by the United Irishmen in the 1790s (Ernest Blythe invoked these to provide a genealogy for his own version of Ulster republicanism), and of attempts to forge alliances on the basis of common concerns. The Tenant League of the early 1850s, which tried to unite Protestant and Catholic land agitators, was a precursor of the Land League, though its disintegration through a combination of rising agricultural prices, sectarian divisions, arguments over taking government office, and failure to achieve sufficient Ulster support, was not a propitious omen.

In the land war of the early 1880s the Land League briefly acquired significant Ulster Protestant support—including rank-and-file Orange defectors. This was defused by Gladstone's 1881 land act and failed to translate into large-scale conversions to nationalism, though some individual Ulster Liberals and tenant-right activists crossed over to the home rule side in the years surrounding Gladstone's conversion, including—after a brief dalliance with liberal unionism—the outspoken north Antrim Presbyterian minister J. B. Armour. The verbal and sometimes physical violence of the Land League could repel as well as attract, and the growth of nationalism in the south (and awareness that the official leadership of British conservatism was willing to intrigue with Parnell for its own ends) led to an Orange-centred counter-mobilisation in 1883–5 and Edward Saunderson's emergence as leader of a quasi-independent 'Ulster party'. Even as late as the 1912–14 Ulster crisis, much Ulster unionist propaganda harked back to the land war to portray nationalism as endemic plebeian violence, and the role of land-war violence in shaping unionist perceptions is underexplored.

The three principal local newspapers of Fermanagh mark the different strands of Ulster politics, and the ways in which the political struggles of the 1880s stimulated the growth of the Irish provincial newspaper industry. The Enniskillen *Impartial Reporter*, founded in the 1820s, had a longstanding reputation as a tenant-right advocate. Its editor/proprietor, William Copeland Trimble, supported the Land League in the early 1880s, but this did not prevent Trimble taking a strong unionist line on the home rule issue and becoming one of the earliest (and most consistently self-publicising) organisers of the Carson-era UVF. The *Fermanagh Times* was created under Orange-landlord patronage in 1880 as a conservative rival to the *Reporter*, and survived until the 1940s. In the 1890s the *Fermanagh Herald* gave the Catholic-nationalist majority in the county its first journalistic voice, becoming part of a network of syndicated newspapers prominent in south and west Ulster, including the Omagh-based *Ulster Herald* and the Newry *Frontier Sentinel*, which after 1916 served as rallying-points for west Ulster nationalists discontented with Redmondite compromise on partition.

Attempts to find another economic formula for converting unionists to nationalism enjoyed only limited success (except, perhaps, in self-deception). Whereas nationalists (and even some unionists) blamed Irish de-industrialisation and de-population on the union, Ulster unionists presented it as the basis of northern industrial prosperity (often with the insinuation that the failure of the rest of the island to follow suit reflected Celtic fecklessness, or Catholic infantilism and refusal to work on religious holidays), downplaying the fact that rural depopulation in south and west Ulster affected Protestants as well as Catholics. When some southern unionist landlords and landlord spokesmen (including Edward Carson and Edward Saunderson) joined the late-1890s nationalist agitation over the statement by the 1896 Childers Commission that the taxation system unduly burdened Ireland, Belfast Chamber of Commerce refused to become involved. The arguments by some nationalist publicists that Leinster was more prosperous than Ulster (because many companies and professionals operated from Dublin and paid tax there), that the linen trade merely enabled landlords to charge higher rents, and that the notoriously low pay and poor working conditions in the Belfast textile industry made it a very dubious blessing, fed into unionist complaints that Ulster industries would not be safe under a home rule parliament dominated by southern farmers (though they also allowed tactical alliances between northern nationalists and trade unionists in highlighting 'bigotry and sweating'). Nationalists and unionists argued over whether living and working conditions were worse in Belfast or Dublin, for good measure disputing whether the higher reported crime rate and number of non-marital births in Ulster indicated lower Protestant moral fibre or greater Catholic expertise in concealment.

Another source of tension lay in the make-up of Ulster nationalism. The relative weakness of the lay Catholic middle-class in Ulster meant that nationalist politics were more dependent than elsewhere on clerical leadership, and the prospect of Protestant revenge lent a salience not felt elsewhere in Ireland to the view that

11

the best interests of Ulster Catholics lay in accepting the leadership of Catholic local elites under clerical guidance, seeking to win concessions by downplaying the wider nationalist agenda. Hence the weakness of Parnellism in Ulster during the Split and the fact that if the clericalist Healyite faction of the Irish parliamentary party that existed during the 1890s had extra-parliamentary support anywhere, it was in the borderlands of south and west Ulster and north Leinster.

Throughout the nineteenth century this *Honoratiorenpolitik* was intermittently challenged by more radical lay nationalists who saw Ulster Catholics' best hope in identifying with a broader nationalist movement. This strain can be detected as early as the 1840s, when the young Charles Gavan Duffy used his Belfast newspaper the *Vindicator* to attack the more compromising *Newry Telegraph*, and tried to pressurise Belfast liberals into endorsing O'Connellism by bringing O'Connell himself to Belfast (leading to sectarian riots inflamed by the Presbyterian cleric Henry Cooke). In the Edwardian era, Joseph Devlin (MP for West Belfast from 1906) inherited this tradition; he built his political fortunes by challenging and eventually displacing the clerical-localist Catholic Association from Belfast municipal politics, with an insistence on integrating Belfast nationalism with the wider national movement. This involved political compromise with the more adroit members of the Catholic hierarchy, and Devlin was widely criticised for imitating many political practices of American ward-bosses and exporting Ulster sectarian divisions to the rest of Ireland through co-option of the explicitly Catholic Ancient Order of Hibernians as a party vehicle. Nonetheless, Devlin's genuine commitment to social reform won him a reputation among many Protestants as well as Catholics as a workers' friend (though this did not necessarily translate into votes). His admission to the inner circle of the Irish party national leadership, and through it his ability to influence the administration of Ireland by post-1906 liberal governments, offered Ulster nationalists a degree of influence they were not to regain until the era of John Hume in the 1980s.

Devlin and his allies were not the only activists seeking to link themselves to a wider nationalist project. In many parts of rural Ulster residual IRB networks survived and were taken over and revitalised by new activists such as Dr Patrick McCartan. The revival of the IRB by a new generation from the late 1890s was as much a Belfast as a Dublin phenomenon, and in both cities it overlapped with a counterculture that drew on existing traditions of antiquarianism and contrasted a heroic past with a suffocatingly conformist present.

For some exponents of the counterculture, the Glens of Antrim, Slieve Gullion and the Mournes, or the Donegal Gaeltacht were remnants of an older culture in tune with the harsher realities of life and with a more glamorous past ignored by the complacent bourgeoisie of the Belfast suburbs. F. J. Bigger and Roger Casement developed a cult of Shane O'Neill—generally depicted as a barbarian—as icon of untamed Gaelic manhood intimately associated with the Glens of Antrim. The overlap of counterculture and separatism is exemplified by the political partnership of Alice Milligan and the short-lived 'Ethna Carbery', Protestant Parnellite-republican-antiquarian and daughter of a Catholic Fenian-Parnellite; their monthly paper the *Shan Van Vocht* (1896–99) played a significant role in the separatist revival before merging into Arthur Griffith's *United Irishman*. Bulmer Hobson recalled that after Milligan introduced him to the glories of Gaelic saga he felt that these were more 'real' than the provincial streets of Lisburn; Patrick McCartan later recalled that his political involvement with separatism unfitted him for what might otherwise have been the life of a provincial doctor participating in the petty-bourgeois pretensions of the Catholic middle class of East Ulster. A darker side of this *fin de siècle* sensibility, and the frustration which produced it, is visible in Milligan's angry contempt for those who disagreed with her on the national question, and her enthusiastic celebrations of the killing of informers in 1798 and of hatred taken even to the extent of the revenger's own destruction.

After Gladstone: Unionist fragmentation and revival

With the apparent demise of the home rule challenge after the fragmentation of the Irish party and the downfall successively of Gladstone's second home rule bill in 1893, Gladstone himself in 1894, and the liberal government in 1895, divisions within the unionist coalition reappeared. Saunderson, an effective leader on the single issue of the union, was reduced to a diehard defender of landlordism, and by his death in 1906 his leadership was largely titular. By the beginning of the twentieth century, official unionism faced a three-pronged electoral challenge, with the liberal unionist former junior minister T. W. Russell running insurgent candidates to exploit Presbyterian and tenant-farmer grievances, particularly the demand for land purchase, and winning by-elections in East Down and North Fermanagh.

In Belfast and surrounding areas, working-class Orange populism re-emerged, with violent protests against alleged 'ritualist' practices by some Belfast and Dublin Anglican clergy and discontent over 'constructive unionist' concessions to nationalism and Catholicism leading to accusations that the unionist government and the Orange leadership were effete aristocrats selling out the Protestant people. Once again ultra-Protestants proclaimed that if only Irish Catholics were presented with the uncompromised gospel they might yet be converted en masse. The secession of the Independent Orange Order and the election of the Orange trade unionist T. H. Sloan to parliament in 1902, and the declarations of the movement's ideologue and publicist Lindsay Crawford that the Independents would work with Irishmen of any persuasion on matters of common concern, could be seen as signs that the nationalist attribution of Ulster unionism to elite manipulation was about to be proved correct. The Independents overlapped with Walkerite labourism, and both movements were willing to co-operate tactically with nationalists where it suited them (as did Russell, who displayed the pre-1885 pattern of a significant Protestant liberal element underpinned by tactical Catholic-nationalist votes). In the 1906 general election Devlin's narrow return in West Belfast and Sloan's re-election in South were facilitated by tactical voting, and (unfulfilled) hopes were expressed that Walker might make a 'third leaf of the shamrock' by winning North Belfast.

Ulster unionism was not dying, however, but being reinvented. As the 1899 local government reforms left the south Ulster landed aristocracy reduced to junior partners at best, or stranded as their traditional areas of influence fell to local nationalist majorities, north-east Ulster came to be dominated by a new elite of local professionals, businessmen and strong farmers, providing a support base for the wealthier professionals and remaining landowners who represented the area at Westminster. Significant members of this elite, such as James Craig (from a Belfast distilling family) and Robert Wallace (whose family combination of long-term connection with the borough and cathedral of Downpatrick and nineteenth-century enrichment as railway lawyers displayed how old elites could adapt to new conditions), had military service in the Boer war as a formative experience underpinning their sense of imperial identity. (Just as many younger nationalists confirmed their sense of political identity through the anti-war demonstrations that unionists saw as evidence of fundamental nationalist disloyalty.) It was this group which led the fightback against the splinter groups, appealing to Orangeism and to the renewed danger of home rule as the unionist government fragmented and a liberal return to power became imminent. This new cadre found organisational expression with the creation of the Ulster Unionist Council in 1905 and organised and drove the Carson campaign after 1910. James Craig's formative political experiences were of the battle to contain the revolt against official unionism (his first electoral contest ended in defeat by a Russellite in North Fermanagh, and he entered Westminster in 1906 by unseating a Russellite in East Down). His subsequent career, before and after partition, was dominated by the desire to preserve Protestant unity around official unionism.

Russellism was defused by the passage of the Wyndham land act (1903). The 1906 general election unseated the two Russellite by-election victors, though Russell held South Tyrone and another Russellite gained the old liberal stronghold of North Antrim. The revival of nationalism and the increasing dependence of Russell on the Liberal government (which appointed him to head the Irish Department of Agriculture and Technical Instruction in 1907) made this a last hurrah. At the January 1910 general election North Antrim reverted to unionism and Russell lost his seat. Russell's return in the 1911 North Tyrone by-election (largely by nationalist votes) could not mask the fact that Ulster liberalism was now a residual network around the *Ulster Guardian* weekly newspaper, financed to a considerable extent by the discontented shipbuilding magnate Lord Pirrie, and made up of tenant-farmer irreconcilables,

15

high-minded intellectual 'mugwumps' and less high-minded professionals suspected by both nationalists and unionists of adhering to liberalism as much from desire for Liberal government patronage (from which consistent nationalists were excluded by the Irish party pledge against office-taking) as from liberal principle. The January 1910 election also saw the final loss of Sloan's seat, the reduction of the Sloanites to a powerless rump, trying to regain relevance by denouncing any partition-based compromise as betrayal of southern unionists, and the departure of Walker from Belfast politics, first to contest a Scottish seat and then to an administrative position under the national insurance act.

The years 1910–14 showed the ability of Ulster to destabilise the British political system. Awareness of its possible consequences if the Great War had not broken out when it did underlay the post-war determination of British politicians to wall off unionist Ulster, as well as nationalist Ireland, from the British political mainstream. Ulster militancy was less unprecedented than it seems in retrospect. Paramilitary mobilisation had taken place in Ulster at the time of the second home rule bill in 1893, and during negotiations in 1913, Bonar Law told Asquith that his statements of support for potential Ulster resistance had not said or done anything not preceded by Salisbury and Balfour during the 1886 and 1893 bills. Nevertheless, the prolonged 1912–14 controversy, as compared to the relatively rapid conclusion in 1893, and the abolition of the house of lords' veto—the existence of which in 1893 had given unionist defiance a certain air of theatricality—gave the later crisis an intensity all its own. Conservative support for the UVF did not merely reflect Bonar Law's personal commitment, but fitted into a wider concern for mobilisation of British citizens and resources to safeguard the empire from the dangers to which it was supposedly exposed by pusillanimous Cobdenite cranks. The UVF may have been created as much to contain potential plebeian violence as to threaten the government, but it was a mobilisation on the basis of the old Plantation structures, the last hurrah of the Ulster gentry as military leaders of an armed citizenry.

For later generations the Ulster crisis was encapsulated in the single figure of Edward Carson. Unionist accounts at the time and since celebrated his personal magnetism and his utter determination as the key to victory and an example to be followed if such dangers ever recurred. Others, emphasising his later lamentations over the fate of southern unionism and his remarks on the need to avoid reducing matters to a straightforward sectarian conflict, note the tragic dimension of a Dublin unionist (his Dublin rather than northern accent was much noted at the time) setting an example for nationalists to resort to physical force. Nationalist commentators cited Carson's laments over his 'betrayal' by the conservative party to support their view of partition as resulting from a cynical and fundamentally illegitimate political manoeuvre, and by accepting the image of Carson as heroic leader could contrast the supposed naïvety of Redmond and echo Sarsfield's alleged words after the battle of the Boyne: 'Change kings and we'll fight you again'.

These discourses tend to disguise the fact that contemporary nationalist and liberal dismissals of Carsonism and the UVF as a gigantic bluff were more plausible at the time than may be realised. Dublin lawyers leading Ulster Protestant resistance to liberal-nationalist alliances were familiar figures throughout the history of the union, and such supposed rebels regularly ended on the judicial bench when a conservative government rewarded their services. Nationalists, too, could present their actions as part of a wider British narrative—the final triumph of British democracy over outworn aristocratic reaction, and the desperate endeavours of the classes to find an election cry to fool the masses into abandoning liberalism and social progress. (Opposition to home rule was one of the few issues uniting a conservative party deeply divided on tariff reform and other matters.) Nationalists declared that to override the wishes of the Catholic-nationalist majority on the grounds of alleged unfitness to rule a Protestant minority seemed tantamount to revocation of Catholic emancipation and denial that Catholics could be equal citizens.

Nationalists also pointed out the incongruity of Carson and his lieutenants declaring that they would prove their loyalty to the empire by taking up arms against it when Tory propagandists were proclaiming that it stood in unprecedented danger from Germany, and threatening to plunge Ireland into civil war to preserve it from anarchy under nationalist rule. It was equally apparent that the UVF, whatever its military pretensions, could not defeat the British army (nondescript rustics shouldering wooden guns featured prominently in nationalist cartoons). Surely everyone could see that this defiance of the rules of the political game was no more than the last trick? Nevertheless, the efforts of nationalist leaders to avoid nationalist mobilisation in Ulster showed they were aware that the danger of sectarian violence, rational or not, was greater than they admitted. The eventual mobilisation of the Irish Volunteers, the Curragh mutiny's revelation of potential discontent in the British armed forces, and the Larne and Howth gun-runnings of 1914 progressively made the unthinkable thinkable, and added to the accumulation of flammable material.

This apparent drift to disaster was accompanied by, and encouraged, another trend. The argument that a minority of the Irish nation should not resist the majority was unquestionable on its own terms. But what if there were two nations? Did not the willingness of Ulster unionists to risk disastrous violence suggest that they ought in prudence to be treated as a separate entity, whatever might be said against this in theory? As Ronan Fanning has recently argued in *Fatal path* (2013), beneath the storm and fury of the 1912–14 Ulster crisis and the apparent dependence of the Liberal government on the Redmondite Irish parliamentary party, both major British parties can be discerned groping for agreement on a partition-based settlement which they could jointly impose on their Irish allies, and which, on partition, prefigured the settlement actually imposed in 1920–22.

Slouching towards partition

As we have seen, partition had been suggested long before 1912–14. From the time of Gladstone's commitment to home rule, it was intermittently suggested that one solution might be to divide the island with Ulster remaining under the Westminster parliament. The 1885 election result, which led to nationalist dominance in the three southern provinces and produced an Ulster divided roughly along a north-east to south-west axis with marginal areas along the Foyle, Clogher and Erne valleys, could be seen as marking the division between two nations. This division was confirmed by the extension of elected local government after 1899, when the same process which swept away the remnants of landed and unionist influence in local government outside Ulster (except for an occasional isolated stalwart with personal influence, and a marginal toehold in the suburban townships of south Dublin) affirmed unionist control in a contiguous block of east Ulster, with a further region of south and mid-Ulster as debatable ground.

During the parliamentary session in which the 1893 home rule bill was debated, even Gladstone expressed willingness to consider partition if sought for its own sake and not as a wrecking device. Gladstone's caveat was important, because early invocations of Ulster distinctiveness were generally undertaken, not to exclude Ulster from the Irish nation but to maintain that—in the absence of an island-wide consensus—a coherent Irish nation did not exist. In 1892 a huge convention held in Belfast to express Ulster opposition to home rule repudiated partition and insisted that Ulster unionists would stand or fall with their southern brethren. The development of Ulster unionism since then had, as we have seen, strengthened a sense of Ulster particularism, but a partition-based compromise in 1914 was hindered both by the question of the area to be excluded (with Tyrone a particular bone of contention) and by fears that liberal-nationalist concessions might be pocketed and used to wreck the implementation of home rule altogether.

In this context the Great War seemed to come as a release, with unionists and nationalists joining a common cause; Redmondism showing that unionist predictions of home rule as a danger to the empire were unfounded, unionists proving their defiance of home rule did not invalidate their professions of loyalty. A minority of Irish Volunteers (some prominent leaders coming from Ulster) broke with Redmond; some unionists wrote angry letters to Carson accusing him of betrayal. More seriously, the two sides operated on the basis of different expectations. Part of the motivation for Belfast nationalist enlistment in the 16th Irish Division was expectation that a militarily trained body of nationalists would be better placed to resist partition; indeed, there is evidence that during Belfast sectarian violence of 1920–22, armed Catholic ex-servicemen engaged in combat independently of the IRA.

The outbreak of war created not a settlement, but a holding operation, relying more and more on wishful thinking, and fatally fractured by the 1916 rising. Subsequent negotiations for an immediate home rule settlement saw the definitive jettisoning of Cavan, Donegal and Monaghan unionists (whatever Carson's later regrets). They also fractured Ulster nationalism, with nationalists in Belfast and the north-east supporting Devlin while many in the west of the six counties broke away, passing through transitional splinter groups such as the Omagh-centred Irish Nation League (derisively called 'the league of seven solicitors') into the reinvented Sinn Féin movement. Devlin's later justification for his support of the abortive compromise—that he had hoped to secure continued rule from Westminster rather than placing Ulster nationalists under a unionist-dominated northern parliament—was an ominous indication of the dangers ahead.

The fall of the Irish party and extension of Sinn Féin into Ulster (despite the survival of Devlinism in parts of east Ulster), rapidly followed by the emergence of the IRA and the development of loyalist vigilante forces on the old UVF framework, led to the fulfilment of the worst nightmares entertained in the pre-1914 era, albeit as a sideshow to the wider Irish and world crisis.

In 1919 the deteriorating Irish situation went largely unaddressed by a British government preoccupied with the peace settlement; in 1920, however, a fourth home rule bill (the Government of Ireland Act) put forward a settlement which included a Northern Ireland parliament. For the British government, this promised that a post-war Britain beset by new social and economic problems would no longer have to deal with the troublesome Irish question. Whatever settlement might eventually be reached with the southerners, an Ulster unionist government in Belfast could be presented as exemplifying self-determination, self-supporting through its industrial base, and keeping matters within its remit from cluttering the agenda at Westminster. The acquiescence of Ulster unionists was a necessary precondition for a settlement with Irish nationalism.

From 1920 sectarian violence was unleashed, with riots in Derry developing into open warfare and spreading to Belfast (with the assistance of incitement by Carson at Belfast's 12 July demonstration in 1920). For two years Belfast burned, with atrocities committed by both sides (though preponderantly by loyalists, often with the tolerance or active co-operation of the nascent state's self-defence forces). The dáil and IRA leadership responded with a concerted boycott of northern firms, intended to drive home northern dependence on the southern economy but in practice widening the gap between the two. Further south and west, IRA units and the Special Constabulary that developed from local vigilante units fought on the borderlands of the new state, often engaging in tit-for-tat retaliation. This did not stop the creation of the new state's administrative apparatus and the election of its parliament and government under James Craig.

The subsequent treaty negotiations, and the debate over the treaty settlement, centred on sovereignty rather than partition. (This should not be overemphasised, however, since many southern nationalists saw partition in relation to sovereignty, not as a separate issue; if the majority on the island were not allowed to override the minority in north-east Ulster because—as nationalists saw it—Britain stood behind the Ulster unionists, Irish sovereignty was overborne or rejected.) The attempt of Michael Collins to defuse the treaty split by directing anti-treaty IRA energies against Northern Ireland failed, and as the civil war erupted in the south, drawing northern IRA men in on both sides, political and military pressure on the Craig government relaxed.

For those nationalists (predominantly in the west of Northern Ireland) who had broken with Devlin after 1916 and formed the core of Ulster Sinn Féin, hope lay in the belief that the boundary commission established under the treaty would award extensive nationalist-majority areas to the Free State. They were disappointed, and their non-recognition of the new state (and loudly-proclaimed revelations about the extent to which nationalist civil servants and policemen subverted the Dublin Castle administration during the southern war of independence) allowed unionists to justify exclusion of Catholics from as many positions of trust as possible and concentration of patronage on the maintenance of a pan-Protestant unionism.

After Aughrim

By 1925 a durable settlement seemed to have emerged. D. P. Moran, the veteran Dublin-based Irish-Ireland editor, expressed relief that nationalist newspapers in the south no longer gave extensive

coverage to 12 July demonstrations (as they had when the speeches
and actions of unionist leaders had implications for the whole island). He suggested that partition had been a blessing in disguise
as it would allow the implementation of cultural and economic protectionist measures through which a Catholic-Gaelic civilisation
would regenerate itself and eventually absorb northern recalcitrants
on its own terms. Some three-county unionists had migrated north,
and others followed over the years; but with no real prospect of irredentist reclamation, others organised at local government level
(and occasionally returned independents to the dáil) to represent
their interests in the new state. For their part, mid-Ulster nationalists
smarted at the failure of the boundary commission to fulfil their
hopes and at the declaration of the Cosgrave government that they
had concluded a 'damn good bargain' by getting their share of war
debt written off—some Ulster nationalists responded that they had
been sold at so much a head. Reuniting with Devlin's followers, they
reluctantly entered the Northern Ireland parliament, where they
found unionists indisposed to compromise from their new position
of power. The memory of nationalist violence and non-recognition
assisted the Ulster unionist government in doing what they would
have done anyway, gerrymandering local authorities to keep as
many as possible under unionist control, and abolishing proportional representation to perpetuate a political system defined around
the single issue of partition. With the aid of gerrymandering and
property-based voting, the nationalist capture of local authorities
such as Derry and Enniskillen after 1914 was rolled back, and the
symbolism of the Williamite siege once more predominated.

The political-sectarian division within the labour movement
was reinforced, with significant sections of the trade union movement incorporated into unionist patronage structures and political
labourism wracked by individual rivalries and subjected to recurring splits between anti-partitionists and those who acquiesced in
the union. A residual liberal and leftist intelligentsia attracted as
much suspicion and as little influence as its counterpart in the
southern state, and, like it, co-existed with an 'official' culture represented by assertions of imperial Britishness and Presbyterian
ruralist nostalgia. The vast neo-classical edifice of Stormont, rising
on a hillside above east Belfast, expressed the new regime's asser-

tion of permanence (though its location away from urban crowds indicated the regime was less secure than it claimed).

In the Northern Ireland parliament, Devlin was treated with a veneer of respect, but found the concerns of his constituents firmly set aside. By his death in 1934 Devlin had been reduced from a national political figure to a ghetto boss struggling to retain political leadership of the Catholic community; his successors lacked his stature and the element of social vision he had possessed, and Ulster nationalism sank into the fragmentation and localism that persisted until the outbreak of the Troubles in 1968–9. An embittered republican subculture, itself divided between Marxists and traditionalists, survived, attracting recruits and engaging in occasional outbreaks but increasingly confined to individual veterans and extended families and unable seriously to challenge the state apparatus. The latter years of Alice Milligan, living in penurious near-isolation in mid-Ulster while caring for ailing relatives who detested her politics, were a sad commentary on the high hopes of the *fin de siècle* revival. The position of Ulster nationalism was further weakened by the departure of many separatist activists to the south, either from ambition or under legal and extra-legal harassment, leaving more provincial and conservative figures in Northern Ireland. The sense of a defeated older generation, the lost hopes and dreams of the cultural revival, echo through Cathal O'Byrne's fragmented and aestheticised urban explorations *As I roved out* (1946), the anatomised nostalgia of Michael MacLaverty, the bitter rebellions of Brian Moore, and the memories of mid-century Derry underlying the work of Seamus Deane and Brian Friel (haunted by the lost Donegal hinterland and the violence and defeat of the 1920s).

The military structures of the Plantation seemed to have emerged anew in the form of the B Specials, and a government dominated by 'millocracy' to have produced an unshakable new aristocracy. Time showed, however, the difficulty of maintaining a state on the basis of sectarian exclusion of a large minority, especially when the industrial power which underpinned the confidence of Ulster unionism was eroded by postwar economic trends that shifted the axis of the British economy away from the traditional heavy industries of Lancashire and Clydeside (and their offshoot in the Lagan Valley) to the new light industries centred in the midlands and south-east of England, and the declining popular resonance of the Victorian whig-Protestant ideology of Britain's greatness made Ulster popular Protestantism a cultural outlier within the United Kingdom. The full implications of these trends were disguised by the second world war and its aftermath, but attempts to adapt Northern Ireland to the modernisations of the 1960s would reveal that the tensions of the late Victorian and Edwardian era remained unresolved beneath the surface modernity of the 'narrow ground'.

A strong case can be made for partition in principle, whatever its flaws in practice. Once the argument for secession was made, Ulster unionists as well as nationalists could appeal to it with equal plausibility. Political 'realists' who argue that the achievement of full sovereignty by an Irish state was necessary in order for Irish nationalism to take responsibility for its own decisions and cease to use the British as an excuse must recognise that such sovereignty might have been delayed or disrupted by the presence of a much larger unionist minority. Those aware of the manner in which, in the late 1920s and early 1930s, Fianna Fáil and organs such as the *Catholic Bulletin* claimed that the Cosgrave government lacked legitimacy because it only held power through the support of ex-unionist deputies from Dublin and the border counties, will see how a long period in which a government supported by a minority of nationalists but retained in power by unionist votes might have destabilised the state and released forces which the post-independence southern state (whatever its shortcomings) confined to the political margins. Yet something was lost by the separation of a provincial Ulster unionism from more metropolitan elements of its heritage (including the traditions of Dublin unionism, of which the Catholic unionist judge Denis Henry and Stormont civil servant A. N. Bonaparte Wyse were relics) and by southern forgetfulness of such an important element of what it is to be Irish. The humiliation and stultification of two generations of northern nationalists would eventually unsettle the 1920–22 settlement, lead to renewed sectarian violence, and threaten the whole island with chaos.

Biographies

Francis Thomas ('Frank') Aiken

1898–1983

Frank Aiken, farmer, revolutionary, and politician, was born 13 February 1898 in Carrickbracken, Camlough, Co. Armagh, seventh child and youngest son of James Aiken, farmer and builder from Co. Tyrone, and Mary Aiken (née McGeeney), of Corromannon, Belleek, Co. Armagh. James Aiken, a prominent nationalist who had built many of the Catholic churches in south Armagh and had declined overtures to stand for parliament, was a member of the county council and the first nationalist chairman of the local board of guardians, where he had adjourned a resolution welcoming Queen Victoria on her visit to Dublin in 1900 'until Ireland became free'.

Early life; war and politics

Frank was educated at the CBS, Newry. He began managing the family farm after his mother's death, when he was 13; although he left school at 16, he was a keen student of agricultural techniques and was elected chairman of the Co-operative Flax-Scutching Society at Camlough in 1917. A member of the Gaelic League and secretary of the local branch from 1914, he became a committed Irish-speaker after several visits to the Donegal Gaeltacht and attendance at Omeath Irish College; from then on he spoke and used the Irish language whenever he could. He was big for his age—15—when in 1913 he was elected lieutenant on joining the local company of the Irish Volunteers, which collapsed after the 1914 split.

Aiken played no part in the 1916 rising, but a lifelong association with Éamon de Valera began in July 1917 when he helped in the Clare by-election campaign. Charged with stewarding a rowdy meeting when he went to hear de Valera speak at Bessbrook during the Armagh South by-election in February 1918, he then organised the Camlough company of Volunteers and was elected captain. He was also active in Sinn Féin from 1917: as an officer of the Camlough club, as secretary of the South Armagh comhairle ceanntair, as constituency representative on the executive in Dublin, and as chief fund-raiser for the Dáil Éireann loan in south Armagh in 1919–20. But he owed his early eminence to military rather than political leadership. He became commandant of the Camlough company in 1919, vice-commandant of the Newry brigade in 1920, and commandant of the 4th Northern Division (comprising north Louth, south and west Down, parts of Tyrone and Antrim, and all Co. Armagh) from March 1921. On the run from autumn 1919 after British forces burned his family home as a reprisal, he frequently commanded his men in action, notably in the derailment near Newry of the troop train carrying the cavalry who had escorted the king at the opening of the Northern Ireland parliament in June 1921. Like Seán Mac Eoin, he won grudging respect from his British adversaries as an honourable antagonist.

Aiken remained a full-time IRA officer after the truce of July 1921 and, when the dáil endorsed the treaty in January 1922, bent his energies to preventing civil war. Hence his opposition to the

call for an army convention before the publication of a new constitution, on the grounds that '"any fool might start a civil war"
because there would then be two armies'; and he was the solitary
senior IRA officer described as 'non-partisan' in a list published in
March 1922 (Skinner, 157–8). Early in 1922 he headed the short-
lived Ulster command, consisting of pro- and anti-treaty officers,
which moved arms from the south to the IRA divisions in Northern
Ireland. His efforts to avert civil war were also reflected in his key
role in the negotiation of the Collins–de Valera pact in May 1922,
in his urging Richard Mulcahy to declare a truce after the attack
on the Four Courts (28–30 June), and in his acting as liaison officer
in a short-lived local truce in Limerick. When these efforts failed
he returned to his own IRA division, which had been responsible
for a reprisal sectarian massacre of six innocent Presbyterians in
Altnaveigh, Co. Down, on 17 June 1922, and which he initially persuaded to remain neutral in the civil war. But the division's refusal
to support the provisional government led to the arrest and imprisonment of Aiken and 200 of his men in Dundalk jail. 'Somebody
wants to goad our division into resistance', he wrote to Mulcahy
(Hopkinson, 170), and on 28 July he led a mass escape of over one
hundred prisoners. He then reorganised his command and, with
'meticulous attention to detail', recaptured Dundalk and its military
barracks on 14 August, freeing the remaining republican prisoners
and imprisoning the 400-strong Free State garrison—much the most
'spectacularly efficient' operation conducted by the IRA during the
civil war (Andrews, *Dublin made me*, 242–3). But Aiken made no
attempt to hold Dundalk, and his division played no further significant part in the war. He declined an invitation to join the IRA
executive until de Valera formed a republican government in
October 1922, and he attended the next, week-long meeting in Co.
Waterford in March 1923, when he supported de Valera's peace
resolution (which was defeated by six votes to five). He was present
on 10 April at the skirmish on the slopes of the Knockmealdown
mountains when Liam Lynch was fatally wounded, and on 20 April
was appointed Lynch's successor as IRA chief of staff, a post he
held until the end of 1925. The mutual respect and understanding
between Aiken and de Valera was instrumental in ending the war:
the timing of de Valera's peace proclamation on 27 April was co-

ordinated with Aiken's simultaneous order to the IRA to suspend all offensive operations and to hide their arms. Although Aiken remained on the run, 'permitted to wander about Co. Armagh unmolested' (Garvin *et al.*, 24) until his dramatic reappearance at a commemoration ceremony in Dundalk in April 1925, his private means cushioned him against the worst hardships experienced by other republicans.

Aiken topped the poll as the Sinn Féin abstentionist candidate in the Louth constituency at the general election of August 1923, a seat he held until his retirement from the dáil fifty years later. His admission to the IRA convention in November 1925, that de Valera's republican 'government' was considering entering the dáil, prompted the IRA's withdrawal of allegiance, which it henceforth vested in its own executive, the army council; it led also to Aiken's expulsion from the IRA. Although he was in the US on a republican fund-raising mission when de Valera founded Fianna Fáil in May 1926, he was on the new party's national executive from the outset.

In 1928 Aiken bought a dairy farm at 'Dún Gaoithe', Sandyford, Co. Dublin, where he lived and farmed for the rest of his life; he was also a part-time inventor who took out various patents—for a turf stove, a beehive, an air-shelter, an electric cooker, and a sprung heel for a shoe (Skinner, 178; Horgan, 67–8).

Public office: defence, lands, and finance

When Fianna Fáil first entered government in March 1932, Aiken's 'almost symbiotic relationship' with de Valera (O'Brien, 217) prompted his nomination as minister for defence. It 'proved an inspired choice...his heart was not in the civil war and he...was probably more acceptable to the Free State officers than any other possible appointment. He soon reconciled the army to the new régime' (Lee, 176). He also sought to reconcile the IRA, and his first official act was to visit the republican prisoners in Arbour Hill prison on the evening of 9 March; they were released next day. Aiken had other ministerial roles in the 1930s. Acting as minister for agriculture in the absence of James Ryan at the Ottawa conference in the summer of 1932, he introduced the use of turf in the Curragh camp. In 1933, when he was acting as minister for lands, he launched the general turf development scheme and always remained passionately interested in the development of the bogs; he was also responsible for the 1933 land act, which reduced the land annuities and accelerated land redistribution.

Much of Aiken's importance in successive Fianna Fáil governments flowed from his influence on de Valera. John Dulanty, the Irish high commissioner in London, told the British government in 1938 that de Valera 'relies upon him to keep the IRA lot quiet and behind the government' (Fisk, 69). He was the most anglophobic of de Valera's ministers and was omitted from the Irish delegation that negotiated the Anglo–Irish agreements of 25 April 1938; the defence agreement handed over the ports retained by the British under the terms of the 1921 treaty and made possible Irish neutrality throughout the second world war, when Aiken held the post of minister for the coordination of defensive measures. His personal direction of a draconian censorship regime became notorious, and he was frequently accused of dictatorial tendencies—one critic, Senator Theodore Kingsmill Moore, spoke of his turning censorship into 'a Frank-aikenstein monster' (Ó Drisceoil, 260). His defence was epitomised in an unapologetic memorandum to government in January 1940, which denounced

> self-styled democrats who would hold on to the peacetime liberalistic trimmings of democracy while the fundamental basis of democracy was being swept from under their feet by the foreign or domestic enemies of their democratic state (Fisk, 141).

Yet when censorship ended, on 11 May 1945, the shy, gruff minister held a dinner for the newspaper editors who had been his severest critics.

When Malcolm MacDonald, the former British dominions secretary, brought a formal plan for the unification of Ireland if it entered the war on the allied side to Dublin in June 1940, he found that Aiken—more than de Valera or Seán Lemass—'took it upon himself to do most of the talking, and was extremely rigid in his opposition'. Although Aiken was then convinced that Britain would lose the war, John Maffey, the British representative in

Ireland, thought him 'anti-British but certainly not pro-German' (Fisk, 69, 174, 184, 264–7). His anglophobia was so deep-rooted that as late as 1979 he acknowledged that throughout the war he had regarded Britain as a greater military threat than Germany, an attitude he had made plain during a stormy White House meeting with an infuriated President Roosevelt during his abortive mission seeking American arms, ships and food in the spring of 1941. It found further expression in 1945 in his support for de Valera's notorious visit to the German legation to offer his condolences when Hitler died, notwithstanding the vehement opposition of the senior officials in the Department of External Affairs.

Aiken's enduring intimacy with de Valera next led to his appointment in June 1945, at his own request, as minister for finance in place of the president-elect, Seán T. O'Kelly. He proved a 'dogged and inquisitive' minister who entertained more independent and unorthodox economic ideas than any of his predecessors in the Department of Finance, one of whom, Seán MacEntee, he had earlier antagonised by his support for the introduction of family allowances. The secretary of the department, J. J. McElligott, was so alarmed by Aiken's espousal of the social credit policies propounded by Major C. H. Douglas that he plucked the young T. K. Whitaker from the ranks to act as the new minister's personal adviser on monetary theory (Fanning, *Department of Finance*, 392–3). But the economic problems of a postwar Ireland struggling to emerge from isolation, compounded by fuel shortages and bread rationing during the hard winter of 1946–7, offered little scope for Aiken's idiosyncratic instincts and necessitated his introducing a supplementary budget imposing further taxes in the autumn of 1947, shortly before Fianna Fáil went into opposition after the February 1948 election.

Foreign policy

In June 1951, when de Valera returned as taoiseach but at last relinquished the foreign policy portfolio he had united with the headship of his successive governments in 1932–48, he chose Aiken to succeed him; the longevity of Aiken's tenure as minister for external affairs (1951–4, 1957–69) has never since been surpassed. Although he was to prefer Lemass as his successor as taoiseach, on foreign policy 'de Valera's heart beat more with that of Aiken' (Williams, 144), who identified with the style as much as the substance of de Valera's foreign policy; he rarely sought the advice of cabinet colleagues, and discouraged public discussion of international affairs both in and out of the dáil. That he had been bequeathed de Valera's mantle made his authority impregnable and, despite the new taoiseach's antipathy for his sitting tenant in Iveagh House, Lemass never felt strong enough to evict him, and made him tánaiste after the 1965 election. The antipathy was mutual but suppressed, and the two men avoided locking horns by keeping out of each other's way. Aiken 'argued that the issues of membership of the EEC and that of Northern Ireland were "constitutional issues" and not his business' (Keatinge, 2); he saw his own role 'as being primarily concerned with the continuation and development of a separate Irish foreign policy at the UN. Lemass increasingly thought in terms of London and Europe' (Williams, 144). 'Lemass "regarded Aiken as a fool" and was delighted to see him disappear over the horizon in the direction of the United Nations for three months every year', according to Brian Lenihan, one of the younger, brasher cabinet ministers who shared that aversion (Horgan, 193). The preferred nomenclature of 'Northern Ireland' in the taoiseach's department under Lemass was another point of difference: Aiken and his officials favoured the traditional and irredentist usage of 'Six Counties'. But Aiken backed Lemass's unprecedented summit meetings in 1965 with the Northern Ireland prime minister, Terence O'Neill.

Aiken's determination to establish a distinctive Irish identity at the United Nations likewise mirrored de Valera's conduct at the League of Nations in 1932–8. Hence his pursuit between 1957 and 1961 of a non-aligned stance on issues such as nuclear non-proliferation, troop withdrawal from central Europe, the Algerian war, UN peacekeeping, and, most controversially, the representation in the UN of the Peoples' Republic of China (in place of nationalist China). That such activism often incurred western— especially American—displeasure bothered Aiken not at all and helped ensure that Ireland was perceived as punching above its weight in the general assembly. So, too, did his passionate support for decolonisation in Africa and Asia—he once told the assembly that the Irish 'know what imperialism is and what resistance to it involves' (Skelly, 125). Such attitudes made Ireland more acceptable in UN peacekeeping missions than most European states, and paved the way for the initial participation of the Irish defence forces, in the Lebanon (1958) and the Congo (1960). But the entry of a host of African and Asian countries, together with the Irish public's rapturous fascination with the Kennedy presidency in the US and the Atlanticist predilections of Lemass, curtailed his freedom of manoeuvre. Indeed 'Ireland's United Nations policy on Cold War issues during the mid to late 1960s was typically formulated within a United States oriented pro-Western context' (Kennedy and McMahon, 207, 252); the most striking example was the Vietnam war, on which Aiken was eloquent only in his silence. When the nuclear non-proliferation treaty was signed in Moscow in 1968 his dedication won international recognition in his being invited to be its first signatory; 'that treaty is Frank Aiken's monument', observed Conor Cruise O'Brien, a leading member of the Irish delegation during his early years at the UN (Skelly, 264).

Aiken's high profile during those years cloaked a deep-seated conservatism. He was opposed to expenditure on new embassies and saw the UN as an alternative mechanism for working with the permanent representatives of the countries where Ireland had no diplomatic missions. And there were echoes of the censorious Aiken of the Emergency in 1967: first, when he refused permission for an RTÉ news crew to go to Vietnam under the auspices of the South Vietnamese government, on the grounds that they could not present an objective report in such circumstances and because it would jeopardise the government quest for American investment in Ireland; and, second, when he prevented a current affairs crew from going to Nigeria because of fears that if Irish public opinion became too pro-Biafran in the Nigerian civil war it would endanger Irish missionaries elsewhere in Nigeria. He also resisted the burgeoning links between Fianna Fáil and business (especially with the building industry) institutionalised in the 1960s by the establishment of Taca (a fund-raising organisation of 500 businessmen who obtained privileged entrée to ministers in return for contributing to the party coffers), to which he denied access to his Louth constituency (Faulkner, 35). Such concerns came to a head when

Lemass suddenly announced his decision to resign as taoiseach in November 1966. A 'very distressed' Aiken, who intensely disliked and distrusted Charles Haughey (1925–2006)—'hated him like poison', according to Kevin Boland—wrote to Lemass from the UN and vainly asked him to stay on for another two years to improve the prospects of the succession of George Colley (Horgan, 333–5). Although Aiken proposed Colley when he unsuccessfully stood against Jack Lynch at the party meeting on 9 November 1966, he was thereafter supportive of Lynch, who reappointed him as tánaiste and minister for external affairs.

Northern Ireland

Aiken's restraint and imperturbability was a source of strength for Lynch when the Northern Ireland crisis erupted in 1968–9, and he instructed members of all Irish missions abroad to 'avoid public addresses or radio or television appearances, specifically dealing with partition or the situation in the north' (Kennedy, 323). In April 1969, when he flew to New York to brief the UN secretary general, U Thant, he practised what he preached by rejecting all requests for television interviews, including that from RTÉ's Kevin O'Kelly, who had accompanied him on the flight from Dublin; he also forswore attempting to bring the crisis to the security council. But this benign dominance in cabinet on Northern Ireland policy came to an end after the election in June 1969, when Lynch effectively sacked a surprised Aiken from the government and replaced him on 2 July as minister for external affairs by the similarly surprised but younger and more European-minded Patrick Hillery.

> In losing Aiken, the Lynch government lost a senior player and the main advocate of common sense and moderation in its Northern Ireland policy...[and] the aggressive Northern Ireland policy advocated by Neil Blaney had no opponent (Kennedy, 328).

Yet when Lynch first learnt of the plot to import arms in April 1970 he turned to Aiken for advice. The response was unequivocal:

you are the leader of the Irish people—not just the Fianna Fáil party. The Irish people come first, the party second and individuals third. If you are asking me what I would do, the whip would be off these men as from now.

His mistrust of Haughey remained so intense that he told Lynch that he would not stand in the 1973 election if Haughey was ratified as a Fianna Fáil candidate and would announce his reasons to the press, suggesting that the party instead approach John Hume or Austin Currie to run in Louth on an independent ticket. It was only after Lynch mobilised pressure from de Valera, Seán MacEntee, George Colley and Paddy Smith that Aiken agreed on 12 February to dissimulate and to say that he was retiring from politics on doctor's orders—a decision announced by Lynch next day at a meeting in Dundalk Town Hall to mark Aiken's seventy-fifth birthday. Further outraged and bemused by Lynch's bringing Haughey back to the opposition front-bench in January 1975, in the last ten years of his life Aiken never attended an ard fheis nor any other party event (Collins, 75, 95–8). He died 18 May 1983 in St Vincent's Hospital, Dublin.

Aiken married (3 October 1934) Maud Davin (Maud Aiken), director of the Dublin Municipal School of Music and daughter of Alderman John Davin, hotel proprietor, and his wife, Mary (née O'Gara); the couple were received in private audience by Pope Pius XI on their honeymoon and later had a daughter and two sons, Aedamar (1938), Proinnsias (1941), and Lochlann (1942).

The best assessment of Frank Aiken is by Todd Andrews (*Man of no property*, 123–4):

He was a brave soldier and a competent one. No man had felt so deeply about the 'split' on the treaty and no man tried harder to prevent the civil war. He had unlimited patience and unusual capacity for detail. He was indifferent to the opinions of either his political friends or opponents or indeed of anyone except de Valera. He could not be insulted because he was never aware of an insult being offered. He was not sensitive to the feelings of others. Nor could he be intimidated... Aiken was a man of ingenuity and imagination. He was the last of the Sinn Féiners.

Ronan Fanning

Sources

Aiken papers, UCDA P 104; *WWW*; Liam C. Skinner, *Politicians by accident* (1946); Ronan Fanning, *The Irish Department of Finance 1922–58* (1978); Patrick Keatinge, *A place among the nations: issues of Irish foreign policy* (1978); C. S. Andrews, *Dublin made me* (1979); T. D. Williams, 'Irish foreign policy, 1949–69', in J. J. Lee (ed.), *Ireland 1945–70* (1979), 136–51; J. L. Rosenberg, 'The 1941 mission of Frank Aiken to the United States: an American perspective', *Irish Historical Studies*, xxii (1980–81), 162–77; C. S. Andrews, *Man of no property* (1982); Robert Fisk, *In time of war: Ireland, Ulster and the price of neutrality 1939–45* (1983); Michael Hopkinson, *Green against green: the Irish civil war* (1988); J. J. Lee, *Ireland 1912–1985* (1989); John Horgan, *Seán Lemass* (1997); J. M. Skelly, *Irish diplomacy at the United Nations, 1945–1965* (1997); Eunan O'Halpin, *Defending Ireland: the Irish state and its enemies since 1922* (1999); John M. Regan, *The Irish counter-revolution 1921–36: treatyite politics and settlement in independent Ireland* (1999), 61–2; Stephen Collins, *The power game: Fianna Fáil since Lemass* (2000); Michael Kennedy, *Division and consensus: the politics of cross-border relations in Ireland, 1925–69* (2000); Ronan Fanning, 'Playing it cool: the response of the British and Irish governments to the crisis in Northern Ireland, 1968–69', *Irish Studies in International Affairs*, xii (2001), 57–85; Máire Cruise O'Brien, *The same age as the state* (2003); Tom Garvin *et al.* (ed.), *Dissecting Irish politics: essays in honour of Brian Farrell* (2004); Pádraig Faulkner, *As I saw it: reviewing over 30 years of Fianna Fáil and Irish politics* (2005); Michael Kennedy and Deirdre McMahon (ed.), *Obligations and responsibilities: Ireland and the United Nations 1955–2005* (2005); Eamon O'Flaherty, 'Aiken: gunman and statesman', *History Ireland*, xv, no. 1 (January–February 2007), 54–5

John Miller Andrews

1871–1956

John Miller Andrews, prime minister of Northern Ireland, was born 17 July 1871 in Comber, Co. Down, eldest of four sons and one daughter of Thomas Andrews, miller, and Eliza Andrews of Ardara, Comber, daughter of James Alexander Pirrie of Belfast, and sister of Viscount Pirrie, shipbuilder, of Harland and Wolff. He was educated at the Royal Belfast Academical Institution and completed an apprenticeship at a Carrickfergus flax-spinning firm. His early career was spent in running the family mill in Comber, and he took little active part in political life until 1912, when he was a member of the organising committee for Ulster Day, and of the provisional government. In 1917 he was associated with the Ulster unionist delegation to the Irish Convention, and subsequently assisted

Edward Carson to organise the Ulster Unionist Labour Association, a political forum for working-class unionists.

In June 1921 Andrews was elected to the new parliament of Northern Ireland as a member for Co. Down, and received the Labour portfolio in Sir James Craig's first cabinet. This post involved responsibility for unemployment benefit, health insurance, and the maintenance of good industrial relations. It was not without significance in the wider political scene: in mid 1922 Andrews was given the task of implementing the relief works agreed as a result of peace talks between Craig and Michael Collins. Given the political tensions of the period, the 'Craig–Collins pact' had few concrete results, and the relative success of the relief-works committee owed much to Andrews's tact and patience.

As the decade progressed, his tenacity was tested even further. The postwar depression did not deal kindly with Northern Ireland, and unemployment spiralled. The anticipated financial benisons of the 1920 Government of Ireland Act did not materialise, and the local unemployment fund actually began with a deficit, which accelerated at the rate of £100,000 a month. The local financial mandarins were anxious to bring the situation under control by reducing benefit below the levels paid in other parts of the United Kingdom. Such a policy was anathema to Andrews, who insisted that all British citizens should be entitled to the same welfare conditions. This policy of parity was the cornerstone of Andrews's political philosophy, based on both compassion and electoral expediency. He regarded Westminster as ultimately responsible for the province's upkeep, and fought hard to have this enshrined in legislation. The first step towards this came in 1926 with the unemployment reinsurance act, a limited measure that provided for some reduction in the province's debt. This legislation was subsequently amended over the following decade in Northern Ireland's favour. Throughout his sixteen-year tenure at the ministry of labour, Andrews defended a number of parity issues, overcoming the opposition of both the Treasury and fellow cabinet ministers. In the late 1920s he campaigned for the introduction of health insurance on British lines, and in the early 1930s he successfully fought for the extension of unemployment insurance to agricultural workers.

In 1937 Andrews succeeded H. M. Pollock as minister of finance. As such, he was effectively Craig's deputy and frequently presided at cabinet meetings. Andrews represented Northern Ireland at the 1938 Anglo–Irish negotiations, and presented a strong case to Neville Chamberlain's government. Much of his work was undermined by Craig, who arrived at a late stage in the talks and reached a private deal with the British premier. Andrews saw very clearly that his prime minister was no longer capable of governing effectively, but loyally refused to press for his resignation. The Stormont administration staggered from crisis to crisis, and the advent of war in 1939 only added to the strain. Andrews was under renewed pressure from the Treasury to pare local spending still further, although his cabinet colleagues did not regard this obligation particularly seriously. Craig increasingly bypassed the cabinet system of government and acted as something of a dictator, albeit a rather incompetent one. He shrugged off all criticism and remained in office until his death in November 1940.

As deputy prime minister Andrews was the most obvious successor and was duly appointed by the governor. He had little real understanding of the military situation and his primary concern was with the government's political situation rather than the war effort. The elderly administration's inefficiency was exposed in a series of crises, including the Belfast air raids, the failure to introduce conscription, and a long-running battle with Belfast corporation, leading to the loss of two safe unionist seats in by-elections. Whitehall was very concerned about Andrews's failure to prevent a series of extensive strikes in the aircraft industry, which earned him a personal rebuke from Churchill. The Treasury mandarins were even more incensed at a speech in which, without consulting them, Andrews announced an ambitious postwar spending plan for the province.

Matters came to a head early in 1943, when a group of backbenchers and junior ministers challenged the prime minister's leadership. Instead of attempting to address the critics' questions, Andrews tried to drum up support in the unionist party outside parliament. However, the rebels prevailed and by 28 April they had been joined by a cabinet minister, Sir Basil Brooke, whose resignation effectively torpedoed Andrews's hopes of staying in office.

At the age of 72, Andrews started life as a backbencher, sitting as MP for Mid Down until 1954. He was appointed a Companion of Honour by George VI and was made a freeman of Londonderry. Andrews also achieved office in the Grand Orange Lodge of Ireland and the Imperial Orange Council. He retired from public life in 1954, and died on 8 August 1956, the last surviving member of the original 1921 cabinet. He married (1902) Jessie (d. 1950), eldest daughter of Joseph Ormrod, stockbroker, of Bolton; they had a son and two daughters. His brother James (Sir James Andrews, lord chief justice of Northern Ireland 1937–51) married Jane, a sister of Jessie. Another brother was Thomas Andrews, chief designer of the *Titanic*. There is no single archive of Andrews papers, but a number of collections are held at PRONI.

Andrews is something of a neglected figure in the historiography of Northern Ireland, mentioned in passing as a rather undistinguished prime minister. However, he was an outstanding minister of labour who earned respect across the political divide for his even-handed stance on social-security issues; and on at least one occasion he intervened to ensure that a Catholic was promoted to a senior civil-service position. Andrews was perhaps the archetypal Stormont politician: with a keen understanding of local needs, but lacking the ability—crucial in wartime—to see beyond them.

David Richardson

Sources

John Burls (ed.), *Nine generations: a history of the Andrews family, millers of Comber* (1958); Patrick Buckland, *The factory of grievances: devolved government in Northern Ireland 1921–39* (1979); Brian Barton, *Brookeborough* (1988); David Richardson, 'The career of John Miller Andrews 1871–1956', unpublished PhD thesis, Belfast, 1998 (detailed bibliography)

James Brown Armour

(1841–1928)

James Brown Armour, Presbyterian minister and political campaigner, was born 20/31 January 1841, youngest of six children of
William Armour and Jane Armour (née Brown), who both came of
Presbyterian tenant-farmer families in Kilraughts, north Co.
Antrim; the Armours lived in Lisboy townland. He was educated
in Ganaby school, Ballymoney Model School, and the Royal Belfast
Academical Institution. In 1860 he entered QCB, and after a year
teaching in Cookstown he transferred in 1863 to QCC, where he
took a general BA (1864). He graduated from Belfast with a master's degree in classics (1866). He intended a career in law, but his
father and brother, dying in 1864 and 1865 respectively, both expressed the wish that he become a minister, and probably as a result

he entered Assembly's College, Belfast, in 1865. On 19 July 1869 he was ordained and became minister in Second Ballymoney, later re-named Trinity, Ballymoney, a few miles from his birthplace. In 1882 he and his congregation built a larger church and hall.

Armour had a lifelong interest in education, and during 1878–83 was principal and sole teacher of Ballymoney intermediate school (later Dalriada school). For twenty-three years until 1908 he was assistant to his wife's brother-in law, James MacMaster, professor of classics in Magee College, Derry, travelling ninety miles (145 km) in unheated trains several days a week. From 1882 he regularly spoke in the Presbyterian general assembly on the need for united secular and separate religious primary education, and after 1900 he advocated a separate state-funded university for Catholics. When QUB was founded in 1908, Armour supported measures to make it more acceptable to Catholic students, and was a member of its senate (1910–14).

Armour contributed in other ways to community life, supporting temperance campaigns and in particular land reform. His eloquent indictments of the hegemony of landlords, and of the injustices done to tenants and labourers, spoke for many in Ulster. He supported liberal candidates and Gladstone's policies, convinced that political liberalism, like 'enlightenment' values, suited Presbyterian traditions of democracy and personal judgement. His contributions to journals such as the *Witness* and his annual appearances at the general assembly made him prominent. Audiences relished his humour and sarcasm, even if, as often happened, his views were unpopular. After 1887 he came to see liberal unionism as dominated by the Anglican and landowning establishment, and home rule (though generally unpopular with Protestants) as good for Presbyterians in the long run. In a special meeting of the general assembly (15 March 1893) Armour asserted that 'the principle of home rule is a Presbyterian principle', and criticised his co-religionists for helping to perpetuate the landlord system, but was interrupted by the hostile majority, and failed to defeat the resolutions against home rule.

His own congregation remained loyal and he retained some support where liberalism persisted, particularly in Co. Antrim. When Armour and his second cousin, the Rev. James B. Dougherty organised a Presbyterian memorial to be sent to Gladstone, they obtained

3,535 signatures without much effort. Gladstone's retirement (1894) and the liberals' 1895 electoral defeat ended any immediate prospect of home rule, and thereafter Armour took less part in politics. In 1906 he became a chaplain to the viceroy, Lord Aberdeen, and when in 1908 Dougherty became under-secretary, Armour had some influence in Dublin. In the 1913 general assembly he strongly advocated home rule, and supported (October 1913) a Ballymoney meeting of Protestants opposing the tactics of Sir Edward Carson. After 1918 he opposed partition and the establishment of the northern parliament, remarking (1923) that northern unionists had had to accept a form of home rule that 'the devil himself could never have imagined'.

Armour resigned (September 1925) after fifty-six years as minister of Trinity, Ballymoney. He died 25 January 1928. He married (19 March 1883) his distant relative Jennie Adams Hamilton, daughter of Alexander Macleod Staveley from Co. Antrim, a Reformed Presbyterian minister in Newfoundland and grandson of William Staveley; she had been a widow for three years, and had two sons. The Armours had three sons: James B. MacM. ('Max') Armour, a Presbyterian minister in England and Canada; J. Kenneth C. Armour, schoolmaster in Campbell College, Belfast; and the eldest son, William Staveley Armour (1883–1940), journalist and author, who was born 28 December 1883 in Ballymoney, Co. Antrim. He was educated at Campbell College, Belfast, and Jesus College, Oxford, and in 1907 became president of the Oxford Union. In 1910, he went to teach in Queen's College, Benares, India, and became inspector of schools in the Lucknow division, but returned to England and became a barrister. He moved to Belfast after the first world war as features writer (later editor) of the *Northern Whig*. In its pages he suggested (1929) that a club should be formed for young people in the country; he had travelled in Denmark in the 1920s and been impressed by the folk high schools there. The article led to the foundation of the Young Farmers' Clubs of Ulster. Armour left the *Northern Whig* after political disagreements, and moved to London, where he wrote *Facing the Irish question* (1935), *Mankind at the watershed* (1936), and *Ulster, Ireland, Britain: a forgotten trust* (1938). His views on society, politics, and Irish affairs were very liberal. He also wrote a biography of his father, *Armour of Ballymoney* (1934). Armour married (10 June 1931) Ruth Marguerite, daughter of Henry Montgomery, Presbyterian minister and moderator of the general assembly (1912), and died childless, 31 December 1940, in England.

Linde Lunney

Sources

J. E. and T. H. Mullin, *Roots in Ulster soil* (1967), 163–5; Thomas J. G. Bennett, *North Antrim families* (1974), 103; S. Alex. Blair, 'Just a youth of fifty-five: the story of the Young Farmers' Clubs of Ulster', *Ulster Local Studies*, ix (1984), 16–19; J. R. B. McMinn, *Against the tide: a calendar of the papers of Rev. J. B. Armour, Irish Presbyterian minister and home ruler 1869–1914* (1985); Len Snodgrass, *Armour's meeting house: the first hundred years* (1985), 41–59

Sir (Richard) Dawson Bates

(1876–1949)

Sir (Richard) Dawson Bates, solicitor and NI cabinet minister, was born 23 November 1876 at Strandtown, east Belfast, son of Richard Dawson Bates, solicitor and clerk of the crown and peace for Belfast, and his wife Mary, daughter of Professor R. F. Dill of QCB. His paternal grandfather John Bates was town clerk and town solicitor of Belfast 1842–55; one uncle was crown solicitor for Belfast, another a judge. Educated at Coleraine Academical Institution, Bates was admitted solicitor in 1900 and entered the family firm. As secretary of the Ulster Unionist Council (1906–21) and joint secretary of the Unionist Associations of Ireland from 1907, he helped to organise the Ulster covenant and Ulster Volunteer Force. He received an OBE (1919) for wartime work for the UVF hospitals and UVF Patriotic Fund. Sir James Craig thought Bates 'knew the mind of Ulster better than almost anyone else', and made him (June 1921) minister of home affairs, a post he held for nearly twenty-two years. Bates was made a knight (1921) and a baronet (1937), and sat in the Northern Ireland parliament for Belfast East (1921–9) and Belfast (Victoria) (1929–45).

With his personal influence in government and central and local unionist organisations, and his ministry's wide powers over security and local government, Bates became a leading architect of the northern state. In unionist eyes, his personal courage and firmness (notably in managing police and special constabulary, and introducing and working the Special Powers Act, 1922) ensured the state's survival. However, his conspicuous distrust of the nationalist minority frustrated initial attempts to secure its cooperation, helped to minimise its power in local government, and encouraged an overtly discriminatory administrative style. As one of the 'step by step' group in cabinet, he resisted cuts in government spending in the 1930s, not only on police but on housing subsidies; but he half-heartedly supported health benefits, rejected rent control, and was reluctant to suspend Belfast corporation for corruption. With the coming of war, he was criticised for general inefficiency and for the specific shortcomings in civil defence revealed by the Belfast blitz (1941). By 1943 Bates and most of his colleagues appeared within their own party as *ancien régime* figures, and were dropped by Basil Brooke from his new cabinet. After leaving office (which he did reluctantly), Bates did not speak in parliament, or stand for reelection. In 1947 he retired to Glastonbury, England, where he died during the night of 9/10 June 1949; he was buried near his former home, Magherabuoy House, Portrush, Co. Londonderry.

He married (1920) Jessie Muriel, daughter of Sir Charles Cleland of Glasgow. Their one son, Sir John Dawson Bates (1921–98) was born 21 September 1921 at Holywood, Co. Down, and educated at Winchester. He was commissioned into the Rifle Brigade in May 1941, won the MC in North Africa (1943), went on demobilisation to Balliol College, Oxford (1946), and graduated in history (1949). After qualifying as a land agent, he joined the National Trust (1957) and became responsible for managing its estates in the south midlands of England and the Isle of Wight. He resided on the Buscot estate, Oxfordshire, until retirement, when he and his wife moved to his mother's house in Somerset. He died 12 July 1998, having been a member of the Orange Order since 1940. He married (1953) Mary Hoult, architect; both were devoted gardeners. They had a daughter and two sons, of whom Richard (b. 1956) succeeded as 3rd baronet.

Richard Hawkins

Sources

Debrett, *Baronetage* (1940); *Belfast Telegraph*, 10, 14 June 1949 (photo); *Times*, 11 June 1949; *WWW*; John F. Harbinson, *The Ulster Unionist Party, 1882–1973: its development and organisation* (1973); Patrick Buckland, *The factory of grievances: devolved government in Northern Ireland 1921–39* (1979); Patrick Buckland, *James Craig* (1980); Brian Barton, *Brookeborough: the making of a prime minister* (1988); *Times*, 21 July 1998 (photo); *Daily Telegraph*, 3 August 1998 (photo)

Francis Joseph Bigger

(1863–1926)

Francis Joseph Bigger, antiquary, nationalist, and Celtic revival polymath, was born 17 July 1863 in Belfast, seventh son of Joseph Bigger, of Belfast, and his wife Mary Jane (née Ardery) of Ballyvalley. F. J. Bigger was educated briefly in Liverpool, where his father worked for a short time, and from 1874 at Royal Belfast Academical Institution. He enrolled to study law at QCB in 1880, was articled to Messrs Henry and William Seeds (1885), and qualified as a solicitor (1887). In 1889 Bigger opened a practice in partnership with George Strahan, whom he had met in Dublin, at Rea's Buildings, Royal Avenue, Belfast.

Aside from his work as a solicitor Bigger's earliest interests, which included Irish history and antiquities as well as the natural sciences, would occupy much of his life. In 1884 he joined the Belfast Naturalists' Field Club (BNFC), which encouraged his interests and where he learned Irish. Under Bigger's direction, as secretary and then president, the BNFC became more actively involved in archaeological and folklore study. In 1888 he was elected a member of the RSAI, becoming a fellow in 1896. In 1894 he had been elected a member of the RIA. Bigger also joined the Gaelic League, becoming a member of its Coiste Gnó (executive committee), which brought him into contact with Douglas Hyde and Eoin MacNeill, who would influence many of his ideas.

Bigger's political beliefs, cultural interests, and social connections naturally led him to approach a political career, which seems to have been curtailed by the events of 1916 and the death of friends such as Roger Casement and Patrick Pearse as well as his increasing isolation amongst Ulster unionists. Although Bigger's political career was unrealised, his cultural activities have left an enduring legacy. His work can be divided into three broad areas: as a writer of books and articles; as an organiser and promoter of social and cultural events and activities; and as a heritage conservationist.

As a writer Bigger was prolific by any standards, producing in excess of 400 articles. As well as being a contributor to Irish antiquarian journals and several daily newspapers, he was also a prolific editor. In 1894 he revived the *Ulster Journal of Archaeology*, and later helped J. S. Crone to establish the *Irish Book Lover*. Several of his articles were issued as pamphlets, including his controversial *The holy hills of Ireland* (1907). His projected series of books, *The northern leaders of '98*, remained unfinished after *Remember Orr* (1906). He also wrote numerous articles on his two favourite pastimes, gardening and bee keeping. Other writings included *Four shots from Down* (1918) and *Crossing the bar* (1926).

Bigger saw his role as promoter of all things Irish, and was involved in the revival of numerous processions, pageants, ceilidhs and feiseanna. His projects were similar in many ways to the European 'to the people' movement and possess some affinity—with their emphasis on the betterment of the urban poor and rural peasantry by rescuing folk traditions—to the culturally philanthropic projects of Ruskin and Morris. Bigger's ideas and endeavours were encouraged by the Rev. George Hill and Fr James O'Laverty (1828–1906), and compared to the work of earlier antiquaries such as George Petrie, Samuel Ferguson, Eugene O'Curry, and John O'Donovan. The 'national romanticism' spirit which pervades Bigger's life and work links him with several other key Celtic revivalists, such as Patrick Pearse and Patrick Geddes (1854–1932).

Bigger was a founder member of the Ulster Literary Theatre, the Irish Folk Song Society, the Irish Peasant Home Industries, the Ulster Public House Association, and schemes for improved labourers' cottages, and he served as a committee member of the Belfast Art Society and the Irish Decorative Art Association. He was a patron of the Dun Emer Guild, the Craftworkers, and the Irish Art Companions, as well as of numerous individual artists, poets and musicians. The year 1898 saw many of Bigger's interests in history, art, literature, and politics coalesce in one single event, the Belfast Gaelic League pageant to mark the centenary of 1798. He also helped organise the Irish harp festival of 1903 and the Samuel Ferguson centenary in 1910. One of Bigger's greatest achievements was the founding of the Feis na nGleann in 1904, which attracted assistance from the Department of Agriculture and Technical Instruction, which, realising Bigger's skills, enlisted him in organising the Irish exhibit for the 1904 St Louis Fair.

As a conservationist he was keen to restore what was left of Ulster's heritage. His enterprises uncovered unique pre-Reformation sculpture and medieval stained glass, and funded restorations of several ancient monasteries and monuments. His greatest achievement was the restoration of the Elizabethan tower house Castle Seán in Ardglass, which became a model building of the Celtic revival and a meeting place for many of its most prominent figures. Bigger also attempted to locate, relocate, or mark the graves of several national figures such as St Patrick, Robert Emmet, and Henry Joy McCracken.

In July 1926 Bigger was conferred with an MA from QUB in recognition of his services to archaeology and local history. In August he went on a research trip to trace the steps of Irish saints from Lindisfarne, Whitby and the Low Countries, but returned home early after falling ill. He died 9 December 1926 at his home, Ard Righ, Antrim Road, Belfast, and was buried in the Bigger family plot at Mullusk two days later. A large collection of his papers is held at the Central Library, Belfast.

Joseph McBrinn

Sources

Obit., *Journal of the Royal Society of Antiquaries of Ireland*, 6th ser., xvii (1927), 73; J. S. Crone and F. C. Bigger (ed.), *In remembrance. Articles and sketches: biographical, historical, topographical by Francis Joseph Bigger M.A., M.R.I.A., F.R.S.A.I.* (1927); Roger Dixon, 'Francis Bigger, Ulster's Don Quixote', *Ulster Folklife*, xliii (1997), 40–7; Joseph McBrinn, 'The peasant and folk art revival in Ireland, 1890–1920: with special reference to Ulster', *Ulster Folklife*, xlviii (2002), 14–69

Ernest Blythe (Earnán de Blaghd)

(1889–1975)

Ernest Blythe, revolutionary, politician, government minister, managing director of the Abbey Theatre, and Irish-language revivalist, was born 13 April 1889 at Magheragall, Lisburn, Co. Antrim, eldest child among two sons and two daughters of James Blythe, farmer, and Agnes Blythe (née Thompson).

Upbringing and education

He was raised as a member of the Church of Ireland, following the religious affiliation of his father. His mother came from a Presbyterian background. He received his formal education at the local national schools at Maghaberry and Ballycarrickmaddy. As he was the elder son, there would have been a conventional assumption that Ernest would succeed his father and spend his life working on their eighty-acre family farm. He failed to satisfy that and many other conventional assumptions during his long life. Blythe's passionate commitment to the promotion of the Irish language was central to the nationalism which he adopted as a young man and persevered with throughout his life. He claimed in his autobiography that his interest in the Irish language dated from his early childhood, sparked both by Catholic servant girls employed on his father's farm and by stories from his mother of her Irish-speaking Presbyterian kinsmen.

Language and early politics

He obtained employment in Dublin in 1905 with the Department of Agriculture and Technical Instruction and soon became acquainted with Sean O'Casey, the future playwright and then a fellow member of the Church of Ireland. When the Rev. James Hannay (George A. Birmingham) made history by celebrating holy communion in Irish in St Patrick's cathedral, Dublin, on St Patrick's day 1906, he had the support of a small group of enthusiastic but unknown young men, including Blythe and O'Casey. Their position on that issue was socially isolating in that their fellow members of the Gaelic League did not approve of activities carried out on a sectarian basis. Perhaps even more so, the great majority of their fellow members of the Church of Ireland were opposed to the use of the Irish language in their church services. Blythe's interest in the revival of the Irish language as the vernacular became a lifelong passionate commitment. Not satisfied with the level of proficiency acquired through Gaelic League classes, Blythe went to live in the west Kerry Gaeltacht in April 1913. He worked there for several months as a labourer on the farm of the family of Thomas Ashe.

His new cultural identity was complemented by clandestine political militancy when in 1906, at the instigation of Sean O'Casey, he joined the Irish Republican Brotherhood (IRB). He recollected in later life that the only public activity in which he was involved as an IRB member was a fruitless attempt in 1907 to break up a meeting in Dublin's Mansion House on the Irish Council bill at which John Redmond and Joseph Devlin were the principal speakers.

Blythe moved in March 1909 to a milieu politically hostile to his nascent separatism when he took up employment as a journalist with the *North Down Herald*, a pro-unionist weekly newspaper published in Bangor, Co. Down. He spent four years writing for that paper, sometimes penning its leading article. At the same time, he was active in the clandestine promotion of the IRB in Ulster. In these years he had first-hand experience of the rise in militant unionist resistance to the 1912 home rule bill. It was an experience shared by very few of those who would come to political prominence in the Irish Free State, and one that shaped much of his political views over many decades, not only on the partition issue but also in relation to the revival of the Irish language.

While employed in Co. Down, Blythe remained in touch with Dublin-based separatists. In October 1910, at the instigation of Tom Clarke, the IRB launched a new separatist monthly newspaper, *Irish Freedom*. Blythe, along with Seán Mac Diarmada, Denis McCullough, Bulmer Hobson, and Dr Pat McCartan, was invited by Clarke to take editorial charge.

IRB and Volunteers

As the political success of Sir Edward Carson in 1912–13 in leading unionist opposition to mooted home rule undermined public confidence in the effectiveness of John Redmond's parliamentary party, advanced nationalists increasingly viewed their counterweight to unionism to be the IRB-influenced Volunteers, not the Sinn Féin party of Arthur Griffith. Blythe reflected that view when he wrote in *Irish Freedom* in December 1913, describing Sinn Féin in somewhat condescending terms as being 'valueless' except as the complement of military organisation. He then enthused also about 'the red tillage of the battlefield', concluding that none was 'worthy of the name of nationalist or citizen or man but the soldier' (*Irish Freedom*, December 1913).

With the outbreak of the first world war and the subsequent split in the Volunteer movement between the larger, Redmondite National Volunteers and the smaller, more radical and IRB-influenced Irish Volunteers, Blythe became a full-time Irish Volunteer organiser, in 1915 working in counties as far apart as Clare and Londonderry. He ensured, as far as he could influence it, that Irish Volunteer officers were also IRB members. This was an important factor in planning the 1916 rising, when the IRB leadership had not yet ensured the agreement of Eoin MacNeill and others on the Irish Volunteers' executive. Blythe's work as a revolutionary organiser was necessarily clandestine and so largely unrecorded. That he had a significant role can be inferred from the fact that he was jailed in autumn 1915 under the Defence of the Realm Act, along with Seán Mac Diarmada and Liam Mellows. A rally held in the Phoenix Park on 12 September 1915 to call for their release was addressed by James Connolly among others, and drew a crowd reportedly in excess of 10,000.

Blythe's release from prison was short-lived: a Dublin Castle security meeting held on 17 March 1916 agreed that Blythe and Mellows posed sufficient danger to warrant deportation to England. The meeting at which that decision was taken was attended by senior members of the Dublin Castle administration, including the British under-secretary for Ireland, Matthew Nathan, and the attorney general, John Gordon. The relative importance ascribed by the Castle administration to Blythe may be gauged from the fact that the same meeting considered it unnecessary to reimprison Tom Clarke 'unless some new offence could be proved'. Blythe spent the succeeding months, including the week of the 1916 Easter rising, in various prisons in Britain, including Oxford, Brixton, and Reading. On release, he spent Christmas 1916 in Limerick at the home of John Daly and in the company of Tom Clarke's widow, Kathleen (née Daly), and her children, though he did not confine himself to seasonal social activities: he also took the opportunity to reactivate Limerick's Volunteer cadre. When the Sinn Féin convention of October 1917 gave that party a new focus as well as a new leadership, reflecting its reinvigorated political status, over a hundred candidates competed for the twenty-four posts on the party's new executive. Blythe, Darrell Figgis and Dr Kathleen Lynn were the only three Protestants to be elected.

Dáil Éireann 1919–21

Blythe's growing public profile was advanced further when he was elected for Monaghan North in the 1918 general election. (He also stood in Armagh North in the same election but lost overwhelmingly to the unionist candidate.) He was returned for Monaghan at successive general elections until 1933. When Éamon de Valera became president of the council of ministers in April 1919 he appointed three non-cabinet directors, with Blythe chosen as director of trade and commerce. Dáil Éireann was soon driven underground, and it met only eight times between September 1919 and July 1921. Blythe was arrested and jailed several times between those dates. Not surprisingly, his administrative achievements in that session were slight, limited largely to the establishment of an industrial resources commission, which carried out its research slowly, if methodically, eventually producing eight separate reports. Blythe's capacity to look at political problems and offer an independent-minded solution was reflected at this stage in his opposition, in Dáil Éireann, to a proposed general boycott of Belfast goods and services. The 'Belfast boycott' evolved in the south as a reaction to major incidents of sectarian attacks on Catholic workers, especially in Belfast. Blythe argued in the dáil that a general economic boycott of Belfast goods would destroy forever the possibility of any north–south union. Instead, he proposed a boycott confined to specific northern individuals and firms who could be demonstrably linked to sectarian attacks on Catholics. As the sole northern Protestant member of Dáil Éireann, Blythe then, and many times later, articulated views sharply at variance with Irish nationalist opinion generally.

Northern policy

Blythe supported the Anglo–Irish treaty of 6 December 1921, arguing, in the course of the dáil debate on its approval, that by the use of 'suitable propaganda' Protestant Ulstermen's latent nationalism could be resuscitated. Positing that Irish nationalists had a right to coerce Ulster unionists, he added that it was inappropriate to attempt to coerce and conciliate them at the same time. Blythe's views on the Ulster question were expressed in more specific terms in the second half of 1922. In the first half of that year the views of Michael Collins on the partition of Ulster had prevailed and his cabinet colleagues had not been fully briefed by him on developments in Ulster. When Collins became commander-in-chief of the national army and withdrew from his ministerial role, the ensuing political power vacuum allowed the direction of northern policy to be moulded by Collins's colleagues in the provisional government, who quickly decided on a substantially different approach. In early August 1922 the provisional government set up a five-man committee, including Blythe, to formulate a coherent northern policy. As an Ulster Protestant, Blythe was probably the only member of the provisional government who had a realistic political insight into how the Ulster Protestant mind worked. He circulated an influential memorandum to the committee, implicitly criticising the northern policy that Collins had pursued since January. He described that clandestine, belligerent policy as 'useless for protecting the Catholics or stopping the pogroms' (quoted in Michael Hopkinson, *Green against green* (1988), 250). Likewise, he saw no prospect for bringing secessionist Ulster into a united Ireland by economic pressure. On 19 August 1922 the provisional government formally adopted a 'peace policy... with north-east Ulster' (Hopkinson (1988), 250). A week later, four days after the shooting of Collins, Blythe's memorandum was circulated to all members of the provisional government. In effect, Blythe's core recommendations were implicitly accepted by that government and, indeed, by successive Irish governments.

Government minister

Blythe's formal ministerial role in the provisional government (from August 1922) and in the early Free State government was that of minister for local government, a position which he vacated in October 1923 on becoming minister for finance. He held that post until the advent in March 1932 of the first Fianna Fáil government. Following the assassination in July 1927 of Kevin O'Higgins, Blythe also took on the office of vice-president of the executive council. After the second general election of 1927 he held both of these roles as well as that of minister for posts and telegraphs. It is, however, in his role as minister for finance that he is chiefly remembered. The nationalist rhetoric of pre-independent Ireland pointed to a prosperous future—once political independence had been achieved. The reality faced by Blythe as minister for finance was entirely different. The Irish Free State had a weak industrial sector, exacerbated by partition, which removed from its political control the most prosperous region and two-thirds of the industrial workforce. The economy of the new state remained closely integrated with that of Britain and Northern Ireland, which accounted for £50.5 m of total Free State exports of £51.58 m in 1924. Prices for Irish agricultural produce, which had risen during the first world war, fell significantly in the post-war era when Britain regained access to other suppliers of food. By 1927 the Free State agricultural price index had fallen below half of the 1920 level. The cost of maintaining the Free State army during the civil war at a strength of over 50,000 was a major burden on the national finances. Over 25 per cent of the total estimates for 1922–3 was allocated to meeting army costs. The top echelons of the Irish banks were dominated largely by men of a pro-unionist background who had little faith in the abilities of the Free State's politicians. As early as 1923 the government was obliged to seek credit facilities from the Irish banks, which responded only when the British Treasury exercised pressure on them. Most of the Free State's senior civil servants had spent the formative years of their careers working in the British civil service and continued to value financial probity, treasury control, and a distaste for economic intervention. In summary, Blythe's time at Finance allowed little scope for radical, developmental innovation in fiscal or economic policies, nor indeed did Blythe seek to promote policies on those lines.

Blythe made little pretence of adhering to either the vague social aspirations of the first dáil's democratic programme, or to the policies of economic self-sufficiency advocated by Sinn Féin's founder, Arthur Griffith. On the contrary, he implemented enthusiastically the then economic orthodoxy of cutting public expenditure and underpinning laissez-faire free trade. Government expenditure fell from £28.7 m in 1923/4 to £18.9 m in 1927/8. Within a month of his appointment in September 1923 as minister for finance, Blythe endorsed the recommendations of his department to cut government spending by measures that would prove to be highly unpopular politically. The measures included salary cuts for national school-teachers and the army, as well as a cut of one shilling in the ten-shilling weekly old-age pension. Blythe's public defence of the pension cut was that the cost of living had fallen significantly since the rate of weekly pension payment had been fixed at ten shillings. Some later comparative research indicates that the Irish old-age pension was, at that time, one of the more generous in Europe as a proportion of average industrial earnings. This arose because the pension rate was set at the UK rate before the Free State's inception, despite the generally lower standard of living in Ireland. Furthermore, in Ireland older age groups formed a greater proportion of the overall population than in the UK. The resulting burden of old age pensions was a major expenditure item in the early Free State, amounting to £3.3 m. of a total public expenditure in 1922/3 of £20 m. Experiencing little assistance from the Irish banks, Blythe accepted his department's strong recommendation to raise a national loan. The expenditure cuts announced by Blythe in November 1923 could be seen as a public commitment to financial orthodoxy, a commitment necessary for the success of the forthcoming national loan. The loan issue was a success. In contrast, the expenditure cuts, especially those applicable to pensioners, remained an outstanding political liability for Blythe and his party for many years.

Blythe was not an innovative minister for finance. The initiative in 1924 to have the first major hydroelectric generation capacity built by the state came from the Department of Industry and Commerce. The decision to implement that proposal was a landmark in the economic history of the Free State. In assenting to the 'Shannon scheme', as the state electricity generation capacity came to be called, Blythe bypassed his departmental secretary, Joseph Brennan, who had a deeply rooted objection to public expenditure on the scale required. Personal relations between Blythe and Brennan deteriorated sharply when Brennan realised that Blythe had not kept him informed of a decision with such major implications for public expenditure. Their relationship never recovered and to a considerable extent led to Brennan's decision in 1927, then aged 39 years, to resign as secretary of the Department of Finance.

Scarcity of economic resources, compounded by the expense of the civil war, undoubtedly greatly circumscribed Blythe's scope for freedom of action as minister for finance. In any case, Blythe was not temperamentally disposed to exercise what scope he had. The parameters of economic policy during Blythe's terms of office were devised and determined by commissions of experts, most notably the fiscal inquiry committee (1923) and the commission on agriculture (1924). Both groups strongly favoured a free-trade economic policy, a policy very much at variance with the economic protectionist policies advocated by Arthur Griffith and pre-treaty Sinn Féin. Blythe's fiscal policy rested on the core assumption that the well-being of the Irish economy was predominantly dependent on agriculture, and that the optimum prospects for agriculture were through increased agricultural exports to Britain. The means to achieve that goal included minimising tariff duties on manufactured goods so as to curtail cost increases for farmers. Blythe imposed tariffs in three successive budgets, 1924–6, but his measures had marginal impact and did little to satisfy the demands of Irish manufacturers for the application of a more rigorous tariff regime.

The enactment of the Tariff Commission Act, 1926, may have been perceived by some as holding out a promise of a significant policy shift on the tariff protection issue. It was not to be. Under the act, three commissioners were appointed (2 December 1926) for a two-year period, appointed respectively by the ministers for finance, agriculture (Patrick Hogan) and industry and commerce (Patrick McGilligan). Accepting the commissioners' recommendations in full did not greatly burden Blythe: during their term of office the commissioners' sole recommendations were the imposition of a 33.3 per cent tariff on rosary beads and a 3d. tariff on each pound of margarine.

Blythe changed the minimalist tariff policy pursued from 1923 to 1929 in his two final years as minister for finance. The change was reactive, driven in large measure in response to the sharp deterioration in the world economy from 1929. Growing internal pressures from the increasingly assertive Fianna Fáil party, and from Irish manufacturers urging the imposition of tariffs on imported goods, also impelled Blythe to amend his fiscal policies. The political convulsion in Britain in August 1931 led to the formation there of a 'national government' committed to protecting British agriculture, most especially those products in which Irish farmers then specialised, such as livestock and dairy products. This move undercut Blythe's tariff policy even further. Against a backdrop of an international economic recession and a virtual halt to emigration from the Free State, Blythe's tariff policies became politically unsustainable. By November 1931, only three months before a general election, Blythe and his cabinet colleagues introduced legislation which gave them power for a nine-month period to impose such import duties as were deemed 'immediately necessary to prevent an expected dumping of goods or other threatened industrial injury' (quoted in Daly, *Industrial development*, 47). In so far as it had any political effect, that action probably confirmed the perception of many voters that Blythe and his colleagues had belatedly come to accept the validity of Fianna Fáil's strongly pro-tariff protectionist policies.

In opposition

Blythe lost ministerial office following the general election in February 1932. He never served in government again. He lost his dáil seat in the 1933 election: the first two seats in his Monaghan constituency were taken by Fianna Fáil candidates; the third and final seat was taken by an ex-unionist candidate, elected with the help of Fianna Fáil transfers. Blythe resumed his parliamentary career when he won a by-election to the senate, and he was reelected in November 1934 in the senate's fourth triennial election. He was placed nineteenth of the twenty-three senators elected. In theory, the first twenty senators then elected were due to hold office for nine years. In reality, the abolition of the senate was impending and Blythe's political focus had already moved to extra-parliamentary activities centred on the Army Comrades Association (ACA, later the Blueshirts).

Blythe's association with the ACA dated from the summer of 1932. His enthusiasm for the new group found expression in different ways. It was on Blythe's recommendation that the colour blue was chosen for the distinctive shirt to be worn by Blueshirts. His belief that the colour of St Patrick's blue would link its wearers to a quasi-nationalist past was more than a little fanciful. He wrote several position papers for the Blueshirt movement on economic and social issues. His papers digressed into details of minutiae and were of no practical political relevance then or later. He wrote and spoke at this stage of his career as an enthusiastic supporter of the corporate and vocational political system. Perhaps disingenuously, and certainly somewhat incongruously for a Co. Antrim-born Protestant, he stressed the importance of Pope Pius XI as the inspiration of that ideology. Blythe urged that the Blueshirt movement should take the leading, overarching role in advancing the corporate system in Ireland, definitely a difference of kind rather than degree with the papal encyclical on vocationalism, *Quadragesimo anno*. The merger of Cumann na nGaedheal, the Centre Party, and the Blueshirt movement in September 1933 was short-lived, not least because of the irascible, exuberant behaviour of the Blueshirt leader, Eoin O'Duffy. By early October 1934 O'Duffy was describing Blythe publicly as a 'damnable traitor' and 'a scandal-monger' (quoted in Manning, *Blueshirts*, 167) who sought to undermine O'Duffy's authority as Blueshirt leader. Blythe certainly played a significant role in the removal of O'Duffy from leadership of Fine Gael, a move that brought that party back unequivocally to exclusively constitutional politics.

In common with several other former leading figures in Cumann na nGaedheal/Fine Gael, Blythe had drifted out of mainstream political activism by the late 1930s. He found employment as secretary of Clondalkin Paper Mills from 1937 to 1941. In 1941 he commenced what would be his longest period of continuous employment with a single employer, becoming managing director of the Abbey Theatre, a position he held until 1967.

The Abbey Theatre

As minister for finance Blythe had ensured in 1925 that an annual grant of £850 would be paid to the Abbey, and had been fêted from the Abbey stage on 8 August 1925 by W. B. Yeats for his enlightened act of patronage, which had returned the theatre to financial solvency. He was again on stage at the Abbey with Yeats and Lady Gregory on 27 December 1925, at a gala celebration marking the theatre's twenty-first anniversary. But the public identification of the Abbey with Blythe, a leading member of the Free State government, was not without its disadvantages for the Abbey. The riot that occurred on 11 February 1926 during the production of O'Casey's *The plough and the stars* was not spontaneous but instigated by well-known anti-treatyites, including Mrs Kathleen Clarke and Maude Gonne MacBride. Anti-treatyite publicists welcomed the riot as a high-profile means of embarrassing the Cumann na nGaedheal government, and Blythe especially, in that it portrayed them as subventing a quasi-sacrilegious attack on the sacred icons and ideals of Irish republicanism.

Blythe became a director of the Abbey Theatre in 1935, at the instigation of Yeats. His appointment, and subsequent rise to being the de facto sole authority figure within the Abbey for virtually three decades, has been portrayed as the culmination of a cunning game plan by Blythe. The reality was more complex. He was one of three new appointees to the expanded Abbey board in 1935. One of the two others, John Weldon (Brinsley McNamara), was a devoutly Catholic playwright who resigned within the year, having denounced his fellow directors for authorising the staging of O'Casey's *Silver tassie*, a play perceived by Weldon as being highly offensive to Catholics. The other appointee, F. R. Higgins, was a neo-romantic poet and on Yeats's recommendation was appointed managing director of the Abbey Theatre in November 1938. Higgins died of a heart attack in January 1941. Blythe succeeded him later that month as managing director, a position that he held from then until 1967. Blythe's appointment filled a power vacuum at the Abbey. Yeats had died in January 1939 and the author Frank O'Connor had been ousted as an Abbey director in August 1939. O'Connor's tenure as a director had lasted less than four years and was ended on the ostensible grounds that he supported divorce, a somewhat ironic basis in view of Yeats's very public defence of divorce in the senate debates of 1925. By September 1943 Walter Starkie was removed from the Abbey's board of directors as he had not complied with the new, more rigorous attendance required of directors. (As director of the British Institute in wartime Madrid, Starkie was scarcely in a position to comply.) By then Blythe's position within the Abbey board had been greatly strengthened as its membership consisted of Blythe, the now ineffectual Lennox Robinson, Richard Hayes, and Roibeárd Ó Faracháin, a close ally of Blythe and then an employee of Radio Éireann. Blythe, Hayes, and

Ó Faracháin shared an enthusiasm for the revival of the Irish language as the everyday medium of conversation, a factor that would influence the artistic direction of the Abbey Theatre for many years.

The balance of retrospective comment on Blythe's managerial role in the Abbey Theatre has been very largely negative. He has been criticised in particular for his zealous promotion of Irish-language plays and pantomimes at the Abbey to the detriment of its artistic standards. He was undoubtedly a cultural and linguistic nationalist, with the greater emphasis on nationalism rather than culture. In that he was very much a man of his time, attempting to implement the re-gaelicisation policy of the government in which he had participated and of its successor in office. Ireland had become increasingly introspective in the 1930s, and the isolationism brought on by the second world war and Ireland's continuing economic malaise had exacerbated that trend. Against that backdrop, Irish theatre audiences preferred pot-boiler farces by George Shiels rather than Yeat's obscure poetry. Existing on a meagre state subsidy, the Abbey was not in any position to offend church or state. The annual grant of £850, approved by Blythe as minister for finance in 1925 and which he increased to £1,000 for the financial year 1926–7, was not increased again until the financial year 1947–8. The Abbey's recurrent offering of forgettable and now forgotten farce, melodrama, and Irish-language pantomimes reflected as much on the preferences of contemporary theatregoers as it did on Blythe and his continuing attempts to balance the Abbey's budget.

The destruction by fire in July 1951 of the Abbey Theatre's premises obliged Blythe to find an alternative venue, the Queen's Theatre, Pearse Street, in autumn 1951. Abbey Theatre programmes laboured the point that the productions were those of 'The Abbey Theatre, Dublin, playing at the Queen's, pending the rebuilding and enlargement of the Abbey'. The envisaged temporary arrangement lasted until July 1966, when the rebuilt Abbey premises reopened at its original site. The larger capacity of the Queen's if anything increased pressure on Blythe to find even more popular box-office successes. The interregnum years at the Queen's worsened already poor staff relations between Blythe and the Abbey's actors, who sought better pay and conditions. When strike notice was served to expire in April 1964, Blythe agreed reluctantly to have the dispute examined by an independent arbitrator, and both sides accepted that the arbitrator's findings would be binding on them. Blythe's reluctance was in part due to his resentment at the actors' challenge to his authority and also to the mutual, long-standing antagonism between him and the arbitrator, C. S. ('Todd') Andrews. Andrews produced an arbitration report within a month which recommended much improved pay and conditions of service and urged the government to increase the subsidy to meet current losses, eliminate accumulated losses, and put in place adequate working capital for the continuance of the theatre.

In accepting part of the Andrews 1964 arbitration recommendations, the minister for finance, James Ryan, decided to increase the number of government nominees on the Abbey board and to widen the base of its shareholders' structure. The net effect was the gradual dilution of Blythe's authority within the Abbey. The enlarged and renewed Abbey shareholders' group sought to circumscribe Blythe's role as managing director by the creation of a new post of artistic director. Blythe was predictably hostile to the proposal and defended his authority tenaciously. The internal debate continued intermittently throughout 1965. The eventual compromise was a face-saving victory for Blythe: Walter Macken was appointed near the end of 1965 as artistic adviser with a consultative remit only. Macken choose to resign from that role by June 1966. The role of artistic adviser was then assumed by Tomás Mac Anna, who had been largely responsible for directing most Irish-language plays produced from 1947 onwards and had considerable experience as a set designer of high repute. Not unimportantly, he had a good working relationship with Blythe. That consideration was seen by some as a ploy by Blythe to retain his influence. Nonetheless, Blythe retired as the Abbey's managing director on 31 August 1967 but retained an office in the theatre and remained on the Abbey's board for five more years.

Irish language

Blythe played several very separate roles in the course of his adult life. The one continuous link over those years was his total commitment to promoting the revival of the Irish language as the language of everyday life. Writing a half-century after Blythe had lost ministerial office, his former private secretary at the Department of Finance, León Ó Broin, described Blythe as being

> less inclined to accept criticisms of [Irish] language projects which, for the most part, he had himself generated, than of the multitude of proposals and expenditure that were submitted for finance consideration (Ó Broin, *No man's man: a biographical memoir of Joseph Brennan* (1982), 128).

Measures initiated during Blythe's term of office as minister for finance included the provision of a subsidised Irish-language theatre at Galway (Taibhdhearc na Gaillimhe); the creation of An Gúm, a state publishing company which made available inexpensive copies of Irish-language textbooks, some new works by writers in Irish, but mostly translations into Irish of well-known novels and histories; the provision of financial assistance to schools teaching through the medium of Irish; and housing grants for Gaeltacht (Irish-speaking) areas. In an era of radical cutbacks on state expenditure, none of these measures could have been introduced without Blythe's full support.

He reaped little or no political dividend from his efforts to advance the everyday use of the Irish language: civil service candidates resented the introduction of compulsory Irish examinations; members of Irish-language revivalist movements mirrored the political split on the treaty issue; would-be Gaelic authors resented the emphasis by An Gúm on translating published works rather than their own creations; Blythe's support for standardised spelling and use of the 'Roman' font in Irish-language print was contested fiercely by dogmatic supporters of the traditional 'Gaelic' font. Blythe's personal preference for speaking Munster Irish engendered paranoia on the part of many supporters of the other Irish-language dialects, who believed that the few opportunities for career advancement on the basis of Irish-language proficiency were being monopolised by those speaking the Munster dialect.

Neither his loss of political office nor the continuing factionalism of other Irish-language revivalists abated Blythe's enthusiasm for Irish. He continued to publish articles in the *Leader* during the late

1930s, urging the introduction of further supportive measures to bolster the position of the Irish language and its speakers. The election in 1941 of an IRA internee as president of Conradh na Gaeilge, then the main Irish-language revivalist body, worsened relations between Éamon de Valera, head of government, and Conradh. That situation in turn contributed to the establishment in 1943 by de Valera of An Comhdháil Náisiúnta na Gaeilge, an overarching co-ordination body, with state subvention, for the various voluntary Irish-language bodies. Blythe was chosen in 1947 as Comhdháil's president. He owed his new position largely to de Valera and Fianna Fáil, his former bitter civil-war enemies, a reflection of the cross-party respect for his unswerving Irish-language revivalist beliefs. Many of the language promotional measures then advocated by Blythe as Comhdháil president were implemented by Fianna Fáil governments. These included state subsidies for Irish-language magazines and newspapers, as well as the creation of a separate department of state with responsibility for the Gaeltacht. Blythe was a Fianna Fáil government appointee to the commission on the revival of the Irish language, as well as to the first Radio Éireann authority, appointed in 1960. His advocacy of the use of film, and even television, as a medium to promote wider use of Irish had been a matter of public record as early as the late 1930s.

Blythe's arguments in favour of greater use of Irish were stated not only on linguistic and nostalgic bases but also on quasi-political grounds. In particular, Blythe in his later life argued vehemently that the abandonment of the Irish language by the majority of Irish nationalists left them without a defining characteristic other than the religious belief of Roman Catholicism, something abhorrent to Protestant Ulster. His corollary was that the Irish language could and should become a badge of nationality shared in common by Irish Catholics and Protestants.

Later attitude to partition

When a major anti-partition propaganda campaign was launched in Ireland, Britain, and the USA in 1949, Blythe was virtually a lone, publicly dissenting voice amongst Irish nationalists in querying the assumptions that then formed the basis for a nationalist consensus 'against partition'. Thus in the early 1950s Blythe wrote, first by a series of letters to newspapers and subsequently in his book *Briseadh na teorann* ('Smashing the border'), on the partition issue from a perspective greatly at variance with his fellow Irish nationalists. While senior Irish establishment figures—even a pragmatist like Seán Lemass—still argued that partition had arisen out of British trickery and that no state could allow a disgruntled minority to opt out of the nation, Blythe in contrast argued that the strident nationalist anti-partition rhetoric over the preceding thirty years had been counter-productive. His basic thesis was that 'the linguistic and cultural apostasy' of Irish Catholics from the nineteenth century onwards made it too difficult for Ulster Protestants to see a national as distinct from a sectarian motive behind the nationalist demand for self-government (Blythe, *A new departure in northern policy: an appeal to the leaders of nationalist opinion* (c.1957), 18). With characteristic pugnacity, *Briseadh na teorann* did not confine itself to philosophical generalities but gave advice on such questions as 'The proper attitude for northern nationalists to toasting Queen Elizabeth; resolutions congratulating the royal family; the display of the tricolour and union jack' (Blythe (1955), 31). From the 1950s until his death in 1975, Blythe argued in favour of the deletion from the Irish constitution of articles 2 and 3, which claimed de jure jurisdiction over Northern Ireland for the Dublin-based government.

Reputation and assessment

Blythe was an outsider by temperament. As an Irish nationalist, he stood apart politically from the great majority of his fellow Protestant Ulstermen. As an Ulster Protestant he encountered recurrent explicit sectarian opposition from nationalist Irishmen. In the aftermath of the 1916 rising, Blythe was categorised editorially in a Kerry Redmondite paper as 'an Orangeman from Belfast'. A successful Fianna Fáil candidate for Blythe's Monaghan constituency argued publicly during the September 1927 general election campaign that Monaghan was a (Roman) Catholic county, which should be represented by Catholics. Blythe contested Monaghan for the last time in 1933. Hostile hyperbole against

Blythe then reached new depths, with one Co. Monaghan Catholic parish priest, Fr Michael McCarville of Scotstown, telling the Monaghan voters that Blythe and his party 'were far worse on the Irish people than Cromwell' (quoted in *Irish Press*, 14 January 1933).

Blythe had a bleak view of his fellow Irishmen. As early as 1922 he had described them as an untrained and undisciplined people with practically everything to learn of the difficult business of organising a national life on a stable basis. He departed little from that view during his career as a party politician and scarcely bothered to conceal it from the electorate. His retrenchment policies as minister for finance were not politically opportune. His hopes for a revival in the everyday use of the Irish language were unrealistic. He was described by a former editor of the *Irish Times* as 'the most reasonable unreasonable man in Ireland' (Douglas Gageby, appreciation of Blythe in *Irish Times*, 1 March 1975). It was a fair summation of a man who held strong if sometimes inconsistent views on many issues and personalities and expressed them trenchantly in public.

Blythe married (13 November 1919) Annie McHugh (d. 25 September 1957), daughter of Patrick McHugh, a Catholic RIC district inspector. She was born in Dunlavin, Co Wicklow. A mathematics and science student at UCD, along with Louise Gavan Duffy, she founded Scoil Bhríde. She played an active role in the Irish Country Womens' Association at a time when that body provided one of the very few outlets for Irish women to associate together outside their home or church.

Blythe died 23 February 1975, survived by his only child, Earnán. He lived at 50 Kenilworth Square, Rathmines, and is buried in Glasnevin cemetery. His portrait, by Seán O'Sullivan, RHA, is held by the Abbey Theatre. Sources for his life include three autobiographical volumes published successively in 1957, 1970 and 1973. His views on politics and public affairs over his lifetime are to be found in various journals, including *The Peasant*; *Irish Freedom*; *An tÓglach*; *The Leader*; *Inniú*; and the *Sunday Independent*. While there are some Blythe papers in NLI, the bulk of his correspondence and other papers is held in UCD archives; TCD Library has his correspondence with Thomas Bodkin.

Patrick Buckley

Sources

Leader, 9 May 1953; Earnán de Blaghd, *Trasna na Bóinne* (1957); Earnán de Blaghd, *Slán le hUltaibh* (1970); Maurice Manning, *The Blueshirts* (1970); David Greene, 'The Irish language movement', in Michael Hurley (ed.), *Irish anglicanism 1869–1969* (1970), 110–19; Earnán de Blaghd, *Gaeil Á Múscailt* (1973); *ITWW*; Nollaig Ó Gadhra, 'Earnán de Blaghd, 1889–1975', *Éire-Ireland*, xi, no. 3 (1976), 93–105; *WWW*; Ronan Fanning, *The Irish Department of Finance 1922–58* (1978); Mary E. Daly, *Industrial development and Irish national identity, 1922–1939* (1992); Arthur Mitchell, *Revolutionary government in Ireland: Dáil Éireann 1919–22* (1995); Roger Blaney, *Presbyterians and the Irish language* (1996), 206–8; *Beathaisnéis*, v; Mike Cronin, *The Blueshirts and Irish politics* (1997); Michael Laffan, *The resurrection of Ireland: the Sinn Féin party 1916–1923* (1999); Mary E. Daly, *The first department: a history of the Department of Agriculture* (2002); Mel Cousins, *The birth of social welfare in Ireland, 1922–1952* (2003); Christopher Fitz-Simon, *The Abbey Theatre: Ireland's national theatre—the first hundred years* (2003); Robert Welch, *The Abbey Theatre 1899–1999* (2003); Gerard MacAtasney, *Seán MacDiarmada: the mind of the revolution* (2004); Philip O'Leary, *Gaelic prose in the Irish Free State, 1922–1939* (2004)

Basil Stanlake Brooke

(1888–1973)

Basil Stanlake Brooke, 1st Viscount Brookeborough, prime minister of Northern Ireland, was born 9 June 1888 at Colebrooke Park, the family estate in Co. Fermanagh. He was the eldest of the five children (three sons, two daughters) of Sir Arthur Douglas Brooke (1865–1907), fourth baronet, of Colebrooke, and his wife, Gertrude Isabella (d. 1918), only daughter of Stanlake Batson, of Horseheath, Cambridgeshire. He succeeded his father as fifth baronet on 27 November 1907.

Background, education and military career

His social class, family background, and Fermanagh upbringing exerted a powerful formative influence on him. His ancestors first moved to Ireland from Cheshire in the late sixteenth century, initially acquiring land in Co. Donegal, and then being awarded estates in Co. Fermanagh, at the expense of leading native Irish families, after the 1641 rising had been repressed. Until the late nineteenth century, the family preserved and consolidated its property in the county. But its most enduring trait was a sustained tradition of military service—the family was known as the 'fighting Brookes'. Fifty-three members of the family served in the first and second world wars (Brooke's uncle Alan Brooke (1883–1963), 1st Viscount Alanbrooke, who became chief of the imperial general staff, was the most prominent); twelve lost their lives.

The family was also politically active. The Brookes fulfilled their prescribed social role in the county, serving as magistrates, sheriffs and lord lieutenants. From the eighteenth century, members of the family sometimes represented Co. Fermanagh in parliament. Though they would not have thought of themselves as other than Irish, they perceived Ireland ultimately in a British context, and when they spoke of standing up for Ireland, it meant standing up for the Protestants of Ireland. Their participation in the Orange Order was almost hereditary in nature, but generally at a local, rather than national, level. Their shared response to the mounting nationalist challenge, which emerged in Ireland from the 1860s, was to act aggressively in defence of the union.

Brooke's early career was typical for a son of an Anglo-Irish gentry family. After attending St George's School, a private institution at Pau in southern France (1896–1901), he went to Winchester College (1901–5), and then Sandhurst (1905–8). Before the first world war, his service with the 7th royal fusiliers (1908–11) and the 10th hussars in India and South Africa imbued him with an enduring commitment to, and pride in, the British empire. Even then, it was evident that he fully identified with the defiant unionism that had characterised his family's recent record of political involvement. In December 1912 (during a period of leave) he helped to initiate the Ulster Volunteer Force in Fermanagh and, in March 1914, he offered to resign his commission and 'return to help the loyalists in Ulster' (Barton, *Brookeborough*, 21).

Though he inherited the family estates in 1913, his military service was extended by the outbreak of the first world war. He served with distinction, on the western front and also in the Dardanelles, rose to the rank of captain in the hussars, and acted as ADC to General Byng. He was mentioned in dispatches, and was awarded the military cross in 1916 and *croix de guerre* with palm. Brooke was deeply affected by his time serving in the army, and lost his religious faith. In 1916, before the Easter rising, he wrote to his sister of his deepening belief that civil war would be 'worse for Ireland' than home rule (Barton, *Brookeborough*, 25).

Return to Fermanagh

Having been elsewhere for most of the previous twenty-two years, Brooke returned to Co. Fermanagh in December 1918. Both from financial necessity and from family duty, he was determined to attend to his neglected estates. These domestic preoccupations appeared to have been reinforced when, on 3 June 1919, he married Cynthia Mary (1897–1970), second daughter and co-heir of Captain Charles Warden Sergison, of Cuckfield Park, Sussex. However, her unionist commitment was to help focus his political ambitions, and her unquestioning loyalty and support, and her social poise, were to help ensure his success. They had three sons, the eldest and youngest of whom were killed in action during the second world war. The middle son, John Warden Brooke, also a soldier, survived the conflict and, in due course, inherited the family estates and entered politics in Northern Ireland.

Whatever his original intentions, on returning home Brooke was drawn into the political turmoil which Fermanagh, and Ireland, were then entering. Acting from family tradition and his own military experience, he organised in June 1920 Fermanagh Vigilance—a numerically small, part-time force, which he established to oppose the gathering IRA campaign, to protect local property, and to defend the union. He avoided the name Ulster Volunteer Force, in order not to deter Catholics from joining. Brooke was active in asking the British government officially to recognise Fermanagh Vigilance, as well as other similar bodies elsewhere in Ulster; he submitted a draft proposal regarding their possible *modus operandi*. When the Ulster special constabulary was established, in

September 1920, Brooke became the Fermanagh county commandant; this was a full-time, paid post from 1922.

Early political career

Through his political activity, Brooke gained a reputation for trustworthiness and became a prominent northern unionist. The first prime minister of Northern Ireland, Sir James Craig, formally recognised his services by awarding him a CBE and nominating him for membership of the Northern Ireland senate. The latter he accepted but had to relinquish: the appointment contravened the Government of Ireland Act (1920) because he held an office of profit under the crown. However, having taken an active part in Fermanagh's public life from his return, Brooke became unionist MP for the county (Lisnaskea division) at Stormont in 1929. He accepted the seat not only from a sense of duty, but also because of political ambition; he described his beloved Colebrooke as 'never enough in itself' (Barton, *Brookeborough*, 15). Soon afterwards, he bought a townhouse in Massey Avenue, Belfast. Brooke's slender, wiry figure—invariably with a cigarette, and his distinct, anglicised accent—was to grace Stormont life for a long time to come. He was to serve as prime minister of Northern Ireland for twenty years, from 1943 to 1963—longer than any other incumbent—and was a cabinet member for an unbroken period of thirty years (1933–63), a record still unsurpassed by anyone at either Westminster or Stormont.

After becoming an MP, Brooke frequently addressed public meetings, where he spoke with the voice of moderation. But on 12 July 1933 he gave a decidedly sectarian speech, the themes of which he was to restate several times in the next nine months. He advised audiences 'to employ good Protestant lads and lassies' only, and not Catholics, as they were 'out with all their force and might to destroy the power and constitution of Ulster' (*Fermanagh Times*, 13 July 1933). He also cautioned that southern nationalists were plotting to 'infiltrate' Northern Ireland and overturn its pro-union majority. The timing of his remarks owed much to the tense political context in which they were delivered. In 1932 the formation of the first Fianna Fáil government by Éamon de Valera, and the great effusion of Catholic and nationalist pride associated with the Eucharistic Congress in Dublin, had generated concern among northern unionists. Meanwhile, a growing economic depression meant that class divisions among the party's rural members were accentuated, and were a threat to party unity. Brooke's remarks also arose from his personal disillusionment at the continued reluctance of northern nationalists to recognise the Northern Ireland state. However, Brooke's open-mindedness in his relationships with political opponents, both as an employer and as a politician, was greater than these notorious comments might imply. In mid-1940 he was even prepared to accept Irish unity, if it meant that de Valera would abandon Éire's neutrality, and so possibly ensure the defeat of Nazi Germany and the survival of the British empire.

The rapid progression of Brooke's political career was owing to several factors: his relative youth combined with already considerable experience, his wide-ranging social network, his willingness to serve, his close relationship with Sir James Craig, and his leadership qualities and personal charm, combined with the lack of other talent on the unionist backbenches at the time. In May 1929 he became junior whip and parliamentary secretary at the Ministry of Finance and in 1933 he was made minister of agriculture. At the Ministry of Agriculture he was associated with the regional implementation of the marketing schemes and other radical initiatives then being introduced at Westminster. Though in later years he was caricatured as 'a lazy man of limited ability' (O'Neill, 40), as a young politician he was known for his ability, enterprise, and vigour. His influence and position, in the government and in the party (especially with backbenchers), rose accordingly.

The second world war

The outbreak of war in 1939 was beneficial for Brooke's career. He was persuaded by Craig not to serve in the military but to remain active in civilian life. His social network and military background became even more important, and there were many more opportunities to demonstrate his pragmatic approach, his capacity for getting things done, and his talent for publicity. He began to look like a possible future prime minister. From the beginning of the war, he was unshakeably committed to allied victory. Partly owing to his leadership, the farmers of Northern Ireland, the only region in the United Kingdom to do so, met and outdid the tillage quota set by Westminster in 1939–40. His achievements were clear, against the background of a government in Stormont being criticised by its own backbenchers for increasing incompetence. However, Craig declined to make the cabinet changes thought essential by his critics.

The government's record did not improve following Craig's death. John Andrews, the ageing minister of finance, succeeded him on 25 November 1940, but he was ill suited to the demands of leadership in a war. Crucially, he did not change the ministers whom he had inherited: he merely reallocated the existing cabinet's portfolios. Brooke was moved to the Ministry of Commerce—a small and, until his appointment, ineffective department, which had been criticised for the region's high wartime unemployment. Again, he showed energy, initiative and a sense of urgency, making the most of his contacts at Westminster when pursuing contracts for Northern Ireland manufacturers from government departments, and trying to raise the poor productivity levels of Northern Ireland's chief heavy industries. By April 1943, unemployment was down to 19,000 (or 5 per cent of the insured population), from about 72,000 in November 1940.

Prime minister of Northern Ireland

But the Andrews government was lurching towards crisis. It was criticised for inadequate preparations for the German air raids of April–May 1941, its incompetent treatment of the conscription question, a temporary suspension of Belfast corporation, an apparent absence of planning for the post-war period, and the ongoing deterioration in labour relations. As a result there was a unionist party revolt, centring on demands for leadership and cabinet change. At a parliamentary party meeting on 28 April 1943, confronted with ministerial resignations and an imminent split in the party, Andrews agreed to resign. His failure to appreciate the degree of opposition caused him to ascribe his fall to the manipulative skills of the man who succeeded him, Brooke. But the evidence suggests otherwise. Brooke had repeatedly encouraged Andrews to re-cast his government and had made no attempt to exploit the premier's palpable weakness; moreover, Brooke also had been taken aback by the scale of the crisis. But he was the only candidate able to form a government with a commons majority, and on 1 May 1943 he was asked to do so by the governor, the duke of Abercorn. He moved straight away to create a new ministerial team, which included Stormont's first non-unionist-party cabinet member, H. C. Midgley. It was largely successful in accomplishing its initial priorities, which were to ensure greater dynamism in the war effort, plan for the post-war years, and defend the constitution.

In 1945 Brooke zealously argued that national service be extended to Northern Ireland so as to confirm the state's constitutional status within the union, reduce unemployment, and also elicit Britain's goodwill. He even proposed that government subsidies to local Catholic schools should be raised in an attempt to lessen that church's opposition to it. However, when the national service bill was introduced at Westminster in 1946, Northern Ireland was excluded. Despite this, by far the most significant political consequence of the conflict for the six counties was the significant improvement in relations between Stormont and Westminster that it caused. This was largely thanks to Northern Ireland's contribution to the war effort, especially in the context of Éire's neutrality. Specifically, the commercial and strategic functions of the province's ports and bases facilitated US imports and protected Atlantic shipping; it supplied munitions, agricultural produce and manpower (including 38,000 volunteer recruits); and it was used as a training ground for allied military offensives in north Africa and Europe. Partly from gratitude, in 1943 the Treasury agreed to greater financial assistance for Northern Ireland in order to put it on a more equal footing with other parts of the UK in such areas as health, education and housing. Brooke greatly welcomed this, in part because he believed that 'the only chance for the political future of Ulster' was that it should become 'so prosperous that the traditional political attitudes are broken down' (Barton, *Northern Ireland in the second world war*, 130).

The formation in London of a Labour administration after the 1945 election (on 9 July) looked as though it might jeopardise the improvement in intergovernmental relations. Brooke feared that that the London administration would pressure his government to accept Dublin rule, and impose socialist legislation. However, he rejected calls by some party colleagues arguing for the refuge of dominion status, regarding this as impracticable given the region's heavy financial dependence on Britain. In fact, his dealings with the Labour leadership soon became unexpectedly cordial. He and his ministers largely welcomed the welfare state legislation introduced at Westminster and its extension to Northern Ireland. They were aware both of its appeal to the Protestant working class and of the extent of local need for such legislation. He also calculated that the measures would create a wide difference in social services between north and south, and so reinforce partition.

The decision by John A. Costello to take Éire out of the British commonwealth and establish a fully independent Republic of Ireland (this took effect from 8 April 1949) was the improbable context for what was, arguably, Brooke's greatest political achievement. Against this background, and an associated campaign against partition, Brooke argued that unionists should be given reassurances, regarding Northern Ireland's constitutional position, through the text of the Ireland bill (Britain's legislation that ratified Éire's change of status). Clement Attlee, the Labour prime minister, responded sympathetically, and appended a clause to the bill that the six counties would remain within the union for as long as a majority at Stormont wished. Attlee anyway considered unionist unease to be justified, and that this amendment would appeal to the British electorate. Moreover, his advice from a government working party was that the province's continued inclusion within the United Kingdom was vital for British strategic interests. Its report affirmed that

> it will never be to Great Britain's advantage that Northern Ireland should form part of a territory outside His Majesty's jurisdiction. Indeed it seems unlikely that Great Britain would ever be able to agree to this even if the people of Northern Ireland desired it (Barton, 'Relations between Westminster and Stormont', 12).

The 1950s and 1960s

Brooke's successes with regard to the constitution, social welfare and the economy helped to ensure that the 1950s and early 1960s were Northern Ireland's most harmonious and promising years; this contrasted with the relative stagnation and isolation of the Republic during the same period. The resulting growth in unionist confidence is evidenced by the greater willingness of some to espouse reform. In 1959 the party conference considered whether the movement should attempt to recruit Catholics and adopt them as candidates. Meanwhile, both the increasing activism of the minority within the six counties' political structures and the collapse of the IRA campaign (1956–62) suggested a greater reconciliation to partition. However, only limited consensus was achieved. Physical force and constitutional nationalists attracted growing support in northern elections during the 1950s and 1960s. There were still many minority grievances: the restricted local government franchise, gerrymandered electoral boundaries, religious discrimination in public bodies and private firms, and perceived shortfalls in state funding for Catholic schools.

The failure at Stormont to introduce such far-reaching reform was largely owing to Brooke's concern for party unity: he feared that division in the unionist party could imperil Northern Ireland's constitutional status. His strategy with regard to the minority was premised on his belief that social reform and economic progress alone would eventually dissolve its nationalist aspirations. Thus he did not support those liberal unionists who, empathetic to the changes taking place in post-war political and social attitudes, favoured recruiting Catholics into the party on equal terms. He considered that this would be politically impracticable and divisive; his private conviction was that public 'speeches [on this issue] will only delay matters' (B. Barton, *A pocket history of Ulster* (1999), 111).

Yet, from the late 1950s, British officials were warning his government of the risk of political disturbances in Newry and Londonderry if action were not taken against religious discrimination. By his failure to act at such an opportune moment, Brooke helped to perpetuate Northern Ireland's endemic, and ultimately fatal, sectarian divisions. It is difficult not to conclude that he lacked that higher quality of leadership that does not simply reflect and pander to its supporters but dares to challenge and dispel their prejudices. Brooke was born into the landed gentry, and became a soldier largely from family tradition and instinct. But, after the first world war, he was impelled into politics primarily from his conviction that the union was threatened, and that it needed to be defended. In his view, the threat to its survival continued during the following decades, and the need to protect it therefore did not disappear. This remained his absolute priority, and thus he never attempted to become a truly national leader with significant cross-community support. He said of himself that he was less 'ecumenical' than others, adding: 'it must be remembered that I lived through...the most troubled of times [in Ireland's history]' (Barton, *Brookeborough*, 234).

Later years

Brooke reluctantly resigned from the premiership on 25 March 1963, owing to a combination of age, poor health, and increasing criticism from the backbenches of his failure to stop either increasing unemployment or the move of unionist voters in Belfast to the Northern Ireland Labour Party. He was succeeded as prime minister by the minister of finance, Captain Terence O'Neill, but retained his seat in parliament until 1968.

Brooke received numerous honours: he had been made a viscount in 1952, and was later offered an earldom for his services to the state; this he rejected, commenting that he had been ennobled enough. In 1965 he was created KG, and he was also awarded an honorary LLD by QUB. In retirement he developed commercial interests, as chairman of Carreras (Northern Ireland), a director of Devenish Trade and president of the Northern Ireland Institute of Directors.

Brooke's wife, Cynthia, who had served in the second world war as senior commandant of the auxiliary territorial service, was created a DBE in 1959. She died in 1970, and the following year Brooke married Sarah Eileen Bell, daughter of Henry Healey, of Belfast, and widow of Cecil Armstrong Calvert, FRCS, director of neurosurgery at the Royal Victoria Hospital, Belfast. Brooke died 18 August 1973 at his family home, Colebrooke, and, three days later, his remains were cremated at Roselawn cemetery, Belfast; in deference to his wishes, his ashes were scattered on the demesne. Probate records suggest that he bequeathed an estate valued at about £450,000. He was succeeded in the viscountcy by John Brooke, the only surviving son from his first marriage. It might seem appropriate, as well as ironic, that John Brooke, then minister of state for finance, should have delivered the final speech from the dispatch box at Stormont before its suspension by Edward Heath's conservative government on 28 March 1972. In it he quoted from Rudyard Kipling's poem 'Ulster', which was written in 1914, about the same time as his father's involvement in the politics of the province began. Its concluding sentiments Basil Brooke fully shared: 'Before an empire's eyes the traitor claims his price. / What need of further lies? We are the sacrifice' (Barton, *Brookeborough*, 234).

Brian Barton

Sources

PRONI, Brooke papers, D3004, 998; PRONI, Northern Ireland government papers; PRONI, Unionist Party papers; *Ulster Year Books* (1926–69); R. Brooke, *The brimming river* (1961); W. D. Flackes, *The enduring premier* (1962); K. Nixon, 'Interviews with Brookeborough', *Sunday News* (January–February 1968); Burke, *Peerage* (1970); Terence O'Neill, *The autobiography of Terence O'Neill* (1972); J. F. Harbinson, *The Ulster Unionist Party, 1882–1973: its development and organisation* (1973); P. Buckland, *The factory of grievances: devolved government in Northern Ireland 1921–39* (1979); B. E. Barton, *Brookeborough: the making of a prime minister* (1988); B. E. Barton, 'Relations between Westminster and Stormont during the Attlee premiership', *Irish Political Studies*, vii (1992), 1–20; B. E. Barton, *Northern Ireland in the second world war* (1995); T. Hennessey, *A history of Northern Ireland, 1920–1996* (1997)

Margaret Byers

1832–1912

Margaret Byers, educationist, suffragist, and philanthropist, was born 15 April 1832 in Windsor Hill, Rathfriland, Co. Down, fourth child and only daughter of Andrew Morrow, farmer and mill operator, and Margaret Morrow (née Herron). After the death (c.1840) of her father, a Presbyterian elder and temperance pioneer, she was reared by paternal uncles in Stoke-on-Trent, England. Educated at the Ladies College, Nottingham, where she also taught for a year, she was deeply influenced by the school's headmistress, a Mrs Treffry, who instilled in her the belief that 'Women can do anything under God' (Jordan, 1). She returned to Ulster and married (February 1852) the Rev. John Byers of Tullyallen, Co. Armagh, who was then commissioned by the American Presbyterian Church to take up a missionary post in China. They subsequently spent a short period in Princeton, New Jersey, USA (where she was greatly impressed by the similarity of education offered to American boys and girls under the high-school system), before moving to Shanghai, where her husband soon became dangerously ill. During this critical time her only child, John, was born. She subsequently organised their return home; however, her husband died during the journey in 1853. On reestablishing herself in Ireland, she refused her missionary widow's pension and briefly considered accepting work as a missionary herself in Agra, before taking up a teaching post at the Ladies' Collegiate School in Cookstown, Co. Tyrone (1854). Her five years there were not particularly happy, and in 1859, with the backing of several influential Belfast Presbyterian clergymen, notably John Edgar and William Johnston, she opened her own educational establishment in Wellington Place, Belfast. The Ladies' Collegiate School (known from 1887 as Victoria College) started with thirty-five pupils, and under her direction soon gained a reputation for educational excellence. It expanded rapidly, and after several changes in location, finally settled into a purpose-built school in Lower Crescent, Belfast.

Byers's primary aim as a headmistress was to improve radically the academic standards of education offered to girls, and in doing so afford them 'the same opportunities for sound scholarship that was [sic] given to their brothers in the best boys' schools' (Breathnach, 56). To achieve this she was initially forced to employ masters, but later found herself able to take on a predominantly female staff, many of whom were her former students. Anxious that women should have access to higher education—after Cambridge University turned down her application to open a centre for holding examinations at her school, on the grounds that the distance was too great—in 1869 she successfully petitioned the Queen's University in Ireland to allow her pupils to take their examinations. She encouraged her brighter students to sit the exams, and they showed themselves well prepared: in 1877 alone, thirty-one Ladies' Collegiate candidates earned certificates from the QUI. She condemned the exclusion of female students from the 1878 intermediate education bill; and, having quickly mobilised support, travelled to London with a deputation that included her colleague and friend Isabella Tod, to lobby the lord chancellor, Lord Cairns, who received an impressive list detailing the achievements attained by girls in QUI exams. Their efforts proved successful, and females were finally included in the act's benefits. After women were given access to both scholarships and degrees from the Royal Colleges of Physicians and Surgeons and the RUI, she opened her own distinct collegiate department within the school (1881). This too was successful and by 1888 the department had educated twelve arts graduates. Women were subsequently admitted to study at the universities, after which the numbers in her department dwindled. She was consistently critical of this trend, maintaining that mixed education was detrimental to women.

An active philanthropist, she was an influential figure in numerous charitable concerns within Belfast. Having become involved in the temperance movement through her work as a superintendent with the Ladies' Temperance Union, she went on to become a foundation secretary of the Belfast Women's Temperance Association and Christian Workers' Union (1874), serving as its president from 1895. Having supported the formation of other branches of the Association throughout Ulster, she was elected president of the newly established Irish Women's Temperance Union in 1894. She was also closely involved with the work of the Prisongate Mission for Women from its inception in 1876; the Victoria Homes for Destitute Girls; and the English-based organisation, the Missionary Settlement for University Women, of which she was a vice-president. Victoria College pupils were always encouraged to assist the poor, and often raised funds for her favourite charities. An advocate of unionism and British imperialism, she was a supporter of the Women's Liberal Unionist Association. She also played a prominent part in the campaign for women's suffrage, and was a committee member of the National Society for Women's Suffrage. A regular speaker at public meetings in Belfast, she produced several articles on women's education, industrial schools in Ireland, and temperance. President of the Ulster Schoolmistresses Association from 1903, she received an honorary LLD from the University of Dublin in 1905, and in 1908 was appointed to the senate of the newly established QUB. Her son John (1852/3–1920), a leading Belfast physician and antiquarian, was knighted in 1906.

Poor health in later years forced her to retire from her active duties. She died 21 February 1912 at her home in Victoria College and is buried in Belfast city cemetery.

Frances Clarke

Sources

Northern Whig, 29 June 1877, 6 February 1879, 22 February 1912; *Belfast News Letter*, 22 February 1912; *WWW*; Anne V. O'Connor, 'The revolution in girls' secondary education in Ireland, 1860–1910', in Mary Cullen (ed.), *Girls don't do honours: Irish women in education in the 19th and 20th centuries* (1987), 31–54; Eibhlín Breathnach, 'Charting new waters: women's experience in higher education, 1879–1908',in Mary Cullen (ed.), *Girls don't do honours: Irish women in education in the 19th and 20th centuries* (1987), 55–78; Maria Luddy, *Women and philanthropy in nineteenth-century Ireland* (1995); Alison Jordan, *Margaret Byers* (n.d.) (photos)

Ethna Carbery

1866–1902

Ethna Carbery, poet, writer, and journalist, was born Anna Johnston on 3 December 1866 into a Catholic family in Ballymena, Co. Antrim. She lived nearly all her life in Belfast, where her father, Robert Johnston, was a successful timber merchant and prominent Fenian organiser who for many years represented the north of Ireland on the IRB supreme council. Her mother Marjory came from Donegal.

Anna Johnston began writing as a young girl and was first published at the age of fifteen. Later she became a prolific contributor of poetry and short stories to a variety of Irish periodicals, among them *United Ireland, Donahoe's Magazine, Young Ireland*, the *Nation*, and the *Catholic Fireside*, sometimes using the pseudonym

Ethna Carbery. She was also published in several American magazines, including *Century* and *Criterion*. In October 1895 she collaborated with her friend Alice Milligan to found the *Northern Patriot*, a radical monthly journal that openly advocated Irish separatism. Following a disagreement with the paper's sponsor, a Belfast workingmen's club, the women ceased their editorship after just three issues. Undeterred, in January 1896 they founded the Belfast-based literary magazine *Shan Van Vocht*, with its editorial offices located in Robert Johnston's timber yard. The two women edited, managed, and contributed to the magazine, which remained in circulation until March 1899. Although it was not allied to any particular political group, it had a strongly nationalist tone which did much to encourage both the Celtic revival and the foundation of Sinn Féin. Arthur Griffith, who took over its subscription list for his *United Irishman*, was a particular admirer of the paper, whose contributors included Katharine Tynan, Nora Hopper, Seumas MacManus and Alice Furlong. The paper also published the early writings of James Connolly though both women distanced themselves from his socialist agenda.

Through the journal Carbery played an active role in the centenary celebrations of the 1798 rebellion and, with Milligan, Maud Gonne, John O'Leary and William Rooney, toured the country delivering lectures on the United Irishmen. In 1900 she assisted in Maud Gonne's Patriotic Children's Treat Committee, established to counter the Phoenix Park celebrations marking Queen Victoria's visit to Ireland. A member of Inghinidhe na hÉireann from its inception at Easter 1900, she became one of its four vice-presidents. Both she and Milligan were already well known in Gaelic League circles for their patriotic short plays which they staged throughout the country, and, on the invitation of Gonne, they performed similar productions for Inghinidhe na hÉireann as part of the organisation's cultural activities.

Carbery married Seumas MacManus (to whom she had already written several love poems) in August 1901, and moved with him to Revlin House, Co. Donegal. She died there of gastritis 2 April 1902 and was buried at Frosses, Co. Donegal. Her poetry, edited by her husband, was posthumously published as *The four winds of Eirinn* (1902). The pathos of her death, at age 36 and so soon after her marriage, enhanced the popularity of the book, which went through ten editions in 1902 alone and many subsequent editions. In the years after her death she was possibly the most widely read poet in Ireland. Two further volumes of stories appeared—*The passionate hearts* (1903) and *In the Celtic past* (1904)—and some of her verse was later anthologised alongside pieces by Milligan and MacManus in *We sang for Ireland* (1950).

Frances Clarke

Sources

Donegal Independent (obit.), 4 April 1902; Ethna Carbery, *The four winds of Eirinn*, ed. Seumas MacManus (1906); O'Donoghue; Charles A. Reade, *The cabinet of Irish literature*, vol. i (n.d.); Alice Milligan, *Poems*, ed. Henry Mangan (1954); León Ó Broin, *Revolutionary underground: the story of the Irish Republican Brotherhood 1858–1924* (1976); Robert Hogan (ed.), *The Macmillan dictionary of Irish literature* (1979); Margaret Ward, *Unmanageable revolutionaries: women and Irish nationalism* (1983); Sheila Turner Johnston, *Alice: a life of Alice Milligan* (1994)

Winifred Carney

1887–1943

Winifred ('Winnie') Carney, trade unionist, feminist, and republican, was born Maria Winifred Carney on 4 December 1887 at Fisher's Hill, Bangor, Co. Down, youngest child among three sons and three daughters of Alfred Carney, commercial traveller, and Sarah Carney (née Cassidy; d. 1933). Her father was a Protestant and her mother a Catholic; the children were reared as Catholics. After her birth her parents moved to Belfast and separated during her childhood. Her father went to London and little more was heard from him; her mother supported the family by running a sweetshop on the Falls Road. Winifred was educated at the CBS in Donegall Street, Belfast, where she became a junior teacher. Independently minded, she later worked as a clerk in a solicitor's office, having qualified as shorthand typist from Hughes's Commercial Academy. In her early twenties she became involved in the Gaelic League and the suffragist and socialist movements. She had a wide range of cultural interests in literature, art and music, had a good voice, and played the piano well.

In 1912 she took over from her friend Marie Johnson as secretary of the Irish Textile Workers' Union based at 50 York Street, Belfast, which functioned as the women's section of the Irish Transport and General Workers' Union (ITGWU) and was led by James Connolly. Her pay was low and irregular, but she and her colleague Ellen Grimley worked with great enthusiasm to improve the wages and conditions of the mill girls, and Carney managed the time-consuming and tedious insurance section of the union. During the 1913 lockout she was active in fund-raising and relief efforts for the Dublin workers. Many of those connected with the ITGWU were drawn into the republican movement and she was present at the founding of Cumann na mBan in Wynn's Hotel, Dublin (2 April 1914). A close friend of Connolly, she joined the Irish Citizen Army (she was a crack shot with a rifle), and became his personal secretary. She appears to have been completely in his confidence and in full agreement with his revolutionary aims. On 14 April 1916 he summoned her to Dublin to assist in the final preparations for the Easter rising, and for the next week she typed dispatches and mobilisation orders in Liberty Hall. She was the only woman in the column that seized the GPO on Easter Monday, 24 April (although several others arrived later). During the rising she acted as Connolly's secretary and, even after most of the women had been evacuated from the GPO, she refused to leave and replied sharply to Patrick Pearse when he suggested she should. She stayed with Connolly in the makeshift headquarters at 16 Moore Street, typing dispatches and dressing his wound, and attending to the other wounded men. After the surrender (29 April) she was interned, first in Mountjoy and from July in Aylesbury prison, and was released 24 December 1916.

In autumn 1917 she was Belfast delegate to the Cumann na mBan convention, and was appointed president of the Belfast branch. In 1918 she was briefly imprisoned in Armagh and Lewes prisons. She stood for Sinn Féin in Belfast's Victoria division in the general election of 1918 (the only woman candidate in Ireland apart from Constance Markievicz), advocating a workers' republic, but she polled badly, winning only 4 per cent of the votes. Afterwards she was very critical of the support she had received from Sinn Féin. In 1919 she was transferred to the Dublin head office of the ITGWU, but did not get on well with colleagues such as Joe McGrath and William O'Brien, and returned to Belfast after a few months. She was Belfast secretary of the Irish Republican Prisoners' Dependants Fund (1920–22). She became a member of the revived Socialist Party of Ireland in 1920 and attended the annual convention of the Independent Labour Party in Glasgow in April 1920.

Never deviating in her hope for the establishment of Connolly's workers' republic, she opposed the Anglo–Irish treaty, and sheltered republicans such as Markievicz and Austin Stack in her home at 2a Carlisle Circus, Belfast. On 25 July 1922 she was arrested by the RUC and held in custody for eighteen days after 'seditious papers' were discovered in her home. She refused to recognise the court and was fined £2. Critical of partition and the social conservatism of Irish governments after independence, she remained in Belfast, concentrating on helping the local labour movement. She refused to accept a pension for her part in 1916, relenting only weeks before her death. In 1924 she joined the Court Ward branch of the Northern Ireland Labour Party (NILP) and was active in the party's radical wing promoting republican socialism. In discussions with colleagues she always praised Connolly and defended the 1916 rising, but was modest about her own part in it and never revealed what she knew of its planning; she also shared Connolly's distrust of James Larkin. Some regarded her as rather austere and sharp-tongued, but close friends spoke of her kindness and charm, and praised her strong personal and political loyalties. She continued to work for the ITGWU in Belfast and Dublin until September 1928, when she married George McBride. McBride (1898–1988), a Protestant, was a textile engineer, staunch socialist, and NILP member, who had joined the UVF in 1913 and fought in the British army (1914–18). They lived at 3 Whitewell Parade, Whitehouse, Belfast, and, despite their disagreements about Irish nationalism, their marriage was very happy; they had no children.

In about 1934 Carney joined the small Belfast Socialist Party, but her health was deteriorating and she took little active part in politics. She died 21 November 1943 in Belfast and was buried in Milltown cemetery, Belfast.

James Quinn

Sources

GRO (Dublin); Cathal O'Shannon, 'Winifred Carney—a link with Easter week', *Torch* (Dublin), 27 November, 4 December 1943; Desmond Ryan, *The rising: the complete story of Easter week* (1949); Margaret Ward, *Unmanageable revolutionaries: women and Irish nationalism* (1983); Michael Foy and Brian Barton, *The Easter rising* (1999); Helga Woggon, *Silent radical, Winifred Carney 1887–1943: a reconstruction of her biography* (2000); Diane Urquhart, *Women in Ulster politics, 1890–1940: a story not yet told* (2000); Sinéad McCoole, *No ordinary women: Irish female activists in the revolutionary years 1900–1923* (2003)

Edward Henry Carson

1854–1935

Edward Henry Carson, Baron Carson of Duncairn, lawyer and politician, was born 9 February 1854 at 4 Harcourt Street, Dublin, second son among six children of Edward Henry Carson, architect and civil engineer, and Isabella Carson (née Lambert). He was educated at Arlington House school, Queen's County (Laois), and at TCD; he qualified as a barrister at the King's Inns, Dublin, in 1877.

Early career, 1881–92

Carson began his career defending the farmer interest in different valuation cases arising out of the 'fair rent' provisions of the land act of 1881; but he swiftly expanded his repertoire to include criminal actions. He also came increasingly to appear for landed clients and for the crown, and particularly after the launch of the Plan of Campaign in 1886. His work was by now commanding the attention of his political and judicial masters, notably Peter O'Brien (later lord chief justice of Ireland, 1889–1913) and Arthur Balfour (chief secretary for Ireland, 1887–91). Just as the Gladstonian land act had provided a spur to his career in the early 1880s, so the Balfourian crimes act of 1887 provided opportunities at the end of the decade: in the summer of 1887 Carson was appointed as counsel to the attorney general for Ireland, and for the following years served Dublin Castle in the fight against the Plan of Campaign. He was a crown prosecutor in some of the most celebrated trials of the period, and forged a reputation that he carried for the rest of his career. The prosecution of William O'Brien after the 'Mitchelstown massacre' (9 September 1887) in itself served to win Carson the lasting contempt of nationalists, and an equally deep admiration within Irish loyalism. Balfour and the Castle establishment were impressed by this and by other displays of moral courage or forensic ability: Carson was appointed as a QC in 1889, and—shortly before the fall of the second Salisbury administration in 1892—served briefly as solicitor general for Ireland. He had Balfour's support when, fighting in the unionist interest, he contested one of the Dublin University parliamentary seats at the general election of 1892. Carson had helped to underpin the success (from the British perspective) of Balfour's administration, but the process was reciprocal, as Balfour freely acknowledged: 'I made Carson, but Carson made me'.

Law and politics, 1893–1910

In 1893 Carson moved his legal practice to London, an upheaval that coincided with his debut in the house of commons. The two events provided a platform for the launch of what Joseph Chamberlain lauded as 'a new force...in politics'. Carson's maiden speech (2–3 February) incorporated a devastating critique of the liberal government's crimes policy, and was further enlivened by his quick-witted handling of interruptions: the result was an instant metropolitan celebrity for a man who, though well known in

Ireland, had as yet made no impression within the British political arena. The speech, and subsequent parliamentary performances (particularly over the second home rule bill), served as a showcase for his courtroom skills; and his business began to accumulate. He took silk at the English bar in 1894, and became embroiled in some of the most celebrated trials of the late Victorian and Edwardian periods. In April 1895 he defended the marquis of Queensberry in the first of the trials that took Oscar Wilde to Reading gaol; and in 1896 he was part of the defence team that sought to extricate Dr L. S. Jameson and his fellow raiders from the tentacles of the foreign enlistment act (on this occasion he was unsuccessful, due partly to the windy perorations of his leader, Sir Edward Clarke). His parliamentary achievements kept pace: he was returned again for Dublin University at the general election of 1895, and was appointed to the Irish privy council in 1896. He distinguished himself as a critic of the new unionist government's Irish administration, mounting an especially ferocious assault on the land bill of 1896. This often highly tetchy opposition underlined the extent to which Carson— even by the standards of the 1890s—was an unconventional, indeed unreliable, party member; it underlined, too, the extent of his independence, even from patrons such as Arthur Balfour. Above all, it was an expression of his concern for the rights of property, and for the integrity of the old, waning landed interest.

The ferocity of Carson's political passions here, as later in his career, raises the issue of the nature of his convictions. As a debater at Trinity he appeared to embrace a number of radical causes: he entered politics in the mid-1880s as a liberal (he was enrolled into the National Liberal Club in June 1886, although by this time he had also professed his unionist convictions). His early legal reputation had been founded on his defence of the farming community and its claims. As late as 1908 he remarked, half ironically, to Lady Londonderry that he looked back with sympathy to the time of the French revolution, when he jokingly imagined that he would have found employment working the guillotine; but the humour was not entirely without point. He grew more conservative with age, however; and by the 1890s he had emerged as the single most gifted champion of the landed establishment. Later he defended the constitutional rights of the house of lords, and led the Ulster unionist fight against home rule; at the end of his life he came out of retirement to champion the cause of British India. In the course of his long career he reversed his stand on women's suffrage.

There are dangers in an over-eager search for consistency, even with a career such as Carson's: but there are, none the less, clearly defined principles or themes within his biography. His devotion to the courts and to legal process was unflagging, even allowing for his association with militant Ulster unionism. His unionism was immovable. He was contemptuous of political fashion: it might be argued that much of his career was spent fighting the tide of history. He was suspicious of the expansion of the Edwardian state; and alarmed by what he saw as government interference in the judicial process or legal right. It is well known that he had strong associations, through his mother's family, with the landed interest; but he had also connections (through his wife's family) with the tenant cause. His enthusiastic landlordism may perhaps be seen as an expression, not of family sentiment, but rather of fear at politically motivated interference in the law of contract and of property.

Carson's career of dissent in the later 1890s in some ways may have strengthened his claims on ministerial preferment; for talented dissidents were threats to the stability of the still vulnerable unionist alliance, and were not infrequently silenced through promotion (T. W. Russell is another Irish example of the rewards of disloyalty). Despite considerable competition, Carson was appointed to the solicitor generalship for England in 1900, acquiring a knighthood on the way; the post meant a reduction in income (Carson by this time was earning around £20,000 a year at the bar), but it was a recognised stepping-stone towards either further ministerial preferment or a senior post in the judiciary. As solicitor general Carson successfully prosecuted Arthur Lynch for high treason, and George Chapman (Severin Klosowski)—one of the contenders for the title of 'Jack the Ripper'—for murder; he acted for the British government in the complex arbitration over the boundary dividing Alaska and Canada. He spurned both ministerial and judicial advancement: in January 1905 he was offered and declined the presidency of the divorce court, and in March 1905 he declined the offer of the chief secretaryship for Ireland. With the fall of the unionist government (December 1905) the possibilities of office for the likes of Carson all but disappeared; but, as a parting gesture, Balfour appointed his former protégé to the privy council. There were other comforts to be drawn from the fall, and subsequent electoral humiliation, of the unionists: while the rout of the British unionists was near complete, their Irish colleagues survived relatively unscathed. One of the eighteen Irish unionists who returned to the house of commons in January 1906 was Carson; and, as one of the relatively few ministerial survivors from the deluge, he was well placed to consolidate his standing, not just within Irish unionism, but within the leadership of the British Conservative party.

Out of office, and as yet relatively untrammelled by the demands of Irish politics, Carson spent much of the later Edwardian period in the courts. This was, perhaps, the apex of his legal career: he was involved in actions where (by the standards of the time) fantastic sums of money were at stake, to say nothing of lives and careers and wider issues of principle. In July 1907 he represented Lever Brothers in a celebrated libel action against the *Daily Mail* and other newspapers within the Harmsworth empire; Carson and the plaintiffs triumphed, extracting damages and costs that reached almost £220,000. In November 1909 he found himself defending the press in a similar action, a case brought by Cadbury Brothers against Standard Newspapers: here again the jury decided in favour of the plaintiffs, but such was the power of Carson's advocacy that the damages awarded to Cadbury's amounted to merely one farthing. By far the most celebrated action of this time, indeed perhaps of Carson's entire career, was his defence of George Archer-Shee, a naval cadet at Osborne, against a charge of stealing a five-shilling postal order. Archer-Shee's case was tried in July 1910, with Carson's most formidable antagonist—Sir Rufus Isaacs—leading the case for the crown. The result was a famous victory for Carson and the complete exoneration of the hapless cadet. Carson, who has entered literary biography as the persecutor of Oscar Wilde, has simultaneously been deified in fiction as the frostily omniscient Sir Robert Morton, KC, in Terence Rattigan's 'The Winslow boy'. This somewhat ambiguous literary fate properly reflects the complexities of Carson himself.

Unionist leader, 1910–14

In February 1910 Carson was invited to assume the chairmanship of the Irish unionist parliamentary party, a position that gave him some claims to lead the wider Irish unionist movement. Carson's acceptance is sometimes read as a withdrawal from British political life, and a renunciation of his claims within the British conservative leadership; it is also sometimes read as an unremarkable or natural development. But the position had been treated by its previous occupant, Walter Long, as a temporary commitment, which could be used for British political advantage: there was, in any case, little to indicate in February 1910 that a leadership contest would soon be in the offing. When in November 1911 the contest for the succession to Balfour came, Carson could still have credibly, even perhaps successfully, pursued his claims. His acceptance did not signal, therefore, any retreat into the minutiae of Ulster loyalism. Nor was the offer of the chairmanship a foregone conclusion: Carson was a Dubliner and had little professional or personal experience of Ulster. He was essentially a southern Irish lawyer who for almost twenty years had lived and practised in England. In addition he had been soft on some—for Orange unionists—pivotal issues, such as the establishment of a Catholic university. Carson may well have been chosen, not so much for his transcendent abilities or reputation, but rather simply because there was no Ulster unionist whose claims were preeminent.

Though it could scarcely have been predicted in February 1910, Carson's new role placed him at the head of the campaign against the third home rule bill. He was a central figure in all the different aspects of Ulster unionist strategy: he was the key speaker at momentous public demonstrations such as that at Craigavon House in September 1911 (when he was first introduced to his loyalist following) or at the Balmoral show grounds in April 1912 (a meeting described as the 'marriage' between toryism and unionist Ulster). He was the centrepiece of the speaking tour that culminated in Ulster Day (28 September 1912), when just under half a million men and women signed a covenant pledging to use 'all means which may be found necessary to defeat the present conspiracy to set up a home rule parliament in Dublin'. He was also the generalissimo in charge of the unionists' parliamentary and high political assault on the home rule bill. In January 1913 he proposed the exclusion of the nine counties of Ulster from the operation of the bill. In December 1913 and January 1914 he met Asquith privately in order to chart the prospects for a settlement. In July 1914, on the eve of the great war, he attended the Buckingham Palace conference, where he argued for the permanent exclusion of six counties from the home rule bill.

Two of the most controversial issues arising from the Ulster unionist campaign were militancy—or the threat of militancy—and the demand for partition. Carson, however, should not be seen as either an uncomplicated partitionist or an untrammelled militant. He was an Irish unionist, who supported the constitutional union between Great Britain and all of Ireland; but he was also an essentially pragmatic politician who by October 1913 (if not earlier) had come to realise that southern unionism was a forlorn hope. Given that an all-Ireland unionism was impracticable, Carson was interested in the notion of a broad federal settlement whereby the constituent territories of the United Kingdom might be given assemblies. Ireland would of course be included in this grand scheme, although the north would of necessity remain bound to the imperial parliament: Carson saw this connection as probably no more than a temporary arrangement. But while such a sweeping constitutional revision interested a few unionist intellectuals and others, it failed to win a wider popularity in 1913–14. Carson threw out some feelers on the issue in May 1914, but was rebuffed by his own supporters: he was forced back on to the expedient of exclusion, firstly in a nine-county formulation, and later in a six-county scheme. Nine-county exclusion, or partition, originally interested Carson because it appeared to represent an effective means of undermining the entire home rule project; later he seems to have been convinced that it offered the best means of guaranteeing both Ulster unionist rights and wider issues of justice; he also seems to have been convinced that it offered the best avenue towards an equitable scheme of reunification. But neither the liberals nor the Irish nationalists were ever likely to endorse the proposal; and more significantly—from Carson's perspective—the unionists of eastern Ulster were (notwithstanding the pledges of the Solemn League and Covenant) relatively unconcerned about the minority unionist communities beyond the heartland of the movement. From the autumn of 1913 it became clear to Carson that the six counties provided the best political vantage-ground upon which to make a stand.

Carson's militancy was also problematic. Numerous letters and platform speeches embody his apparently uncomplicated militant convictions: he told James Craig in July 1911 that he was 'not for a mere game of bluff, and, unless men are prepared to make great sacrifices which they clearly understand, the talk of resistance is no use'. He sanctioned the formation of the paramilitary Ulster Volunteer Force in January 1913; and he helped to found the Ulster provisional government of September 1913. The British government had banned the importation of weapons into Ireland on 4 December 1913; but in January 1914 Carson inaugurated the gun-running adventure that culminated at Larne (24–5 April). On the other hand, there is evidence that depicts Carson battling to moderate the hardliners within his own movement: at key unionist meetings on 15 December 1912 and in May 1913 Carson counselled restraint. Although he alone was responsible for setting in motion the gun-running conspiracy, he seems to have been under very considerable pressure at this time from within the ranks of the Ulster Volunteer Force. After January 1914 it is arguable that the relationship between Carson and his militant support changed, and that the disciplined paramilitarism that he had helped to fashion and sought to control now obtained a momentum and vitality of its own. In January 1914—at the time when he was under pressure from the UVF—Carson 'confessed' to Horace Plunkett 'his inability to control his own forces'; in April 1914 he emphasised to Plunkett that he wanted a settlement, but that if one were not forthcoming and the Ulster unionists acted illegally or put 'themselves hopelessly in the wrong' or compelled troops to intervene, then 'in such an event he would very likely resign the leadership'. Given his political sensitivities, and later fondness for histrionic resignations, this testimony carries some conviction. 'Nobody supposes that at my age I prefer strife to peace', Carson proclaimed on 29 April 1914; 'only a fool would fight if there is a hope of accommodation', he affirmed on 5 May. Throughout 1914 Carson's speeches were often tinctured by calls for public order. All this should not be seen as evidence for an essentially quietist Carson. It is clear, however, that Carson was more cautious and pragmatic than has often been grasped; and that his uncertain, even manic, temperament, as well as his very finely tuned strategic sense, gave rise to more nuanced political signals than has often been allowed. Carson seems to have believed in the political usefulness of paramilitary menace; but he also seems to have believed in the potentially disastrous nature of paramilitary violence.

World War 1, 1914–18

The outbreak of the European war ended Carson's career as a rebel, and gave him the opportunity to augment his majesty's troops (through the offer of the Ulster Volunteers) rather than conspire to shoot them. In addition, the formation of the Asquith coalition government brought the first ministerial appointment that had come his way in ten years: on 25 May 1915 he accepted the post of attorney general of England. But his tenure was brief: he was increasingly alarmed by the prodigious waste of lives and resources during the British campaign in Gallipoli, and he was appalled by what he saw as the Allied betrayal of Serbia. He resigned on 12 October 1915, retiring to the backbenches from where he coordinated a wider assault on the coalition government: in January 1916 he was elected leader of a parliamentary ginger group, the unionist war committee, whose purpose was to encourage a more vigorous mobilisation of British military resources. The position suited Carson, who was now in effect leader of the opposition: by November 1916 he had joined forces with Lloyd George and a reluctant Bonar Law in order to divert the listless Asquith away from the war effort. Asquith struggled to maintain his ascendancy, but on 5 December was forced into resignation: Robert Blake has said that 'more than any single person, [Carson] was responsible for Asquith's fall'. Carson was now at the peak of his parliamentary influence, with nomination to the premiership a clear, if still remote, possibility. He was content, however, to subordinate his own claims, and to accept the first lordship of the admiralty from Asquith's successor, Lloyd George. He held this, one of the most demanding of wartime offices, between December 1916 and July 1917: these were months of mounting U-boat attacks on Allied shipping, with associated threats to the supply of food and other essential materials to the home front and the trenches. Criticism of Carson and of his *laissez-faire* managerial style grew; and on 30 April Lloyd George descended to the admiralty building, where he demanded, and won, changes. Convoy protection for merchant shipping was introduced, and helped to reduce losses. Carson and his most trusted admiral, Jellicoe, had considered this initiative, but too hesitantly for the taste of Lloyd George; other necessary reforms seemed unlikely to be enacted by the plodding first lord and his nervous subordinates. Carson was therefore moved out of the admiralty in July 1917, ostensibly in a promotion to the war cabinet as a minister without portfolio. But the particular responsibilities that he was given in his new role were of secondary importance; and the 'promotion' could thus barely disguise the taint of failure and humiliation. In January 1918, after barely five months tenure, he resigned from his new post, in part because of the dismissal of Jellicoe, but professedly because of the looming crisis in Ireland.

Carson's ministerial preoccupations inevitably meant a slackening interest in Irish politics. He was involved in the Lloyd George negotiations of May–July 1916, and succeeded in winning support in Belfast for the enactment of home rule beyond the six northeastern counties of Ulster: but the wider initiative was rejected by southern unionist sympathisers within the cabinet. He was alarmed by the Irish Convention (1917–18), and by the direction taken by the southern unionist representatives led by Lord Midleton; it was partly in order to reserve his position on the Convention that he resigned from the war cabinet in January 1918.

Disengagement, 1918–35

In the December 1918 general election he stood for the newly formed Duncairn division of Belfast, and was returned with a triumphant majority of some 9,200 votes over his nearest (nationalist) rival. But on the whole these were years of disengagement from Ulster unionism and indeed from mainstream politics. In July 1919 he threatened to call out the UVF in a speech that appeared unacceptably extreme to British opinion. While Carson resumed his legal career, his lieutenant James Craig served successfully as a junior minister in the new coalition government, and emerged in 1920 as a significant influence over the evolving government of Ireland bill; Craig was perceptibly warmer towards this, the founding charter of Northern Ireland, than was Carson. Despite the overt sympathy between the two men, differences were opening up: in January 1921 Carson was offered the chance to lead the new northern government. But he passed the invitation over to Craig in an irritating and slighting manner. He resigned from the leadership of Ulster unionism on 4 February 1921. But some of his subsequent actions created political difficulties for Craig: Carson was, for example, a bitter opponent of the Anglo–Irish treaty, and his parliamentary speech on the question (14 December 1921) 'greatly embarrassed' and angered his former lieutenant.

On 21 May 1921 Carson accepted a lordship of appeal in ordinary, and took the title of Lord Carson of Duncairn. He served as a law lord till November 1929, when ill health and old age compelled his resignation. But his time in the lords provided a certain symmetry to his long career; for an abiding concern here was the condition of the community into which he had been born—the loyalists of the south of Ireland, and their travails under the Free State dispensation. His education as an ultra-tory was now reaching completion: in his last years he denounced what he saw as the weak-minded revision of the Book of Common Prayer, and the betrayal of the empire-builders in India. In the early 1930s he was a contemptuous observer of the dismantling of the treaty of 1921.

Family matters provided some, not always happy, distraction in his later years. Carson's first wife, Sarah Annette Foster Kirwan, whom he married on 19 December 1879, died on 6 April 1914 after a series of strokes; the couple had two sons and two daughters. The marriage had been happy, although not altogether without troubles: Annette never fully adjusted to the grand manner of living that was expected of Edwardian legal stars; and some of their children proved equally wayward. Carson married his second wife, Ruby Frewen, on 17 September 1914. There was one child, a son, from this union. Edward Carson died 22 October 1935 at his home in Kent.

Assessment

Carson had been a brilliantly successful lawyer; and a gloriously eloquent advocate of lost causes in politics. He began his career as a liberal unionist, and he retained a whiggish devotion to the landed interest, and to the British constitution, at least in its pre-1911 formulation. He had a ferociously emphatic professional and political style. But he matured as an ultra-tory; and his determined public manner obscured a degree of private pragmatism, even hesitation. He had the temperament of a manic depressive. His time in government, except perhaps for his periods as a law officer, was undistinguished: his somewhat neurotic and disengaged manner was unsuited to the demands of (especially wartime) ministerial responsibility. On the other hand, his years in opposition, whether as an advocate of Ulster unionism in 1912–14 or as a critic of the Asquith coalition in 1916, displayed his formidable gifts to the full. Carson unquestionably contributed to the success of the Ulster unionists' demand for six-county exclusion, even though this form of settlement held little intrinsic appeal. Equally, he contributed decisively to the overthrow of Asquith in December 1916, even though he profited little from this, and came swiftly to despise Lloyd George ('a mass of corruption'). However indirect his contribution, Carson may none the less be seen as an architect of the British victory in 1918, and of the partition settlement of 1920.

He contributed a stylistic legacy, too. Given throughout his political and legal career to brilliantly argued but often emotive or even belligerent speechifying, he had a weakness for melodramatic exits from uncongenial political debates or negotiations. He preferred resignation and disengagement to political wars of attrition. He was happiest as a prosecution counsel, rather than in what might have been seen as more constructive roles. He was one of the founding fathers of modern unionism, and an example of the faith to his successors. To these he bequeathed a model of tactical brinkmanship and histrionic style.

Alvin Jackson

Sources

PRONI, Carson papers; Ronald McNeill, *Ulster's stand for union* (1922); Edward Marjoribanks and Ian Colvin, *Life of Lord Carson* (3 vols, 1932–6); H. Montgomery Hyde, *The life of Sir Edward Carson, Lord Carson of Duncairn* (1953); A. T. Q. Stewart, *The Ulster crisis: resistance to home rule, 1912–14* (1967); A. T. Q. Stewart, *Edward Carson* (1981); Alvin Jackson, *The Ulster party: Irish unionists in the house of commons, 1884–1911* (1989); Alvin Jackson, *Sir Edward Carson* (1993); John Hostettler, *Sir Edward Carson: a dream too far* (1997); Geoffrey Lewis, *Carson: the man who divided Ireland* (2005)

Sir George Smith Clark

1861–1935

Sir George Smith Clark, shipbuilder and politician, was born 8 November 1861 in Paisley, Renfrewshire, Scotland, second of three sons of James Clark, a partner in J. and J. Clark, thread manufacturers, and provost of Paisley 1882–5, and his wife Jane, daughter of George Smith, a Glasgow shipowner and founder of the City Line. Clark's younger brother, James, became a shipbuilder in Troon, Ayrshire.

Clark was raised a Presbyterian and educated at Merchiston Castle School, Edinburgh. He left school at the age of 17 and received some business training in Edinburgh before moving to Belfast at the age of 19 as an apprentice engineer with Harland and Wolff. In 1880 he went into partnership with his cousin Frank Workman (related by marriage to the Smiths), who had founded (1879) the shipbuilding firm of Workman and Co. (located on four acres at Thompson's Point on the Antrim side of the River Lagan). The firm was renamed Workman and Clark in 1881. It became Workman, Clark and Co., Ltd in 1891 when joined by a third partner, Charles Allan (a Glasgow second cousin of Clark and a member of the family that founded the Allan Shipping Line); at this time the firm expanded to the south bank of the Lagan, beginning with nine acres and moving steadily outwards. Workman concentrated on the technical side of the shipyard (as later did Allan, who oversaw the company's move into engine manufacture; it had previously concentrated on hull construction, and built thirty large steel-built four-mast sailing vessels between 1880 and 1896). Clark primarily handled the administrative and sales side of the business (though his admirers recounted how he sometimes took a hand in heavy physical jobs while making tours of inspection of the growing yard). In 1894 the company absorbed the shipyard and engineering works of the rival firm of McIlwaine and Coll, which had gone bankrupt. From small beginnings, the business grew rapidly (with the assistance of Clark's family connections, who dominated the firm's order books in its early years). It eventually became one of the largest shipyards in the world, employing over 9,000 men on a 130-acre site, known with increasing irony as 'the wee yard'. (It was also often referred to as 'the Belfast shipyard', with Harland and Wolff's known as 'the Queen's Island'.) Clark's *Irish Times* obituary described it as 'one of the greatest romances of industry in Irish history'.

The yard specialised in medium-sized cargo/passenger vessels; they were pioneers in the development (in which Clark took a personal interest) of the turbine engine invented by Charles Parsons, and in the construction of insulated and refrigerated fruit-carriers for the United Fruit Co. of Boston and of chilled-meat vessels for the South American trade. In 1903 the company acquired its own electrical power station in the North Yard; in 1905 the firm completed the turbines for *Victorian* (one of a pair commissioned by the Allan Line), earning the distinction of building and equipping the first turbine-propelled ocean steamer. It did move into the ocean liner market associated with Harland and Wolff (where its customers included R. and H. Holt of Liverpool), but tended to concentrate on smaller and slower ships for less glamorous routes than its rival. On two occasions the output of the yard was the largest in the world (1902, 1909) and between 1895 and 1909 the proportion of UK tonnage it launched rose from 5 to 14 per cent. As managing director, Clark provided the principal impetus behind this progress.

Clark's position within a network of Scots and Ulster business dynasties was cemented by his marriage (28 September 1881) to Frances Elizabeth, daughter of Henry Matier, a linen manufacturer, of Dunlambert, Belfast. She died intestate 3 May 1929, leaving personal estate of £140,506; letters of administration were granted to her husband. They had two sons, including Sir George Ernest Clark (1882–1950). The family lived at Dunlambert, Fortwilliam Park, Belfast. (Clark was a founding member of Fortwilliam presbyterian church in 1885, and an active and generous participant in the congregation throughout his life.) Clark's *Northern Whig* obituarist noted that either directly or by marriage Clark was connected with the Ulster business families of Corry, Workman, Smiley, Dixon, and Matier as well as the Clarks and Kerrs of Paisley.

The interlocking business dynasties of east Ulster (with their links to Scotland) were not only the leaders of the Ulster business community; they also formed the nucleus of the new Ulster-particularist leadership that from the late 1890s progressively displaced the old landed elite (dominated by south Ulster landlords such as Edward Saunderson) as leaders of Irish unionism. Clark's first prominent political participation came during the Ulster opposition to Gladstone's second home rule bill (1892–3); he addressed political meetings in Britain and Ireland in opposition to the bill, and at a semi-militarised Belfast rally (attended by A. J. Balfour) shortly before the bill's introduction, Clark led a contingent of 2,000 Scottish loyalists in the march-past.

Clark was a prominent Orangeman, a member of LOL No. 7. He was a founder-member of the Ulster Unionist Council in 1905 and unionist MP for Belfast North 1907–10, having defeated the Labour candidate William Walker in a by-election caused by the death of Sir Daniel Dixon. (An incident where Clark allowed Walker to address a meeting within the Workman and Clark yard, after the harbour police had prevented its being held outside, was cited as proof of Clark's sporting instincts, though it may also have indicated his confidence that the Belfast Labour electoral challenge to unionism had peaked.) Clark retired from parliament at the January 1910 general election to devote more time to business. In 1912 he personally led a large contingent of his workers to the Balmoral (south Belfast) rally at which Edward Carson pledged to resist home rule by force of arms, and Bonar Law promised to support him to the last. In 1913 Clark was widely condemned for acquiescing in the expulsion of Catholic workers from the yard during riots and suggesting that the victims showed themselves lacking in pluck by running away rather than standing their ground. He was a member of the military committee of the Ulster Unionist Council and was appointed chairman of the UUC arms committee in 1913; Workman and Clark made significant financial contributions to the UVF (in which Frank Workman was also active; both Workman's and Clark's sons were UVF officers). Clark was a member of the Ulster Unionist delegation at the Irish convention (1917–18). As chairman of the Duncairn Unionist Association, he invited Carson to contest this newly formed north Belfast constituency in December 1918. In 1920 the workers of Workman and Clark led the movement to expel Catholics from the shipyards and other major Belfast factories; in contrast Harland and Wolff, as in 1913, made some attempt to restrain their workers.

During the first world war Workman, Clark and Co. concentrated almost exclusively on admiralty work (primarily repairs and refurbishment) and the manufacture of munitions, employing 9,000 men with a weekly wage bill of over £22,000. Clark's brother James was killed at Ypres in 1915 while commanding the 1/9th (Dumbartonshire) Battalion of the Argyll and Sutherland Highlanders; Clark's younger son Henry also served in the regiment. On 6 July 1917 Clark was made a baronet for services to the industry during the war. After the war he served on a government commission on the state of the British shipbuilding industry.

By the end of the war Workman was largely inactive (though he remained on the board), Allan was about to retire, and Clark was suffering from the strains of age and long labour. The firm thus found itself with a succession crisis at a time when the British shipbuilding industry was undergoing a period of upheaval and readjustment. In February 1920, as part of a wider process of postwar speculative consolidation, the Northumberland Shipping Co. (chaired by Workman's nephew) bought up a majority shareholding in Workman and Clark. Clark resisted the merger and even undertook a lawsuit in order to prevent it, but since the majority of shares were against him (partly because of a large 1919 share issue) he failed. The new owners undertook two further share issues in 1920, which increased the capital considerably; this money was largely spent on retiring Northumberland Shipping's debt rather than developing the yard (as had been promised). Clark and his son George Ernest (whom he may have regarded as a future head of the firm) profited considerably from these manoeuvres, though it is unclear how far they were aware of their full extent. In January 1921 the Clarks and Workman disposed of their shares and resigned from the company. The new owners found themselves saddled with a huge burden of fixed-interest debt, while the shipbuilding industry plunged into depression (partly through the existence of large-scale excess shipping capacity built during and immediately after the war). By 1927 Workman and Clark was on the verge of bankruptcy and defaulted on its payments to debenture shareholders, several of whom sued the company and several named individuals (including Clark) for misrepresentation, fraud, conspiracy, breach of trust, and breach of contract, arising out of the allegedly misleading prospectus the company had issued in 1920. (Clark's defenders claimed the new owners had recklessly dissipated the company's financial reserves.) The company lost on appeal and went into liquidation; the case, which was eventually settled out of court, made legal precedent. The receivers asked Clark to resume control of the company since he was less deeply implicated in the dubious dealings than his partners and retained a good personal reputation, but he declined on health grounds. A syndicate of Belfast businessmen then launched the Workman, Clark (1928) company, but this failed to thrive and was fatally damaged by the post-1929 depression.

Clark was chairman of the Great Northern Railway (1926–34) and a director of the Bank of Ireland (1926–34), Henry Matier and Co. Ltd (linen manufacturers), the Scottish Maritime Investment Co., Irish Shipowners Co. Ltd, Ardan Shipping Co., and the Ulster Steamship Co. A member of the Belfast harbour board and Belfast chamber of commerce, and of the committee of the British Corporation for the Survey and Registry of Shipping, he was DL for the city and county of Belfast and a member of the senate of Northern Ireland (1925–35). As a young man Clark played rugby for North of Ireland and Windsor RFC; although his busy lifestyle left little time for sport, he occasionally hunted with the Killultagh Harriers and the County Down Staghounds. His yacht *Feltie* was well known (his brother Robert and nephew Maurice Clark were also well-known yachtsmen) and at the time of his death he was the oldest member of the Royal Ulster Yacht Club. He was a member of the Carlton Club, London, and the Ulster Club, Belfast.

Clark died 23 March 1935, having suffered from cardiac trouble for some time. He left personal estate in England valued at £718,027, personal estate in Northern Ireland valued at £502,236, and personal estate in the Irish Free State valued at £20,961. Two months after his death the firm of Workman, Clark ceased to exist; most of its remaining assets were acquired by Harland and Wolff, which absorbed the South Yard and sold off the North Yard under conditions which ensured it could never again be used for shipbuilding. Clark's career reflects the role of the 'Glasgow–Liverpool–Belfast' triangle in the industrial growth of late Victorian Belfast, and its political as well as economic implications.

Patrick Maume

Sources

'Is the Bank of Ireland mad?', *Irish Truth*, 23 October 1926; *Belfast Newsletter*, 25, 27 March 1935; *Belfast Telegraph*, 25, 26 March, 14 June 1935; *Irish Times*, 25 March 1935; *Northern Whig*, 25, 27 March 1935; *Times*, 25 March, 14 June 1935; *Workman, Clark (1928) Ltd: Shipbuilding at Belfast 1880–1933* (1935); *WWW*; H. Montgomery Hyde, *Carson* (1953); A. T. Q. Stewart, *The Ulster crisis* (1967); Burke, *Peerage* (1970 ed.); Henry Patterson, *Class conflict and sectarianism* (1980); David Johnson, 'Sir George Smith Clark', D. J. Jeremy (ed.), *Dictionary of business biography* (1984); Cormac Ó Gráda, *Ireland: a new economic history 1780–1939* (1994); John Lynch (ed.), *Forgotten shipbuilders of Belfast: Workman, Clark 1880–1935* (2004) (reprint, with introduction, of 1903 and 1933 promotional volumes); Timothy Bowman, *Carson's army: the Ulster Volunteer Force, 1910–22* (2007)

James Craig

1871–1940

James Craig, 1st Viscount Craigavon, first prime minister of Northern Ireland, was born 8 January 1871 at Sydenham, Co. Down, seventh among the eight children of James Craig of Tyrella and Craigavon, Co. Down, and Eleanor Gilmore Craig (née Browne). He was educated locally and at Merchiston School, Edinburgh (1882–7).

Early career

In April 1892 he established a stockbroking company, Craigs and Co., and was later one of the founding members of the Belfast stock exchange. Here he learned the meticulous business habits that distinguished, if not his later political career, than at least his work against the third home rule bill in 1912–14. Craig was a careful but unenthusiastic broker who happily forsook his business in March 1900, when the opportunity arose to fight in South Africa: he applied for, and was awarded, a commission in the 3rd Royal Irish Rifles. He was captured by the Boers at Lindley, where he was also injured; he was later able to rejoin the British forces and obtained the appointment of deputy assistant director of the imperial military railways. He was finally invalided home in June 1901. His time in South Africa had been relatively brief, but none the less decisive. He had acquired a military and logistical training that would later stand him in good stead. He had acquired injuries that would plague him throughout his life. He had, as St John Ervine affirmed in a suggestive anecdote, willingly flexed the law in his pursuit of suspected Boer spies. And, as Ervine further emphasised, Craig acquired in South Africa an understanding and appreciation of the empire: a theoretical political concept had been converted into a thrilling reality.

Ulster Unionist, 1903–14

If South Africa supplied Craig with a basic political education, then his finishing school was to be found in the muddy byways of rural Ulster, during the electoral struggle in 1903 between the Ulster unionists and T. W. Russell. Russell, a junior minister in the third Salisbury administration, had broken with the unionists in 1900 over the issue of compulsory purchase; an advocate of compulsion, Russell was intellectually and politically aggressive, and he carried his fight with conservative unionism into a series of angry by-election struggles. Here Craig tested the strategic skills and political insights that he had honed in South Africa: he assisted his brother, Charles Curtis Craig, in the contest for Antrim South (February 1903); and he conducted his own fight against Russellism in Fermanagh North (March 1903), where he lost to Edward Mitchell. At the general election of 1906 he was able to unseat the Russellite member for Down East, James Wood; and he held the constituency until the boundary changes of 1918, when he moved to Down Mid. He remained here until July 1921. The campaign against Russell revealed Craig's essential political style: unflappability, a ponderous but accessible wit, and a genial cussedness. The campaign, and indeed the wider circumstances of Ulster unionism in the early and mid Edwardian period, left Craig with a pronounced fear of internal unionist schism. In this sense, Russellism helped to form the highly defensive unionism—the embattled and carefully patrolled movement—which dominated the Northern Ireland state under Craig's leadership.

Craig's apparent stolidity concealed a considerable level of political ambition, and some degree of dexterity both as a networker and as a tactician. Craig had inherited a fortune of some £100,000 on the death of his father (1900): his marriage (March 1905) to Cecil Mary Nowell Dering Tupper, daughter of the assistant comptroller of the royal household, gave him an *entrée* into fashionable circles. He had, thus, both social access and the means to make something of his connections. He had strong links within the Ulster Protestant professional and commercial elite as well as within the Orange Order. He had, therefore, both high-political and local networks. He was never a dazzling public performer; and his personal style was emphatically uncharismatic. He was never likely (at least in the short term) to clamber up the parliamentary greasy pole; but on the other hand, he was well equipped for the political long haul. His shrewdness—still less his obstinacy—ought not to be underestimated. When Walter Long, the leader of the Irish unionists, formally retired (1910), Craig, though popular and well connected in the house of commons and in Ireland, had not yet established a commanding position over his contemporaries. The evidence is somewhat uncertain, but it is probable that Craig engineered the nomination of Edward Carson as Irish unionist leader. It is possible that, given the number of young turks contending for prominence within late Edwardian Ulster unionism, the selection of Carson as leader was a compromise solution, which averted any damaging rivalry. Whatever the politics of Carson's election, a bond between him and Craig was speedily formed; and it was through this that Craig achieved the wider prominence that had as yet eluded him.

Carson and Craig together dominated the unionist campaign against the third home rule bill. It is sometimes remarked that Craig acted as impresario to Carson's star turn; it might equally be suggested that Craig acted as high priest to Carson's deity. Either way, it was Craig who stage-managed his leader's public appearences in Ulster, beginning with an impressive rally at

115

Craigavon (September 1911) and peaking (arguably) with the demonstrations preceding and accompanying Ulster Day (28 September 1912). Craig's home at Strandtown, on the south-eastern outskirts of Belfast, served as a kind of protective shrine for Carson: here Craig might interpret his leader's oracular views, or induct devotees into the great man's presence. Here some of the most solemn ceremonial rites of unionism were performed (such as the introduction of Carson to his Ulster following, or the launch of the Solemn League and Covenant). Craig supplied Carson with the local knowledge and insights that he lacked; he seems to have been a more committed hardliner than his leader in so far as he had military experience (which Carson had not), was actively involved in the Larne gun-running of April 1914 (he helped to land weapons in Donaghadee), and does not appear among the ranks of those who (like Carson and Lord Londonderry) periodically counselled restraint. Indeed, from an early stage in the development of the constitutional crisis (at least as early as April 1911, when he was writing to Fred Crawford, the chief gun-runner) Craig was directly involved with the importation of weapons. Carson had charisma; but Craig had a populist flair. Craig helped to create the context within which Carson enjoyed a form of apotheosis: Craig's fertile imagination brought forth the Covenant as well as the Boyne banner, a tattered silk flag that had once fluttered beside King William III, and which was now carried before King Carson. Craig helped to create the means by which Ulster unionism, that most fissile of movements, sustained a unity and discipline in the face of grinding pressures. Craig, rooted in eastern Ulster, helped to popularise the advocacy of six-county exclusion among northern unionists. Craig, much more than Carson, may thus be seen as an architect of the partition settlement that evolved between 1912 and 1920.

War and partition, 1914–20

With the outbreak of European war in August 1914, Craig threw himself into the creation and development of the 36th (Ulster) Division: he held the office of assistant adjutant and quartermaster-general in the new unit. But the division went to the front without Craig: in the spring of 1915 he fell seriously ill, and by April 1916 he felt compelled to resign his commission. Craig returned to the safer battlefields of Belfast and Westminster, fighting for the acceptance of permanent six-county exclusion during the Lloyd George diplomatic offensive of the early summer of 1916. With the creation of the second wartime coalition in December 1916, he was given junior office as treasurer of the household; he acted thereby as one of the government whips, a task for which, with his combination of affability, tenacity and menace, he was particularly well equipped. With Carson, he resigned from the government in January 1918, although it seems that he was more reluctant than his leader to forgo the fruits of office. He had, however, been awarded a baronetcy in the new year's honours of 1918.

Craig returned to office in January 1919 as parliamentary secretary to the ministry of pensions (an appointment that owed much to his popularity with Edward Goulding, a close associate of Bonar Law and of Beaverbrook, and one of the Svengalis of conservative politics in this era). He was translated in April 1920 to the admiralty, where he was financial secretary, still a relatively junior appointment but one made more significant by the prolonged illness at this time of the first lord of the admiralty, Walter Long. There were three particularly important features of this, Craig's swansong within British ministerial politics. First, Carson returned to the lawcourts in 1919, and thereby freed Craig from both his support and his protection; this period marks the beginning of a noticeable drift in their relationship. Second, Craig, unlike his leader and patron, was a success in his executive roles; and in this era of relatively large and often uncharismatic governments—an era when, given the divisions within conservatism, a number of 'second eleven' figures attained prominence—it might have been expected that Craig would have flourished further. Third, Craig was well placed to direct the evolving strategies of the coalition with regard to Ireland—and all the more emphatically, given that his ministerial chief, Long, headed the cabinet committee responsible for devising a government of Ireland bill. Craig was a significant influence behind the committee's decision to draft a measure based on a six-county partition scheme. As in June 1916, so in March 1920 Craig was a prominent advocate of the six-county formula before the Ulster unionist council.

Premier of Northern Ireland, 1921–25

The invitation was offered at first to Carson; but it was Craig who in January 1921 accepted nomination for the premiership of the new Northern Ireland. Craig defined the emergent state: he had persuaded the elders of Ulster unionism to accept the government of Ireland bill (a by no means foregone conclusion); he fought for the creation of a new police reserve (the Ulster Special Constabulary, drawn largely from a reactivated Ulster Volunteer Force) to protect its frontiers; and with the civil servant Ernest Clark he oversaw the creation of the seven ministries that together formed the government of the territory. The first Northern Ireland parliament was elected in May 1921, and was opened by George V in June; it was therefore launched on the eve of the somewhat uneasy truce between the IRA and the forces of the British crown. But Northern Ireland was born into trouble; and it fell to Craig to fend off the political challenges arising from the Anglo–Irish treaty negotiations and the military challenge supplied by the IRA through 1921 and into 1922.

He showed considerable physical courage as well as a measure of political adventurousness at this time: he met de Valera on 5 May 1921 in a tense but unproductive session orchestrated by the British government's intermediary, Alfred ('Andy') Cope. He fought off the siren charms of Lloyd George in November 1921, when the British prime minister was seeking to include Northern Ireland within the framework of an all-Ireland polity: Craig, however, judged the treaty exclusively from the northern perspective; and, while angry over the boundary commission proposal, was much less concerned than Carson by its wider terms (indeed, Carson's speech in the lords during the treaty debate 'greatly embarrassed' his former lieutenant). In early 1922 he sought to defuse the IRA campaign within Northern Ireland by negotiating with Michael Collins. The first of their meetings, which took place in London on 24 January 1922, brought hopes for a lasting reconciliation: Craig was unexpectedly 'impressed' with Collins, and later joked that the proposed new parliament building for Northern Ireland might, if not needed, be used as a 'lunatic asylum'. A tentative deal was struck on the issue of the boundary commission and the southern boycott of Belfast business; Collins proposed the joint meeting of the two Irish parliaments, while Craig countered with the much less ambitious (but still startling) suggestion that the two governments might occasionally meet in joint session. But the auguries were misleading, and at a later meeting (2 February) Collins came to the table with hefty demands for the acquisition of northern territory. The breakdown of this session was followed by an intensification of IRA and loyalist violence, which after weeks of struggle gave no side a clear political or military advantage, and thus brought Craig and Collins back into negotiations. The result of this diplomacy was the Craig–Collins pact of 29 March 1922, which in ten clauses outlined a strategy for peace and reconciliation, and speedily collapsed in a welter of political recrimination and civil and military violence. A form of peace eventually came to Northern Ireland, but only because of the severe policing strategies of the unionist government, and because Collins and the provisional government in Dublin were now distracted by the challenge of republican dissent within their own borders.

The most important remaining statutory challenge to Craig's Northern Ireland arose from the provision made within the Anglo–Irish treaty for a boundary commission. Craig's handling of the commission negotiations in 1924–5 illustrates his tactical finesse as well as his relationship with the broader unionist movement. His stand was tough-minded but not without scope for movement: in February 1924, when the prime minister, Ramsay MacDonald, suggested (as part of the wider Labour initiative over the commission) that the British government's powers in Northern Ireland be temporarily ceded to the joint administration of the Belfast and Dublin authorities, Craig was sympathetic. When the Labour government moved to form the commission, Craig refused to co-operate; but he was prepared to support the notion that Carson might be appointed by MacDonald as the northern representative. Craig's hesitant agreement was, however, countermanded by his ministerial partners in Belfast; as Lord Balcarres observed (September 1924), 'Craig would like to be more forthcoming than his colleagues will permit'. In the event, the commission operated within a very tightly defined brief, and collapsed in late 1925; Craig's ingenuity was therefore not seriously tested. It had doubtless been useful for him to be seen in London as a moderating force within Ulster unionism; but there are some grounds for viewing his actions in 1924–5 as being more than tactical pirouetting.

Consolidating the state, 1925–1940

The collapse of the IRA challenge in 1922, and fixing of the boundaries of the northern state in 1925, might well have given Craig and the Ulster unionists an opportunity to seek reconciliation with northern nationalists; the survival until 1932 of the relatively friendly Cumann na nGaedheal administration would have eased any overtures of this kind. These did not occur. The security apparatus laid down during the military crisis of the period 1920–22 survived into the 1930s and beyond with only some amendments: the Ulster Special Constabulary (USC) was scaled down in 1925, but was sustained; while the Special Powers Act of 1922, ostensibly a temporary measure, not only survived but was given permanence. Both the USC and the Special Powers Act weighed heavily on the northern minority. The abolition of proportional representation in local government elections (1922) and later in parliamentary contests (1929) affected minority representation and morale; the implementation of the Leech commission's proposed boundary changes overturned nationalist control in several local government authorities, and gave rise to accusations of gerrymandering. Employment opportunities in the state sector (and not only the state sector) shrank; Craig asked critics to 'remember that in the south they boasted of a Catholic state. All I boast of is that we are a Protestant parliament and a Protestant state'.

Had Craig shown a greater magnanimity towards his nationalist compatriots, he might well have consolidated his regime and his state more effectively than by more militant strategies; on the other hand, there are no grounds for believing that an Ulster unionist campaign of 'killing home rule by kindness' might have been any more successful than the earlier British unionist ventures. Had Craig shown a greater magnanimity, he might well have alleviated the economic and political sufferings of his Catholic compatriots; but, given the parlous condition of the northern economy in the interwar period, it is hard to imagine how real economic suffering might have been eliminated from any section of the community. A magnanimous Craig could have created a Northern Ireland characterised by a greater egalitarianism and greater social justice; but these were not, and never had been, central to his political vision. A magnanimous Craig would, by definition, have risen above the bloody tensions of the home rule and revolutionary era: but an ascent such as this, difficult to imagine in any circumstances, could scarcely have been undertaken by a populist tory rooted in Orangeism and in military and political turmoil. Craig's political achievement was not, and was not intended to be, aerodynamically sound.

Community reconciliation in Northern Ireland in the Craig era was scuppered by the attitudes of the governing elite, by divisions and demoralisation among nationalists, and by the economic condition of the state. Northern Ireland in the inter-war period was, beyond a small and overwhelmingly unionist economic elite, characterised by widespread inter-communal poverty; the economic condition of the state threatened its survival more dangerously than the IRA campaigns of the early 1920s. Here Craig was hampered both by the field on which he had to play (namely the Government of Ireland Act), and by his own feeble grasp of the rules of the macroeconomic game. Craig was keen to improve the economic relationship between Belfast and London laid down in the act of 1920; and he pressed for, and won—through the Colwyn committee reports—a better deal for his administration. Equally, he supported the different Loans Guarantee Acts (1922–36) by which the Northern Ireland government sought to bolster the shipbuilding industry; and he supported, too, initiatives to diversify the northern economy, and in particular the New Industries (Development) Acts of 1932 and 1937. He was susceptible, not just to local clamourings, but also to imperial needs: in 1927, despite intensive lobbying from within Northern Ireland, he did not press the British to protect the linen trade, for fear of the political consequences. More notoriously, in 1938, during the negotiations that produced the Anglo–Irish agreement, Craig took personal charge of the Northern Ireland case, and glibly promised his support for the wider deal provided that the Belfast government was adequately compensated (his particular desire that Stormont be bought off with armaments contracts for Belfast astonished those, like Wilfrid Spender, in the know). This was seen by Spender, and by subsequent commentators, as a defining moment in Craig's 'little Ulsterism'; while it does reflect an intensely limited approach to politics, it also points to Craig's imperial susceptibilities—and also (as with the linen episode) to an irreducible sense of the vulnerability of the northern polity.

In 1938 Neville Chamberlain had successfully appealed to Craig by pointing to the role that a settlement with Dublin might play in the wider imperial diplomatic initiative. In April 1939, with the failure of this initiative and with war looming, Craig and the unionist government sought to make provision for the introduction of conscription into Northern Ireland. Chamberlain again appealed to Craig's broader loyalties in order to avert the possibility of a damaging controversy on the issue. But the limits of Craig's imperial vision were determined when Chamberlain sought, as Lloyd George had earlier done, to undermine the partition settlement in the wider British interest. An attempt in May–June 1940 to trade the unification of Ireland for Dublin's military engagement elicited a telegram from Craig that (even allowing for the constraints of the medium) conveyed a carefully calculated rage. Craig fought off this, and earlier, challenges to his state: he died peacefully, his pipe and a detective story by his side, on 24 November 1940.

Assessment

Craig's political outlook had been formed within the commercial and professional classes of eastern Ulster; he had been moulded by his experiences in South Africa and in the campaign against Russellism. His concern for the unity of unionism was, arguably, the underlying thrust of his strategies in 1912–14; it remained a central goal through the years of his premiership. South Africa provided an imperial outlook and helped to make warfare familiar, even perhaps normal; it was thus an important underpinning for his work in fighting home rule and, later, the IRA. But it did not make Craig a proactive imperialist. He had been born into a tightly knit society, where the ties supplied by church, by business, and by the Orange Order created a supportive but ultimately exclusive and parochial community. Craig's career hovered between this 'little Ulster' and a wider imperial engagement: he fought for empire in South Africa, but fought for a conservative Ulster unionism in the byways of east Down. He defended his home turf in 1912–14 but served successfully in the government of the empire. He was both master of an Orange lodge and a viscount of the United Kingdom (a creation of 1927). In 1921–5 he fought his corner with tenacity, but he was capable of rising above a merely obstructionist unionism. After 1925 the implicit tension between the sectional leader and the imperial statesman was largely resolved in favour of the former role. Craig emerged as the paterfamilias of unionist Ulster, 'distributing bones' of patronage, and looking after his own.

Alvin Jackson

Sources

PRONI, Craig papers (and papers of Lady Craigavon); Ronald McNeill, *Ulster's stand for union* (1922); Hugh Shearman, *Not an inch: a study of Northern Ireland and Lord Craigavon* (1942); St John Ervine, *Craigavon: Ulsterman* (1949); A. T. Q. Stewart, *The Ulster crisis: resistance to home rule, 1912–14* (1967); Patrick Buckland, *The factory of grievances: devolved government in Northern Ireland, 1921–1939* (1979); Patrick Buckland, *James Craig, Lord Craigavon* (1980); Alvin Jackson, *The Ulster party: Irish unionists in the house of commons, 1884–1911* (1989); Bryan Follis, *A state under siege: the establishment of Northern Ireland, 1920–1925* (1995)

Frederick Hugh Crawford

1861–1952

Frederick Hugh Crawford, soldier and UVF gun-runner, was born 21 August 1861 in Belfast, son of James Wright Crawford of Cloreen, Malone Road, Belfast, owner of a chemical factory, and Madge Crawford (née Mathews) of Portadown, Co. Armagh. The family were Methodist and Frederick was educated at Methodist College, Belfast, and University College School, London. He began work in Harland and Wolff's shipyard as a premium apprentice, later qualifying as an engineer. In December 1881 he managed to rescue several men who had fallen into the shipyard dock after a gangway collapsed, for which he was awarded a medal by the Royal Humane Society. He then spent a year at sea as an engineer with the White Star Line and some time travelling the world.

Returning from Australia in 1892 to take up the family business, he found unionists agitated at the prospect of home rule. He was strongly opposed to home rule, which he believed should be resisted by force of arms. To this end in 1892 he was a founder member of Young Ulster, an armed secret society modelled on continental national sporting clubs, and was involved in drilling its members and in the first of many attempts to import weapons. He was also a member of Lord Ranfurly's Ulster Loyalist Union (1893), and appears to have considered a plan to kidnap Gladstone and take him to a remote Pacific island, where he would be marooned with a few necessities and a good library of classics. It seems, however, that Ranfurly refused to put up the funds needed to finance the operation.

Crawford was commissioned second lieutenant in the artillery militia in 1894 and served in the Donegal Artillery in South Africa (1900–01); he rose to the rank of major, was decorated and mentioned in dispatches, and learned a great deal about modern weapons and warfare. After the war he remained on the reserve. In 1906 he was secretary of the Ulster Reform Club, but resigned when his efforts to import 10,000 rifles were revealed. This episode intensified his exasperation at the failure of fellow unionists to support their threats against home rule with armed force. He generally believed that Ulster unionists were under siege: he regarded the 1907 Belfast strikes as a nationalist plot to destroy Belfast's prosperity and denounced Protestants who participated in industrial action as either dupes or demagogues. From 1911 he was a member of the Ulster Unionist Council, and was a key figure on its secret military committee. For the next three years he tried various schemes to import arms into Ulster and, although often unsuccessful, he gained valuable experience and contacts in the international arms trade. He helped to raise the Young Citizen Volunteers, and commanded the guard that escorted Edward Carson on Covenant Day (28 September 1912). He was a founder member of the Ulster Volunteer Force (31 January 1913), and was appointed director of ordnance on the UVF headquarters staff.

Throughout 1913 he managed to import into the north hundreds of rifles, some machine guns, and a large quantity of ammunition, using various ingenious ruses to hide them from the customs authorities. In June 1913, however, customs in Belfast and Dublin and police in London managed to seize several hundred rifles that Crawford had imported. By now he was frustrated by piecemeal efforts to arm the UVF and pressed for a single large-scale purchase of weapons. Despite a royal proclamation prohibiting the importation of arms into Ireland (4 December 1913), his proposal was approved by Carson in January 1914, and Crawford was commissioned to undertake the task. In February, using a defence fund subscribed to by British and Irish unionists, he bought 20,000 rifles and 2,000,000 rounds of ammunition in Hamburg and spent the next two months arranging their shipment to Ulster. Using a Norwegian collier, the *SS Fanny,* he managed to ship the arms alongside Tuskar Rock, where they were transferred to the *Clyde Valley* and landed at Larne, Bangor and Donaghadee on the night of 24–5 April 1914; they were then distributed to UVF units throughout Ulster. The successful landing and efficient distribution of the arms greatly boosted the morale of the UVF and its credibility as a fighting force.

After the outbreak of the first world war Crawford was promoted to lieutenant-colonel and appointed OC Royal Army Service Corps in northern Ireland, and undertook an instruction tour in France in 1916. During the violence of 1920–22, he maintained that Ulster Protestants could not rely on the British army and would have to protect themselves and he played a leading part in reviving the UVF. He also formed the Ulster Brotherhood, an armed undercover body nicknamed 'Crawford's Tigers', and discussed plans to infiltrate the IRA in Dublin and to kidnap Arthur Griffith, but concluded that his strong Belfast accent might put him at a disadvantage. Although his efforts to seek legal status for the UVF were unsuccessful, many of its members were incorporated into the Ulster Special Constabulary and he was appointed commandant of the South Belfast B Specials. In April 1920 he published a leaflet, *Why I voted for the six counties,* in which he argued that it was essential for the safety of the British empire that the Northern Ireland state be predominantly Protestant. At the opening of the Northern Ireland parliament in 1921 he was created CBE by George V. By 1923 his chemical manufacturing business was failing and he applied to the Northern Ireland government for employment. He was appointed contracts and stores officer of the Ministry of Home Affairs

(1925–36) with responsibility for an arms depot. At the age of 78 he volunteered for active service in the second world war, but was turned down. His gun-running activities were recorded in *Guns for Ulster* (1947). He died 5 November 1952 in Belfast.

He married (1896) Helen Wilson of Lincolnshire; they had two sons and three daughters.

James Quinn

Sources

Fred H. Crawford, *Guns for Ulster* (1947); *Belfast Telegraph, Times,* 6 November 1952; *WWW*; A. T. Q. Stewart, *The Ulster crisis: resistance to home rule 1912–14* (1967); Sir Arthur Hezlet, *The B Specials* (1972); Patrick Buckland (ed.), *Irish unionism 1885–1923: a documentary history* (1973); Michael Farrell, *Arming the Protestants* (1983); Michael Hopkinson, *The Irish war of independence* (2002); Keith Haines, *Fred Crawford: Carson's gunrunner* (2009)

(Robert) Lindsay Crawford

1868–1945

(Robert) Lindsay Crawford, journalist, Orangeman, and diplomat, was born 1 October 1868 at Tonagh, Lisburn, Co. Antrim, son of James Crawford, scripture reader, and Matilda Crawford (née Hastings). Educated privately, he worked for a time in business before becoming the founding editor (1901–6) of the evangelical *Irish Protestant* and a founding member (1903) of the Independent Loyal Orange Institution of Ireland. The 'IOL' had been formed in the wake of events that followed the election (1902) to Westminster of Thomas Sloan. Sloan, a shipyard worker, was highly critical of the middle-class complacency of the unionist party, and in 1902 he succeeded in defeating its Westminster candidate for the seat of Belfast South. Sloan's victory was too much for the more conservative elements within the Orange Order, and he was expelled. Several of the more radical Belfast Orange lodges, including that of Donegall Road, headed by Alex Boyd, split from the original and founded the IOL.

The IOL attempted to articulate a socially radical and egalitarian philosophy and Crawford became its greatest exponent and principal theoretician. He outlined the new order's democratic manifesto in *Orangeism, its history and progress: a plea for first principles* (1904). The new order gained momentum, and in May 1904 the Ulster Protestant Electoral Union was established with the aim of securing more democratic representation in parliament. Crawford, Sloan, and their followers were fiercely critical of the unionist party at Westminster, which they accused of blindly surrendering Ireland's interests for the sake of maintaining the union. On 15 June 1905 Crawford delivered a lecture that outlined his assessment of the situation in Ireland, and this was later published (24 June 1905) as a pamphlet, *Irish grievances and their remedy*, based on the report in the *Irish Protestant*. He believed that the act of union had failed and that Irish Protestants had been 'frightened' out of the right to Irish citizenship. Crawford viewed unionism as utterly negative, and Irish nationalism as too much under the thumb of the Catholic clergy. He stated that

> it was the failure of Irishmen, both Protestant and Roman Catholic, to form a true conception of nationality, that enabled English parties to sit in the market place and buy the Irish vote.

In July 1905 Crawford published what he later considered to be the greatest achievement of his life, and what became known as 'the Magheramorne manifesto'. In this polemic he called on Irishmen of all creeds to unite on a basis of nationality, focused not on religion but on Irish interests. He attacked the Ulster Unionist Council and argued for compulsory land purchase and a national university for Ireland.

The radical nature of Crawford's ideas, which could be interpreted as favouring home rule at the very least, if not a form of republicanism similar to that espoused by Theobald Wolfe Tone, unsurprisingly proved too much for the unionist community. The Magheramorne manifesto was in reality the beginning of Crawford's transition from unionist to republican nationalist. Denounced as a devolutionist document, the manifesto led to Crawford's dismissal from the *Irish Protestant* in May 1906. The IOL and Sloan continued to support him, but in November 1906 he suffered a heavy defeat at a by-election in Armagh North, which signalled that there was little support for his radicalism. He accepted a position as editor of the *Ulster Guardian* (from January 1907), the official publication of the Ulster Liberal Association, but in May 1908 Crawford's radical ideas led to his enforced resignation from the *Ulster Guardian* and his expulsion from the IOL.

Unable to find employment in Ireland, he emigrated to Canada (June 1910), where he secured a post on the editorial staff of the *Toronto Globe* (1910–February 1918). Retaining his interest in Irish affairs, Crawford, as magazine editor, recrossed the Atlantic to cover the passing of the third home rule bill in 1914 and sent back sixty dispatches to Canada between April and early July. His later editorials argued that the causes of the 1916 rising were economic rather than political, and he urged clemency. To Crawford, Irish self-government was the only solution to unrest. As the political climate in Canada changed to favour the liberal unionists, so too did the *Toronto Globe,* and Crawford (who supported Sir Wilfrid Laurier) was dismissed in February 1918.

In July 1918 he became the founding editor of the *Statesman,* a journal modelled on the *Nation* (London), in which he ran articles attacking British policy in Ireland and British imperialism. Outside journalism, Crawford started the Protestant Friends of Irish Freedom in New York and was to the fore in the Self-Determination for Ireland League of Canada and Newfoundland, a movement that boasted a membership of 20,000 after just three months in existence in 1920.

Critical of the constitution of the Irish Free State, Crawford, now a self-confessed republican, accepted it as a means towards complete sovereignty. In December 1922 he was appointed acting consul by T. A. Smiddy and served as trade representative of the Irish Free State in New York (December 1922–October 1929). He died in New York in 1945.

Pauric J. Dempsey and Shaun Boylan

Sources

NAI, DFA 31, 200–210; *Times*, 30 May 1904; R. L. Crawford, *Irish grievances and their remedies* (1905); *Toronto Daily Star*, 27 January 1923; *American Biography*, xxxv (1928), 261–4; J. W. Boyle, 'The Belfast Protestant Association and the Independent Orange Order, 1901–10', *Irish Historical Studies*, xiii (1962–3), 117–52; C. Desmond Greaves, *The ITGWU: the formative years 1909–23* (1982); John W. Boyle, 'Robert Lindsay Crawford, 1910–1922; a Fenian Protestant in Canada', in Robert O'Driscoll and Lorna Reynolds (ed.), *The untold story: the Irish in Canada* (1988), 635–46; R. Fanning *et al.* (ed.), *Documents on Irish foreign policy*, i *1919–1922* (1998), ii *1923–1926* (2000); Kevin Haddick-Flynn, *Orangeism: the making of a tradition* (1999)

Joseph ('Joe') Devlin

1871–1934

Joseph ('Joe') Devlin, nationalist leader, was born 13 February 1871 at Hamill Street, Belfast, fourth son of Charles Devlin, car driver, and Elizabeth Devlin (née King), both recent migrants from the Lough Neagh area of east Co. Tyrone. Educated to elementary level from the age of 6 at CBS, Divis Street, Devlin proceeded to employment in Kelly's Cellars public house near the city centre. From this unpromising background (throughout his life opponents made condescending references to him as a Belfast bottle-washer) Devlin rose through a combination of ability, connections, and ambition to journalism with the *Irish News* (1891–3) and *Freeman's Journal* (1895) and political position.

Early political career: the AOH

The young Devlin was active in various local debating societies, where his associates included Cathal O'Byrne; they always retained a personal friendship despite later political differences. A committee member of the Belfast branch of the Irish National League in 1890, Devlin joined the anti-Parnellite faction during the O'Shea divorce scandal (1891), becoming local secretary of the Irish National Federation. His political model at this time was Thomas Sexton, MP for Belfast West, whose campaign he organised at the general election of 1892.

Although Healyism was strong in Catholic Ulster (where Catholic lay elites were weaker, and clerical political leadership correspondingly stronger, than elsewhere in Ireland) Devlin aligned himself with the faction led by John Dillon and—from 1899—with the United Irish League (UIL), founded by William O'Brien. From the late 1890s this brought Devlin into conflict with the Catholic Representation Association of Dr Henry Henry, bishop of Down and Connor (1895–1908); this organisation, though sometimes regarded as Healyite, was essentially based on the view that mass nationalist political mobilisation in Belfast could only bring trouble and ostracism, and that Catholic interests were best represented by allowing a small group of lay and clerical notables to broker concessions from the unionist majority. After a series of local election contests in Catholic wards and controversies between the pro-Devlin weekly *Northern Star* and the clerically controlled *Irish News*, Devlin succeeded in marginalising the politically maladroit Henry by 1905; in the process, however, he took on some of the qualities of his 'Catholic establishment' opponents. (The *Irish News* came to be dominated by Devlin, who eventually served as one of its directors.) At the same time, Devlin moved onto the national political stage.

Returned unopposed for Kilkenny North (1902–6), he was appointed secretary of the United Irish League of Great Britain (1903) and of the parent body in Dublin (1904). A speaking tour of the US in 1902–3 convinced him of the organisational potential of Catholic fraternal organisations, and in 1905 he took over the presidency of the Board of Erin faction of the Ancient Order of Hibernians (AOH), a specifically Catholic body which Devlin proceeded to develop as an organisational arm of the nationalist party. Under his tutelage the AOH expanded from 10,000 members in 1905 to 60,000 in 1909, despite opposition from some Catholic bishops (notably Cardinal Logue) who distrusted it because of its close affiliation to Dillonism, its secrecy, and its habit of staging dances and other entertainments without paying what they regarded as due deference to local priests. Devlin's AOH also faced opposition from a rival separatist body, the Irish-American Alliance AOH; though far less numerous, this group was able to draw on the support of separatists within the American AOH and hinder Devlin's attempts to mobilise the American organisation in his support. The AOH expanded further after 1910, and was strengthened by becoming an approved society under the National Insurance Act of 1911.

Belfast was where Devlin's political career began and where it ended. Organisational skill contributed substantially to his hold on the largely working-class seat of Belfast West, which he won in 1906 on a platform that sought to transcend religious boundaries by combining labour issues with the home rule demand—a platform born of Devlin's acute social conscience, and consistent with the nationalist party's efforts to forestall the independent political mobilisation of Irish labour through incorporating its concerns within the party's agenda. A lifelong bachelor, Devlin, though short in stature (he was known in Belfast as 'Wee Joe'—and by Tim Healy, less affectionately, as 'the duodecimo Demosthenes' (Brown, 155)), was apparently highly attractive to women, and took a special interest in their problems, no doubt mindful of the influence they might have on the political behaviour of their spouses. He was to found a holiday home for working-class women. When the scholar Betty Messenger interviewed former Belfast linen workers in the late 1960s and early 1970s, she was startled to discover the extent to which Devlin was remembered as a champion of the workers decades after his death; this image persisted among Protestant workers as well as Catholics, and he was generally credited with various ameliorations of workplace conditions even when he had not in fact been responsible for them.

Organiser of the Irish party

Possessed of great oratorical skills and even greater organisational ability, Devlin effectively became the key organiser of the nationalist party from the early years of the twentieth century, relieving the party leader, John Redmond, of a great deal of the administrative burden of party affairs, and becoming well known abroad through fund-raising trips, especially in North America. His personal geniality made him a great favourite at Westminster, and Irish socialists were dismayed at the willingness of British Labour MPs to accept him as an authentic Labour representative. Several MPs elected after 1906 can be identified as his protégés, and groups of Hibernian strong-arm men upheld the party leadership in such contests as the 1907 Leitrim North by-election and the 1909 'baton convention' which witnessed the final departure of William O'Brien and his supporters from the UIL. He was the only post-Parnellite MP to be admitted to the tight leadership group around Redmond (to the dismay of some party intellectuals such as F. Cruise O'Brien and Francis Sheehy-Skeffington, who regarded him as a 'brainless bludgeoner' and a Tammany Hall boss). In 1913 Devlin was a leading organiser of the Irish National Volunteers.

When William O'Brien embarked on his personal initiative to deal with the Ulster problem through conciliation in the early Edwardian period, he found a stern critic in Devlin and in turn demonised the 'Molly Maguires' as sectarian corruptionists—though it has been suggested that O'Brien's denunciations, and their exploitation by unionists, actually assisted the Order's growth by associating it with loyalty to Redmond's leadership. Personally non-sectarian, Devlin, like other party leaders, endorsed the shibboleth that home rule would prove a panacea for Ireland's problems, including Ulster, and used his credentials as a labour representative to dismiss popular unionism as a mere product of elite manipulation—a position more excusable for southern nationalists, with only a limited knowledge of the province, than it was for him. In a period when the Vatican's *Ne temere* decree on religiously mixed marriages was heightening Protestant fears about the 'tyranny' of Rome, Devlin seemed to be oblivious to how his integration of Hibernianism and nationalism was exacerbating that problem (as seen in the attempts of Frederick Oliver Trench, Lord Ashtown, to use the AOH's alleged foundation by Rory O'More as 'proof' that the Irish party wished to repeat the 1641 massacre of Protestants). As the third home rule bill passed through parliament and the Ulster Volunteer Force mobilised, Devlin encouraged the

Irish party leaders in the view that the Ulster unionist campaign was a gigantic bluff, dismissing contrary opinions even when held by other nationalist MPs. During these years the AOH clashed with the Irish Transport and General Workers' Union during the Dublin lockout (though there was some overlap between AOH and trade union membership in provincial centres such as Sligo), and from late 1913 the AOH spearheaded the Redmondite attempt to take over and dominate the Irish Volunteers.

War and partition

Devlin endorsed Redmond's support for the British war effort and engaged in extensive recruiting activity (leading his old opponent James Connolly to denounce him as 'a recruiting sergeant luring to their death the men who trusted him and voted him into power' (Connolly, *Collected works*, 364–5). He seems to have been motivated, at least in part, by the belief that after the war nationalist ex-soldiers could be used to overawe the Ulster unionists by the threat of force. According to Stephen Gwynn, Devlin wished to apply for an officer's commission but was asked not to do so by Redmond on the grounds that the party needed his organisational skills.

Devlin's career was decisively shaped by his decision to use his influence to persuade northern nationalists to accept temporary partition, in fulfilment of the flawed agreement arrived at between Lloyd George, Sir Edward Carson, and Redmond in the aftermath of the 1916 rising. Devlin later claimed he had been decisively influenced by the prospect that under this agreement the excluded area would be governed directly from Westminster, rather than by a local Orange-dominated parliament. Other motives may have included personal loyalty and deference to Redmond. Devlin forced the agreement through a Belfast-based convention despite protests from west Ulster nationalists, but the proposals collapsed after it transpired that Lloyd George had made incompatible commitments to nationalists and unionists. Northern nationalism immediately split between west and south Ulster dissidents and Devlin's loyalists (predominant in Belfast and east Ulster), and the next year saw massive secessions of AOH members outside Ulster to Sinn Féin. Although Devlin retained a core of loyal supporters, he was reduced from a national to a sectional leader. As a member of the Irish convention (1917–18) Devlin sided with Bishop Patrick O'Donnell against Redmond on the issue of seeking a compromise settlement with southern unionists on the basis of home rule without fiscal autonomy. Devlin was offered the leadership of the nationalist party on Redmond's death in 1918, but conceded the honour to his long-standing mentor, John Dillon.

Devlin held Belfast West until 1918, and easily swept aside an attempt by Éamon de Valera to displace him from the Falls division of Belfast at the general election of that year, though the electoral decimation of the nationalist party elsewhere left him leading a rump of only seven MPs (five from Ulster, one from Liverpool). In the ensuing parliament he was an outspoken critic of government policy towards Ireland, and highlighted sectarian violence against northern nationalists. Clearly discouraged and with boundary changes militating against retention of the Falls seat, Devlin unsuccessfully contested the Exchange division of Liverpool (which had a large Irish population) as an Independent Labour candidate in 1922. Elected for Co. Antrim and Belfast West to the parliament of Northern Ireland in 1921, he eventually took his seat (Belfast West) in 1925, holding it till 1929, when he combined representation for Belfast Central with that for Fermanagh and South Tyrone at Westminster.

Last years; death and legacy

Only after the boundary commission ended the border nationalists' hopes of speedy incorporation in the Irish Free State was Devlin able to assert leadership of northern nationalism as a whole on the basis of attendance at the northern parliament; even then he was considerably handicapped by recriminations over the events of 1916–25. He embarked on his last significant political campaign in 1928, when he sought to unite minority politics through the agency of the National League of the North. The initiative, emphasising social reform, was unsuccessful. Devlin's own political baggage was a hindrance to the unity of the factions that minority politics had thrown up over the previous ten years, while the minority community itself was politically demoralised by the fate that had overtaken it, and the unionist government showed itself unwilling to make concession to Devlin. The project, moreover, coincided with the onset of the gastric illness (exacerbated by heavy smoking) that would take Devlin's life on 18 January 1934. For some time before his death he had ceased to attend the Northern Ireland parliament.

Devlin's political career was one of great promise only partially fulfilled, its ultimate realisation undermined first by the fallout from the Easter rising that destroyed the vehicle of his political ambitions, and second by the sequence of events that led to the creation of a constitutional entity so constructed that all nationalist politicians, regardless of talent, were effectively denied a route to power. Only at his death did the unionist regime adequately acknowledge Devlin's political stature. His funeral was attended by at least three Northern Ireland cabinet ministers, together with representatives of the government of the Irish Free State. Northern nationalism never again produced a leader of his ability in the Stormont era; his ability to use Westminster to promote the interests of Ulster nationalists is comparable to John Hume's use of Europe for the same purpose from the mid 1970s. After his death the nationalist party in Belfast grew increasingly reliant on middle-class leadership and was eventually displaced by nationalist labour splinter groups, some of whose prominent activists, such as Harry Diamond, had begun their careers as election workers for Devlin. A portrait of Devlin by Sir John Lavery is held by the Ulster Museum, Belfast. His papers are in the PRONI.

James Loughlin

Sources

Stephen Gwynn, *John Redmond's last years* (1919); Maurice Craig, article in *DNB*; William Francis Brown, bishop of Pella, *Through windows of memory* (1946); Betty Messenger, *Picking up the linen threads; a study in industrial folklore* (1978); Michael O'Riordan (ed.), *James Connolly: collected works*, i (1987), 364–5; Austen Morgan, *Labour and partition: the Belfast working class 1905–23* (1991); Eamonn Phoenix, *Northern nationalism: nationalist politics, partition and the Catholic minority in Northern Ireland 1890–1940* (1994); A. C. Hepburn, *A past apart: studies in the history of Catholic Belfast, 1850–1950* (1996); Patrick Maume, *The long gestation: Irish nationalist life 1891–1918* (1999); A. C. Hepburn, article in *ODNB*

John Ferguson

1836–1906

John Ferguson, publisher, home-ruler, and land reformer, was born
18 April 1836 in Belfast, the son of Leonard Ferguson (d. 1844?),
who was in the provision trade there and whose family were tenant
farmers in Co. Antrim and related to the United Irish martyr
William Orr. After Leonard Ferguson's early death his widow,
Charlotte (née Ferris), moved with her son and daughter Margaret
to Glenavy, Co. Antrim, where her father occupied large tracts of
land on the shore of Lough Neagh. After schooling nearby at
Crumlin the young John Ferguson was apprenticed to a stationer
in Belfast. On some evenings he attended lectures provided by QCB
and was much influenced by T. E. Cliffe Leslie, an economist
interested in agrarian reform. He devoted his Saturday evenings to
improving himself by reading history and learning German and

French. His father had been a Presbyterian, his mother was an episcopalian Protestant. On Sundays he attended St John's, an episcopalian church, until he quarrelled with the minister, Charles Seaver (1820–1907), an evangelical and a conservative.

Aged 24, Ferguson left Ireland for Glasgow and eventually went into partnership with a publisher, Duncan Cameron. In Scotland he became a fervent Irish nationalist and cosmopolitan radical. When visiting Dublin he was persuaded by the publisher Henry Gill to bring out works of interest to Irish nationalists, which he began doing with *The green flag of Ireland*, a collection of popular songs. Many more such works followed with the imprint 'Cameron & Ferguson, Glasgow'. Ferguson may be considered the founder of the Home Rule Confederation of Great Britain, a body that gave rise to the Irish home-rule and land reform movements of the 1870s and 1880s. It was he who organised and presided over a well-attended public meeting in the Choral Hall, West Nile St., Glasgow, on 19 December 1871 that resulted in the formation of an Irish home-rule association, the first of many formed in British industrial towns in the 1870s and organised by Ferguson, John Barry and Martin Waters Kirwan into the Home Rule Confederation of Great Britain. Kirwan (d. 1899) had commanded Irish volunteers fighting with the French in the Franco-Prussian war (1870–71).

When Joseph Gillis Biggar stood as a home-rule candidate at a Londonderry city by-election, Ferguson crossed over to Ireland to organise his campaign (August–November 1872). While there he joined the council of the Home Government Association of Isaac Butt. Respected in Fenian circles (though not a member of the IRB) and always inclined gently to criticise Butt for his moderation, Ferguson was active behind the scenes and then in the public eye at the conference held at the Rotunda in Dublin to form a successor body, the Home Rule League (18–21 November 1873). From his base in Glasgow, from which he would often travel to Ulster on publishing business, Ferguson gave much moral and practical support to Butt and later to Charles Stewart Parnell. He was present on Kingstown pier to welcome three released Fenian prisoners (13 January 1878) and at Irishtown, Co. Mayo, at the famous meeting of tenant farmers (20 April 1879). On the formation of the Irish National Land League (21 October 1879) he became a member of the first committee, joined the executive a few months later and chaired the Land League rally at the Rotunda (29 April 1880).

Ferguson was to the political left of his fellow Irishmen in Glasgow and was no less active in promoting land reform in the Scottish Highlands than in Ireland, which, because most highlanders were Protestants, aroused suspicion among many Glasgow Irish. At the famous Mid Lanark by-election (1888) he worked tirelessly for the independent labour candidate James Keir Hardie to the disgust of most other Irish in Scotland, who favoured Hardie's liberal opponent. After the split in the Irish home-rule party (1890), Ferguson was elected to Glasgow burgh council as a representative of the Fourth or Calton ward (1893) and later appointed magistrate (1896). At the parliamentary elections of 1905 he organised the Irish vote for liberal and labour candidates in Glasgow. A radical intellectual, admirer of Gladstone and Bright, devotee of J. S. Mill and Herbert Spencer, and associate of Henry George, Ferguson was inclined to regard land reform as a panacea and at the time of his death was the leading advocate of taxation of land values. John Ferguson died 23 April 1906 at his home, Benburb House, Lenzie, and was buried in Old Aisle Cemetery, Kirkintilloch, a United Free Church minister officiating. Earlier in Glasgow he had been a communicant at an episcopalian church.

He married (1862) Mary Ochiltree, daughter of Matthew Ochiltree of Markethill, Co. Armagh, a well-educated woman who fully shared his enthusiasm for home rule and land reform. They lived at first in West Cumberland St., bordering the Gorbals and Tradeston. They had four children: John (b. 1865), William Bertram Ochiltree (d. 1867?), who became a physician at Newcastle-upon-Tyne, Anna (b. 1869), who died unmarried, and Elizabeth, who died young.

C. J. Woods

Sources

Irish Times, 24 April 1906; *Glasgow Observer*, 28 April 1906, portr.; David Thornley, *Isaac Butt* (1964), 134–5, 141, 163–6, 269, 292–3; T. W. Moody, *Davitt and Irish revolution* (1981); E. W. McFarland, *John Ferguson, 1836–1906: Irish issues in Scottish politics* (2003); A. G. Newby, '"Scotia major and Scotia minor": Ireland and the birth of the Scottish land agitation, 1878–82', *Irish Economic and Social History*, xxxi (2004), 29–30, 34–40

Mary Galway

1864–1928

Mary Galway, trade unionist, was born 6 September 1864 in Taglanneg, Moira, Co. Down, daughter of Henry Galway and Elizabeth Galway (née Magennis), linen weavers. She later moved with her family to Belfast, living initially in 85 Leeson St., before settling in 31 Crocus Street, off the Springhill Road, after her father's death. She and her sisters all found work in the linen industry (which then dominated Belfast), describing themselves as handkerchief stitchers in the 1901 census. She subsequently told a government inquiry that she had worked for eleven years as a machinist. A member of the Textile Operatives Society of Ireland (TOSI; the only women's trade union in the linen industry) from its earliest days, she evidently became active soon after joining, given her attendance at the Trade Union Conference held in Belfast in 1893. This continued throughout the period that followed, so that by January 1897, when Belfast's linen workers went on strike, she had come to occupy a central role in the union. It was as president of TOSI (an elected and voluntary post) that she represented the Belfast trades council in the ensuing negotiations between workers and employers on the implications of the 1896 Truck Act, during which she and her colleague Susan Cockbill secured concessions from employers. Having made a favourable impression during these negotiations, she was appointed TOSI's general secretary after Cockbill left the job in the summer of that year. At the time of her appointment she faced a difficult task, given the appalling conditions faced by many working women. She later recalled how women of 'long experience and skill' received a mere ten shillings for a fifty-four-hour week (Moriarty MS, p. 12). Added to such problems was the fact that her union's membership remained relatively small, and though it reached a pre-war peak of 3,000 in 1908, it never had anything close to a majority of the workforce. While poorly represented in the larger mills, it gained a greater foothold in the smaller factories such as Kennedy's, where Galway organised a successful strike in 1900. She has been accused by some of concentrating her recruiting efforts on the more skilled workers in the 'making-up' section of the industry; nevertheless she was a familiar figure to most mill-workers, who recalled her standing outside the factories as early as 5.45 a.m., urging employees to become unionised.

Her position within Belfast trade-union circles was further consolidated in 1898 when she was elected to the executive of the city's trades council. A close colleague of William Walker, with whom she had a good working relationship, she earned a reputation for moderation. However, she could be extremely determined when pursuing the needs of her members, as is evident in her public attack on her own trades council at the Irish TUC for its perceived indifference to women workers (1901). She came to play a significant part in Belfast's union campaigns, most notably during the 1906 linen strike, and in 1907 when she addressed rallies and collected funds on behalf of the striking carters and dockers led by James Larkin. At national level she was well known through her attendance at the ITUC from 1898, where she regularly contributed to the debates. As a member of its parliamentary committee (1907–13) and vice-president (1909–10), she was included in the trade union delegation that met the chief secretary, Augustine Birrell. Her conservatism could frustrate some colleagues: her opening address at the 1910 congress, in which she proposed a vote of condolences on the death of the king, infuriated William O'Brien (d. 1968), who opposed the motion on the grounds that 'our sympathy had much better be extended to the victims of the colliery disaster at Whitehaven' (ITUC annual report, 1910). Similarly, radical members of her own trades council at times voiced opposition to her conciliatory style.

Galway was, however, an extremely effective trade unionist. She was a persistent and influential campaigner in securing the first woman factory inspector in Ireland (having approached in person the president of the Board of Trade in London); her demands were finally met in 1905. She was similarly active in the campaign for outworkers, which came to a head in 1910 after the publication of a highly influential and much quoted annual report by Belfast's medical officer, H. W. Bailie. She played a central role in the establishment of a trade board specifically for outworkers (1915), to which she was subsequently appointed. Among the other issues she addressed were the need for improved sanitation and safety in the workplace, the system of fining employees for allegedly spoiled work, and the question of 'half-timers' (whereby children divided their week between school and the factory). An early member of the Belfast branch of the Worker's Education Association, in 1924 she contributed an article on the significance of the linen industry in Ulster to William G. Fitzgerald's *The voice of Ireland*, in which she highlighted the contribution made by skilled women workers.

Despite these contributions, Galway is probably best known for her very public clash with James Connolly in the autumn of 1911. The conflict initially arose when Connolly, then recently settled in Belfast, agreed to represent striking workers from the York Street mill. This in turn led to his establishing a rival union for the women, which he named the Irish Textile Workers Union. Galway clearly regarded it as unwanted competition, and felt threatened enough to organise a counter-demonstration to denounce the strike. In December 1911 she asked the trades council to disaffiliate the new union, but Connolly repudiated her claims of poaching members, and pointed out that she had left the vast bulk of textile workers unorganised. The council took no decisive action, and the dispute simmered on at the 1912 congress, where she repeated her claims of poaching and accused Connolly of organising his union along sectarian lines.

With the setting up of the government of Northern Ireland in 1921, Galway was appointed to a number of parliamentary committees associated with her industry. She remained general secretary of TOSI at the time of her death in Crocus Street, Belfast, 26 September 1928. She was buried in the Galway family plot in Hillsborough, Co. Down.

Frances Clarke

Sources

Belfast Weekly Telegraph, obit. and death notice, 6 October 1896 (photo); *Reports of the Irish Trade Union Congress* (1901–13); Mary Galway, 'The linen industry in the north and the betterment of working conditions', in William G. Fitzgerald (ed.), *The voice of Ireland* (1924); John Fitzsimons Harbinson, 'A history of the Northern Ireland Labour Party 1891–1949' (M.Sc. Econ. thesis, QUB, 1966); Samuel Levenson, *James Connolly: a biography* (1973); Norbert C. Solden, *Women in the British Trade Union 1874–1976* (1978); Betty Messinger, *Picking up the linen threads* (1980); Austen Morgan, *Labour and partition: the Belfast working class 1905–23* (1991); Peter Collins, 'Mary Galway', *Labour History News*, no. 7 (summer 1991), 14–15 (photo); Penny Holloway and Terry Craden, 'The Irish Trade Union Congress and working women, 1894–1914', *Saothar*, xxiii (1998), 47–59 (photo)

James Hamilton

1838–1913

James Hamilton, 2nd duke of Abercorn and MP, was born 24 August 1838 in Brighton, Sussex, eldest son of James Hamilton, 1st duke of Abercorn, and his wife Louisa Jane, second daughter of the 6th duke of Bedford. He was educated at Harrow School and at Christ Church, Oxford, graduating BA (1860) and MA (1865). Though one of two conservative representatives for the Abercorn stronghold of Co. Donegal from 1860, he rarely attended the house of commons during the first part of the 1860s, having inherited royal favour and court office from his father. After taking part in a mission to the Danish court in 1865, he accompanied the prince of Wales on a state visit to Russia in early 1866, and was lord of the bedchamber to the prince (1866–86). Irish landed political equipoise had been little shaken by October 1868, when he went without fear of contest to the hustings in Donegal, with an affable appeal to Catholic voters to support a principled stance against disestablishment of the Church of Ireland in order to secure the foundations of society. Again, in the general election of February 1874 he found that nationalist feeling had made little headway among the Donegal electorate and, despite the emergence of contenders for the county interest, he headed the poll on the strength of a vague statement of respect for continuance of the Ulster custom. Scenting future difficulty, however, he unsuccessfully urged the tory party in June 1874 to prepare its own amendments to the 1870 Land Act.

By early 1880 the bonds of sentiment between tory and liberal unionists had unravelled, and Hamilton affirmed the unpopularity of tory government in the north to the party whip, explaining that the old fear of 'popery', among Presbyterian voters in particular, was now strongly outweighed by an appetite for agrarian reform. Though he was the sole tory candidate presented for Donegal at the general election in April, he found that emollient promises of fair hearing for the tenant case did not avail to preserve his seat. During 1884 and 1885 he endeavoured to mend fences between tory and liberal unionists in north-west Ulster, and managed to acquire the backing of the Tyrone Liberal Association for his selection as north Tyrone candidate for the forthcoming elections, on the basis of a deal in which the proposed conservative candidate gave way to a liberal in east Donegal. He was replaced as candidate by his younger brother, Lord Ernest Hamilton, when he succeeded to the dukedom on the death of his father in October 1885.

A pronounced sense of urgency in the face of the forthcoming introduction of the first home rule bill in 1886 prompted unceasing attempts on his part at regrouping unionist forces. He played an active role in the quiet establishment of the Irish Loyal and Patriotic Union (ILPU) in Dublin in May 1885, specifically an effort to set up a vehicle for the non-sectarian and cross-party expression of unionist conviction, north and south. When the ILPU announced itself publicly in late 1885, seeking to set up an independent unionist body in parliament, the primacy of northern middle-class and Orange elements in the unionist alliance was reflected in the failure of Abercorn's bid for leadership. The struggle for control of unionism played itself out over several decades, however, and the reckoning was delayed by the success with which Abercorn established a consultative intimacy with the inner circles of tory power in early 1886. In January he founded the North-West Loyalist Registration and Electoral Association, with the Tyrone liberal, E. T. Herdman, in order to intensify a registration programme in the area, and to coordinate the different wings of local unionism. On the one hand, Abercorn discovered that there was great difficulty in raising subscriptions in the area, and as a consequence electoral and registration funding tended to fall on his shoulders; on the other, liberal and Orange unionists resisted the conservative embrace.

He had a less frustrating task trying to bring about concerted action by the unionist peerage in the house of lords. During March and April 1887 he led the Irish landed assault on a proposed amendment to the 1881 land act, securing the removal of disadvantageous clauses protecting bankrupt tenancies, while bowing to the inevitable with regard to the introduction of a triennial revision of judicial rents under the land courts, on condition that limits to possible reduction be set for fear that 'the door would be open to absolute confiscation' (quoted in Curtis, 340), as he put it. It was no surprise that he was one of the principal agents in the formation of the hard-line Irish Landowners Convention (ILC), set up in early 1888 to defend the rights of landed property in Ireland, was elected its first president, and held the office for at least a decade.

Abercorn kept continuously abreast of the currents of political feeling within the inner circle of conservative politicians through correspondence with the marquess of Salisbury, among others. During the campaign against the second home rule bill of 1893 he struck a chord with the mass of unionism by the rigid dignity of the phrase 'We will not have home rule', enunciated first at a farmers' meeting in Enniskillen, but with greatest plangency and effect at the enormous convention held in Belfast on 17 June 1892, where he got the 12,000 people attending to raise their hands and repeat it after him. It became a somewhat unlikely slogan over the next two decades. In the spring of 1893 Abercorn presided at a huge meeting in opposition to home rule at the Albert Hall, London. He mustered effective opposition against the bill in the house of lords, helping to bring it to defeat that year. During the early 1890s he carried on a running battle against radical unionism, particularly in the shape of T. W. Russell, whom he characterised as a 'vicious, little, teetotal, radical, Scotchman' (Gailey, 155), and his fellow campaigners for compulsory land purchase.

The comprehensive exercise of patronage through manipulation of his contacts within the conservative ruling caste was one of the instruments by which he attempted to hold the ground against populist unionism, with its threat to principles more fundamental than the union. While this ironically remained a standing option with regard mainly to superior office (the appointment of Sir John Ross as a land judge in 1896 being one of his coups that year), the increasing regulation of clerical and other lesser public offices by competitive examination made patronage at this level much more difficult. Even his genial mastery of the unionist peerage within the house of lords proved of diminishing effect. Despite frequent tactical meetings at Hampden House in late 1896, and the achievement of getting 138 peers to gather and defeat on six separate divisions a bill designed to enhance tenant security, he was ultimately unable to halt the legislation, for which his brother, Lord Claud Hamilton, voted in the house of commons. Some compensation was offered when Salisbury encouraged calls in April 1897 by the ILC for a commission of inquiry into the operation of the 1881 Land Act. Shortly after the report of the commission came out on the landed side, Abercorn made known, in private audience with Salisbury, landed and broad unionist discomfort with the provisions of the local government bill of November 1897. Swayed as much by the aura of intimacy and courtesy projected by Salisbury as by any definite promise of safeguards to either interest, Abercorn warmly supported the progress of the bill in early 1898. A unionist strategy based on fellow-feeling within a decaying caste was clearly open to exploitation by government more than by the Abercorn lobby. By the middle of 1899 the ILC under Abercorn had extracted a tithes rent charge act of minor assistance to the landed interest out of the largely redundant Fry report. Abercorn rejected an invitation to the land conference proposed by John Shawe-Taylor in late 1902, but proved 'pleasantly surprised' by the text of its report and moved a resolution at a meeting of the ILC on 7 January 1903 that it should receive the serious consideration of the government. Accordingly he oversaw the broad cooperation of the landed right wing with the progress of the Wyndham land bill of 1903, intervening to carry through a crucial compromise amendment by John Redmond at a meeting of the ILC in the Westminster Palace Hotel on 20 June.

Chairman of Tyrone county council from 1899, Abercorn scotched efforts by nationalists in late 1904 to turn a fledgling general council of county councils into a forum for discussion of general political matters, and led the withdrawal of northern council delegates. Several months later he was elected the first president of the Ulster Unionist Council, established at Glengall Street, Belfast, on 3 March 1905, as a link between Ulster unionists and their MPs. Increasingly no more than a figurehead for the movement and laid low by bouts of illness, he now appeared less often on protest platforms. Presiding to nostalgic acclaim at Carson's Londonderry meeting of 20 September 1912, and present among those delegates assembled to consider schemes for an independent Ulster at the Ulster Hall on 24 September, he was too ill to sign publicly the Ulster Solemn League and Covenant several days later, signing instead a copy of the document at his residence in Baronscourt, Co. Tyrone. He died 3 January 1913 at 61 Green Street, Mayfair, London. His body was returned by steamer and train to Baronscourt, where he was buried to the sound of a Scottish lament by the Hamilton pipe band.

He married (7 January 1869) Mary Anne Curzon, fourth daughter of Richard William Penn, 1st Earl Howe. They had seven sons and two daughters.

Desmond McCabe

Sources

Gaelic-American, 5 November 1904; *Times*, 4, 7, 8, 9, 10, 11 January, 11 February 1913; Earl of Dunraven, *Past times and pastimes*, ii (1922); A. G. Gardiner, *The life of Sir William Harcourt*, ii (1923); Ian Colvin, *The life of Lord Carson*, ii (1934); Pamela Hinkson (ed.), *Seventy years young: memories of Elizabeth, countess of Fingall* (1937); L. P. Curtis, jr, *Coercion and conciliation in Ireland, 1880–82: a study in conservative unionism* (1963); A. T. Q. Stewart, *The Ulster crisis* (1967); Patrick Buckland, *Ulster unionism and the origins of northern Ireland, 1886–1922* (1973); John Flint, *Cecil Rhodes* (1976); Desmond Murphy, *Derry, Donegal and modern*

Ulster, 1790–1921 (1981); John Biggs-Davison and George Chowdharay-Best, *The cross of St Patrick: the Catholic unionist tradition in Ireland* (1984); J. R. B. McMinn, *Against the tide: a calendar of the papers of Rev. J. B. Armour* (1985); James Loughlin, *Gladstone, home rule and the Ulster question, 1882–93* (1986); Andrew Gailey, *Ireland and the death of kindness: the experience of constructive unionism, 1890–1905* (1987); Mark Bence-Jones, *Twilight of the ascendancy* (1988) (port.); Alvin Jackson, *The Ulster party: Irish unionists in the house of commons, 1884–1911* (1989); Brian Walker, *Ulster politics: the formative years, 1868–86* (1989); Lawrence W. McBride, *The greening of Dublin Castle* (1991); Alvin Jackson, *Colonel Edward Saunderson: land and loyalty in Victorian Ireland* (1995)

Cahir Healy

1877–1970

Cahir Healy, nationalist politician and language revivalist, was born Charles Everard Healy, on 2 December 1877 at Doorin, near Mountcharles, Co. Donegal, the son of Patrick Healy, a small farmer and merchant. A Catholic, he was educated at Drimcoo interdenominational national school, which must have contributed to the spirit of broad-minded tolerance that marked his long political career. After study at Derry Technical School he became a journalist, working for the *Fermanagh News*, *Roscommon Herald*, and *Sligo Times*, and in 1897 married Catherine Cresswell of Enniskillen, who belonged to the Church of Ireland. About 1900 Healy left journalism and became an insurance supervisor, settling at Enniskillen, Co. Fermanagh.

The product of a bilingual household, Healy was active in the Gaelic revival of 1893–1916: he wrote articles and verse for *Shan Van Vocht*, an advanced nationalist journal published in Belfast by Alice Milligan and Anna Johnston (under 'Ethna Carbery'), frequented F. J. Bigger's advanced nationalist 'Ard Righ' circle in Belfast, and was a founder of the Gaelic League and the GAA in Co. Fermanagh in the early 1900s. A founder of the Fermanagh feis, he brought in the later revolutionary Patrick Pearse to open it in 1916. He was present when Sinn Féin was launched by Arthur Griffith at a historic meeting in Dublin in 1905; as a convinced separatist, he strongly supported Sinn Féin's novel policy of dual monarchy, and subsequently campaigned for the party with Griffith during the North Leitrim by-election in February 1908. When Sinn Féin was defeated Healy joined the revolutionary IRB; although he was not involved in the 1916 Easter rising, following the 'blood sacrifice' of the IRB leaders his admiration for them intensified until he could eulogise them as: 'Ye holy dead Who died that we Might taste the sweet of liberty' (*Catholic Bulletin*, 1918).

By 1918 Healy was a leading member of the Sinn Féin movement in Ulster and he was prosecuted for opposing wartime conscription. He campaigned for the party in the election of December 1918, which saw the return of Griffith in North-West Tyrone and Sean O'Mahony in South Fermanagh. During the war of independence of 1919–21 he took advantage of the peripatetic nature of his job to promote the revolutionary movement over a large area of Fermanagh, Leitrim and Sligo, where he set up republican arbitration courts. As a northerner, Healy was preoccupied, above all, with preventing partition, and in August 1921 he led a deputation from the nationalist-controlled Fermanagh county council to Dublin to impress on Éamon de Valera the county's claim to be included in an Irish state. Although the stand against partition failed, when the Anglo–Irish treaty was signed in December 1921 Healy shared the ill-fated optimism of border nationalists—reinforced by assurances from Griffith and Michael Collins—that the boundary commission set up under the treaty would ensure the transfer of Fermanagh and Tyrone to the Irish Free State. In an attempt to undermine the authority of the new Northern Ireland government, Healy threw his support behind

Collins's policy of 'non-recognition' of the northern state in education and local government from January 1922 onwards, but he was later to criticise 'the rather jumpy efforts which, with Collins, passed for statecraft' (*Ulster Herald*, 21 February 1925). None of the Sinn Féin leaders, he declared, understood the 'northern situation or the northern mind'.

In April 1922 Collins appointed Healy to serve on the provisional government's north-eastern advisory committee, set up to formulate a northern policy following the breakdown of the agreement between Collins and James Craig, the so-called 'Craig–Collins pact' of 31 March. His membership of this body, together with his efforts to prepare the Fermanagh nationalist case for the boundary commission, indicted him in the view of the unionist authorities, and he was interned in May 1922, along with 500 republican suspects, on the *Argenta*, a converted cargo vessel in Belfast Lough. It was not until he had been twice elected to the Westminster parliament—in 1922 and 1923—as a Sinn Féin MP for Fermanagh and Tyrone that the Craig administration grudgingly acceded to appeals from the British and Free State governments for his unconditional release in February 1924. The Irish government was determined that Healy, as 'one of the sanest and most far-seeing leaders of northern nationalism' (Phoenix, *Northern nationalism*, 294), should take his seat so as to keep the boundary issue alive. While opponents of the treaty attacked his 'fruitless apostasy' in the press, Healy believed that de Valera's irregulars were the real betrayers because their 'reckless actions' had delayed a decision on the boundary.

During 1924–5 Healy worked closely with the Free State boundary bureau in preparing the case of the border nationalists for presentation to the boundary commission. He demanded that the Irish government should insist on a plebiscite in border districts but his appeal was ignored, and he was vindicated in his expectation of failure when in November 1925 the commission collapsed following a leaked report confirming that it had recommended only minor changes in the 1920 boundary. The tripartite agreement of 3 December 1925, by which the Free State government recognised the 1920 border in return for financial concessions and the suppression of the report, led to an irreparable breach in Healy's relations with the pro-treaty administration: the northern nationalists, he declared, had been 'sold into political servitude for all time' (Healy to editor, *Irish Independent*, 30 November 1925; Healy papers, PRONI, D2991/B/1/10A).

Healy was elected to the Northern Ireland parliament as a nationalist MP for Fermanagh and Tyrone in 1925. He took the realistic view that a reconciliation between his own border supporters and the home rule remnant under the Belfast politician Joseph Devlin was the only means of reuniting nationalism and providing effective political leadership for the demoralised minority. In 1928 he and Devlin founded the National League of the North, a nationalist party committed to bringing about Irish unity by consent and constructive opposition in parliament. But his desire to promote a less sectarian political system was thwarted by Craigavon's abolition of proportional representation in 1929, and by 1932, when all hope of pursuing their ends by constitutional means seemed futile, Healy, Devlin, and their small party walked out of the Northern Ireland parliament in frustration.

When Devlin died in 1934, Healy assumed the role of nationalist leader. However, his Sinn Féin background and Fianna Fáil orientation made him suspect among the old Redmondite wing of the party, which identified with the Belfast MP T. J. Campbell, and he faced increasing opposition from republicans and the advocates of an abstentionist policy. Until 1935 Healy, in common with the majority of his colleagues, boycotted Stormont and waited for de Valera—now returned to power in Dublin—to reopen the partition question. In 1936, at Healy's instigation, the British National Council for Civil Liberties (NCCL) mounted an inquiry into the operation of the Northern Ireland Special Powers Act; the result was a damning indictment of the unionist regime. Healy always regarded Westminster as a valuable forum in which to air the minority's sense of injustice, and he played an active role there during two further periods as an MP (1931–5 and 1950–55).

Healy was bitterly disappointed by de Valera's failure to gain concessions on partition at the 1938 Anglo–Irish negotiations, but during the second world war he hoped that Britain's defence requirements might result in a British offer of Irish unity in return for the use of Irish ports by British forces. In July 1941 a letter that he had written to a Fermanagh parish priest about the likelihood of a German victory was intercepted and he was interned in Brixton prison for eighteen months under the Defence of the Realm Act. Among his fellow prisoners was the British fascist leader, Sir Oswald Mosley, with whom he formed a lasting friendship.

After the war Healy sought to mobilise world opinion against the partition of Ireland, and to that end in 1945 co-founded the broadly based Anti-Partition League (APL), along with James McSparran and Malachy Conlon. He also helped Hugh Delargy, a Labour MP at Westminster, to establish the Friends of Ireland, a parliamentary pressure group. The decline of the APL coincided with the IRA border campaign of the 1950s; Healy was a vigorous opponent of the use of force and continued to advocate peaceful constitutional means for achieving Irish unity, both during his last years as a Westminster MP and until he retired from political activity some ten years later. He was the author of the pamphlet *The mutilation of a nation* (1945), which sold 20,000 copies and became the 'bible' of every anti-partition orator, including de Valera. Moreover, in his later years he became convinced that the abstentionist policy that he had earlier supported was unavailing. He was scathing towards his inflexible republican opponents, accusing them of failing to 'face realities' and 'thriving on a diet of theories' (Healy to O'Kelly, 1 May 1948, PRONI, D2991/A/166B, Healy papers).

Despite his passionate commitment to Irish unity, Healy was sceptical of nationalist attempts in the post-war years to gain admission to the dáil for the representatives of the northern minority. 'We have no work to do in the dáil', he wrote in 1950, 'we are needed outside badly' (Healy to Canon T. Maguire, 5 November 1950, PRONI, D2991/B/4/11B, Healy papers). His desire for dialogue between the two traditions in Northern Ireland led him to support the ill-fated 'Orange and Green talks' between leaders of the Ancient Order of Hibernians and the Orange order in 1962–3. (In an effort to promote greater north–south understanding, he had been instrumental in arranging in 1949 a private meeting between the Northern Ireland prime minister, Sir Basil Brooke and the Irish minister for external affairs, Seán MacBride). He was sensitive to the mounting criticism of the image and structure of the Nationalist Party from such middle-class ginger groups as National Unity in the early 1960s, and suspected that such critics really wished to supplant the traditional party. However, he was alive to the possibility of Westminster intervention after the return of the Labour government in 1964, and sought to draw Harold Wilson's attention to the system of gerrymandering and discrimination in Northern Ireland.

When Healy finally retired from Irish public life in 1965 at the age of 87, having been returned by Fermanagh South in every Stormount election from 1929, he had attained an almost patriarchal status within the legislature whose very creation he had opposed. In his last years he turned his attention to Irish history and folklore, on which he wrote numerous articles for the Irish, British and United States media. He was a founder member and trustee of the Ulster Folk Museum in the 1960s. His personal friendships were eclectic and included the unionist MP and historian H. Montgomery Hyde, the left-wing socialist republican C. Desmond Greaves, Seán MacBride, and Sir Shane Leslie, writer and cousin of Winston Churchill.

Healy's career provides a focus for a study of the political fortunes of the northern nationalist minority from the onset of partition until the late 1960s. He represented a distinctive strand within the nationalist movement whose political origins lay with the original Sinn Féin party rather than with the Irish party of Redmond and Devlin. A member of the IRB after 1908 and an early admirer of the Easter rising, he was later to combine the rejection of physical force with an unswerving attachment to the ideal of a united and independent Ireland. A fervent supporter of the view that the boundary commission would render the fledgling northern state non-viable, he recovered from his deep sense of betrayal by the Free State government and joined with Joe Devlin in creating a constitutional nationalist party in 1928. In 1932, despairing of any hope of achieving reform at Stormont, he looked to de Valera and, to a lesser extent, the British government to undo partition. He saw the Irish language as a badge of national identity for nationalists and identified the Nationalist Party closely with its revival in the 1930s and 1940s. In later years, Healy adopted a more conciliatory attitude towards Ulster unionism and expressed the view that the 1916 rising had made partition inevitable.

He died 8 February 1970 at the Erne Hospital, Enniskillen, Co. Fermanagh, and was buried three days later in Breandrum cemetery. His wife predeceased him in 1948. He was survived by his three children, Victor and Peter (both bank managers) and Dr May Leavy, a medical doctor in Co. Monaghan. Apart from *The mutilation of a nation* (1945), he was the author (with Cathal O'Byrne) of a volume of poetry, *The lane of the thrushes* (1907) and wrote an unpublished account of his internment experiences of 1922–4 entitled 'Two years on a prison ship' (PRONI D2291/C).

Healy stands out as one of the few leading Sinn Féin figures from Ulster in the years 1917–22, as a significant leader of constitutional nationalism in the Northern Ireland under Stormont, and as a largely self-educated man who made a wide-ranging contribution to Ireland's literary and cultural heritage. Personally charming and erudite, Healy, with his quiet advocacy of a tolerant, non-sectarian form of nationalism, earned the respect of political opponents.

Eamon Phoenix

Sources

Cahir Healy MSS, PRONI, D2991; Cahir Healy, letter to the editor, *Irish Independent*, 30 November 1925 (copy in PRONI, Healy Papers); F. J. Whitford, 'Joseph Devlin, Ulsterman and Irishman' (MA dissertation, University of London, 1959); *Irish Weekly*, 12 February 1970; E. Phoenix, 'Introduction and calendar of the Cahir Healy papers' (MA dissertation, Queen's University, Belfast, 1978); *Irish Times*, 2 January 1980; E. Phoenix, 'Nationalist father figure', *Irish Times*, 9 June 1982; E. Phoenix, *Northern nationalism: nationalist politics, partition and the Catholic minority in Northern Ireland, 1890–1940* (1994); E. Phoenix, 'Cahir Healy (1877–1970) northern nationalist leader', *Clogher Record*, xviii, no. 1 (2003), 32–52

Denis Stanislaus Henry

1864–1925

Denis Stanislaus Henry, lawyer and politician, was born 7 March 1864 in Cahore, Draperstown, Co. Londonderry, one of five sons and two daughters of James Henry, businessman, and Ellen Henry (née Kelly), both of Draperstown. Educated at the local national school, he attended the Marist College in Dundalk, before enrolling at the age of fourteen in the Jesuit College of Mount St Mary's near Chesterfield, Derbyshire, England. He subsequently read law at QCB, where he won every available law scholarship possible, before being called to the Irish bar in 1885. Henry established himself as a successful figure in the north-west circuit, becoming a QC in 1898.

Like so many prominent lawyers of this era, he was closely involved with politics. While at one time a firm liberal, he declared his support for the unionist cause when Gladstone endorsed home rule in 1886. Henry's early participation in politics was active and varied. He supported unionist candidates in the 1895 election in Derry South and Donegal East, while his latter endorsement provoked a form of scornful contemporary criticism from nationalists which was to feature in his early life. A unionist delegate at the inaugural meeting of the Ulster Unionist Council in 1905, Henry became unionist candidate in the Tyrone North election of 1906, losing the contest by nine votes. Rejecting the legal advice for a recount, he accepted defeat with characteristic good grace. In 1907 his attempt to win Tyrone North in a by-election witnessed bitter defeat by a mere seven votes. His commitment to the union, and his warm personality, won Henry much admiration and respect from contemporaries of all political outlooks.

He rapidly emerged as one of the most outstanding advocates in Ireland, becoming father of the north-west circuit as well as establishing a successful practice in the Four Courts. In 1898 he had the unusual experience of appearing in three murder cases at a single assize, in which convictions were recorded. In January 1914 Henry, along with S. L. Brown, KC, headed a commission of inquiry into the circumstances of the riots that followed the Larkinite demonstration in Dublin in August 1913. Henry's quiet, courteous, and economical courtroom manner was evident during the proceedings. W. E. Wylie regarded Henry as the quickest thinker and most brilliant advocate that he had known, while A. M. Sullivan recalled that Henry was the best man that the Irish bar had produced in his time. In August 1916 Henry formed part of a royal commission of inquiry into the deaths of Francis Sheehy-Skeffington and two other men during the Easter rising. The commissioners found no possible justification for the conduct of Captain John Bowen-Colthurst, the officer responsible.

By this stage Henry had entered parliament, having won the Londonderry South by-election in May 1916. He was soon promoted to Irish law officerships: solicitor general in 1918, and attorney general in 1919. From then until August 1921, he served two Irish chief secretaries: Ian MacPherson and Sir Hamar Greenwood. His tenure was as troublesome as it was eventful. Badly briefed, and with Greenwood often absent from the commons, he at times appeared defensive when answering questions about allegations of misconduct by crown forces during the Anglo–Irish war, the revelations of reprisals, and the application of coercive measures such as the 'drumhead' courts. Henry was unrepentant in his vindication of government policy, and in cabinet opposed making truce offers to Sinn Féin. In spite of many heated parliamentary debates, he maintained good personal relations with all sides of the house. Testimony that Henry's reputation remained intact came with his appointment in August 1921 as the first lord chief justice of Northern Ireland. The truce in the Anglo–Irish war and the prospects of formal negotiations between Sinn Féin and the British government dominated the political agenda, which partly explains why unionists made little play with the fact that the newly created state had a Catholic leading the judiciary. In an atmosphere of uncertainty about the stability of the northern state, nationalists speculated that Henry's appointment would be short-lived.

Henry left Westminster for the last time on 5 August 1921, vacating his Londonderry South constituency that he had retained in the 1918 general election. Sworn in as lord chief justice on 15 August, he was charged with the task of assembling the machinery of a new judiciary at a time of great lawlessness. All aspects of the workings of the new judiciary fell to Henry, who displayed great energy and initiative, applying his notable qualities of working with others to good use. He secured the use of the county courthouse, Crumlin Road, Belfast, as temporary accommodation for the supreme court. He was directly involved in the recruitment of officials to staff the new judiciary, adopting a policy originated by the prime minister, Sir James Craig, that when candidates of equal merit were considered, the deciding qualification should be that the applicant was Ulster-born. Even the more mundane tasks of ensuring adequate pension rights for newly appointed staff and the purchase of furniture came under Henry's brief. He worked hard to foster good relations with members of the northern bar, who accepted an invitation to dine with Henry and his other judges in June 1922. He was also at the centre of several notable cases, which reflected the turbulent times in which the northern state functioned in its early years. In July 1922, Henry ruled against the plaintiff in the case of O'Hanlon v. Governor of Belfast Prison, which mounted a challenge to the legality of the Special Powers Act. In November 1923 he ruled against claims for compensation for the victims arising out of the well-publicised Cushendall ambush of 23 June 1922, arguing that the deaths of the three Catholic youths arose out of unlawful assembly. The cumulative impact of his work after 1919 took its toll, and he died 1 October 1925 at his home, Lisvarna, Windsor Avenue, Belfast, and was buried at the family plot in Straw cemetery in Draperstown.

He married (1910) Violet, third daughter of Hugh Holmes, lord justice. They had five children: James, Denise, Alice, Denis, and Lorna.

A. D. McDonnell

Sources

PRONI, SCH/665/1/1 Records of Draperstown national school for boys, 1870–1903; LR/141, will of James Henry and family members; *Banbridge Chronicle*; *Belfast News Letter*, *Belfast Telegraph*; *Coleraine Chronicle*; *County Down Spectator*, *Derry Journal*; *Impartial Reporter*, *Irish News*; *Irish Times*; *Irish Weekly*; *Londonderry Sentinel*; *Northern Constitution*; *Northern Whig*; *Strabane Chronicle*; *Times*; *Tyrone Constitution*; *Ulster Guardian*; PRONI, CAB/4/48/11, CAB/4/79/6, CAB/4/140/7, CAB/6/57, CAB/8/B/11, CAB/9D/9/11; Carson papers, D/150/F/11/11–16, D/1507/F/11/11 (photo, with Carson and others), D/2298/16/1, letters held by Wilson and Simms, solicitors, Strabane; *Hansard*; Henry family papers; *Incorporated Law Society's Calendar and Law Directory for 1920*; *Irish Law Times and Solicitors' Journal*; *Irish Law Times Reports*; Mount St Mary's College archives; *Thom*; unpublished memoirs of W. E. Wylie; G. Hill Smith, *The supreme court of judicature of Northern Ireland* (1926); J. Ross, *Pilgrim scrip: more random reminiscences* (1927); T. M. Healy, *Letters and leaders of my day* (1928); *WWW*; M. Healy, *The old Munster circuit* (1935); interview with Sir James Henry in London, 29 July 1979; L. McBride, *The greening of Dublin Castle* (1991); J. Casey, *The Irish law officers* (1996)

Bulmer Hobson

1883–1969

(John) Bulmer Hobson, nationalist, was born 14 January 1883 at 5 Magdala Street, Belfast, the son of Benjamin Hobson, a grocer who was from a Quaker family established in Ireland since the time of Oliver Cromwell, and his wife, Mary Ann Bulmer, a Yorkshire radical.

Family influences and early life

Hobson's father was a Gladstonian home ruler. His mother was active in the Belfast Naturalists' Field Club (lecturing on archaeology) and the suffragette movement. Her friends included Ada MacNeill, a member of the Gaelic League, who maintained a lifelong connection with Hobson. (He later mistakenly claimed that MacNeill was the fiancée of Roger Casement.) Mary Ann Hobson belonged to the Irishwomen's Association organised by Alice Milligan and 'Ethna Carbery' (Anna Johnston); Milligan acquainted Bulmer with the works of Standish James O'Grady, which 'opened up...new ranges of hitherto unimagined beauty'. The ancient heroes 'became my constant companions...far more real than the crude town in which I lived' (Hobson, 1). Hobson subscribed to Milligan's and Carbery's separatist monthly, *Shan Van Vocht* (1895–8). The 1898 centenary of the rebellion of the United Irishmen added them to his pantheon, and he became a republican. He soon also joined the artistic and antiquarian circle around F. J. Bigger.

Hobson was educated at the Friends' school, Lisburn. After leaving school at the age of sixteen, Hobson supported himself through haphazard clerical jobs. In 1900 he founded the Ulster Debating Club for boys. In 1901–2 he was secretary of the Belfast Tír na nÓg branch of the Gaelic League. As secretary of the first Antrim county board of the GAA, he successfully resisted proposals that policemen should be permitted to join, though he resigned over the GAA's reluctance to encourage youth clubs. In 1902 he founded a boys' group, Fianna Éireann, which was soon crippled by financial problems and Hobson's other commitments. At the first Glens of Antrim feis in 1904 Hobson befriended Casement and they corresponded regularly. Casement saw Hobson as a substitute son; Hobson admired Casement's idealism, anger at injustice, and financial sacrifices for cultural and political nationalism. They shared a love for the Glens of Antrim, where they often hiked and camped; in later life Hobson recalled these excursions as proof of Casement's heterosexuality, on the grounds that Casement had never taken advantage of this close proximity to make advances to him.

In 1901–3 he trained as a printer, and he retained a lifelong interest in publishing and fine printing. In 1902 he and David Parkhill decided: 'Damn Yeats, we'll write our own plays!' (Hanna Bell, 1), and in 1904 they co-founded the 'Ulster branch of the Irish Literary Theatre'; it had to be renamed the Ulster Literary Theatre, after the Abbey Theatre in Dublin (which had developed out of the Irish Literary Theatre, founded by W. B. Yeats and his associates) refused responsibility for it. Its first production was Hobson's historical drama 'Brian of Banba', inspired by a poem by Milligan offering the apparently hopeless struggle of the young Brian Bórama (Boru) as a model for modern separatists. The theatre was associated with a literary magazine, *Uladh* (1904–5), the contributors to which included Joseph Campbell. Because of his political commitments Hobson drifted away from the group, which survived into the 1930s, its programme dominated by kitchen comedies.

Membership of the IRB

From 1901 Hobson belonged to Cumann na nGaedheal, a front organisation for the Irish Republican Brotherhood, and in 1904 was sworn into the IRB by Denis McCullough; they joined other young men (including Seán MacDermott and Patrick McCartan) in displacing the older Belfast leadership of the brotherhood. In 1906 they founded the Dungannon Clubs, another front organisation for the IRB, which maintained republican separatism against the dual-monarchist 'Hungarian policy' of Arthur Griffith. The clubs' mouthpiece was the *Republic*, a Belfast weekly established by Hobson in December 1906, which published several writers associated with Bigger and the Ulster theatre. Hobson also debated with home rulers at public meetings in Ulster and Scotland. His working life was precarious: he lost one job because of his membership of the Gaelic League and another through his anti-recruiting activities. He visited America early in 1907, where he met IRB veterans and established contact with John Devoy, becoming Irish correspondent for Devoy's *Gaelic American*.

In May 1907, the *Republic* merged with the Dublin journal the *Peasant*, edited by W. P. Ryan with Hobson as deputy editor. When the Dungannon Clubs merged with Griffith's Sinn Féin shortly afterwards, Hobson became vice-president of the merged organisation. From 1907 younger IRB men associated with the Belfast group (including Hobson), and the veteran former prisoners Tom Clarke and John Daly challenged the IRB leadership in Dublin, which was finally deposed in 1911. Hobson moved to the capital in 1908, and became 'centre' of the Teeling circle of the IRB; in 1911 he was elected chairman of the Dublin centre's board and the Leinster board, and a member of the IRB supreme council. He was a particular friend of Clarke, who idealised him as a new John Mitchel and hoped that he could one day win over Ulster Protestants to separatism. In 1909 the *Peasant* became the *Irish Nation and the Peasant*, remaining under Ryan's editorship with major contributions by Hobson.

In August 1909 Hobson and Constance Markievicz co-founded a republican boy scout movement, Na Fianna Éireann, which borrowed its name and some characteristics from Hobson's Belfast youth club but was more explicitly military in its orientation. Hobson was its first president, though Markeivicz later replaced him. Hobson and Markievicz briefly shared a large house in Co. Dublin, combining Fianna duties with an unsuccessful horticultural enterprise, which gave rise to some tension with Markievicz's husband. (Hobson's son later interpreted some of his father's descriptions of eccentric behaviour by the countess as indicating sexual advances that Hobson was too idealistic and sexually naïve to recognise or reciprocate; Hobson himself did not regard them in this light.) In 1912 Hobson founded an IRB circle for Fianna members.

Nationalist power struggles

After reading the writings on popular resistance by James Fintan Lalor in 1901, Hobson had begun to advocate this form of action; in 1909 his handbook, *Defensive warfare*, was published by the west Belfast branch of Sinn Féin. But the following year Hobson and his allies resigned from Sinn Féin over policy differences with Griffith, and founded a monthly journal of their own, *Irish Freedom* (edited by Hobson), and several Freedom clubs.

In July 1913 Hobson organised drilling for members of the IRB in Dublin in preparation for the founding of a volunteer force, and he was one of the IRB group that persuaded Eoin MacNeill to found the Irish Volunteers, against the advice of MacNeill's old friend and Gaelic League associate P. H. Pearse, who warned him against such extremists as Hobson. Hobson became secretary of the Volunteer executive in December 1913, to the disquiet of the Clarke–MacDermott group within the IRB, who were alarmed at Hobson's assumption of such a prominent position. Hobson believed that once the Volunteers had been founded, IRB members should regard non-IRB Volunteers as colleagues and work with them on equal terms within a broad group encompassing nationalists of different opinions. By contrast, Clarke and MacDermott and their associates believed that the IRB should be controlled by a tight-knit internal caucus, which could manipulate the Volunteers as a whole and use non-IRB members of the leadership for its own ends while keeping them ignorant of its true strategy.

These tensions were compounded by Hobson's arrogant air: he was acutely conscious that he had already been a separatist when MacDermott was a member of the Ancient Order of Hibernians, and he later claimed that MacDermott had never quite shaken off the Hibernians' fondness for wire-pulling and intrigue. Hobson was also compromised by his friendship with Casement, whose eccentricities and government service aroused suspicions that he was a government spy. Hobson used *Irish Freedom* to promote Casement's view that Ireland's best interests lay in forming an alliance with Germany against Britain; during an American speaking tour in March 1914 Hobson passed a message to this effect from Casement to Devoy for transmission to the German ambassador.

In the first half of 1914 Hobson drew closer to MacNeill, becoming his principal adviser. In June, when John Redmond threatened to set up his own volunteer organisation if he was not allowed to nominate half of the Volunteers' executive committee, most of the IRB element in the Volunteer leadership favoured refusal. Hobson, however, persuaded MacNeill and the executive majority to accept Redmond's nominees, thereby avoiding a crippling split. Clarke, suffering from the after-effects of long imprisonment and the tensions of his political activity, interpreted Hobson's actions as treason: he accused Hobson of selling himself to Dublin Castle and they never spoke to each other again. Pearse, whom Hobson had sworn into the IRB, was now allied with the intransigents, but he accepted Hobson's good faith and interceded when Devoy sacked Hobson from the *Gaelic American*. Rather than split the IRB, Hobson left the supreme council and the editorship of *Irish Freedom*, but he retained his other IRB positions and remained active in the brotherhood, helping to organise the Howth and Kilcoole gun-runnings in July 1914. At this time he also resigned from the Society of Friends, having long abandoned Quaker pacifism; he remained a non-denominational Protestant, and later had difficulty obtaining a dispensation to marry a Catholic.

The Easter rising and its aftermath

After the outbreak of the first world war and the split between Redmondite and MacNeillite Volunteers, Hobson became the driving force of the MacNeill group, which favoured a defensive strategy and guerrilla warfare. When he discovered that the Pearse group was actively preparing a pre-emptive rising, in March 1916 Hobson urged MacNeill to confront them, but MacNeill refused to press the issue after receiving assurances from Pearse. On the Thursday of holy week 1916 Hobson learned of the impending insurrection and notified MacNeill; they confronted Pearse but MacNeill failed to act decisively against the plotters, and on the evening of Good Friday Hobson was lured to a meeting and detained until the outbreak of the rising.

Believing that the rebels had wrecked Ireland's hopes, Hobson took no part in the fighting; unlike MacNeill (who was more receptive to political symbolism and less unbending) he evaded arrest. Thereafter he was excluded from mainstream Irish nationalist politics: he was barred from the meeting at the Mansion House in 1917, when the second Sinn Féin party was founded, and ostracised by many former friends. He continued to believe in the efficacy of guerrilla warfare and held its effectiveness during the war of independence vindicated his original strategy. In 1918 he published the first volume of *A short history of the Irish Volunteers* (no more appeared) followed by an abridged edition of the life of Wolfe Tone, and in 1921 a selection of Tone's letters.

Later career

On 19 June 1916 Hobson married (Mary) Clare Gregan, formerly a secretary in the Irish Volunteer offices; they had a daughter and a son. On the foundation of the Irish Free State, Hobson became deputy director of the stamping department in the Office of the Revenue Commissioners; he held this position until his retirement in 1948. In 1929 he edited *A book of Dublin* for Dublin Corporation and in 1932 edited the *Saorstát Éireann official handbook*, a multi-author account of Irish life and culture commissioned by the government of W. T. Cosgrave. He took a strong interest in the

Gate Theatre during its early period, helping to recruit support for it at the time of its foundation; he edited and published in 1934 the *Book of the Gate Theatre*. He also took an interest in Esperanto.

Hobson detested the cautious economic policies of post-independence Irish governments, describing them as 'economic unionists'. From 1923 he advocated reafforestation, believing that spin-off industries would end rural depopulation and stabilise the Gaeltacht. His position as a civil servant obliged him to publish much of his writing on such matters anonymously, as, for example, *The new querist* (1933), whose authorship Hobson acknowledged only when he reprinted it in his memoir of 1968. In 1935 he founded a monthly journal, *Prosperity* (which became *Social Justice* in 1936 and folded in 1937), advocating the proto-Keynesian social credit theories of Major C. H. Douglas; these argued that economic growth could be secured by printing extra money to finance public works while controlling the speculative activities of the banks. Hobson joined the Catholic social activists Father Edward Cahill SJ and Mrs Berthon Waters in the League Against Poverty. In 1936 they founded a monetary reform group, the League for Social Justice; they drafted the minority report of the banking commission (1938) equating monetary reform with the social doctrine of the papal encyclicals. Orthodox economists, including George O'Brien, were utterly dismissive of Hobson and his associates. Although monetary reform had cranky, far-right overtones, it was a serious, if underdeveloped, response to the deflation of the 1930s. Many poets and artists advocated social credit in the 1930s and several prominent British adherents of this policy were lapsed Quakers. Hobson's former Volunteer associate Eimar O'Duffy (whose satirical *King Goshawk* trilogy was published under Hobson's 'Martin Lester' imprint from the late 1920s), was also a monetary reformer. After his retirement Hobson informally advised Clann na Poblachta on such matters as reafforestation and breaking the link with sterling; his criticisms of the banks' dominance of the Irish economy were occasionally quoted by the Irish Green Party in the 1990s.

A major preoccupation of Hobson's later career was his support for Roger Casement and his denial of Casement's homosexuality. He denounced the accusation as despicable propaganda, a charge that was foreshadowed in 1908, when, in the *Gaelic American*,

Hobson had publicised the Irish crown jewels scandal, with its homosexual overtones, as evidence of British degeneracy; he expanded on this in his 1968 memoir. Hobson and McCartan encouraged W. J. Maloney (who was based in America) to write *The forged Casement diaries* (1937), which advanced the now exploded theory that the diaries were Casement's transcription of material written by a Peruvian criminal. Hobson became Maloney's Dublin research assistant and oversaw the publication.

Last years and assessment

On his retirement from the staff of the Revenue Commissioners in 1948, Hobson moved from Dublin to Roundstone, Co. Galway. He was frequently consulted by scholars about the Volunteers and the events of 1916, and significantly influenced scholarly reassessments of the Easter rising. In retrospect Hobson criticised Pearse as a 'sentimental egotist' with a 'strain of abnormality', whose financial irresponsibility inflicted severe damage on vulnerable creditors (Edwards, 157, 337–8). Shortly before his death Hobson published a fragmentary memoir, *Ireland yesterday and tomorrow* (1968). Increasingly blind, he spent his last years with his daughter in Castleconnell, Co. Limerick, where he died on 8 August 1969.

Hobson's was a life of achievement, though the potential greatness once seen in him never came to fruition. His expectations were arrogantly high, his disappointment and frustration profound. 'The Phoenix of our youth has fluttered to earth such a miserable old hen', he lamented in 1953 (Dudgeon, 16). Many, like Sean O'Casey, thought Hobson vain and manipulative; others, like MacNeill, revered his quiet determination and selflessness. MacNeill's nephew, the novelist Brian Moore, who chose to have his ashes scattered at the Connemara graveyard where Hobson is buried, wrote: 'his body lay here in this small Connemara field, facing the ocean, under a simple marker was somehow emblematic of his life' (Patricia Craig, *Brian Moore* (2002)).

Hobson's papers are in the NLI, including his copy of the *Irish Freedom* anthology *The voice of freedom*, annotated with the authors of the anonymously published articles. The Maloney

Papers in the New York Public Library have his extensive correspondence with Maloney in connection with *The forged Casement diaries*. UCD holds letters to Denis McCullough (McCullough papers, UCD Archives Department, P120) and Desmond Ryan (Ryan papers, UCD Archives Department, LA10). Police reports on Hobson's separatist activities are in the NAI. A few items of correspondence may be found in the *New Statesman* archive at the University of Sussex Library.

Patrick Maume

Sources

Belfast Telegraph, 29 March 1960; 25 July 1964; 9 August 1969 (interview with Hobson); *Irish Times*, 6 May 1961; F. X. Martin, *The Irish Volunteers, 1913–1915* (1963); F. X. Martin, *The Howth gunrunning* (1964); Bulmer Hobson, *Ireland yesterday and tomorrow* (1968); *Irish News*, 14 November 1968; 9 August 1969; *Irish Independent*, 9 August 1969; *Newsletter* (Belfast), 18 August 1969; Sam Hanna Bell, *The theatre in Ulster* (1972); F. X. Martin and F. J. Byrne (ed.), *The scholar revolutionary: Eoin MacNeill, 1867–1945, and the making of the new Ireland* (1973); León Ó Broin, *Revolutionary underground: the story of the Irish Republican Brotherhood, 1858–1924* (1976); Ruth Dudley Edwards, *Patrick Pearse: the triumph of failure* (1977); Michael Tierney, *Eoin MacNeill: scholar and man of action, 1867–1945*, ed. F. X. Martin (1980); Kathleen Clarke, *Revolutionary woman: Kathleen Clarke, 1878–1972*, ed. Helen Litton (1991); Thomas Hennessy, *Dividing Ireland: World War I and partition* (1998); Billy Mitchell, 'Hobson's choice', *Fourthwrite*, no. 2 (summer 2000); Jeffrey Dudgeon, *Roger Casement: the black diaries* (2002); Ben Levitas, *The theatre of nation: Irish drama and cultural nationalism, 1890–1916* (2002); W. J. McCormack, *Roger Casement in death; or, Haunting the Free State* (2002); Marnie Hay, 'Bulmer Hobson: the rise and fall of an Irish nationalist' (Ph.D. thesis, UCD, 2004); local history newscuttings, Belfast Central Library collection

Sir Samuel Robert Keightley

1859–1949

Sir Samuel Robert Keightley, barrister, politician, and novelist, was born 13 January 1859 in Belfast, the eldest son of Samuel Keatley of Belfast, who may have been a pawnbroker but later became a successful clothier and outfitter and was a JP, and his wife, Catherine (née Brennan). Keightley was educated privately and then at QCB, where he was a scholar in both classics and law, graduating BA in 1879, LLB in 1882, and LLD in 1884.

He published, at the age of nineteen, *A king's daughter and other poems* (1878), having written the poem that gave the volume its title when he was sixteen. But despite this early foray into letters, Keightley initially devoted himself to practising law. Spelling his name Keightley (though his father continued to use the form

172

Keatley until the 1890s), he was called to the Irish bar in 1883 and the following year joined the north-east circuit, where he established a successful practice, though somewhat unusually he confined himself to appearing at courts in Belfast and the surrounding area.

Keightley's first novel was *The crimson sign* (1894), a vivid, though somewhat romanticised, description of the siege of Derry. It was followed by *The cavaliers* (1895), *The last recruit of Clare's* (1897), *The silver cross* (1898), *Heronford* (1899), *A man of millions* (1901), *The pikemen: a romance of the Ards of Down* (1903), *Barnaby's bridal* (1906), and *A beggar on horseback* (1906)—all, except *A man of millions* and *Barnaby's bridal*, historical novels. An excellent evocation of the rebellion of the United Irishmen in the Ards peninsula of Co. Down in 1798, *The pikemen* is his best work, offering a well-constructed, rapidly moving narrative with some fine characterisation; it ran to four editions by 1906, and in 1936 the government publications office in Dublin published an Irish translation (*Lucht picí a's sleagh*). Although now forgotten, Keightley's novels enjoyed considerable success, and were popular in the USA. Although uneven in quality, they are never dull, and 'despite some tendency to long-windedness, have a lot of incident and some good characterization' (Hogan, i, 648).

Notwithstanding the demands of his practice and his writing, in the early 1900s Keightley became active in Ulster political life when he joined the Ulster Farmers' Union, a small group devoted to the expropriation of estates by compulsory purchase from their landlords. T. W. Russell MP joined the organisation when he resigned from the South Tyrone Unionist Association in 1901, and it was renamed the Ulster Farmers' and Labourers' Union and Compulsory Purchase Association; Keightley became one of its two joint secretaries. Russell was a liberal unionist, dismissed from his post in the conservative government in 1900 because of his fervent advocacy of land reform; he built up a formidable movement of independent unionists (usually referred to as 'Russellites') in several Ulster constituencies in the early 1900s. He initially relied on the votes of Presbyterian tenant farmers, and on those of nationalist voters when there was no other candidate to attract their support; by 1906, however, he was increasingly dependent upon the nationalist vote, and in 1907 accepted office under the liberals.

Keightley unsuccessfully contested South Antrim in 1903 and South Derry in 1906, on both occasions as a Russellite. In 1906 he stood on an anti-home rule platform and lost by a narrow margin of seventy-one votes; despite ostensibly opposing policies espoused by the liberal party, as the polls closed Keightley helped to found the pro-liberal *Ulster Guardian*. Proclaiming himself a liberal (though in later years he maintained that he had always been a unionist), he became a prominent member of the Ulster Liberal Association. He continued to champion the cause of the tenant farmer in the columns of the *Ulster Guardian*, and again stood unsuccessfully in South Derry in 1910, this time as a liberal.

In February 1911 Keightley and the Rev. J. B. Armour of Ballymoney were appointed as government nominees to the first senate of the Queen's University of Belfast—Keightley gaining his place thanks to Armour's urging his appointment on the liberal government. Keightley was an active member of the senate until his term of office expired in 1914, and in 1912 unsuccessfully proposed that it pass a resolution sympathetic to home rule. He was knighted in 1912 but, despite his efforts and those of Armour in the liberal cause, neither was reappointed to the senate by the liberal government in 1914, a notable slight to two of its leading supporters in Ulster. Keightley withdrew completely from public life after this. He lived at Fortwilliam Park and at 9 Mountpleasant, both in Belfast, then at The Fort, Lisburn, and Drum House, Drumbeg, Lisburn, both in Co. Antrim. In the early 1930s he moved to Dublin, where he lived for the rest of his life.

Keightley was married twice. In 1892 he married Gertrude Emily Smith (Gertrude Keightley), younger daughter of Henry Smith of Northampton, with whom he had two sons (both of whom joined the British army—one died of influenza in 1919 after serving throughout the first world war). Gertrude died in 1929, and in 1930 he married Anne, widow of Colonel Vowell. He died on 14 August 1949 at Grattan Lodge, Naas, Co. Kildare.

A. R. Hart

Sources

Admission papers, King's Inns, Dublin; NAI: PRONI, D / 1792 / A3 / 1/24, D /1792 / A3 / 3/1; records and senate minutes, 1912–13, Queen's University of Belfast, pp 5 ff.; *Slater's Directory of Ireland* (1856); *Belfast Street Directory*; G. Hill-Smith, *The north-east Bar* (1910); *Belfast Newsletter*, 1 January 1912; *Ulster Guardian*, 6 January 1912; *Catholic Bulletin* (June 1938), 519; *Irish Times*, 16 August 1949; *Belfast Newsletter*, 17 August 1949; *Northern Whig*, 18 August 1949; St John Ervine, *Craigavon, Ulsterman* (1949), 102–3; *WWW*; T. W. Moody and J. C. Beckett, *Queen's Belfast, 1845–1949: the history of a university* (2 vols, 1959), i, 450; Alvin Jackson, 'Irish unionism and the Russellite threat, 1894–1906', *Irish Historical Studies*, xxv (1987), 376; K. Rankin, *The linen houses of the Lagan valley* (2002), 122; Rolf Loeber and Magda Loeber, *A guide to Irish fiction 1650–1900* (2006)

Richard Lyttle

1866–1905

Richard Lyttle, land campaigner, nationalist, and non-subscribing Presbyterian minister, was born 6 March 1866 at Barnhill, a farm near Dromore, Co. Down, owned by his father, Richard Lyttle, a merchant in Dromore whose family had been gentlemen farmers near Donaghcloney. His mother, Mary (née McWilliam) of Banbridge, came from a family connected with the linen trade. In later life he liked to speak of himself as possessing mixed 'Celtic and Teutonic' blood. His family were unionists, but as a boy Richard became a nationalist through reading nationalist newspapers and works of Irish history. His discontent with the existing state of affairs was strengthened during his boyhood when Barnhill was lost to his family through a defective title, and his father's legal claim against the landlord for £2,000 compensation for tenant right was disallowed.

At the age of 14 Lyttle entered Lurgan College; after studying there he was briefly apprenticed in a solicitor's office before deciding to become a minister, rather than a lawyer as his parents had intended. In 1884 he entered the Unitarian College at Manchester, where he studied for three years. He won a scholarship to Owens College, Manchester (latterly Manchester University, then part of the federal Victoria University) where he studied for two years but left without graduating. This was due to eyestrain caused by overwork and to a feeling that the recent death of his only sister and the declining health of his parents made it necessary for him to return to Ulster to help them. During his stay in Manchester Lyttle was prominent in Irish nationalist and liberal activities. He was also a successful athlete, and was offered a place on the Irish national rugby team, which he declined for health reasons.

On 24 January 1889 Lyttle was called to the non-subscribing Presbyterian congregation of Moneyreagh, Co. Down, taking up his ministry in July. This area of east Down had a strong tradition of Presbyterian, liberal, and tenant-farmer radicalism dating back to the United Irishmen; a previous minister of Moneyreagh (1879–84), the Rev. Harold Rylett, had been a prominent Land Leaguer and retained links with the area after moving to a congregationalist ministry in London. Lyttle's parents lived with him in the manse till they both died in May 1897. Lyttle was a renowned preacher and an active and conciliatory minister who resolved disputes within the congregation over its denominational affiliation, increased its membership, raised funds to repair the meeting-house, and formed an active and successful temperance guild. His pastoral dedication and the non-subscribing denomination's traditional emphasis on private judgment won him acceptance even among those who did not share his home rule views. In the early 1890s Lyttle organised Ulster Protestant home rulers to campaign for Gladstonian by-election candidates in Britain, going over himself whenever he could spare a few days. He was a leading promoter of the Ulster Protestant petition in favour of home rule presented to Gladstone in 1893. He engaged in extensive controversies in the correspondence columns of the liberal unionist *Northern Whig* and often wrote for the nationalist *Irish News*. Lyttle associated himself with the Dillonite wing of the anti-Parnellites. At the 1896 Irish Race Convention he recalled Catholic O'Donnells and Protestant United Irishmen, and predicted that falling agricultural prices and rising wages would convert Ulster unionist farmers to home rule. In 1900 he campaigned for the nationalist candidate in the marginal Tyrone East constituency.

In 1894 he participated in the foundation of a cultural nationalist body, the Irish Women's Association, which brought him into contact with Alice Milligan and Ethna Carbery. His cultural nationalism also found expression in the establishment of a Gaelic League branch at Moneyreagh, and in 1896–7 Lyttle helped organise nationalist excursions to the grave of Betsy Gray. His pamphlet *The origin of the fight with the Boers* (1899) went through several editions and was widely reviewed and quoted by nationalist newspapers. It denounced the Boer war in terms reminiscent of British pro-Boer radicals, rather than the advanced nationalist view that Britain's difficulty was Ireland's opportunity.

After the defeat of the second home rule bill, Lyttle was active in the Ulster Tenants' Defence Association, an umbrella organisation for local tenant and Presbyterian groups which resented landlord and anglican influence. From 1900 this body became the Ulster Farmers' and Labourers' Union (UFLU), led by T. W. Russell, liberal unionist MP for Tyrone South, which campaigned for land purchase and opposed official unionists at the polls. Lyttle was one of Russell's principal lieutenants as joint secretary of the UFLU.

Lyttle's health was undermined by his political exertions and pastoral labours; from 1894 he was responsible for the neighbouring congregation of Ravara as well as Moneyreagh, and from 1901 for a newly formed Carrickfergus congregation. He died suddenly on 22 October 1905 in Bristol, while returning from a conference of unitarians at Geneva; he was buried at Moneyreagh, and a memorial fund organised by the congregation and the UFLU built the Lyttle Memorial School, which existed from 1908 to 1961.

Patrick Maume

Sources

[Rev. Daniel F. McCrea], *History and album of the Irish Race Convention which met in Dublin the first three days of September 1896...With memoirs, list of delegates, proceedings &c.* (1897), 133–8, 260 (photo), 301–2; Richard Lyttle, *The origin of the fight with the Boers* (5th ed., 1900, with additional material); *Belfast Newsletter*, 24 October 1905, 7; 25 October 1905, 9; 26 October 1905, 4; *Freeman's Journal*, 24 October 1905, 5; *Irish People*, 28 October 1905, 5; Anon., *In memoriam Reverend Richard Lyttle, Moneyrea* (1906); Hugh Frame, *A short history of the Lyttle Memorial School, Moneyrea* (1932); Rev. William McMillan, *A history of the Moneyreagh congregation 1719–1969* (1969); Hugh C. Thompson, *A history of Moneyrea* ([1981]); Hugh C. Thompson, 'Rev. Richard Lyttle: a home rule Protestant', *Familia*, ii, no. 2 (1986), 95–100 (photo); Roger Blaney, *Presbyterians and the Irish language* (1996), 177–8; copies of local publications supplied by Sandra Gilpin, Comber, Co. Down

Sean (John) Francis MacEntee

1889–1984

Sean (John) Francis MacEntee, revolutionary, politician, and engineer, was born 1 January 1889 at Mill Street, Belfast, eldest among seven children of James MacEntee, publican, and Mary MacEntee (née Owens), who both came from Co. Monaghan. James MacEntee owned three public houses in Belfast, and had been a member of the IRB and a supporter of Charles Stewart Parnell. Sean MacEntee was educated at St Malachy's College and went on to study electrical engineering at the Belfast Municipal College of Technology. His daughter, Máire Cruise O'Brien, observed that although he was always bitter at being denied a university education, engineering was his proper bent as he was 'thoroughly a man of the twentieth century' (O'Brien, *Same age as the state*, 33). However, he was also interested in cultural nationalism and joined the Gaelic League and the Ulster Literary Theatre. A volume of his poetry was published in 1917 and some of his poems were also included in the anthology *Poets of the insurrection* (1918). In 1914 he was appointed assistant chief engineer at the Dundalk electricity works.

Radical politics and war

MacEntee's interest in politics had been stimulated by James Connolly and in 1910 he joined Connolly's Socialist Party of Ireland. In his memoir *Episode at Easter* (1966) MacEntee explained how he had been radicalised by the challenge of the Ulster unionist leader, Edward Carson: 'he not only preached rebellion, he openly armed and prepared for it. And he did so with impunity.' MacEntee joined the Dundalk corps of the Irish Volunteers in January 1914. At the end of that year he was planning to leave Ireland but decided to stay, and after the split in the Volunteers in the summer of 1914 he joined the wing led by Eoin MacNeill. By 1915 the Dundalk corps numbered only 120 men. When the Easter rising started on 24 April 1916, MacNeill's countermanding order caused considerable confusion. The Dundalk Volunteers had mobilised on Easter Sunday and marched to Slane in Co. Meath to wait for orders which never came. MacEntee eventually made his way to Dublin, but on the journey an affray occurred at Castlebellingham in which an RIC constable was killed. MacEntee was later charged with his murder. In *Episode at Easter* MacEntee wrote a vivid account of the last days and hours in the GPO with incisive portraits of the leaders, Patrick Pearse, Connolly, Thomas MacDonagh and Éamonn Ceannt. In a 1972 interview MacEntee recalled how he felt after the failure of the rising:

> It had been in every sense of the word, an adventure. People felt toughened and hardened by the fact that they had ran so close and not to be pushed over [*sic*] (UCDA, MacEntee papers P67/776 (11); interview for BBC, November 1972).

MacEntee was sentenced to death for his role in the events at Castlebellingham but was reprieved. He was imprisoned at Dartmoor, Lewes and Portland but was released in June 1917. Later that year he was elected to the Volunteer national executive. In May 1918 he was rearrested after the discovery of the alleged 'German plot'. During his imprisonment at Gloucester jail he started to write a narrative of the rising in Louth which was the basis for *Episode at Easter*, although it was not published for another fifty years. In December 1918 he was elected Sinn Féin MP for Monaghan South and was returned unopposed in May 1921. In the same election he also stood for Belfast West in a deal brokered by the northern nationalist MP Joseph Devlin, but he was unsuccessful. He was vice-brigadier and then brigadier of the IRA's Belfast Brigade (1919–21), in what was some of the most hostile terrain of the war of independence.

He married (May 1921) Margaret Browne, whom he had first met in 1917 at a ceilidh for released prisoners. The Brownes were a prominent republican family from Co. Tipperary. Margaret's brothers were Mgr Pádraig de Brún, president of UCG, Maurice Browne, priest and novelist, and Michael (David) Browne, Dominican friar and cardinal. Margaret took a double first in Irish and modern languages at UCD and was awarded an MA in 1917. She had joined Cumann na mBan before the Easter rising and had acted as a courier for Liam Mellows in Galway. She worked for the Sinn Féin election campaign in 1918 and then for the Belfast boycott in 1920–22.

MacEntee opposed the 1921 Anglo–Irish treaty and made the most forceful and prophetic denunciations of its Ulster clauses, which, he argued, would make partition permanent. He remained a consistent critic of southern nationalism's failure to appreciate the depth of Ulster unionist feeling. In 1922 he set up a short-lived consulting engineering firm but this collapsed after the start of the civil war in 1922. MacEntee was interned at Kilmainham and Gormanston and was released at Christmas 1923. Their daughter Máire was born in April 1922, and during his internment Margaret worked long hours teaching and continued to pay the rent for her husband's engineering office. MacEntee was released from prison because he had been engaged to work on the street lighting for Wexford, and the mayor of Wexford refused to pay the contractors until he was released. He resumed his engineering career while Margaret, who had lost her job at Rathmines technical school because she refused to make a declaration of loyalty, joined the teaching staff of Alexandra College, whose headmistress merely asked her to keep her political views from the parents. The couple had two more children, Séamus (b. 1924) and Barbara (b. 1928). Margaret remained at Alexandra until the early 1930s, when she was appointed to a lectureship in Irish at UCD.

Return to the dáil; minister for finance

MacEntee contested the Co. Dublin constituency for Sinn Féin in 1923 and 1924 but was unsuccessful. When asked why he returned to politics when Fianna Fáil was founded in 1926, MacEntee replied:

> Just the determination not to be beaten. It wasn't a case of going out of politics. In internment, you're in politics. You're surrounded by politicians (Interview for BBC, November 1972).

In the split with Sinn Féin, he was typically trenchant on the question of Ulster: for Sinn Féin to argue that the new policy of Éamon de Valera made partition permanent was nonsense, he argued, as republican policy generally had achieved this since 1922. MacEntee was elected to the dáil for Co. Dublin in June 1927 and, with the other Fianna Fáil TDs, took the oath of allegiance and became part of the official opposition. He was reelected in September in the second general election of 1927. The leaders of the new party criss-crossed the country, setting up new cumainn and building up a formidable political machine. MacEntee later recalled:

> For more than five years hardly any of us were at home for a single night or any weekend. Lemass bought up four or five 'old bangers' and with them we toured every parish in the country founding Fianna Fáil branches on the solid basis of Old IRA and Sinn Féin members. They were all marvellous people (McInerney, *Irish Times*, 22–5 July 1974).

MacEntee was one of the party's treasurers and was elected to the party's national executive, on which he served until he retired from politics in 1969.

When Fianna Fáil won the general election in February 1932, fears of political and social revolution were rife. De Valera's decision to make MacEntee minister for finance was intended as a reassuring appointment. There was considerable pressure from the Fianna Fáil grassroots to purge the civil service of officials who were considered disloyal, but MacEntee refused. He had last met the secretary of his new department, James McElligott, when they were both escaping from the GPO in 1916, but apart from this bond they both espoused conservative fiscal, social and administrative policies, opposing increased taxation and demands for state provision of social services. In 1934 MacEntee appointed a commission to examine banking, currency and credit in the Irish Free State. Given the conservative composition of the commission, the conclusions of its report in 1938 were unsurprising: it criticised the government's social programmes, particularly housing, and also the sharp increase in the national debt. It also concluded that the banking system was adequate. MacEntee had been against the establishment of a central bank in 1933, but he accepted the commission's recommendation that one should be set up, which happened in 1942.

MacEntee played an important role in the events that led to the passing of the External Relations Act in December 1936, following the abdication of King Edward VIII. He urged de Valera to take advantage of the abdication to remove the British crown from the internal and external affairs of the Irish state. However, other aspects of de Valera's constitutional policy were more controversial within the MacEntee household: Margaret MacEntee was vehemently opposed to the clauses of the 1937 constitution on the place of women in the home. During the six-year economic war with Britain (1932–8) MacEntee consistently pressed de Valera to reach a settlement, and a memorandum he wrote in November 1937 spurred de Valera to open negotiations with the British government, which started in January 1938. During the four-month-long talks, MacEntee frequently vented his exasperation about de Valera's negotiating strategy in letters to his wife. He wanted to conclude the finance, trade, and defence agreements and thought it hopeless to hold out for concessions on partition, as de Valera wanted.

Relations with Lemass

MacEntee served in all of de Valera's administrations until 1959, but his relations with his colleagues were often difficult. There are six letters of resignation in his papers, dating from the late 1930s to the early 1950s, none of which, however, actually resulted in his resignation. He displayed a certain obtuseness in suggesting several times to de Valera that he take over the external affairs portfolio, which was firmly rejected by the taoiseach. He also took a combative approach to journalists and pursued a number of successful libel cases, despite advice from colleagues not to do so. But it was the political rivalry between MacEntee and Seán Lemass that was to be a dominant theme in Fianna Fáil politics from 1932 to 1959. However, while they certainly differed on economic and financial policy, they were closer on other issues. As Dublin TDs they were consistently critical about the deficiencies of Irish agriculture. They were also united in their opposition to the report of the commission on vocational organisation, which was published in 1944. When the second world war broke out in September 1939, Lemass was given the new Department of Supplies, which had the task of ensuring the country's economic survival during the conflict. To achieve this, he had no intention of being constrained by the conservatism of the Department of Finance, and MacEntee was moved first to Industry and Commerce (1939–41) and then to Local Government and Public Health (1941–6).

MacEntee loved cinema, theatre, and jazz. He gave up poetry in the late 1920s but maintained an interest in literature; he was particularly proud of his eldest daughter's career as a poet. In 1942 he pressed de Valera to give a subsidy to *The Bell*, the journal of Sean O'Faolain. In 1946 he took up the cudgels on behalf of one of his officials, Brian O'Nolan (alias 'Flann O'Brien' and 'Myles na Gopaleen'), when the Department of Finance refused to sanction his promotion because of his journalism. The refusal was 'nothing short of victimization', he protested to the minister for finance (UCDA, MacEntee papers, P67/281).

MacEntee was always a voracious reader and his papers testify to the wide range of journals and newspapers that he read from all over the world, copies of which he frequently sent to reluctant cabinet colleagues. During the Emergency he became increasingly concerned by the encroachment of the state, and this reached a pitch after the publication (1942) of the Beveridge report on social insurance in Britain. The report received wide coverage in Ireland, and MacEntee feared that this would produce unrealistic expectations of similar provisions by the Irish government. He bombarded his colleagues with a flood of articles and newspaper reports attacking state socialism. Despite this, the government introduced children's allowances in 1944 and MacEntee himself was largely responsible for drafting the 1947 health act, which introduced extensive reforms in the Irish health service.

In the 1948 elections MacEntee was returned for the new Dublin South-East constituency but Fianna Fáil was defeated. His fellow constituency TDs included the new taoiseach, John A. Costello, and the new minister for health, Dr Noel Browne. MacEntee was friendly with Costello and other opposition politicians, including Desmond FitzGerald and Michael Hayes, but he was scathing about Browne and remained so. MacEntee refused to participate in the all-party anti-partition campaign which started later in 1948, arguing that once again southern nationalism was displaying its ignorance of Ulster unionism.

The 1950s and 1960s

When Fianna Fáil returned to power in 1951 MacEntee returned to the Department of Finance, a sign that Lemass's dominant role during the war and the postwar years was waning. His influence with the trade unions was also declining, and for the first time commentators began to express doubts about Lemass's assumed succession to de Valera. MacEntee was in the ascendant, but this did not survive his 1952 budget, which was called the 'famine budget'. When he returned to Finance in 1951 there was a trade deficit of £123 million, and to rectify this the budget included increases in income tax and in the cost of petrol, tobacco, spirits, ale, stout, tea and sugar. MacEntee and Lemass agreed that Irish external assets should not be frittered away on imported goods for domestic consumption. But while the budget was successful to the extent that the trade deficit declined sharply, industrial production was lower and unemployment rose. This bore particularly on the urban workers who were Lemass's constituents in Dublin. MacEntee later wrote that Lemass had

> a strong bias in favour of the worker and of organised labour. If he had a weakness in his approach to such matters, it was for the more spectacular solution, and this, when I was minister for finance, sometimes set us at variance with each other. Which, given our respective responsibilities and personal dispositions, was unavoidable (obituary of Lemass, *Irish Press*, 12 May 1971).

The differences between MacEntee and Lemass continued when Fianna Fáil left office again in 1954. In 1955–6 Lemass made important speeches on full employment and the need for foreign investment. When another general election was called in early 1957 the outgoing taoiseach, Costello, highlighted the economic disagreements between MacEntee and Lemass. But with the return of Fianna Fáil to power in 1957, the supporters of financial orthodoxy lost ground as the government gradually dismantled protection, liberalised external trade, and actively promoted foreign investment. In 1959 de Valera retired as taoiseach to make way for Lemass and to stand for the presidency. Despite the past tensions between them, Lemass appointed MacEntee tánaiste, a position he held until 1965. MacEntee wanted the external affairs portfolio, but this remained with Frank Aiken. MacEntee later wrote that, like de Valera, Lemass had the ability to pick a good team although he had a more difficult job as he had a wider choice of able young men eager for promotion. Explaining why he promoted MacEntee, Lemass wrote that

> it would have seemed a rebuke to him if I did not appoint him as tánaiste so I did appoint him. It is far more important to maintain goodwill and harmony than seek a more effective distribution of responsibility (Quoted in Brian Farrell, *Seán Lemass* (1991), 101).

MacEntee combined the health and social welfare portfolios until 1965. One of the most contentious pieces of legislation passed during his tenure was the Health (Fluoridation of Water Supplies) Act, which introduced mandatory fluoridation of drinking water (Ireland was the first country in Europe to implement this in 1964). The act was challenged in the supreme court in *Ryan* v. *Attorney General* (1965), but the court held that the act did not infringe the plaintiff's right to bodily integrity.

Final years

Relations between MacEntee and Lemass deteriorated after the 1965 election. MacEntee had planned to retire but his constituency organisation put pressure on him to stand again—which he did, much to Lemass's annoyance. But MacEntee was vitriolic when Lemass decided to retire in October 1966, declaring that Lemass was ten years younger than he was and had 'let us all down', squandering de Valera's 'great heritage' (UCD, MacEntee papers, P67/734). He was clearly unaware of the toll that the strain of office was taking on Lemass's health. MacEntee finally retired from politics in 1969. When the northern troubles erupted that year he urged the taoiseach, Jack Lynch, to take a new approach to Northern Ireland, stating that 'the hard fact [is] that the Unionist party does represent the traditions and deeply-held convictions of a large majority of the people in that area' (MacEntee papers, P67/520; letter from MacEntee to Lynch, 6 November 1969). He gave unstinting support to Lynch in 1970 when the latter dismissed Charles Haughey (1925–2006) and Neil Blaney from his government after an attempt to import arms for northern republicans.

Lemass died in 1971 and de Valera four years later. The obituary of Lemass which MacEntee wrote for the *Irish Press* was generous, perceptive, and testified to the comradeship that lay beneath their long and often difficult working relationship. After de Valera's death in August 1975 he wrote to de Valera's son Vivion that he looked back on his years working for de Valera 'with pride, but also with awe' (MacEntee papers, P67/479 (13); MacEntee to Vivion de Valera, 30 August 1975). Margaret MacEntee died in September

1976. MacEntee remained active until his last illness at the end of 1983. His kidneys failed but he refused dialysis and insisted on going home to die. He died 12 January 1984.

Deirdre McMahon

Sources

UCDA, Sean MacEntee papers; *The poems of J. F. MacEntee* (1917); Sean MacEntee, *Episode at Easter* (1966); Sean MacEntee, 'Sean Lemass', *Irish Press*, 12 May 1971; Michael McInerney, 'Sean MacEntee', *Irish Times*, 22–5 July 1974; Máire Cruise O'Brien, *The same age as the state* (2003)

Thomas MacKnight

1829–99

Thomas MacKnight, newspaper editor and political writer, was born 15 February 1829 at Gainsford, Co. Durham, son of Thomas MacKnight and his wife Elizabeth. He was initially educated at the Rev. Dr Bowman's school at Gainsford. After his parents moved to London he studied medicine at King's College (1849–51), where he won several prizes and came under the influence of the Christian socialist F. D. Maurice who regarded him as a particularly talented protégé. He also acquired a knowledge of foreign languages, which proved useful in his subsequent editorial career, as it enabled him to consult continental news sources directly. An address to a student society on contemporary literature (1851) and a prize essay on Shakespeare (1852) were published as pamphlets. He also published two Burke-related articles in *Frazer's Magazine* in 1851.

Political and biographical writing; marriage and scandal

In 1851 MacKnight left King's College 'to devote himself to literature'. On 26 July 1851 he married Florence Fanny Holland Smith. The marriage produced two children, a boy and a girl. MacKnight's insistence on living precariously off publishers' advances in order to concentrate on major works, rather than engaging in ephemeral but more profitable journalism, contributed to tensions within the marriage. (The first surviving MacKnight letter in the Gladstone papers, dated March 1854, was caused by Florence writing to Gladstone seeking financial assistance without telling MacKnight first; the letter suggests MacKnight saw this as both personally humiliating and politically compromising.)

MacKnight had just published, anonymously, *The Right Honourable Benjamin Disraeli M.P.: a literary and political biography* (1854), which attacks Disraeli as an opportunistic adventurer who is corrupting English political life, cites numerous embarrassing passages from Disraeli's novels, criticises his view that the Jews are a superior race, and derides his claim to be a disciple of Edmund Burke. The book went through two editions (Disraeli took it seriously enough to co-author an anonymous review in his own newspaper), and it served as a resource for later critics of Disraeli such as T. P. O'Connor. MacKnight later pointed out that the book praised Gladstone (then a Peelite rather than a whig) as proof of the depth and sincerity of his own Gladstonianism. It was followed by *Thirty years of foreign policy* (1855), which argued that the foreign policies of lords Palmerston and Aberdeen, traditionally seen as rivals but now serving together in a whig–Peelite coalition, had both been inspired by a common desire to defend British-style constitutional government against the absolutist principles upheld by tsarist Russia. MacKnight predicted that the Crimean war, which had just begun, would be an epoch-making showdown between the forces of freedom and despotism. The book was allegedly used as a textbook for trainee diplomats.

Meanwhile, MacKnight's marriage continued to deteriorate. After several disputes, which F. D. Maurice tried to mediate, the couple parted in 1856; Florence later alleged that MacKnight had deliberately deserted her and that verbal or physical violence had been involved. In 1859 MacKnight formed a new relationship with the actress Sarah Thorne (1836–99) and from February 1860 they lived together after telling friends that they had married. Thorne left the stage at this point, and they had a son and a daughter. Florence MacKnight claimed that her husband contributed nothing to the support of her and their children; his financial situation remained precarious, and he suffered health problems including depression.

MacKnight's *History of the life and times of Edmund Burke*, which he regarded as his *magnum opus*, was published (1858–60) (Gladstone assisted MacKnight to retain his copyright in *Burke* by lending him £100 to be repaid on the publication of the first volume, MacKnight having refused to take it as an outright gift; MacKnight felt lifelong personal gratitude towards Gladstone over this), and was followed in 1863 by *The life of Henry St John, Viscount Bolingbroke* (which, MacKnight told Gladstone, contained an anti-Disraeli subtext in its criticisms of Bolingbroke, Disraeli's political hero). Despite generous advances from his publishers, Chapman and Hall, MacKnight sank into debt and was obliged to apply for assistance from the Royal Literary Fund in July 1859 and June 1863, receiving payments of £35 on the first occasion and £50 on the second. He told one of his referees that while Gladstone would have been willing to help him, he wished to avoid being politically compromised.

One week after MacKnight received the second payment, Florence MacKnight sued for divorce on the grounds of his adultery with Thorne. She received a decree nisi on 17 June 1863, and the reports of her evidence which appeared in *The Times* and the *Morning Post* the next day led the Fund to write to MacKnight's referees demanding an explanation, and Chapman and Hall (who had acted as one of his referees) breaking off their business relations with him. In August 1863 Sarah Thorne returned to the stage, and this may be seen as the end of their relationship. It is not clear what contacts, if any, subsequently took place between MacKnight and his two families. MacKnight apparently survived this personal and financial catastrophe by becoming a leader writer on a 'great London daily' (*Northern Whig*, 20 November 1899).

Northern Whig editor; Belfast liberalism

In February 1866 MacKnight moved from London to Belfast to take up the position of editor of the Belfast daily *Northern Whig*. The paper was regarded as the voice of Presbyterian tenant farmer politics, and MacKnight liked to recall that, since its foundation in the 1820s, it had consistently opposed both Orangeism and repeal. When he arrived its fortunes were at a low ebb, owing to the suspicion that its proprietors favoured Unitarianism (one Belfast conservative newspaper habitually called it 'our infidel contemporary') and its support for the northern side in the American civil war.

MacKnight's arrival in Belfast was soon followed by the final campaign for the disestablishment of the Church of Ireland; this, together with a renewed campaign for tenant-right legislation (partially answered by Gladstone's 1870 Land Act) and the enfranchisement of many tradesmen by the 1867 Reform Act, led to an upturn in the political fortunes of Ulster liberalism and the readership of the *Northern Whig*. MacKnight, in search of a congenial place of worship, experienced some difficulty in finding a Belfast Church of Ireland congregation whose services were not dominated by denunciations of disestablishment and of popery, and eventually settled on St Thomas's Church of Ireland in Eglantine Avenue in south Belfast. (Despite his marital misadventures, MacKnight remained a devout Anglican; his obituarists noted that he read the New Testament daily in the original Greek.) While believing that Irish circumstances made disestablishment necessary, he was not opposed to established churches in principle; his mentor Maurice saw establishment as symbolising the moral bonds holding a nation together and MacKnight was probably influenced by this view. He hinted that he wished Irish disestablishment could have been averted by earlier Catholic emancipation and concurrent endowment; in later life he opposed church disestablishment in Scotland and in England and Wales.

MacKnight played a significant role (as go-between and editorial advocate) in the informal electoral alliance between the independent Orangeman William Johnston (1829–1902) and the liberal Thomas McClure, which led to the defeat of the two conservative MPs for Belfast at the 1868 general election; after the election he was presented with a service of silver plate by Belfast liberals to commemorate his role in the victory. He rapidly came to be seen as a perceptive and knowledgeable analyst of Irish affairs. He resumed contact with Gladstone, who had apparently lost touch with him after the scandal, and occasionally wrote to him concerning Belfast political matters. At this period he regarded Gladstone as a Burkean hero, the embodiment of enlightened reform based on moral integrity and consistent adherence to principle; he remained fiercely hostile to Disraeli. With Gladstone's discreet approval, MacKnight vehemently opposed a proposal that the conservative prime minister should visit Ireland in 1874, and he tried to persuade Gladstone to include Ulster in his 1877 Irish visit. Gladstone's willingness to regard MacKnight as a personal friend and invite him to his own house despite his marital situation reflects the liberal leader's distinction between personal failings and public bad example, which later influenced his attitude towards Charles Stewart Parnell. MacKnight kept in touch with British high politics by paying annual visits to London in May or early June, staying at the Devonshire Club and mixing socially with liberal leaders. He was one of the few Irish liberals who regarded Gladstone as a personal friend, and he was annoyed that some Belfast liberals accused him of compromising on denominational education under Gladstone's influence. Except when absent from Belfast on these visits, MacKnight wrote two leading articles for the *Northern Whig* every day. He modelled his literary style on Macaulay, whom he admired as a stylist though not as a thinker (noting that Orangemen regularly quoted Macaulay's description of the siege of Derry while omitting the associated condemnation of Orange demonstrations), and his editorials made copious references to Edmund Burke.

From 1874 MacKnight associated with the circle of Catholic liberals around Lord O'Hagan, with whom he was on terms of close friendship; many of these, like O'Hagan himself, achieved official positions under Gladstone's first two administrations and were regarded as traitors by more radical nationalists. MacKnight later liked to recall their hostility to home rule, which was shared by some of their Catholic episcopal friends. He emphasised that the belief of militant anti-Catholics that the Irish bishops were the secret masters of the nationalist party was incorrect, and that in matters not specifically religious they were obliged to follow their flocks. While celebrating Gladstone's disestablishment of the Church of Ireland and the passage of the 1870 Land Act, MacKnight regretted that Gladstone had tried (albeit unsuccessfully) to solve the Irish university question, which was guaranteed to divide his Irish followers along sectarian lines. MacKnight strongly defended the view that education should be based on shared secular and separate religious instruction; he opposed the replacement of the Queen's University in Ireland by the Royal University of Ireland because it would endanger this principle, and denounced any suggestion that a Catholic university should be recognised by the state.

MacKnight was dismayed by Gladstone's 1875 pamphlets against the declaration of papal infallibility, which he publicly denounced as exaggerated in their argument, as logically implying that Catholic emancipation was a mistake, and as unnecessarily offensive to Catholic liberal voters. He complained that even Ulster Orangemen seemed embarrassed at being outdone in 'No popery' rhetoric by their old political enemy.

Opposition to home rule and break with Gladstone

MacKnight was a consistent opponent of home rule, which he believed would throw Ireland into the hands of classes who would not govern fairly or competently, and would therefore lead to economic ruin, sectarian civil war, and an eventual reconquest by Britain. His sympathy for Maurice's Christian socialism should not be confused with socialism in the modern sense of the term: MacKnight was essentially a whig, whose belief in social reform and responsiveness to the well-being of the poor coexisted with fear of 'demagogues'. He supported household suffrage at the time of the third reform act of 1884, describing the political damage this inflicted on Irish liberalism as a necessary sacrifice to the liberal principle of equal laws, but declared that a government in which the propertyless majority ruled the propertied minority would prove disastrous to both, and described the house of lords as an inviolable 'estate of the realm'. He strongly supported the British empire as (among other things) an invaluable outlet for the talents of such Irishmen as his friend Lord Dufferin, and believed that home rule would inevitably lead to separation, followed by civil war in Ireland and the loss of imperial prestige (with particularly damaging consequences in India).

While MacKnight gave extensive coverage in the *Northern Whig* to Ulster tenant-right agitation and advised Gladstone on the 1881 land act, he declared boycotting 'contrary to all laws, human or divine', and was a strong supporter of the coercive measures undertaken by W. E. Forster and Earl Spencer in the early 1880s. His retrospective account of the growth of the home rule party emphasises the role of disgruntled tories in its creation and the willingness of home rulers to form cynical alliances with conservatives against Ulster liberal candidates.

In the run-up to the 1885 election, MacKnight prided himself on the *Northern Whig*'s continued loyalty to Gladstonian liberalism, despite increasing Ulster liberal fears (which he privately shared) that Gladstone was unsound on home rule. After a last attempt to persuade Gladstone against home rule and a final despairing letter in which he told Gladstone that Ulster tenant farmers would always be grateful for his past services, MacKnight threw his support behind the liberal unionists led by Lord Hartington, whom he praised as a model of Burkean statesmanship and consistency; thereafter his contact with Gladstone was intermittent and unfruitful. MacKnight lamented that Gladstone had fallen victim to delusion, and that most of his lieutenants had been misled by despair or opportunism. He excepted John Morley, whom he acknowledged to have behaved consistently and sincerely. They shared a friendship based on their common interest in Burke; Morley's study of Burke draws heavily on MacKnight, though they differed on Burke's view of the French revolution. MacKnight's obituary for Gladstone (*Northern Whig*, 20 May 1898) generally eulogises his achievement while lamenting 'the disastrous change which clouded the closing years of a brilliant career'.

MacKnight's *Ulster as it is, or, Twenty-eight years' experience as an Irish editor* (2 vols, 1896) written over the five years preceding its publication, may be compared (in terms of format, if not political sentiment) to *New Ireland* by A. M. Sullivan (1830–84) as a political autobiography written in the form of a narrative of recent Irish political events. The book is devoted to disproving

Gladstone's claims that the liberal unionists of Ulster were renegade liberals who had turned into virtual Orangemen, and it remains the most accessible contemporary statement of the liberal unionist case that Gladstone had betrayed liberal principles by abruptly abandoning his faithful followers to pursue the reckless project of home rule; it is still consulted by historians as well as by latter-day liberal unionists seeking historical predecessors. It may profitably be contrasted with contemporary works by R. Barry O'Brien, which argue that Gladstonian home rule was the logical extension of previous liberal reforms. Completed just after the unionist landslide victory of 1895, the book ends by applauding the continued economic growth of Belfast and predicting that the union will be cemented by the construction of an underwater tunnel between Ireland and Scotland.

In his later years MacKnight was a strong supporter of constructive unionism, hailing the land purchase legislation and infrastructural development pursued by A. J. Balfour and Gerald Balfour as important steps towards the solution of the Irish question. When he died of heart failure at his home at 28 Wellington Park, Belfast, on 19 November 1899, MacKnight was revising his Burke biography, preparing an annotated edition of Burke's works, and finishing a history of political progress in the nineteenth century for a Canadian publisher. This last was published as *Political progress in the nineteenth century* (1902), having been revised and completed by C. C. Osborne. Newspapers as politically distinct as the ultra-tory London *Globe* and the outspokenly liberal *Westminster Gazette* praised him as an honest and open defender of the union and of liberal principles; the conservative *Belfast Newsletter* remarked that even in the days before the struggle against home rule brought the two papers together it had always recognised the editor of the *Northern Whig* as a scrupulously fair-minded controversialist, while the nationalist *Irish News* called him a link with the old days when Catholics and Presbyterians had fought side by side against Anglican privilege and for 'fair land laws'.

MacKnight was a founder of the Irish district of the Institute of Journalists; when this was disrupted by the conflict over home rule, he organised the Ulster branch of the institute, becoming its first president. He was also an enthusiastic member of Royal Portrush golf club. MacKnight's letters to Gladstone are in the Gladstone papers in the British Library and his dealings with the Royal Literary Fund are recorded in its files at the British Library (Registered Case 1511).

Patrick Maume

Sources

Thomas MacKnight, *Ulster as it is, or, Twenty-eight years' experience as an Irish editor* (2 vols, 1896); *Belfast Newsletter*, 20 November 1899; *Irish News*, 20 November 1899; *Northern Whig*, 20–23 November 1899; *ODNB*; Patrick Maume, 'Burke in Belfast: Thomas MacKnight, Gladstone and liberal unionism', in D. G. Boyce and Alan O'Day (eds), *Gladstone and Ireland: politics, religion and nationality in the Victorian age* (2010), 162–85

Eoin MacNeill

1867–1945

Eoin (John) MacNeill, Gaelic scholar and nationalist politician, was born 15 May 1867 in Glenarm, Co. Antrim, sixth of eight children of Archibald MacNeill, baker, sailor and merchant, and his wife Rosetta (née Macauley).

Family background and education

MacNeill was profoundly influenced by his upbringing in the Glens of Antrim, a Catholic enclave which still retained some Irish-language traditions and was to become a major focus for Ulster-based Gaelic revivalists (especially in the period before the Great War). The fact that local Protestants shared with Catholics a

199

veneration for St Patrick based on his association with Slemish, the existence of a few Irish-speaking Presbyterians in the Glens, and the strength of the Presbyterian liberal tenant-right tradition in Co. Antrim, led MacNeill to see Ulster unionism as a superficial product of elite manipulation; this perception might have seemed less convincing in the embattled borderlands of south Ulster. His father had been prosecuted in 1872 for participating in a demonstration against the first Orange march in the Glens by a lodge recruited among the Protestant lumpenproletariat by the local rector and land agent.

The MacNeill family attached considerable importance to education. All five sons had distinguished educational records, and the youngest daughter became a hospital matron and inspector of industrial schools. (Her two elder sisters ran the family business.) MacNeill received his primary education in local schools, and his secondary education (1881–5) at St Malachy's College, Belfast, in whose collegiate division from 1885 he began his studies for the (examination-only) RUI after securing a modern languages scholarship. He secured a degree in constitutional history, jurisprudence and political economy in 1888 having attended law lectures at TCD and King's Inns.

In 1887 MacNeill obtained a junior clerkship in the accountant-general's office in Dublin law courts. He was the first clerk in the office to be appointed by competitive examination rather than patronage; he was also the first not to be a member of the Church of Ireland. (When he left in 1909, nine of the eleven clerks were Catholic; the others were Englishmen.) MacNeill's position as a civil servant attracted some criticism from separatist opponents within the Gaelic League. When MacNeill assisted in disrupting a meeting organised by William Martin Murphy to gather public support for a proposed Dublin international exhibition (denounced by Irish Irelanders as a denationalising project), the *Irish Independent* sneered at 'a civil servant masquerading as Robert Emmet' and MacNeill narrowly escaped dismissal.

MacNeill, the Irish language and the Gaelic League

From 1887 MacNeill took up the study of Irish. In 1890 he began to study Old and Middle Irish in his spare time under the Jesuit scholar Edmund Hogan; this led him to study Irish history and to learn spoken Irish through annual visits to the Aran islands (1891– 1908). These studies, and the bitter political factionalism of the Parnell split (in which MacNeill was strongly anti-Parnellite), led MacNeill to develop a theory of Irish identity which stressed cultural factors (especially the language) over state power; in later life he accused those historians (generally imperialist) who equated the progress of civilisation with the growth of state power of 'worshipping the Beast and his image'. This distrust of state absolutism echoed his strongly held Catholicism, though he was not necessarily clericalist.

He contributed articles on the Irish language to the *Irish Ecclesiastical Record* and the *Gaelic Journal*, and in 1893 took a leading role in the group of clerks who founded the Gaelic League under the inspiration of Douglas Hyde's *The necessity of de-anglicising Ireland*. From 1893 to 1897 MacNeill acted as unofficial (and unpaid) secretary to the Gaelic League. The burden of work this entailed brought on a nervous breakdown which left him with an abiding lassitude and a distaste for correspondence. (He developed a tendency to write letters forcefully setting out his position, but not posting them.) MacNeill edited the *Gaelic Journal* (1894– 7), co-edited *Fáinne an Lae* (1898–9), and became the first editor of *An Claidheamh Soluis* (1899–1901), without pay. In 1898 he nominated Patrick Pearse as a member of the Gaelic League executive, and they worked together on the publications committee. The fact that Pearse and MacNeill are generally thought of in connection with their roles in the Irish Volunteers tends to obscure the length of their personal friendship and professional association in the Gaelic League; this underlay MacNeill's willingness to accept Pearse's assurances in 1914–16, and his lasting indignation at the revelation that his friend had systematically misled him.

In 1902 MacNeill took a leading role in establishing an Irish-language printing business, which eventually involved him in heavy losses. In 1903 he became vice-president of the Gaelic League in succession to Fr Michael O'Hickey. In 1909 he was appointed to the chair of early (including medieval) Irish history at UCD (incidentally forfeiting his civil-service pension rights); he took a leading role in the campaign to make Irish compulsory for matriculation in the new university, publishing *Irish in the National University: a plea for Irish education* (1909).

The Irish Volunteers

On 1 November 1913 MacNeill published an article, 'The North began' in *An Claidheamh Soluis*. He claimed that the creation of the Ulster Volunteers marked the inception of a popular movement which would end by overthrowing the decayed feudal leadership of unionism, suggested that Edward Carson was a crypto-nationalist, and called for the formation of Irish Volunteers on the Ulster model. (MacNeill's view of Carson as crypto-nationalist, which he only abandoned after the outbreak of the Great War, reflected the unionist leader's participation in a protest campaign against Irish over-taxation in the late 1890s; MacNeill attached great importance to the taxation issue as a means of converting Ulster unionists. His practice of advocating cheers for Carson at early Irish Volunteer meetings caused some difficulties.) As a result of his article, MacNeill was approached by a group of separatists associated with the Irish Republican Brotherhood, who asked him to take the lead in organising the Irish Volunteers (launched 11 November 1913).

MacNeill is often seen as a straightforward Redmondite loyalist manipulated by the IRB. In fact, it is clear that he had his own agenda; he hoped that John Redmond could use the Volunteers' existence to demand an end to compromise and pressurise the liberals into granting home rule. (MacNeill believed H. H. Asquith never intended to grant home rule and was secretly encouraging Ulster resistance to provide a pretext for abandoning the bill; this belief derived from memories of Asquith's earlier association with the liberal imperialist faction who had regarded home rule as a political liability after the retirement of Gladstone.) When Redmond, having initially opposed the Volunteers, demanded that as civil leader of the Irish nation he should control this military force, MacNeill replied that a nation's military forces should not be controlled by the leader of a single party and suggested that by joining the Volunteers the Irish people had given MacNeill a mandate independent of Redmond. When Redmond threatened to establish his own rival organisation, MacNeill was persuaded by Bulmer Hobson to give in to avoid nationwide disruption; this set the pattern for the organisation's subsequent history in which a faction led by MacNeill with Hobson as his chief counsellor was intrigued against by IRB militarists centred on Tom Clarke and allied to Pearse.

MacNeill and 1916

On the outbreak of war in August 1914, MacNeill initially hoped that Redmond's suggestion in parliament that the Volunteer forces should take over the defence of Ireland represented an attempt at non-involvement, but Redmond's Woodenbridge speech (20 September) advocating recruitment for overseas service precipitated the final split. As editor of the weekly *Irish Volunteer* newspaper, MacNeill accused Redmond and his followers of mental and moral corruption, while proclaiming that both British parties were joined in a conspir-atorial 'continuity coalition' to defeat home rule, and only the existence of the Volunteers could prevent this. This view of the gov-ernment as determinedly and systematically hostile underlies both the MacNeill group's resistance to the IRB project of a pre-emptive rising (they believed it would inevitably be suppressed by the gov-ernment, which would take the opportunity to abandon home rule) and MacNeill's reluctance to split the Volunteers by confronting the conspirators. (A memorandum which MacNeill prepared for presen-tation to the Volunteer executive but never produced for discussion advocates the defensive strategy on both practical and moral terms; the contrast between the sensibilities of MacNeill and Pearse is indi-cated by the difference between MacNeill's invocation of Catholic casuistry on the conditions for a just war and Pearse's deployment of apocalyptic and devotional rhetoric to present the rising as a supreme act of sacrificial faith.) MacNeill's associates appear to have had a better grasp of the prospects for guerrilla warfare than their opponents, though the latter could see the defensive strategy as leav-ing the initiative with the government.

Early in April 1916 the IRB group convinced MacNeill that a crackdown was imminent by producing a forged 'Castle document' (possibly based on genuine contingency plans). Only on Maundy Thursday (20 April) did he discover that the IRB group was using preparations for a general mobilisation on Easter weekend to bring about a rising on Easter Sunday. MacNeill initially acquiesced, but after discovering that an arms ship sent from Germany had been sunk and that the Castle document had been forged, he sent out messengers around the country ordering a general demobilisation, following this up with an advertisement in the *Sunday Independent*. This decision delayed the rising for a day and largely frustrated it outside Dublin. MacNeill was arrested after the suppression of the rising, court-martialled, sentenced to life imprisonment, and deprived of his UCD chair (he was reinstated after his release in June 1917).

Political career 1918–27

Despite recriminations he took an active role in the reconstituted Sinn Féin party. In 1918 he was elected to the first Dáil Éireann for Sinn Féin as agreed nationalist candidate for Derry City and as representative of the NUI. In May 1921 he was re-elected for both constituencies in the elections for the northern parliament and southern parliament (second dáil) respectively.

In January 1919 MacNeill was appointed minister for finance in the first dáil government; he was relegated to minister for industries when Michael Collins was appointed to the finance portfolio in April 1919. MacNeill's three eldest sons were active in the IRA. In mid 1920 he witnessed large-scale sectarian violence in Derry city. He was arrested in November 1920 and remained in jail until released on 30 June 1921. In August 1921 he was elected speaker of the second dáil. In this capacity he presided over the Anglo–Irish treaty debates, attempting unsuccessfully to get both sides to agree to ratify the treaty with an explanatory declaration on disputed points. He spoke in favour of the treaty, but as speaker did not vote.

In 1922 MacNeill was elected as a pro-treaty TD for Clare; he was re-elected in 1923. During the civil war he was a strong supporter of the government's reprisal policy. He is alleged to have been one of the two strongest advocates (with Ernest Blythe) of the summary execution of four imprisoned republicans in retaliation for the assassination of Seán Hales; when Thomas Johnson, the Labour leader, protested in the subsequent dáil debate that such measures were rendering the government morally indistinguishable from the previous British administration, MacNeill retorted that the old regime had used force to suppress the will of the people, whereas the current government was stern in order to uphold the people's will. MacNeill experienced personal tragedies. His sister Anne McGavock, already suffering terminal illness, came south from Glenarm to plead unsuccessfully for the life of Erskine Childers; the siblings quarrelled and were not reconciled. His second son, Brian, joined the anti-treaty forces and was killed during fighting in Sligo; MacNeill convinced himself that (authentic) reports that his son and those with him had been killed after surrendering were republican propaganda devised to torment him.

As minister for education (1922–5), MacNeill was largely inactive, because he saw the primary responsibility for education as lying with the churches rather than the state; his principal legacy was the stringent implementation of compulsory Irish. In these respects he set a pattern for state education policy which lasted until the 1960s. His ministerial role was further diminished in 1924, when he became the Irish representative on the boundary commission. There is some evidence that he expected the failure of the commission and accepted the position in the knowledge that he would serve as a scapegoat, but his maladroit behaviour made his position worse. Seeing the commission as a quasi-judicial body, he made no attempt to inform his cabinet colleagues of developments (he was not imitated in this by the Northern Ireland representative) and by acquiescing when he was outvoted on the points at issue he strengthened the legal position of the other commissioners. In November 1925, when a leak revealed that the border would be virtually unchanged, he resigned as commissioner and as minister. In the June 1927 general election he stood as a Cumann na nGaedheal candidate for the NUI, but received little support from his party.

Academic career 1927–45

His narrow defeat ended his political career and he returned to academic life. He chaired the Irish Manuscripts Commission from its foundation in 1928; he was president of the newly founded Irish Historical Society (1936–45), the RSAI (1937–40) and the RIA (1940–43).

On 19 April 1898 MacNeill had married Agnes Moore; they had four sons and four daughters. He retired from his professorship in 1941 and died of abdominal cancer on 15 October 1945 at his residence, 63 Upper Leeson Street, Dublin.

Intellectual achievement

MacNeill's interest in early Irish history grew out of his interest in the Irish language. According to himself, it was a chance remark of his father's that awakened his interest in the language, but it was also the circumstances of time and place. The Glens of Antrim were one of those districts in which, in the second half of the nineteenth century, the language was just slipping beyond the horizon. A sense of the loss of a language and of the culture embodied in the language, and a consequent impoverishment of national distinctiveness, a sense of a break with a shared tradition that had lasted since the dawn of Irish history—all this was enough to make him desire to recover what had been lost. This desire would, in him, work towards making him an historian, especially of that first period of Irish history, just as it led him to learn the language and to promote it in the Gaelic League. His first ambition was to learn the Irish of the Glens, about which he would later write, but a meeting in 1890 with Eugene O'Growney, professor of Irish at Maynooth, and a subsequent decision to become a pupil of Edmund Hogan (1917), widened his ambitions. In 1891, on O'Growney's advice, he visited Inishmaan in the Aran islands, the principal resort at that time for scholars wishing to learn to speak Irish. He returned annually until 1908. At the same time he soon became not so much Hogan's pupil as, in MacNeill's own words, 'my professor's apprentice'. Hogan, as Todd professor in the RIA, was working on an edition of the Middle Irish text 'Cath Ruis na Ríg'. MacNeill became his assistant, subsequently writing that 'he made me do all the spade-work', a contribution handsomely acknowledged by Hogan. This was hugely advantageous, since MacNeill was thereby introduced, under supervision, to skills he would later need: reading and comparing manuscripts, establishing a text, translation, textual commentary, and compiling a vocabulary. When he himself, with Hogan's encouragement, went on to edit texts on his own, he chose three Middle Irish poems about the legendary Battle of Mucrama; here he was dealing with one of the principal Irish 'origin legends', stories that purported to recount the beginnings of the early Irish political order. One of his major contributions was his discussion of 'the Irish synthetic historians' and their construction, partly out of such origin legends, of a pre-Patrician history for Ireland.

MacNeill's contributions to early Irish scholarship may be placed under three headings: first, 'Where does Irish history begin?', the title of one of his lectures; second, the history and hagiography of St Patrick; and third, early Irish law. The first was his main preoccupation up to the Great War, the second a comparatively brief phase arising out of his imprisonment in Mountjoy, while the third occupied him especially from 1923 to 1934. The synthetic historians had been successful in creating a history that established a line of narrative from the book of Genesis to early Christian Ireland. This history was later given memorable expression in Geoffrey Keating's *Foras Feasa ar Érinn*; and, down the centuries, what began as a learned construction became the standard view of the Irish past. A scholarly Irish history could not exist until the Milesian legend embodied in *Lebor Gabála Érenn*, 'The book of the settlement of Ireland', had been analysed and mere fiction separated from what might be history and from what was history. For MacNeill, establishing a scholarly history did not entail throwing away all early Irish narrative about the centuries before St Patrick: the strategy was to isolate those stories and aspects of stories that were inconsistent with the Milesian legend. The most important of these was the Ulster cycle, which cast doubt on the antiquity of an all-Ireland kingship of Tara.

Another prerequisite was a critical analysis of the medieval collections of genealogies, which in their overall structure presupposed the Milesian legend and yet contained a mass of essential material about early Irish royal dynasties: MacNeill's 'Notes on the Laud genealogies', published in 1911, supplied a model study of how to work on these extraordinarily voluminous sources. A further approach to the half-known period between the fall of the Western Roman Empire and the seventh century was epigraphy, a subject mainly cultivated by MacNeill's colleague, R. A. S. Macalister. MacNeill wrote two papers for the RIA that occupy a central position in his most fertile period as an historian, 1900–14. One was principally linguistic, 'Notes on the distribution, history, grammar, and import of the Irish ogham inscriptions', in one section of which he proposed a rule (subsequently known as 'MacNeill's law') governing an early Irish sound-change. The other, 'Early Irish population-groups: their nomenclature, classification, and chronology', used evidence from the ogham inscriptions, in conjunction with annals, genealogies, and hagiography, to establish changes in the way collective groups were described from the time of Ptolemy's Geography up to the Viking period. In these two papers, MacNeill's conjunction of linguistic and historical skills can be seen to their best effect. In his more general books, *Phases of Irish history* (1919) and *Celtic Ireland* (1921), his preoccupation with the beginnings of Irish history are just as apparent as in his more specialised work.

At the same time, MacNeill was also giving major assistance to Hogan's last and greatest work, *Onomasticon Goedelicum*, taking over a position that had been occupied by his elder brother, Charles (1862–1958). The *Onomasticon* has ever since been an indispensable tool for early Irish historians and editors of texts: not only did it collect together a vast mass of references to places, peoples and dynasties from medieval Irish texts, only some of them in print, but it also drew on the pioneering work of John O'Donovan and William Reeves. MacNeill was always concerned with the where as well as the when of Irish history: perhaps the most valuable strand in his work on St Patrick from 1923 to 1934 was his analysis of the topography of the Tripartite Life of St Patrick. This source offers the first comprehensive single view of the geography of power in Ireland and the related geography of churches; and MacNeill's account corrected several misconceptions, and has ever since been a *vade mecum* for early Irish historians.

Two elements in MacNeill's account of the Patrician material have not endured so well. The first is his over-valuation of the evidence linking St Patrick with Ulster. MacNeill is seen at his best and at his worst close to home—at his best in his correction of earlier views on the boundary between Dál Riata and Latharna (the church of Glore and, therefore, his birth place, Glenarm, belonged to the latter); and at his worst in his attempt to show that the *Silva Focluti*, 'the Wood of Fochloth', mentioned in Patrick's *Confessio* was to be located in Ulster, and, therefore, that the story of Patrick in slavery on Slemish propounded by the seventh-century hagiographers, Tírechán and Muirchú, was historical. The other contention that soon came under damaging fire was his claim that the Tripartite Life embodied Tírechán's own revision of his earlier *Collectanea*.

MacNeill was capable of misjudging texts and issues, as in his dating 'The Book of Rights', *Lebor na Cert*, to the reign of Brian Bórama. Yet even his mistakes were often fruitful for the discipline, since they usually contained some element of truth and they elicited further research. Sometimes his views now look closer to the truth than they did to his immediate successors, as with the kingship of Tara. Sometimes, too, the occasional rash speculation has been exaggerated: he did not think that the Book of Rights as we have it went back to the time of Benignus, disciple of St Patrick, merely that Benignus could have been responsible for an earlier text on the same topic, a text written in Latin. Moreover, his mistakes pale into insignificance beside what the leading Irish medieval historian of the next generation, D. A. Binchy, called 'his uncanny sense of communion with a long-dead past'. The truth is that he had read widely and sympathetically in the primary sources, and he had a sense of how all the elements of society fitted together into a functioning whole. He was the first historian of early medieval Ireland of whom this can be said, and his work thus marks the start of a new era in the subject he made his own.

Political reputation

MacNeill's reputation has been dominated by his role in relation to the 1916 rising. Early accounts written by admirers of Pearse generally presented MacNeill as comically ineffective or even treacherous, and displayed little concern for accurately recounting his actions or for understanding his motives. MacNeill's later years were distressed by this; he frequently explained himself to friends, and composed fragmentary memoirs. His version of events, however, attracted little attention until 1961 when F. X. Martin edited for publication in *Irish Historical Studies* two self-justificatory memoranda prepared by MacNeill in 1915 and 1917. MacNeill's historical reputation was further rehabilitated through the efforts of his son-in-law Michael Tierney, who arranged the publication of the essay collection *The scholar revolutionary* (edited by F. J. Byrne and F. X. Martin), and who himself undertook an official biography of MacNeill (edited for publication by F. X. Martin after Tierney's death). The Northern Ireland crisis after 1969 and the reassessment of Pearse's messianic nationalism in an Ireland increasingly less receptive to Catholic valorisations of sacrifice contributed to the re-evaluation of MacNeill; it is arguable that this exaltation of MacNeill as 'man of peace' underestimates the extent to which he and Pearse shared terms of reference, while differing on strategy. Even MacNeill's sceptical and iconoclastic nephew Brian Moore revered his integrity, and saw him as embodying the idealism of the Revival generation (as well as some of its limitations). In the long run, MacNeill's reputation is more likely to rest on his epochal contributions to language revival than on his ambivalent and chequered political career, which combined selfless dedication with weak execution and considerable capacity for self-deception.

Patrick Maume and Thomas Charles-Edwards

Sources

MacNeill papers in UCD Archives and NLI; Eoin MacNeill, *Shall Ireland be divided?* (1915); *Dictionary of national biography 1941–1950* (London) (entry by D. A. Binchy); F. X. Martin and F. J. Byrne (ed.), *The scholar revolutionary: Eoin MacNeill, 1867–1945, and the making of the new Ireland* (1973); Michael Tierney, *Eoin MacNeill: scholar and man of action 1867–1945*, ed. F. X. Martin (1980); Charles Townshend, *Political violence in Ireland* (1983); Pádraig Ó Snodaigh, *Two godfathers of revisionism: 1916 in the revisionist canon* (1991); J. A. Gaughan (ed.), *The memoirs of Senator Joseph Connolly: a maker of modern Ireland* (1996); Patrick Maume, *The long gestation: Irish nationalist life 1891–1918* (1999); Patrick Maume, 'Anti-Machiavel; three Ulster nationalists in the age of de Valera', *Irish Political Studies* (1999); *Oxford dictionary of national biography* (2004)

Patrick McCartan

(1878–1963)

Patrick McCartan, medical doctor, revolutionary, and politician, was born 13 May 1878 in Carrickmore, Co. Tyrone, third among two sons and three daughters of Bernard McCartan, farmer and engineer, originally from Rostrevor, Co. Down, and Bridget McCartan (née Rafferty), of Carrickmore. Educated at Tandragee national school, a Latin school in Termonmagurk, St Patrick's College, Armagh, St Macartan's seminary, Monaghan, and St Malachy's College, Belfast, he first became interested in Irish nationalism in 1898 during the centenary of the United Irish rebellion, when he was influenced by the *Life of Theobald Wolfe Tone* by Alice Milligan. Leaving school, he went to the USA and worked as a barman in Philadelphia, where fellow Carrickmore native Joseph McGarrity initiated him into camp 428 of Clan na Gael.

Returning to Ireland (1905) to study medicine in UCD with financial assistance from McGarrity, he transferred from Clan na Gael to the IRB and became a member of the Teeling circle and its close counterpart the Keating branch of the Gaelic League. He remained in close contact with McGarrity, informing him of developments in Ireland, and was Irish correspondent of the *Gaelic American* for John Devoy. Having established Dungannon clubs in Carrickmore and among students in Dublin, he joined Sinn Féin when it was formed and in 1908–9 was elected a member of Dublin corporation. He continued his studies at the RCSI, graduating in 1910 and becoming a fellow of the college in 1912. He then worked in the Mater and Cork Street hospitals in Dublin before being appointed as practitioner to the Gortin district dispensary in Tyrone in 1913. Editor of the IRB journal *Irish Freedom* for a time, in 1911 he caused a disagreement within the IRB by openly opposing the visit to Ireland of King George V, which resulted in the resignation of many of the old IRB leaders and their replacement by younger, more radical men. Having organised the IRB and Irish Volunteers in Tyrone, in 1914 he went to the USA to explain the Volunteer split, raise funds for the IRB and Patrick Pearse's St Enda's school, and discuss plans with Roger Casement for the formation of an Irish brigade among prisoners of war in Germany. He was coopted to the IRB supreme council in July 1915, but during the 1916 Easter rising his plans to link up with Denis McCullough and join Liam Mellows in rebellion in Connacht failed because of confusion over the countermanding order from Eoin MacNeill. On the run until February 1917, when he was arrested and deported to England, he returned to Ireland in May to campaign in the Longford South by-election.

Intending to go to Russia in July 1917 as an IRB representative to seek recognition for Irish independence, he was diverted to the USA to deliver a memorandum from the released Irish rebellion leaders to President Woodrow Wilson. Arrested (October 1917) in Halifax, Nova Scotia, while trying to travel to Germany with Liam Mellows to buy munitions, in May 1919 he was fined $250 for impersonating an American seaman. In the meantime he had been defeated as Sinn Féin candidate in the Armagh South by-election (February 1918), during which he was criticised for allegedly having assisted the Larne gun-runners in 1914, but was elected unopposed in the King's County (Tullamore) by-election (April 1918) and was reelected unopposed for King's County in the 1918 general election. Active in campaigning against the conscription of Irishmen living in the USA in 1917 and 1918, in March 1918 he was appointed editor of McGarrity's newly established *Irish Press* in Philadelphia. In 1919 he became embroiled in the acrimonious Clan na Gael split, supporting the McGarrity faction against that of John Devoy and Daniel Cohalan, which was exacerbated by the US tour by Éamon de Valera in 1919–20, during which McCartan accompanied him on a number of speaking trips. He returned briefly to Ireland in February 1920 to explain de Valera's controversial 'Cuban analogy' speech to the dáil cabinet, although he did not agree with de Valera's position. From December 1920 to July 1921 he undertook an unsuccessful mission to Moscow, seeking Russian support for Irish independence. Although deeply dissatisfied with the provisions of the Anglo–Irish treaty, which he saw as a betrayal of the north and of the republic, he voted for it reluctantly, feeling that rejection would lead to war. Having been reelected to Dáil Éireann for Leix–Offaly in the 1921 general election, he was defeated in 1922 when he stood as a pro-treaty candidate, after which, disillusioned, he left politics to concentrate on a private medical practice in New York, where he lived at East 68th Street. In 1937 he returned to live in Ireland.

Returning to politics in 1945 as an independent candidate in the presidential election, supported by Labour, Clann na Talmhan, Farmers, and independents, he campaigned on his non-party affiliation and promised to do 'the utmost to hasten the reunion of our partitioned country' (*Irish Independent*, 9 June 1945). Although beaten into third place behind the victor Seán T. O'Kelly (Fianna Fáil), and Seán Mac Eoin (Fine Gael), his 19.6 per cent of the vote, and the distribution of his transfers overwhelmingly in favour of Mac Eoin, signified voter dissatisfaction with Fianna Fáil. Left-wing and republican in his political views, he was a founder member of Clann na Poblachta in 1946, and an unsuccessful party candidate in three general elections for Cork borough (1948), Dublin South-East (1951), and Dublin North-East (1957). He was a member of Seanad Éireann (1948–51), nominated by Clann na Poblachta. In 1959 his presidential election nomination was declared invalid because of an insufficient number of nominations.

During the interregnum of his political career he became a close friend of W. B. Yeats, helping him raise funds in the USA for the Irish Academy of Letters, endowing the academy's O'Growney award for Gaelic literature, seeking American plays for the Abbey theatre, organising a testimonial committee to provide financial security for the remainder of Yeats's life, and raising funds to return Yeats's body for burial in Ireland in 1948. *A speech and two poems by W. B. Yeats* (December 1937) included a poem of dedication to McCartan, and he was awarded the Irish Academy of Letters Gregory medal. He was among a group of people who presented the Sam Maguire memorial trophy to the GAA in 1928. In 1932 he published *With de Valera in America*, an account of his time in America in 1917–20. Interested in native Irish industry, he owned the Kilquaid Sand Co. and St Patrick's mines in Glendalough, and established Donegal Carpets with his close friend Joe McGrath. He died 28 March 1963, leaving an estate valued at £1,502.

He married (30 June 1937) Elizabeth Kearney, actress, daughter of Thomas Kearney and Margaret Kearney (née Reidy), Ballydesmond, Co. Kerry, whom he had met at Irish-language classes in New York. The McCartans lived at 'Karnack', Greystones, Co. Wicklow, with their son and daughter. His daughter Deirdre (d. 2007) married the ballad singer Ronnie Drew. His papers are in the NLI and in the possession of his son, Pádraig McCartan, SC. His statement to the Bureau of Military History is in the military archives.

Marie Coleman

Sources

NLI, Patrick McCartan papers; Patrick McCartan, *With de Valera in America* (1932); Diarmuid Lynch, *The I.R.B. and the 1916 insurrection* (1957); 'Extracts from the papers of the late Dr Patrick McCartan', *Clogher Record*, v (1963–4), 30–45, 184–212; F. X. Martin (ed.), 'The McCartan documents, 1916', *Clogher Record*, vi (1966), 5–65; John Unterecker (ed.), *Yeats and Patrick McCartan: a fenian friendship* (1967); Sean Cronin, *The McGarrity papers* (1972); F. M. Carroll, *American opinion and the Irish question, 1910–23* (1978); Arthur Mitchell, *Revolutionary government in Ireland: Dáil Éireann, 1919–1922* (1995); Kevin Rafter, *The Clann: the story of Clann na Poblachta* (1996); Ronan Fanning *et al.* (ed.), *Documents on Irish foreign policy, i, 1919–1922* (1998); David McCullagh, *A makeshift majority* (1998); Michael Laffan, *The resurrection of Ireland: the Sinn Féin party, 1916–1923* (1999); information from Pádraig McCartan (son)

Timothy McCarthy

1868–1928

Timothy McCarthy, journalist, was born in Cloghroe, Inniscarra, Co. Cork, where his father, Denis McCarthy, ran the family farm. He was educated at the local national school and later his studies continued under a private tutor. While still in his teens McCarthy began his journalistic career on the *Cork Herald* and *Cork Weekly Herald* and often covered the activities of the National League. Most notably he was in attendance at one of the most notorious political meetings of the 1880s, in Ennis, Co. Clare, when William O'Brien, Michael Davitt, and other parliamentary representatives were 'dragooned' by the military and 'the streets ran red with the blood of the people' (*Irish News*, 31 December 1928) after disturbances took place. In 1893 he left Cork to take up an appointment in Dublin with the *Freeman's Journal*, the leading Irish nationalist paper of the time and a fervent supporter of John Redmond. His stay was, however, brief; he went on to edit the *Dublin Evening Telegraph* and then was invited to London by T. P. O'Connor, who was later to describe him as the 'greatest political and most versatile journalist in the country' (*Irish News*, 31 December 1931), to work as a sub-editor, news editor, and leader writer on the staff of the *Evening Sun*. On the occasions of O'Connor's trips to Ireland and the USA in support of the cause of home rule, McCarthy's expertise and abilities were recognised, as he was entrusted with sole responsibility for the publication of the paper along with its stablemate the *Star*. Then, after an offer from the noted journalist W. T. Stead, who had begun to publish the *Daily Paper* in London, he took up a position on it, becoming one of Stead's principal assistants as well as contributing a series of articles on Ireland. In 1897 he finally returned to live and work in Ireland, first as editor of the Belfast *Northern Star*, the paper of Joe Devlin; then as acting editor of the *Irish People*, the official journal of the United Irish League. This was followed in 1904 by his appointment as editor-in-chief of the North West group of newspapers (1904–6), based in Omagh, Co. Tyrone, and by 1906 he was back in Belfast when he was made editor of the *Irish News*, the leading nationalist daily newspaper in the north of Ireland, a position he held till his death in 1928.

Throughout his long journalistic career McCarthy was a committed Irish nationalist, and his commitment on occasions brought him into conflict with the authorities. For instance, his strong attack in the *Irish People* on a royal visit by Edward VII to Ireland in 1903 led to the paper's being suppressed and his receiving a six-month prison sentence. His own political philosophy was based on support for a strictly constitutional approach and he was, therefore, a fervent supporter of the Irish parliamentary party (IPP) and its campaign for home rule. This became clear in his editorials in the *Irish News* as the prospects for home rule grew after the return to power of the liberals at Westminster in 1906. Along with other nationalist papers and journals of the time, the *Irish News* poured scorn on the threats of Edward Carson and other unionists, especially their threats to use bodies such as the UVF to oppose the introduction of a devolved administration. He also ruled out the prospect of partitioning Ireland as a possible solution to the crisis. On the outbreak of the first world war he joined with the IPP in calling for the people of Ireland to assist the British war effort, on the basis that the fight was for the 'freedom of small nations' (Phoenix, *A century*, 22).

While he had shown some sympathy for the objectives of the Gaelic revival of the late nineteenth and early twentieth century, McCarthy was less benevolent to the physical-force tradition of the IRB, and hostile also to the objectives of Arthur Griffith and Sinn Féin, even though both he and Griffith were at first committed to non-violent means. Instead, he viewed Sinn Féin and similar political movements as causing unnecessary division among nationalists in the quest for home rule. It is no surprise, therefore, to find that along with other spokesmen for constitutional nationalism, McCarthy attacked the motives and intentions of those behind the Easter rising in Dublin in 1916. However, he warned the British government that the policy of executing the leaders was allowing public sympathy for the rebels to grow. In the wake of the rising, McCarthy and his paper played a crucial role in ensuring that nationalists in the north of Ireland backed Lloyd George's proposal for home rule to be introduced immediately, with the proviso of the temporary exclusion of six Ulster counties. It was not long after these events that constitutional nationalism came under threat from militant republicanism by way of the growing electoral strength of Sinn Féin and its demand for an independent Irish republic. In the general election of November 1918 the *Irish News* remained loyal to the IPP cause, but (as in the rest of Ireland) nationalist opinion was now badly divided. As the Anglo–Irish war erupted in the rest of Ireland after 1919, McCarthy recorded the plight of the minority Catholic community in the north, especially in Belfast, and described their ordeal as a 'concerted pogrom'. He roundly condemned the formal introduction of partition with the election of the first Northern Ireland parliament (May 1921), but backed the Anglo–Irish treaty in the hope that it would pave the way for unification. As for the position of nationalists after the collapse of the boundary commission in 1925, McCarthy suggested the time had come for them to accept the political reality of the situation, and to unite within one political movement in order to defend their interests against perceived unionist domination. By the time of his death this objective had not been achieved, but more alarming was the precarious financial state of the *Irish News* due to falling sales. Partly this was the impact of partition, cutting it off from some of its readership, but more importantly the paper's support of constitutional nationalists such as Devlin had alienated many with a more radical approach.

After a long battle against illness McCarthy died at his own home on the Antrim Road, Belfast, on 30 December 1928. He was survived by his wife Katie, daughter of Denis McLynn of Sligo; they had no children.

Brendan Lynn

Sources

Belfast Telegraph, Northern Whig, 31 December 1928; *Irish News*, 31 December 1928, 2 January 1929; *WWW*; Hugh Oram, *The newspaper book: a history of newspapers in Ireland 1649–1983* (1983); Eamon Phoenix, *Northern nationalism: nationalist politics, partition and the Catholic minority in Northern Ireland 1890–1914* (1994); Eamon Phoenix (ed.), *A century of northern life: the* Irish News *and one hundred years of Ulster history 1890s–1990s* (1995); Patrick Maume, *The long gestation: Irish nationalist life 1891–1918* (1999); Enda Staunton, *The nationalists of Northern Ireland 1918–1973* (2001)

Denis McCullough

1883–1968

Denis McCullough, revolutionary and businessman, was born 24 January 1883 in Divis Street, Belfast, son of Daniel McCullough, publican, and Margaret McCullough (née Magee), of Quilly, Dromore, Co. Down. Educated locally by the Christian Brothers, he served an apprenticeship as a piano tuner with Messrs Crane and Sons, High Street, and was employed with Charles Hardy and Son, Anne Street, before establishing his own businesses at 8 and 12 Howard Street.

A member of the Gaelic League in the 1890s and a founder of the first hurling club in Belfast, he was sworn into the IRB by his father c.1900 and purged the Belfast circles of their older members (including his father), replacing them with younger men, including

Seán MacDermott. Chairman of the Ulster provincial council from 1905, and Ulster representative on the supreme council 1907–16, he was responsible, along with Bulmer Hobson, MacDermott, and Tom Clarke for the greater militancy of the IRB after 1907. In 1905, with Hobson, he established the Dungannon Clubs—a non-sectarian, republican, separatist organisation named after the eighteenth-century Irish Volunteers' Dungannon convention—which eventually merged with Cumann na nGaedheal and the National Council of Arthur Griffith to form Sinn Féin. A member of the Irish Volunteer executive in 1913, he established several Volunteer corps in Belfast. Disobeying an order to leave Ireland in 1915 under the Defence of the Realm Act, he was imprisoned (August–November 1915), and was elected president of the IRB supreme council in September 1915. However, he was largely kept in the dark about plans for the Easter rising, during which his efforts to join the uprising led by Liam Mellows in Connacht failed, and he was imprisoned in Richmond barracks, Knutsford, Frongoch, and Reading before his release on 6 August 1916.

Having left the IRB after the rising, feeling he had been sidelined, he remained an ordinary Volunteer during the war of independence, much of which he spent in prison: Belfast, Arbour Hill, and Gloucester (May 1918–March 1919); Belfast (April–July 1920); Belfast and Mountjoy (October 1920–January 1921); and Belfast, Holywood, and Ballykinlar (January–December 1921). A supporter of the Anglo–Irish treaty, he undertook between March and June 1922 a mission to the USA, aiming to reunite the warring Irish-American factions, in particular Clan na Gael (at which he was unsuccessful); convince them to abstain from Irish party politics; establish control of dáil funds for the provisional government; and get publicity on the Ulster question. A member of Belfast corporation (1918–22) and elected MP for Tyrone South in the 1918 general election, he was defeated as a Sinn Féin candidate in Belfast West in the election for the first Northern Ireland parliament in 1921. Travelling to Germany in 1922, he convinced Colonel Fritz Brase to become director of the Army School of Music. He was elected Cumann na nGaedheal TD for Donegal in a 1924 by-election, but resigned from the party in 1925 in protest at the government's handling of the boundary commission. He retired from politics in 1927.

Forced by the Belfast boycott to move his business to Dublin, he had to rebuild his premises at 56 Dawson Street, after their destruction by an anti-treaty IRA landmine in December 1922, and he continued in business as McCulloughs Ltd, merging in 1967 with Pigotts Ltd to form McCullough Pigott. Later he served as vice-president of the Royal Irish Academy of Music, and supported the establishment of the Gate Theatre in 1928. An influential figure in Irish industrial development after independence, he was vice-president of the Federation of Irish Manufacturers, Irish representative at an inter-parliamentary commercial conference in Rio de Janeiro (1927), and employers' adviser to the Irish delegation at the twentieth session of the International Labour Conference in Geneva (1936). Chairman of the New Ireland Assurance Company (1922–64), and of Clondalkin Paper Mills, James Crean and Sons (1936) Ltd., Moore Clothing Ltd, M. Duan and Co. Ltd, and Weartex Ltd, he was a director of the Irish National Insurance Company Ltd, Bowater's Irish Wallboard Mills, C. B. Paper Sacks Ltd, and Drimnagh Paper Mills Ltd.

He married (16 August 1916) Agnes, daughter of John Ryan, farmer, of Tomcoole, Co. Wexford, sister of Dr James Ryan, and sister-in-law of Richard Mulcahy and Seán T. O'Kelly, whom he had met while she was teaching in the Dominican Convent, Belfast. They had four sons and two daughters and lived at 4 Leeson Park (1921–35) and 12 Oakley Road, Ranelagh (1936–68). He died 11 September 1968 in Dublin, leaving an estate valued at £46,379. His papers are in the UCD archives department, and there is a portrait of him by Seán O'Sullivan, RHA, in the New Ireland Assurance Company.

Marie Coleman

Sources

UCD archives, Denis McCullough papers; Diarmuid Lynch, *The IRB and the 1916 insurrection*, ed. Florence O'Donoghue (1957); *Irish Independent, Irish Press, Irish Times*, 12 September 1968; León Ó Broin, *Revolutionary underground* (1976); Tim Pat Coogan, *Michael Collins* (1990); Walker; Ronan Fanning *et al.* (ed.), *Documents on Irish foreign policy*, i: *1919–1922* (1998); Michael Laffan, *The resurrection of Ireland* (1999); John M. Regan, *The Irish counter-revolution* (1999); information from Joseph McCullough (son)

Alice Leticia Milligan

1866–1953

Alice Leticia Milligan, novelist, playwright, and political activist, was born in Gortmore, Co. Tyrone, one of eleven children of Charlotte (née Burns) and Seaton Milligan (1836–1916), writer and antiquary. From 1877 to 1887 she attended Methodist College, Belfast, where she wrote short stories for the school magazine, *Eos*. From 1887 to 1888 she studied English history and literature at King's College, London, and completed a teacher-training course in Belfast and Derry (1888–91). Alice Milligan and her father (an executive of the Bank Buildings, Belfast, antiquary, and member of the RIA) published a political travelogue of Ulster and Sligo, *Glimpses of Erin*, in 1888. Continuing the theme of travel, her first novel, *A royal democrat* (1890), tells of a disguised English king who

ventures across Ireland to win home rule for the Irish while securing a greater English monarchical presence in Ireland. From
January to August 1891 Milligan lived in Dublin, where she met
the architects of the Irish cultural revival. After the unexpected
death of Parnell in October 1891, she became an ardent nationalist
and began a lifelong career writing for the Irish nationalist papers.
In 1892 she formed a women's branch of the Irish Industries
Association in Derry and contributed a series of *tableaux vivants*
to Lady Aberdeen's 'Irish village' at the 1893 Chicago World's Fair.

Milligan's nationalist politics became more overt and radicalised
when in November 1894 she and Jenny Armour founded branches
of the Irish Women's Association in Belfast, Moneyreagh, and
Portadown. As the IWA's first president, Milligan promoted the organisation as the northern voice of Irish female nationalism. In
February 1895 she helped to establish the Henry Joy McCracken
Literary Society in Belfast and was elected its first vice-president.
In October of the same year the McCracken Society founded its
own Belfast-based journal, the *Northern Patriot.* Under the editorship of Alice Milligan and Anna Johnston ('Ethna Carbery') the
paper was defined by a strongly regionalist agenda. The editors
were dismissed in December 1895 after the paper's sponsors discovered that Anna Johnston's father, Robert, was an active Fenian.
In the midst of great controversy, the women launched their own
'national' literary journal, the *Shan Van Vocht* (1896–9). The paper
supported Irish nationalist initiatives such as the '98 centenary, the
amnesty movement, and the Gaelic League. In September 1897
Milligan was elected to three of the five subcommittees set up to
bolster the effectiveness of the '98 centenary. While serving on the
Dublin-based executive, she continued as secretary of the Belfast
centenary committee, and was also elected the representative for
Letterkenny's '98 centenary association.

A pioneer in the formation of Irish National Theatre, she 'began
to have premonitions of a dramatic movement' as early as 1897
when she started to bring theatre to diverse communities across
Ireland and its diaspora, in places that lacked resources and dedicated venues. She staged plays and *tableaux vivants* with groups in
theatre venues, school halls, on city streets and in fields (where
people watched sitting on benches carved out of felled trees.)

Milligan always worked collaboratively, never alone. On a break from his human rights work in the Congo, her close friend Roger Casement joined her in Antrim where they cleared fields and constructed stage sets for local Irish *tableaux* and drama shows. Audiences attending her performances were not passive, ticket-buying, anonymous consumers, but active participants in the creation of national theatre and cultural independence. Those who built the stages made the costumes; those who performed the shows sourced the props and invented stage effects out of local materials. Looking back during the civil war at the intervention that Alice Milligan made in imagining a cultural republic, Susan Mitchell reflected that she was 'the most successful producer of plays before the Abbey Theatre started on its triumphant way'.

From 1898 Milligan's interests in the amateur theatre movement developed and she wrote eleven plays that were staged by the Irish Literary Theatre, Inghinidhe na hÉireann, and the Gaelic League (these included 'The green upon the cape' (1898), the 'Ossianic trilogy' (1899), and 'The escape of Red Hugh' (1901)). In November 1904 Milligan was appointed by the Gaelic League as a full-time travelling lecturer. She toured the 'English-speaking districts of Ireland' raising funds by staging plays, magic-lantern shows, and *tableaux vivants* until 1909, when the care of her aging parents took priority. Along with Francis Joseph Bigger, Milligan organised the 1910 Samuel Ferguson centenary in Belfast.

She was in London during the 1916 Easter rising—a year that also brought the death of her parents and her sister Charlotte Milligan Fox (1865–1916), founder of the Irish Folk Song Society. After attending the trial of Roger Casement, she joined the fundraising campaign in support of Irish political prisoners and their families. During this time she ran an Irish book shop in Dawson Street, Dublin, and her poems relating the plight of Irish prisoners appeared in *New Ireland*. Milligan supported Éamon de Valera in his opposition to the treaty—a decision she believed was supernaturally made for her by the automatic writings of her brothers Ernest and William. After 1921 she and William (a member of the British army) went to live with relatives in Bath, England, later settling in the north with his wife and son. The family eventually settled at the rectory in Mountfield, Omagh, Co. Tyrone. Despite Milligan's social and political isolation (she complained in letters to friends that she was 'an interned prisoner', existing among family who opposed her views) she remained politically active and continued to write. In the 1930s she became a founding member of the Anti-Partition League and published articles and poetry in the *Derry Journal* and other northern nationalist and American newspapers. She died 13 April 1953 at the age of 87 in Tyrcur, Co. Tyrone.

Milligan's literary and political career was excluded from all major accounts of the Irish cultural renaissance, and her papers remained scattered and uncollected. Until the 1990s very little had been written about her. However, the publication of *Alice Milligan and the Irish cultural revival* (2012), based on a fifteen-year project by Catherine Morris, has considerably heightened awareness of Milligan and led to television documentaries based on her life, and to exhibitions featuring her work, notably at the NLI (2010) and IMMA (2015). In 2012 Catherine Morris gifted her entire research archive on Alice Milligan to Omagh Public Library. Milligan's descendants have since gifted her diary to the NLI. Other important Milligan archives can be found in the Francis Joseph Bigger papers, Belfast Central Library, and the Brother Allen Library, O'Connell Schools, Dublin.

Catherine Morris

Sources

Henry Mangan, introduction to *Poems by Alice Milligan* (1954); Sheila Turner Johnston, *Alice: a life* (1994); Brighid Mhic Sheain, 'Glimpses of Erin. Alice Milligan: poet, protestant, patriot', supplement to *Fortnight* (April 1994); Catherine Morris, 'In the enemy's camp: Alice Milligan and *fin de siècle* Belfast', in Nicholas Allen and Aaron Kelly (ed.), *Cities of Belfast* (2003), 62–73; Catherine Morris, 'Becoming Irish? Alice Milligan and the revival', *Irish University Review*, xxxiii, no. 1 (2003), 79–98; Catherine Morris, 'Alice Milligan: republican tableaux and the revival', *Field Day Review*, vi (2010), 132–65; Catherine Morris, *Alice Milligan and the Irish cultural revival* (NLI, 2010); Catherine Morris, *Alice Milligan and the Irish cultural revival* (2012); El Lissitzky, *The artist and the state* (IMMA, 2015)

Thomas Moles

1871–1937

Thomas Moles, MP and journalist, was born 13 November 1871 in Belfast, second son of Edward Moles of Ardmore, Ballymena, Co. Antrim, and Margaret Jane Moles (née Carson). He was educated at the old Collegiate School in Ballymena and was subsequently appointed to the staff of the *Ballymena Weekly Telegraph*. He then moved to Armagh to take up the position of editor of the *Ulster Gazette*. During this time he came under the notice of Sir Robert Baird, managing director of the *Belfast Telegraph*, and was invited to join the staff of the *Telegraph* in 1902. In 1909 he became chief leader writer and in 1924, following the death of A. W. Stewart, he was promoted to managing editor and held this position until his death. He was made a fellow of the Ulster District Institute of Journalists in 1925 and also sat on the committee of the Belfast branch of the Newspaper Press Fund.

As one of the leading assistants of Edward Carson, Moles was prominently identified with the anti-home-rule campaign. His main contribution was in the field of propaganda, and his 'open letter' to A. G. Gardiner, editor of the *Observer*, was a *tour de force*. As well as advocating the position of the Ulster unionists in the pages of the *Telegraph*, he produced a number of pamphlets including *The Ulster situation* and *The real Ulster* (1917). *The leadership of Edward Carson* was originally written for inclusion in an album presented to Carson but was later made available to the public. In 1911 he was appointed Irish representative on the British press visit to Canada, and he was the only journalist who knew in advance of the Larne gunrunning. He witnessed and took part in the landing of the consignments of rifles from the *Mountjoy* and subsequently wrote a description of the event. In 1917 he was invited by leading members of the Ulster party to join the secretariat of the Irish Convention, and kept an extended record of its proceedings.

His parliamentary career began in December 1918 when he was elected as the unionist member for Ormeau in the imperial parliament. In November 1922 he was returned unopposed to Westminster for Belfast South and he held this seat until 1929. During this period he was involved in protracted negotiations over the financial implications of the Government of Ireland Act. Both Moles and H. M. Pollock considered that the scheme of finance on offer from Westminster was inadequate, and insisted on the setting up of the joint exchequer board. The Colwyn committee was appointed by this board and ultimately conceded many of Moles's and Pollock's demands. In keeping with one of his election promises Moles also successfully redressed the demands of the prewar RIC pensioners, whose allowances did not take account of postwar living costs.

In May 1921 he was elected for Belfast South in the first election to the Northern Ireland parliament and had the distinction of being the first member declared elected. Given his experience as an MP at Westminster, he was appointed deputy speaker of the new house and chairman of the committee of ways and means. In 1929, however, he suffered two attacks of nephritis and resigned his seat in the imperial parliament. On hearing this, Carson wrote:

> all through our campaign in Ulster and in the house of commons you were a very devoted and able comrade and I could never thank you sufficiently for all the loyalty and help you lavishly devoted to myself (*Belfast Telegraph*, 3 February 1937).

Moles continued his parliamentary career in the Northern Ireland house of commons as the representative for Belfast (Ballynafeigh) from May 1929 until his death in 1937.

Outside politics, his recreations included cycling, football, boxing and shooting, and he did a great deal to foster such outdoor pursuits. He was a leading figure in the Ballymena cycle club and was largely responsible for the construction of a cement racing track in the town. He was also responsible for the promotion and organisation of sporting events such as the 'Ballymena walk' and the 'cyclists' parade'. He later held a unique record in that he sat on the governing bodies of five different sports. He was a member of the council of the Irish Football Association and the international selection committee; president of the Northern Ireland Amateur Athletic Association; president of the Ulster Centre National Cycling Union; and patron of the Belfast Sports Club. In later years he became an ardent motorist and made frequent contributions to the athletic and cycling press.

Moles had a long association with the Masonic order and was a member of the Tower of Lebanon Masonic Lodge No. 285, the Rosetta Masonic Lodge, and the Press Lodge No. 432. As a member of Star of Down LOL and Preceptory, the Friendly Sons of Ulster LOL, London, and Avonmore Royal Arch Chapter, No. 26, he was prominently identified with the Orange order and frequently addressed Twelfth of July demonstrations. He was also a member of the Walker club apprentice boys of Derry.

A member of the Church of Ireland, he was connected to the congregation of St Jude in Belfast. In 1923 he was appointed as a privy councillor for Northern Ireland and was the first working journalist to receive this honour. He married (1901) Charlotte Douglas, third daughter of M. Branigan of Ballycastle; they had one son and two daughters. He died on 3 February 1937 at a private Belfast nursing home.

Anna Bryson

Sources

GRO, Belfast; *Thom IWW* (1923); *Belfast Telegraph*, 3, 5 February 1937; *Belfast News Letter*, 4, 6 February 1937; *Northern Whig, Times*, 4 February 1937; *WWW*; John F. Harbinson, *The Ulster Unionist party, 1882–1973: its development and organisation* (1973); *Walker*; www.election.demon.co.uk/stormont/biographies.html (accessed 4 August 2003)

Hugh de Fellenberg Montgomery

1844–1924

Hugh de Fellenbery Montgomery, landowner and Northern Ireland senator, was born 14 August 1844 in Blessingbourne, Fivemiletown, Co. Tyrone, the only child of Hugh Ralph Severin Montgomery (1821–44), landowner, and his wife Maria Philipina, daughter of Philip Emmanuel de Fellenberg of Hofwyl, educationist of Berne, Switzerland. His father died in the year of his birth and his mother when he was two years old. He was educated privately and at Christ Church, Oxford, graduating in 1868. That year he succeeded to the family estates of 7,996 acres in Fermanagh and 4,552 acres in Tyrone. In addition he inherited land from his mother in Switzerland.

Mongomery lived all his long life at Blessingbourne and devoted himself to the interests of the area, with which his family had been associated since 1618. He was a captain of the Fermanagh militia and high sheriff of Fermanagh (1871) and Tyrone (1888). A model landlord, he helped his tenants in times of distress by granting rent reductions and contributing to relief committees—on one occasion he was the only landlord along the Fermanagh–Tyrone border to contribute to the Fivemiletown relief committee. His generosity was impressive since despite the substantial valuation of his estates—in 1878 their annual income was £4, 924—he was never without financial difficulties. He married (1870) Mary Sophia Julia, daughter of the Rev. Charles Maude, rector of Enniskillen, and was soon father to a large family of sons. Of eight born, six survived, with the only daughter dying in her first year. To house his growing family he had a mansion built (1870–74) in Blessingbourne to the designs of Pepys Cockerell at a cost of £8,000.

Montgomery was strongly interested in progressive German ideas of farming, and hoped that the Irish would eventually be 'Prussianised'. He established a local railway and was a prominent member of Horace Plunkett's Irish Agricultural Organisation Society (IAOS). Other members found him opinionated, impatient and arrogant: R.A. Anderson, Plunkett's right-hand man, wrote:

> To him cooperation was nothing more than a highly organized system of business in which sentiment had no place...I used to watch him, curling his lip in proud disdain, while his pale-blue eyes were fixed coldly on any of us who referred to the spiritual side of the movement. He was intensely materialistic. (Anderson, 126–7)

Originally a liberal and a strong supporter of Gladstone, Montgomery was also a firm unionist and defender of landlordism, and became alarmed in the 1880s by the twin threats of the land league and home rule. He was highly critical of the Land Act of 1881, which established the principle of dual ownership by landlord and tenant, believing it conceded too much to the latter. His lengthy correspondence with Gladstone on the question of whether Edmund Burke would have been a home ruler was eventually published in 1886. Montgomery rejected the analogy

Gladstone drew between the American colonists whom Burke championed and the Irish Catholics, since the Irish had the privilege of being represented in Westminster.

Montgomery equated unionism with landlordism and was highly suspicious of T. W. Russell's populism, which he felt would wreck the union. In 1885 he took an executive position on the Irish Loyal and Patriotic Union, founded to defend the union, and in the run up to the election that year he proposed that liberals and conservatives unite against home rule. He held a violent correspondence on this point in the *Irish Times* and the *Northern Whig* with another leading Tyrone liberal, Thomas Dickson (1833–1909), MP for Dungannon (1874–80) and Co. Tyrone (1881–85) who was sympathetic to land reform and home rule. On 1 April both announced their candidature as liberals for South Tyrone—both subsequently withdrew but their feud prevented liberals from choosing another candidate, and the nationalist William O'Brien won the seat.

The threat of home rule also helped reconcile Montgomery to the Orange Order. An active member of the synod of the Church of Ireland, he first dismissed the order as mischievous, and in 1871 caused resentment when he removed their flags from a church in Fivemiletown, but by 1893 he was allowing Orangemen celebrate the 12 July in a field opposite his house—though he only permitted lemonade and soda water to be drunk. On the formation of the Ulster Unionist Council in 1905, he became a member of its advisory committee, and helped to draft the Solemn League and Covenant (1912). A prominent member of the Irish Landowners Convention, he maintained close contacts with southern unionists. In 1892 he assured them that Ulstermen would not sit still 'and set up a little home rule shop of our own…while the yoke of a Healyite parliament was being firmly strapped on your necks' (McDowell, 23), but by 1916 he believed that Ulster unionists had no choice but to accept Lloyd George's proposal for a six-county Northern Ireland. Although he advised Carson not to send delegates to the 1917 Irish Convention as they would be unable to secure agreement to the exclusion of the six counties, would have to withdraw, and would be blamed for wrecking the conference, in the event he went himself. In fighting form, he rejected any compromise and told Lloyd George that his threat that the failure of the Convention would harm the war effort was bunkum. He became a Northern Ireland senator in 1921 and died in office in Tyrone on 8 October 1924 at the age of 80, being vigorous till the last. His papers (1865–1924) are held in PRONI.

Memorably described by Anderson (125) as

> a man of fine presence and stature, always standing stark and erect...he seemed to have stepped straight out of the frame of one of his Cromwellian ancestors' portraits,

Montgomery was a difficult, seemingly contradictory figure: nominally a liberal but a 'thoroughgoing Conservative of the die-hard breed' (Anderson, ibid); he castigated all 'Southerners' as Fenians but allied himself in the IAOS with the North Tipperary Nationalist, T. P. Gill; he was also an atheist who supported the Church of Ireland, a virulent 'anti-papist' who built a church for his Catholic tenants, and a Gladstonian liberal who decried home rule. However, all his actions were consistent with two dominant traits: his craving for order and efficiency, and his unionism.

Bridget Hourican

Sources

Irish Times, Times, News Letter, 9 October 1924; *WWW;* D. C. Savage, 'The origins of the Ulster Unionist Party, 1885–6', *Irish Historical Studies,* xii (March 1961), 189; R. B. McDowell, *The Irish Convention, 1917–18* (1970); Burke, *IFR* (1976); R. A. Anderson, *With Plunkett in Ireland* (1983), 125–7; Patrick Buckland, *Irish unionism,* i, The *Anglo-Irish and the new Ireland 1885–1922* (1972); Patrick Buckland, *Irish unionism 1885–1923: a documentary history* (1973); John Kendle, *Walter Long, Ireland, and the Union, 1905–20* (1992); David Burnett, *Unionism in modern Ireland* (1996); Charles Dillon and Henry A. Jeffries (ed.), *Tyrone, history and society* (2000)

Peadar O'Donnell

1893–1986

Peadar O'Donnell, socialist and writer, was born 22 February 1893 in Meenmore, near Dunglow (Dungloe), Co. Donegal, youngest among six sons and three daughters of Biddy and James ('Sheáin Mhóir') O'Donnell. He was greatly influenced by his upbringing in the Rosses, in north-west Donegal, one of the poorest and most remote parts of Ireland. His father, a popular local fiddler, earned a living through his smallholding, seasonal labouring in Scotland, and winter work in a local corn-mill. His mother, who came from a radical labour and nationalist political background, worked in a local cooperative store. O'Donnell attended Rampart national school and Roshine national school, near Burtonport, where he was a monitor (pupil-teacher) for four years. In 1911 he won a scholarship to attend St Patrick's teacher training college in Drumcondra,

Dublin, and returned in 1913 to the Rosses, where he spent two years teaching on Inishfree Island. In 1915 he was appointed head of Derryhenny national school, near Dunglow, and the following year became principal of a national school on Arranmore Island, where he began to write. O'Donnell had long been concerned by the poor conditions of the local 'tatie-hokers' (potato-pickers) who migrated annually to Scotland, and in the summer of 1918 he travelled there to help organise the Scottish Farm Servants' Union. While there he was influenced by left-wing radicals such as Willie Gallacher, later a communist MP, and Emanuel 'Manny' Shinwell, later Baron Shinwell. In September 1918, against a background of rising labour militancy, O'Donnell left teaching to become a full-time organiser for the Irish Transport and General Workers' Union (ITGWU) in the west Ulster area. The following year O'Donnell organised one of Ireland's first 'soviets' when the attendants and nurses of Monaghan's lunatic asylum occupied the grounds and appointed O'Donnell as governor until their demands were met.

In early 1919 he joined the IRA in Monaghan, resigning from the ITGWU for full-time IRA service in late 1920. He led the 2nd Battalion, Donegal IRA, from the summer of 1920. In December 1920 he went 'on the run' and led a flying column in west Donegal until May 1921, when he was wounded. Regarded as insubordinate and militarily inexperienced, O'Donnell was unpopular among the other senior officers of 1st Northern Division. O'Donnell, in turn, was disappointed by the lack of social radicalism among the nationalist leadership. He opposed the treaty, was placed in command of the minority anti-treaty 1st Northern Division, and was a member of the IRA executive that occupied the Four Courts in Dublin in defiance of the provisional government. Arrested in June 1922, O'Donnell shared a prison cell with Liam Mellows and influenced his radical 'Notes from Mountjoy', an important document for subsequent left-wing republicans. O'Donnell spent the next two years in various prisons and internment camps; his execution was widely expected to follow those of 8 December 1922. In August 1923 O'Donnell won a seat in Donegal in the general election called after the end of the civil war. He went on hunger-strike for forty-one days in late 1923 and succeeded in escaping from the Curragh in March 1924. In June 1924, while on the run, O'Donnell married Lile

O'Donel, a wealthy Cumann na mBan activist who had smuggled communications for republican prisoners. O'Donel, a radical and member of the Communist Party, was the daughter of Ignatius O'Donel, a prominent landowner from Mayo. They had no children but raised their nephew, Peadar Joe, as their own son after the death in New York of O'Donnell's brother Joe.

O'Donnell began writing seriously in jail and remained a prolific writer, journalist, and editor until the 1960s. His first novel, *Storm*, set in the war of independence, was published in 1925. One of his most highly regarded books, *Islanders*, was published in 1928. *Adrigoole* (like *Islanders* a story of poverty and starvation in rural Ireland) was published the following year. *The knife* (1930) and *On the edge of the stream* (1934) soon followed. The most significant of his later novels was probably *The big windows* (1954). Foremost among O'Donnell's qualities as a writer was his empathy for the people, life, and landscape of rural Ireland. But his novels have been criticised for their slow pace, excessive detail, and didactic nature. O'Donnell claimed his writing was incidental to his political activism. His trilogy of autobiographical non-fiction, *The gates flew open* (1932), *Salud! An Irishman in Spain* (1936), and *There will be another day* (1963), which respectively concern the Irish civil war, his activism during the Spanish civil war, and his role in the land annuities agitation, remain highly regarded. O'Donnell's other important literary achievement was with *The Bell*, an innovative literary and political magazine which played a useful dissenting role in an insular and conservative period. He founded *The Bell* with the writer Sean O'Faolain in 1940 and edited it from 1946 until it ceased publication in 1954.

O'Donnell exercised an influential role in the interwar IRA, particularly through his editorship of *An Phoblacht* (1926–9), which he attempted to divert from militarism to socialist agitation. His ultimate aim was for a thirty-two-county socialist republic. His most successful campaign was organising small farmers against the payment of land annuities to the government in the late 1920s and early 1930s. This campaign was later adopted by Fianna Fáil and contributed to their electoral success in 1932. O'Donnell was less successful in radicalising the IRA. After the failure of Saor Éire, a left-wing IRA front which provoked clerical and popular hostility against the IRA, increasing tensions between the IRA's left-wing and the leadership led O'Donnell (along with Frank Ryan and George Gilmore) to split from the IRA to establish the short-lived Republican Congress in 1934. Although O'Donnell claimed he was never a Communist Party member, he played a central role in forging links between republicans and the revolutionary left (both in Ireland and internationally) and invariably supported the Communist Party line at critical junctures. After the failure of Congress, O'Donnell (who had been in Spain when the Spanish civil war broke out) took up the cause of the Spanish republic. His championing of unpopular causes such as communism and Spain entailed a good deal of frustration. He was physically attacked at political meetings and in 1932, despite having never visited the Soviet Union, lost a high-profile libel action against the Dominican *Irish Rosary*, which claimed he had studied in Moscow's Lenin College. He was banned from entering the United States for several decades, although he maintained: 'My relations with all the great powers continue to be friendly.'

O'Donnell continued to support radical campaigns until his death. He was an outspoken advocate of Irish emigrants. He was prominent in the Irish Campaign for Nuclear Disarmament and served as its president in the early 1960s. He was a leading protester against the Vietnam war and a supporter of African anti-colonial movements such as that against apartheid. In later years he was involved in the 'Save the west' campaign, highlighting the problems of the west of Ireland. After several months of ill-health following a heart-attack, O'Donnell died in Dublin, aged 93, on 13 May 1986. He was cremated in Glasnevin and his ashes were buried at his wife's home in Swinford, Co. Mayo. Although O'Donnell once remarked that every cause he fought for was a failure, he is now regarded as one of the most influential socialist republican theorists and an important voice of dissent in twentieth-century Ireland.

Fearghal McGarry

Sources

Irish Times, Irish Press, 14 May 1986; Uinseann MacEoin, *The IRA in the twilight years* (1997); Peter Hegarty, *Peadar O'Donnell* (1999); Fearghal McGarry, *Irish politics and the Spanish civil war* (1999)

Eoin O'Duffy

1890–1944

Eoin O'Duffy, soldier, policeman, and politician, was born 28 January 1890 on the family farm at Carrickaduff (Cargaghdoo), near Castleblayney, Co. Monaghan, youngest among five sons and two daughters of Eugene ('Owen') Duffy and Brigid Duffy (née Fealy) of the nearby parish of Donoghmoyne. A frugal and melancholy childhood, marked by successive sibling emigration, was compounded by the death in 1902 of his mother, and in 1903 of his eldest brother, Peter, in America. Raised by his father, he balanced a basic education at Laragh national school with labour on the farm. At school he became influenced by the Irish language movement and the 'Irish Ireland' campaign of the Gaelic League. He took an early and lifelong interest in the Gaelic Athletic Association

(GAA), serving as secretary of its Ulster council 1912–22, subsequently as a national council member until 1934.

Forsaking the option of a teaching career, he became a clerk in Monaghan county council in 1910, held a short apprenticeship in Co. Wexford c.1913, and served in Monaghan as surveyor, engineer, and architect, mainly for the Clones district. As he was left without property at his father's death (1915), when the farm passed to his brother Patrick, and deprived of both remaining brothers, who had migrated to Scotland, Duffy's aloofness and self-reliance became more pronounced. Deeply impressed by the 1916 rising, he joined the Irish Volunteers and Sinn Féin (1917) and campaigned for that party's general election victory of December 1918, leading to the formation of Dáil Éireann on 21 January 1919. A member of the IRB supreme council, he also held command of Monaghan Brigade IRA in the war of independence (1919–21). Nationalist sympathies in the local authority facilitated his general absence from official duty. He adapted his name to O'Duffy, sometimes opting for the Gaelic form 'Ó Dubhthaigh'. He led the first IRA raid on an Ulster RIC barracks 15 February 1920, at Ballytrain, Shantonagh, near his family home. One policeman was fatally wounded but O'Duffy prevented further loss of life by successfully forcing surrender of the barracks. Shortly afterwards he was arrested and imprisoned briefly in Crumlin Road gaol, Belfast. Released when he and others went on hunger strike, he continued raiding for arms, keeping casualties low by contemporary standards. Presenting an heroic image of himself, O'Duffy was one of three Monaghan candidates elected to the second dáil in May 1921.

Supporting the Anglo–Irish truce in July, at which time he was IRA director of organisation, O'Duffy became deputy chief of staff to Richard Mulcahy and Michael Collins at GHQ in Dublin, as Brigadier Dan Hogan became commandant of the Monaghan IRA's new 5th Northern Division. GHQ sent O'Duffy to liaise with the Ulster IRA, influencing the northern divisions to accept the Anglo–Irish treaty (6 December 1921).

In February 1922 he became chief of staff of the National Army, forerunner of the Free State army, containing pro-treaty IRA and new members, many of whom had formerly been in the British army. O'Duffy attempted to reconcile the anti-treaty IRA through frantic diplomacy and strategic meetings with the mainly southern dissidents led by Liam Lynch and Rory O'Connor. His efforts only postponed civil war. In the general election of 16 June 1922 he was reelected for Co. Monaghan on the 'coalition treaty' ticket, representing a desire to heal the republican split.

O'Duffy was appointed with Collins and Mulcahy in July 1922 to a war council in which he was named GOC South Western Command, a 'poisoned chalice' jurisdiction in the Kerry area where some of the hardest fighting took place, the worst of it after O'Duffy's further relocation in September 1922. In that month he became commissioner of the Civic Guard (*An Garda Síochána*), an unarmed police force that he intended would conform to his own national ideals in contrast to the semi-military RIC which it replaced. Shortly after the civil war, his military authority was temporarily restored as both inspector general and general officer commanding the forces, conferring him with near-dictatorial powers to restore army discipline in the 'mutiny' crisis of March 1924. He undermined the seniority of the defence minister, Mulcahy, by insisting on absolute command, and redrew the army's organisational structure, established by Mulcahy under defence legislation. Reverting exclusively to his police role in 1925, he was an able commander who expected unfailing obedience.

O'Duffy imbued the force with his conservative Catholic standards and a Gaelic identity, promoting the Irish language, making moral pronouncements, and writing didactic articles in *Iris an Gharda* (*Garda Review*). He was popular though feared, enjoying the high visibility his position afforded, and loyally serving the Free State government against all opponents; his Special Branch counter-insurgency made him the special enemy of republicans, whom he viewed as subversive and possibly communist. He was hardly less suspicious of Fianna Fáil, the leading opposition party in the dáil from 1927. He clashed with government over the increasing vigour of Garda methods (especially against political crime) but was deemed irreplaceable, particularly after the assassination (10 July 1927) of Kevin O'Higgins.

He travelled widely and led Garda pilgrimages to religious shrines in Europe, exposing him to the spectacular propaganda of fascist Italy and the turbulence of France and Germany. The experience reinforced his conservatism at home. Reputedly intent on usurping Fianna Fáil's election victory in 1932, he demurred and enjoyed some late glory as ceremonial commander at the eucharistic congress in Dublin and as president of the Olympic Council of Ireland for the successful California games of that year. Indeed, leadership in sport might be seen as his most positive legacy outside of policing, ranging from presidency of the Irish Amateur Handball Association to patronage of the Irish Native Breeds Society (founded to promote native strains of Irish dogs).

O'Duffy was mesmerised by the glamour of fascism and its seeming compatibility with Christianity. He veered towards its disciplined, 'corporatist' ideals of vocationalism and the radical right. For him, opposition to godless communism was its greatest credential. In 1932, confusing semblance with substance, he became involved with the Army Comrades Association (ACA) led by Colonel Edmund Cronin. Standing for 'free speech' in politics, its members were pro-treaty army veterans who had served the late Cumann na nGaedheal administration. Fianna Fáil, lacking 'full confidence' in O'Duffy as commissioner, replaced him with Éamonn Broy in February 1933. Turning down a sinecure as controller of prices, O'Duffy was pensioned out of office. Without delay, he rose quickly within the ACA to become leader in July 1933. Sharing conservative, Catholic views with most fellow 'Blueshirts' (so-called from a distinctive uniform adopted in the previous March), O'Duffy and his followers bore the appearance of continental fascist movements and held some similar though less extreme aspirations, chiefly to thwart communism and the IRA and to oppose Fianna Fáil. They upheld the interests of those (largely farmers) affected by the 'economic war' and protected Cumann na nGaedheal politicians from attack at public meetings. Blueshirt social and athletic clubs were formed in clear opposition to jazz culture.

Under O'Duffy the ACA confusingly changed its official title several times in less than six months: National Guard (July 1933), Young Ireland Association (November 1933), and League of Youth (December 1933). The last was technically a new organisation, responding to government prohibition (the first in August 1933, to offset a 'march on Dublin') under the previous titles. Meanwhile, in September 1933 O'Duffy became president of a new United

Ireland Party or Fine Gael, a tripartite merger of Cumann na nGaedheal, the Centre Party, and National Guard. His presidency of Fine Gael exposed his political naivety, punctuated by extreme language, with bellicose references to Northern Ireland and encouraging Blueshirts to defy the authorities. Forced to resign (September 1934), he presided over a confused and declining Blueshirt movement. He became more admiring of European fascism, apparently ignorant or in denial of its record on civil rights. His loss of direction and the growth of dissatisfaction with his leadership caused a split in 1935 into two Blueshirt movements. O'Duffy led a breakaway faction while the main body, under Cronin, remained within Fine Gael until dropped from the party in October 1936. O'Duffy's short-lived National Corporate Party (NCP), founded in June 1935, opposed communism, capitalism, and dictatorship, anticipated an all-Ireland corporate state, and retained a variation of the Blueshirt uniform, changing it to green in 1936.

The NCP was practically moribund as the Spanish civil war began in June 1936. O'Duffy identified the conflict as a simple battle between Christian virtue and communist evil. He supported the nationalist rebellion of General Francisco Franco against the left-wing coalition of the Spanish republic. The Dublin government declared Ireland to be neutral over Spain, but both sides attracted ideological volunteers. Requested by the rebels to form a brigade, O'Duffy claimed thousands of responses but recruited only about 700 volunteers, including Blueshirt veterans. He took them to Spain in the winter of 1936–7 to fight for 'Christian civilisation'. In six dismal months the *bandera irlandesa* lost enough men in sickness and battle to demoralise the rest, who endured climatic and other physical hardships until a majority voted to go home in June 1937. O'Duffy published an account of his adventure as *Crusade in Spain* (1938). His NCP faded away and he retired from political life. Briefly, in 1939, the Germans courted him as a possible link to the IRA but this came to nothing. He instead offered his services to the state for the duration of the Emergency but was not called. He maintained a pro-German viewpoint but concentrated his failing energy on sport, renewing in 1942 his previously held presidency of the National Athletic and Cycling Association. The name of his last home, 'Farney', at Merrion Park, Blackrock, Co. Dublin, recalled his rural

Monaghan origins. He died 30 November 1944 in a Dublin nursing home at 4 Pembroke Street, and received a state funeral to Glasnevin cemetery with full military honours. Monaghan County Museum has an oil portrait by Gillian Bourke, and photographic portraits are held by the Garda Museum and Archive, Dublin.

Patrick Long

Sources

Irish Law Times and Solicitors' Journal, 19 September 1931; Eoin O'Duffy, *Crusade in Spain* (1938); *Irish Independent*, 3 December 1944; *Spearhead* (journal of Army 2nd Division), December 1944 (NAI, Military Archives); *Garda Review*, January 1945; Captain Denis J. O'Kelly, *Salute to the Gardai: a story of struggle and achievement, 1922–1958* (1958), 20–21; Captain Liam Walsh, 'General Eoin O'Duffy—his life and battles' (unpublished MS, n.d., NLI); *Cuimhneachán Mhuineacháin* (1966); Conor Brady, *Guardians of the peace* (1974); Peadar Livingstone, *The Monaghan story* (1980); Maurice Manning, *The Blueshirts* (2nd ed., 1987; reprint 1988); Patrick Lindsay, *Memories* (1992), 54–5; Maryann Gialanella Valiulis, *Portrait of a revolutionary: General Richard Mulcahy and the founding of the Irish Free State* (1992); Mike Cronin, *The Blueshirts and Irish politics* (1997); Patrick Long, 'Organisation and development of the pro-treaty forces, 1922–1924', *Irish Sword*, xx, no. 82 (winter 1997), 308–30; Liam McNiffe, *A history of the Garda Síochána* (1997); Robert Stradling, *The Irish and the Spanish civil war* (1999); Gregory Allen, *The Garda Síochána: policing independent Ireland 1922–82* (1999); Risteárd Mulcahy, *Richard Mulcahy (1886–1971): a family memoir* (1999); John M. Regan, *The Irish counter-revolution 1921–1936* (1999); Fearghal McGarry, *Irish politics and the Spanish civil war* (1999); Eunan O'Halpin, *Defending Ireland: the Irish state and its enemies since 1922* (1999); Fearghal McGarry, *Eoin O'Duffy: a self-made hero* (2005); information from Military Archives, Garda Museum and Archive, and Fearghal McGarry

Kevin Roantree O'Shiel

1891–1970

Kevin Roantree O'Shiel, barrister and land commissioner, was born 23 September 1891 in Omagh, Co. Tyrone, eldest of four sons and two daughters of Francis Shields, solicitor, and his wife Elizabeth, daughter of D. J. Roantree, school inspector. While his father retained the name 'Shields', his mother and the rest of the family used the form 'O'Shiel'. His great-uncle was James Shields, US soldier and politician. Educated at Mount St Columba's CBS, Omagh, convent preparatory schools in Oxford and Bath, St George's School, Surrey, and Mount St Mary's Jesuit school, Derby, O'Shiel studied law at TCD and the King's Inns, and having been called to the bar (Michaelmas term 1913) joined the north-west circuit.

A member of the Irish Volunteers until the split in 1914, he was initially a home rule nationalist, but became disillusioned by the postponement of home rule in 1914, and with the policies of the Irish party. Increasingly influenced by separatism, in 1916 (after the Irish party had accepted the exclusion of Ulster from home rule) he joined the Anti-Partition League (later the Irish Nation League), formed by Ulster nationalists opposed to the Irish party. Having campaigned for Sinn Féin candidates during the 1917 by-elections in Roscommon, Longford and Clare, he joined that party in 1917 after the dissolution of the Irish Nation League and became a member of the Owen Roe branch in Omagh, which he represented at the Sinn Féin convention in October 1917. Prominent in the anti-conscription campaign in mid Tyrone in 1918, and supervisor of the Ballyjamesduff district for Sinn Féin in the Cavan East by-election (June 1918), he was an unsuccessful Sinn Féin candidate in the 1918 general election in the constituencies of Fermanagh North and Antrim South. Recruited as land commissioner by Arthur Griffith in May 1920 to deal with the resurgence of land agitation in the west, from September 1920 he was judicial commissioner of the newly established dáil land commission. Noted for the sagacity of his judgments, together with Conor Maguire he was largely responsible for the success of the dáil land courts, although their effectiveness was curtailed during 1921 by British efforts to suppress the republican courts. In 1921 he wrote a series of articles arguing that a boycott of British goods would be of economic benefit to Ireland.

A supporter of the Anglo–Irish treaty, in 1922 he was assistant legal adviser to the provisional government, during which he was involved in drawing up plans for the pact election, conducted an inquiry into a May 1922 mutiny by garda recruits, and supported action by the government to secure the release of republican internees on the *Argenta* prison ship in Belfast, among whom was his friend Cahir Healy. He served in 1922 as adviser to Michael Collins on Northern Ireland affairs, and in 1922/3 was assistant legal adviser to the provisional government and the Irish Free State. In January 1923 he wrote a memo urging the government to hasten the end of the civil war, and from October 1922 to November 1925 was director of the Free State government's North-Eastern Boundary Bureau, which was established in October 1922 to compile data for the boundary commission. As part of this work he was sent to Geneva to examine material from other boundary commissions at the League of Nations archives. From 1923 he served as commissioner with the Irish Land Commission until his retirement in 1963. The author of a number of articles on the history of partition and Irish land settlement, his principal publications include *The rise of the Irish Nation League* (1916), *The making of a republic* (1920), a history of the American revolution, and (with T. O'Brien) *The land problem in Ireland and its settlement* (1954). His hobbies included reading, ornithology, botany, and walking. He lived at 28 Kenilworth Road, Dublin, and died 12 July 1970 in Dublin, leaving an estate valued at £738.

He married (6 September 1922) Louise F. Conry, daughter of John Conry, medical doctor, of Dublin; they had two sons who did not survive infancy, and after her death he married (15 October 1929) Cecil, daughter of T. A. Smiddy, economist and diplomat, of Cork, and his wife Lilian, daughter of Cornelius O'Connell, of Cork. They had two daughters. O'Shiel's papers, including an unpublished memoir of the revolutionary period, were left in the possession of his daughter Eda Sagarra, MRIA, professor of German at TCD.

Marie Coleman

Sources

Kevin O'Shiel, 'The times that were in it' (unpublished memoir); Kevin O'Shiel, 'Memories of my lifetime', *Irish Times*, November 1966; Mary Kotsonouris, *Retreat from revolution: the dáil courts, 1920–24* (1994); Eamon Phoenix, *Northern nationalism* (1994); Arthur Mitchell, *Revolutionary government in Ireland: Dáil Éireann, 1919–22* (1995); Michael Laffan, *The resurrection of Ireland: the Sinn Féin party, 1916–1923* (1999); Eunan O'Halpin, *Defending Ireland* (1999); John M. Regan, *The Irish counter-revolution, 1921–1936* (1999); Ronan Fanning *et al.* (ed.), *Documents in Irish foreign policy*, ii, *1923–1926* (2000), p. xxiv; Mary E. Daly, *The first department* (2002); information from Eda Sagarra (daughter)

Herbert Moore Pim

1883–1950

Herbert Moore Pim, writer and political activist, was born 6 June 1883 in Belfast, son of Robert Barclay Pim and Caroline Pim (née Moore). The Pims were a leading quaker business and professional dynasty; his father was secretary of the Friends Provident Insurance Company. Pim was educated at Friends School, Lisburn, and public schools in Chester and Bedford, then spent four years studying in Grenoble and Paris. He detested English schools, and became a Francophile.

Pim became an insurance agent and an active member of the YMCA. He also dabbled in occultism. In June 1903 he married Amy Vincent Mollan, daughter of a Presbyterian linen merchant. From the age of 17 he circulated manuscript annual collections of his stories and poems. The son and only child of his first marriage, Terence (b. 1908), claimed Pim published pornography and religious tracts simultaneously under pen-names; he certainly published two fantasy novels, *A vampire of souls* (1901, by 'H. M. P.') and *The man with thirty lives* (1903, by 'Herbert Pym'). Pim was persistently unfaithful and the marriage broke up in late 1916.

Initially conservative in politics, Pim developed liberal sympathies after meeting upper-class Belfast liberals, then joined the United Irish League (UIL), converted to Catholicism (1910), and joined the Ancient Order of Hibernians. By 1914 he was a prominent UIL activist and contributor to the *Irish News* under the pseudonym of 'A. Newman' (he had become 'a new man' on conversion).

In 1914 Pim published *The pessimist*, a novel whose central character hopes to end suffering by the extinction of all life. He joined the Irish Volunteers; at the outbreak of war he declared himself a separatist and lost his job. He may have joined the IRB; he wrote regularly for the *Irish Volunteer* (as 'A. Newman') and published a pamphlet series, *Tracts for the times*. Pim preached blood sacrifice in *Why the martyrs of Manchester died* and *The significance of Emmet in 1915*; Pearse's four final manifestoes appeared as *Tracts* in early 1916. Pim was one of four separatists imprisoned (July–September 1915) for seditious activities; he published a tract about his jail experiences, *What it is like* (1915). Early in 1916 he founded a Belfast-based literary and political monthly, *The Irishman*. Pim joined the Volunteer muster in Coalisland at Easter 1916, and was arrested after the rising and deported to Reading gaol. He was released in September 1916, restarted the *Irishman* as a weekly, and claimed to represent the prisoners. He set about reviving Arthur Griffith's Sinn Féin party, circulating tracts on Sinn Féin policy, and claiming leadership. After internees were released in December 1916 Pim was marginalised, but remained politically active.

The Irishman combined Sinn Féin propaganda and campaigns against sexual immorality with encouragement of local writers and artists; Forrest Reid was a contributor; John McBurney and R. Ponsonby Staples provided illustrations. Pim was joined in these campaigns by Lord Alfred Douglas; *The Irishman* published many of Douglas's poems. Pim also founded *Young Ireland*, a children's journal. His *Selected poems* were published in 1917, as was

Unknown immortals in the northern city of success, sketches of picturesque Belfast street-people.

In early 1918 Pim's health broke down; *The Irishman* and *Young Ireland* were taken over by the Dublin Sinn Féin leadership. In June 1918 Pim and his mistress Dorothy Hungerford resigned from Sinn Féin and advocated conscription. He published *Unconquerable Ulster* (1919), arguing that Ulster unionists were of Gaelic descent while nationalists represented a pre-Celtic slave race. (*A short history of Celtic philosophy* (1920) argues that the druids were Platonists.) Pim unsuccessfully offered his services to the Ulster unionists, then left for London.

Douglas and Pim campaigned against an alleged German plot to corrupt the British upper classes by homosexuality. Douglas established a weekly, *Plain English* (1919–21), 'die-hard, anti-Sinn Féin, and anti-Semitic'. Pim became assistant editor and serialised a self-glorifying memoir, *Adventures in the land of Sinn Féin*. He also published a pamphlet, *Sinn Féin: an illumination*, and *Songs from an Ulster valley* (both 1920) and joined the far-right Britons Society. Pim's and Douglas's next journal, *Plain Speech* (1921–2), accused Winston Churchill of manipulating war news to benefit Jewish speculators. This led to Douglas's imprisonment for libel. Pim and Douglas quarrelled over their poetic achievements when Pim published *New poems and a preface* (London, 1927).

Pim took French citizenship and married Germaine Eleanor Dussotour; they had one daughter, Françoise (b.1930). In 1927 his novel *French love* (a self-serving fabulation portraying his life as he would have liked it to have been) accused his first wife of unspeakable perversions, and portrayed Pim as a devout Catholic and Ulster unionist who spends the war spying in Germany. It was banned in Ireland. Thereafter he produced pamphlets of doggerel verse and polemics (published by Douglas's chief eulogist, the Scottish journalist W. H. Sorley Brown) expressing extreme right-wing views. After some years residence in France and Italy (where he dabbled in fascism) Pim returned to Britain by 1937 and died at Hove, Sussex, on 12 May 1950. The H. M. Pim papers are in the library of QUB.

Patrick Maume

Sources

Belfast Telegraph, obit., 13 May 1950; *Irish News*, 15 May 1950, 4; Cathal O'Shannon, 'Herbert Moore Pim—an appreciation', *Irish Times*, 15 May 1950; *Irish Times:*, 17–19 May 1950 (letters to the editor by 'Old Irish-Irelander', Aodh de Blacam, Cathal O'Shannon, and 'Thoolemaraun'); Ralph Bossence, 'Aunt Jane boiled bones' [on Pim's *Unknown immortals*], *Belfast Newsletter*, 12 October 1966; Ralph Bossence, 'Diary', *Belfast Newsletter*, 19 October 1966; Ralph Bossence, 'More about Herbert Moore Pim', *Belfast Newsletter*, 2 November 1966; Ralph Bossence, 'Words and a man of action', *Belfast Newsletter*, 22 November 1966; J. A. Gaughan (ed.), *Memoirs of Senator Joseph Connolly (1885–1961)* (1996); León Ó Broin, *Protestant nationalists in revolutionary Ireland: the Stopford connection* (1985); Rosalie Kerr, 'Songs from an Ulster valley: the unconventional career of Herbert Moore Pim', *New Ulster* (Spring 1994), 11–15

William James Pirrie

1847–1924

William James Pirrie, 1st Viscount Pirrie, shipbuilder and politician, was born 31 May 1847 in Quebec, Canada, the only son of James Alexander Pirrie, shipping merchant (and son of a shipping merchant, Captain William Pirrie), of Conlig, Little Clandeboye, Co. Down, and his wife, Eliza Swan, daughter of Alexander Montgomery, of Dundesart, Co. Antrim. Returning with his mother to the ancestral home at Conlig in 1848 after the death of his father in the same year, most of William's life was spent in Co. Down. Educated privately and at the Royal Belfast Academical Institution (RBAI), he entered the growing Belfast shipbuilding firm of Harland and Wolff, 23 June 1862, aged fifteen, as an apprentice. In 1874, after rising rapidly from draughtsman to manager at Queen's Island shipyard, where he thoroughly absorbed practical and commercial knowledge of the business, he joined the board of directors as a partner to Walter H. Wilson (who resigned in 1877) and the company's founders, Edward J. Harland and G. W. Wolff. When the founders retired from active partnership in 1884 they left Pirrie in virtual control of the business. At Harland's death in 1895 Pirrie became chief executive and also, on Wolff's retirement in 1906, chairman.

As a pioneer in Ireland's most industrialised city, Pirrie developed local shipbuilding beyond the iron-hulled (e.g. *Oceanic*, 1871) to the steel-built Belfast passenger liner, an international byword of marine engineering. He advanced it in terms of volume and awe-inspiring splendour (e.g. *Teutonic*, 1889) in the way that his fellow Irishman, Charles Parsons, simultaneously increased motive power and speed at sea with marine turbine engines. Pirrie also presided over engine-building at Harland and Wolff, adopting innovations as they emerged. After a devastating fire in 1896 he greatly improved shipyard facilities and erected a massive gantry which, when enlarged, could accommodate several ships at once. By 1914, with orders from many clients, the oldest including the renowned Bibby and White Star Lines, he had extended the business to Glasgow and Liverpool with smaller works in the Belfast and Dublin areas. He encouraged the interdependence of local industries, such as linen and glassmaking, with shipbuilding, supporting a comprehensive economic system in and around his extensive yards.

Pirrie was prominent in philanthropy and public education, partnered by his dynamic wife (and first cousin), Margaret Montgomery Carlisle, daughter of John Carlisle, professor of the RBAI, whom he married in 1879. A woman of formidable influence and organising ability (especially in health care), she became first female honorary burgess (1904) and first female JP (1922) of Belfast, and a life member (1926) of Belfast chamber of commerce. Pirrie himself entered local politics in Belfast corporation as a liberal unionist. He was lord mayor of Belfast in 1896 and 1897 (initiating the construction of the city hall and other major institutions), a privy counsellor in 1897, and first honorary burgess (freeman) of Belfast in 1898. He was high sheriff of Co. Antrim (1898) and Co. Down (1899).

Such distinctions (and honorary university degrees) aside, conservative unionism attempted to chasten him in 1902 by denying him a candidacy in the South Belfast by-election. Disappointed but accelerated further into liberalism by the experience, he became Baron Pirrie (1906) for his work on behalf of the liberals in the general election of that year. He was created KP (1909) and appointed Belfast city lieutenant (1911). Then, to the outrage of many (unionists above all), he supported Irish home rule in 1912. Illness, however, shielded him from public view for long enough to offset recrimination, and in later years he reverted to a unionist position.

Meanwhile, having been chairman of the chamber of shipping of the UK in 1900, he greeted the twentieth century with ever-greater business plans and projects. He influenced the formation of the International Mercantile Marine Co. (1902), a major Anglo-American shipping cartel for the Atlantic trade. He became sole director of Harland and Wolff (1904) and was a member of several client boards, not least the White Star Line; his promotion of Harland and Wolff's 'floating hotels' (using Charles Parsons's turbine engine technology) reached its high point with the White Star liners *Olympic* (1910), *Titanic* (1911), and *Britannic* (1914). *Titanic*'s tragic maiden voyage in April 1912, endemic financial strains, skilled-labour shortages, and disputes with Belfast harbour commissioners over land lease, all failed to buckle the monumental self-confidence which sustained Pirrie through the world war of 1914–18. He immediately turned over Harland and Wolff's entire peacetime enterprise to war production, converting *Britannic* into a hospital ship (it was later sunk in the Mediterranean), and created an unprecedentedly large company workforce in Britain and Ireland, though one that was sometimes fraught with sectarian conflict. He produced warships and other military hardware, and was appointed comptroller general of merchant shipbuilding by the admiralty in March 1918, as the war entered its final phase.

Through the brief postwar shipping boom of 1918–20, Pirrie acted with as much vigour as political upheaval and the subsequent economic recession of 1920–22 would allow, including the further purchase of works in Scotland. He was created a viscount (1921) and a unionist senator in the new Northern Ireland parliament; his other offices included JP, comptroller of the household to the lord lieutenant of Ireland, pro-chancellor of QUB, and member of the committee on Irish finance and of the road board. A Belfast sports ground, Pirrie Park, was named after him. He had houses at 24 Belgrave Square, London; at Witley Park near Godalming, Surrey; and Harland's old home, Ormiston, at Strandtown, Belfast. Professionally, he was MICE and MIME; and he was a member of the Ulster Club (Belfast), Kildare Street Club (Dublin), and Reform Club (London). Less well known are the many family relationships through which he undoubtedly advanced his social and economic fortunes; among others, he was cousin to the Heyns who owned the Ulster Steamship Co., to the Carlisles of the Blue Star Line, to the Sinclairs of Liverpool, and even (more distantly) to the Harlands and the Wolffs.

Pirrie's extraordinary career, weighed down by titles, citations, and latterly by ill health (mainly prostate trouble) and company debt (largely to the Midland Bank), ended suddenly when he died 7 June 1924 while travelling by sea on company business to South America. As he had no children, his peerage died with him. Lady Pirrie, although appointed in that year as life president (until her death in 1935) of Harland and Wolff, had a difficult relationship with her husband's successor, Sir Owen Cosby Philipps (Lord Kylsant) (1863–1937), whose unenviable task it was to chair and continue the business of an industrial autocrat whom the journalist W. T. Stead and Sir Shane Leslie, saw as the greatest shipbuilder since Noah.

Patrick Long

Sources

Robert M. Young, *Belfast and the province of Ulster in the 20th century: contemporary biographies* (1909), 314; *Annual Reg., 1924*; *WWW*; Shane Leslie, *The Irish tangle for English readers* ([c.1930]), 153; Art Byrne and Sean McMahon, *Great northerners* (1991), 199–201; Flann Campbell, *The dissenting voice: Protestant democracy in Ulster from plantation to partition* (1991), 320, 385, 417; Robin Gardner and Dan van der Vat, *The riddle of the Titanic* (1995); *New History of Ireland*, vi (1996), 299; J. P. Lynch, *An unlikely success story: the Belfast shipbuilding industry, 1880–1935* (2001); John Bradbury, *Celebrated citizens of Belfast* (2002), 77–8; John Wilson Foster, *The age of Titanic: cross-currents of Anglo-American culture* (2002); Sir Bernard Crossland and John S. Moore, *The lives of great engineers of Ulster*, i (2003), 115–23

Sir John Ross

1853–1935

Sir John Ross, judge, politician, and last lord chancellor of Ireland, was born 11 December 1853 in Derry, eldest son among eight children of the Rev. Robert Ross (d. 1894), Presbyterian minister and moderator (1886–7) of the general assembly of the Presbyterian Church in Ireland, and Margaret Ross (neé Christie). He was educated at a small private school and a new model school in Derry before entering Foyle College; with the assistance of a small scholarship from Foyle, he progressed to TCD. Once there, he excelled academically and in other aspects of student life. He won a classical sizarship, graduated BA, and was president of the Philosophical Society in 1877. In 1878 he was auditor of the College Historical Society. He also captained the hockey club and founded the lawn tennis club, numbering Lord Glenavy and Edward Carson among his acquaintances. In 1879 he graduated with an LLB and was called to the Irish bar, but he retained lifelong links with Trinity and was elected president of the College Historical Society (1913) and Dublin University Athletics Union (1909). He also maintained his interest in the classics, becoming president of the Classical Society of Ireland (1914).

He refused invitations from conservatives to contest the constituencies of Londonderry county or Tyrone at the election of 1880 and instead built up a very successful practice on the north-west circuit and in Dublin, becoming a QC in 1891. He often represented landlords during agrarian disputes. In 1892 he accepted an offer to stand in the constituency of Antrim North, but changed his mind and stood as unionist candidate in Londonderry city. After an exciting campaign, he defeated Justin McCarthy by twenty-six votes. He does not appear to have harboured long-term political ambitions, regarding his time in parliament as an enjoyable—if costly—break from his legal career and an opportunity to accumulate anecdotes; he regarded himself as a raconteur. He lost the seat to E. F. Vesey Knox (1865–1921), the anti-Parnellite nationalist, by a margin of thirty-nine votes at the general election of 1895.

The financial strain of being an MP had been relieved when in 1894 his wife, Katharine (m. 1882; d. 1932), daughter of Colonel Deane Mann, inherited her father's estate at Dunmoyle, Co. Tyrone. They had another residence in Fitzwilliam Square, Dublin. In the wake of his election defeat he returned to the circuit, but in April 1896 was appointed land judge of the chancery division of the high court of justice in Ireland, following lobbying on his behalf by the 2nd duke of Abercorn and others. At the time, he was the only Presbyterian (perhaps a factor in his appointment) and the youngest candidate to achieve such a senior judicial post. In 1902 Ross became a privy counsellor and encouraged a reluctant George Wyndham to take the job of chief secretary for Ireland. He assisted in drafting the Irish Land Act of 1903 (the 'Wyndham act') and had sole responsibility for drafting the 1904 Land Act. His position gave him enormous responsibility in the implementation of these acts and in the attempts to control land agitation; among those he jailed for agrarian activities were the MPs P. A. McHugh and Laurence

Ginnell. As a judge he attained a formidable reputation for fairness and legal acumen.

In 1914 he suffered a duodenal haemorrhage during a ceremony to confer him with an honorary LLD at Trinity, but recovered. He was asked to sit on the commission that adjudicated on internments after the 1916 rising, but this invitation was withdrawn. He did, however, serve as chairman of the advisory appeal committee that monitored internments in Ireland (1920–21). In general he seems to have advised against excess in the state's response to the revolution. He became a baronet in 1919, but it was a surprise when in 1921 he was appointed lord chancellor of Ireland, a position he held until the abolition of the office in 1922.

He held a variety of other public positions, including commissioner of charitable endowments and bequests (1898), commissioner of national education (1905), chairman of the St John's ambulance service (1914), member of the joint war committee of the British Red Cross, and honorary bencher of the inn of court of Northern Ireland (1926). A competent golfer, he was captain of Royal Dublin Golf Club (1909). During retirement he concentrated on writing and produced two volumes of memoirs, *The years of my pilgrimage* (1924) and *Pilgrim scrip* (1927), and a collection of speeches and journalism, *Essays and addresses* (1930). He died of bronchial pneumonia 17 August 1935 at Dunmoyle. He had two daughters and one son, Ronald, 2nd baronet, who was MP for Londonderry (1929–51) at Westminster.

William Murphy

Sources

John Ross, *The years of my pilgrimage* (1924); John Ross, *Pilgrim scrip: more random reminiscences* (1927); *Belfast News Letter, Belfast Telegraph, Irish Times,* 19 August 1935; *Times,* 19, 20 August 1935; *WWW; DNB*; Walker; *DIH*; Lawrence W. McBride, *The greening of Dublin Castle* (1991), 74–5, 283, 294; Newmann; Ball, *Judges* (1993 ed.), 320–28; Michael Hopkinson (ed.), *The last days of Dublin Castle: the diaries of Mark Sturgis* (1999), 14, 161, 193; *ODNB*

George William Russell ('Æ')

1867–1935

George William Russell, journalist, writer, artist, and cooperator, was born 10 April 1867 in William Street, Lurgan, Co. Armagh, son of Thomas Elias Russell (d. 1900), a bookkeeper, and Marianne Russell (née Armstrong; d. 1897).

Early life and marriage

The youngest of three children, Russell attended the model school at Lurgan before the family moved to Dublin in 1878; they lived at 33 Emorville Avenue and then at 67 Grosvenor Square, Rathmines. Russell attended Dr Power's school in Harrington Street and night classes at the Metropolitan School of Art, before entering

Rathmines school, which he left in 1884. Russell met William Butler Yeats that year at the Metropolitan School, and the two became firm friends. Russell spent the next six years in various jobs, then in 1890 entered Pim's drapery store as a clerk.

Russell later reported trances and visions throughout his adolescence, experiences encouraged by his friendship with Charles Johnston, whom he met in Dublin in 1885. Johnston, son of the northern unionist MP William Johnston, founded the Dublin lodge of the Theosophical Society in 1886. Theosophy was the synthetic doctrine of Madame Blavatsky, a Russian émigré whose book *The secret doctrine* was an attempt to reconcile the various faith systems of the world in one spiritual revival. Russell, an other-worldly youth, was known to the Yeats sisters as 'the Strayed Angel'. He entered the Theosophical Society in 1890, moving into its lodge in Upper Ely Place, which was also the home of a Scottish engineer, Frederick Dick. Russell contributed occasional writings to mystical journals such as *Lucifer* and the *Irish Theosophist* which constitute the beginning of his literary career; they also brought about the genesis of the pen name by which he is best known, 'Æ' (or A.E.), derived from 'Aeon' (the first sound in the universe). Russell began to publish as Æ regularly after 1893. He continued to paint, and the murals with which he decorated the halls of the lodge survive in the National Gallery of Ireland.

Russell's occult self-expression found register in his first collection of poetry, *Homeward: songs by the way* (1894). There followed a period of rapture in the imagined presence of the ancient Irish gods: influenced by the two-volume *History of Ireland* of Standish O'Grady, Russell began to find a form for his occult beliefs in the magical character of Cú-Chulainn (Cuchulain). Russell's excitement rose in 1896 when, with many of his theosophist colleagues, he developed a belief, expounded in early pamphlets such as *Ideals in Ireland: priest or hero?* (1897), that a Celtic saviour was due to return to the world. Russell's prose retains some of the evangelical fire he had experienced in his Ulster childhood. (John Butler Yeats derided Russell to his son, calling him a 'Portadown boy'). His next poetry collection was *The earth breath* (1897).

Russell's life now took two important new turns. In 1897 he left Pim's for employment with the Irish Agricultural Organisation

Society (IAOS) of Horace Plunkett; and on 9 June 1898 he married his fellow spiritualist Violet North (1869–1932). Plunkett, a son of the 16th Baron Dunsany and a unionist MP, founded the IAOS in 1894 to develop cooperative societies in dairy farming and credit banking, on a model already successful elsewhere in Europe. His intentions were political in their practicality. By working together he felt that Irish people of all creeds and beliefs might develop a new understanding. Russell left for Co. Mayo in December 1897 to speak to local communities about the potential of the IAOS. He reported his work in the society's journal, the *Irish Homestead*, and found a subject for his social and spiritual conscience in the figure of the local moneylender, or 'gombeen man', whose influence on rural life Russell spent much of his career fighting. Plunkett recognised Russell's abilities and appointed him Dublin-based assistant secretary to the IAOS in June 1898.

At this time Russell and his wife lived at 28 Upper Mount Pleasant Avenue. Their first child, a son, born in March 1899, died soon after birth. Russell continued his literary activity, writing reviews and poetry, while travelling to rural areas to promote cooperation. His second son, Brian, was born in 1900, and the family moved to 25 Coulson Avenue, Rathgar; a daughter was born there in July 1901 but she died a month later. The Russells' third son, and last child, Diarmuid, was born in November 1902. Russell's public profile had begun to rise. His play *Deirdre* was produced alongside Yeats's *Kathleen ni Houlihan* in April 1902, Maud Gonne, Russell's neighbour in Coulson Avenue, playing Yeats's lead character. Russell never wrote another play for production, but he accepted the role, with Gonne and Douglas Hyde, of joint vice-president of the Irish National Theatre Society in February 1903; Yeats was president, an arrangement that lasted until 1904. Russell drew up a constitution for the society in August 1905.

Russell's house soon became known for his Sunday evening salon, which attracted the literati; George Moore became a close friend and James Joyce, who first attended the salon in August 1902, an associate. The stories that would be published as *Dubliners* first appeared in the *Irish Homestead*, thanks to Russell's influence (then as a collection, edited by H. F. Norman, in 1904), and Russell later appeared in *Ulysses* as the yogi-bogey box. Joyce's mockery of Russell should not obscure the importance of his support at a time before Joyce was widely known or respected. At this time two more collections by Russell were published: *The divine vision and other poems* (1904) and *The mask of Apollo and other stories* (1905).

The *Irish Homestead* and nationalism

Russell entered a crucial phase of his life when he assumed the editorship of the *Irish Homestead* in the summer of 1905. This weekly journal, published every Saturday, was designed to promote the ideal of cooperation between rural communities and agricultural societies and found its way all round the country. Russell's genius was to use this organ as a means to promote ideals of citizenship and self-help crucial to the formation of an independently functioning Ireland. The cooperative movement was publicly non-political, but its economic programme coincided with a cultural revival that reinvested Irish identity with a confidence nearly destroyed by the famine. Using his weekly columns as editor to attack dishonest traders and inefficient producers, Russell bridged the gap between material and intellectual reform. He translated the epic language of the heroic revival, of Cuchulain and the ancient heroes, into a practical discourse of reform, neatly sidestepping the established controversies of constitutional politics by appealing to agricultural improvement, so avoiding the dilemma of land reform. Week in week out, first from offices in Lincoln Place, then (starting in 1908) from an office at the top of 84 Merrion Square, the walls of which he had painted himself, Russell wrote on everything from butter preservation to poetry, encouraging his readers to exercise careful stewardship of their resources. His assistant editor was Susan Mitchell. In the wake of his appointment as editor of the *Irish Homestead* Russell and his family moved to 17 Rathgar Avenue in early 1906.

Russell met George Bernard Shaw at the NGI in late September 1908; both men afterwards claimed that they had held a long conversation with an unknown stranger. In November Russell published in *Sinn Féin* his polemical poem 'On behalf of some Irishmen not followers of tradition', an idealistic expression of separatist nationalism that suggests the radicalism submerged in Russell's weekly editorials. From 1908 the IAOS was under severe pressure from T. W. Russell, vice-president of the Department of Agriculture and Technical Instruction, and nationalist MPs led by John Dillon, partly because of the cooperative movement's success in modifying relations between small traders and farmers. Owing to Plunkett's aristocratic background, claims persisted that the IAOS was a covertly anti-national project, that an amelioration of rural conditions cloaked the basic structural inequalities of land ownership. Advanced nationalists nevertheless recognised Russell's potential. In 1911 he wrote a series of essays entitled 'The problem of rural life' for the *Irish Review*, a journal edited by Padraic Colum and supported by a coterie that included Patrick Pearse, Thomas MacDonagh, and Joseph Mary Plunkett. Russell continued with his advocacy for mutual aid in *Co-operation and nationality: a guide for rural reformers from this to the next generation* (1912). Uneven and energetic, *Co-operation and nationality*, which the *Irish Review* compared to an indistinct impressionist painting, is part Fabian social report, part polemic, and part mystic rapture.

Russell's increasing social militancy found focus in 1913 in the lockout by William Martin Murphy of tram workers trying to organise as part of the ITGWU. James Larkin, the workers' leader, was imprisoned, and Russell shared a platform with James Connolly, who Russell felt was 'a really intellectual leader', at a demonstration at the Royal Albert Hall in London on 1 November. Larkin was released twelve days later. Russell's speech, which was highly critical of state and church authorities, particularly the police and William Walsh, archbishop of Dublin, caused fury in the constitutional nationalist press, the *Freeman's Journal* accusing him of hiding anti-Irish sympathies in his socialism. *Sinn Féin* and *Irish Freedom* remained sympathetic. Russell was saved and his position on the *Irish Homestead* preserved by Plunkett's silence during the controversy. There followed an exchange of views in print between Russell and Connolly, each reading and responding to the other's theories of social and political organisation through the columns of the *Irish Homestead* and Connolly's books on labour in Ireland. Each offered the other a constituency difficult to reach—in Russell's case the urban worker, in Connolly's the farm labourer and smallholder.

For all this flirtation with republicanism, Russell, like Yeats, was surprised by the outbreak of the Easter rising; he travelled to the home of Edward MacLysaght in Co. Clare on Good Friday and did not arrive back in Dublin until the following Wednesday, 26 April 1916. His first report of events was published on 13 May in the *Irish Homestead*, in which he argued that the rising was the logical outcome of the oppression of Dublin's working class, and perhaps portended a larger change to come. He was distraught at Connolly's execution. Connolly himself asked his wife to contact Russell to arrange for his family's emigration to America; having raised £101, Russell secured permission from General John Maxwell for them to leave, but the licence was revoked when the British authorities awoke to the propaganda use to which the Connollys' departure might be put. Russell was enraged.

Some of this anger is manifest in Russell's *The national being* published in September 1916. Composed from March 1914, the text is Russell's prediction of apocalypse and recovery, Ireland surviving the displacements of world war and national convulsion by a commitment to the spiritual economy of cooperation. Russell found practical focus for his thinking in the last major attempt to reconfigure constitutional relations between Britain and Ireland, the Irish Convention, held at Regent House, TCD, from 25 July 1917 to 5 April 1918. With the election of Éamon de Valera for Sinn Féin to the constituency of East Clare in June 1917, there was pressure for a new settlement to replace an increasingly outmoded Irish Home Rule Act, which had been languishing on the statute books since 1914. Russell secured his government nomination to the Irish Convention as a representative of advanced nationalism by means of a media campaign that culminated in the publication of his 'Thoughts on Irish settlement' in the London *Times* of 31 May 1917; this was followed by a declaration of support for Russell's ideas from a group that included Alice Stopford Green, Douglas Hyde, and, most surprisingly, Russell's former adversary William Walsh. Russell took his seat at the first meeting of the convention on 25 July 1917, accompanied by MacLysaght, who kept Sinn Féin informed of the convention's progress through the intermediary of Eoin MacNeill. Russell remained a member until 1 February 1918. The experience disheartened him, especially the encounter with the intransigence of Ulster unionism, which was at odds with his own vision of a single island nation. In his last speech to the delegates Russell warned of a revolution to come of the kind that had happened in Russia.

Russell turned his energies back to the *Irish Homestead* and the writing of *The candle of vision* (1918). An obscure book even by Russell's standards, *The candle of vision* surprised its author by quickly going into a third edition. A precursor to Yeats's *A vision* (1925), Russell's work argues for art, from Shakespeare to Shelley, as a means by which to divine the future, the medium through which to see the trembling behind the veil. With the ending of the first world war in November 1918, a speech that Russell had written for the first anniversary of the Easter rising but never delivered was published in the *Voice of Labour*, a journal edited by Cathal O'Shannon. A former contributor to Connolly's *Worker's Republic*, O'Shannon saw the cooperatives as a useful tool in the creation of a socialist state, as was proved at Ballina, Co. Mayo, in 1919, when a Dublin cooperative society opened a store in the town to supply workers locked out by local employers. As the war of independence began, O'Shannon went on the run to avoid arrest by the RIC.

Russell, meanwhile, was identified publicly with the cause of revolutionary nationalism by Sir Hamar Greenwood, chief secretary for Ireland, in a speech to the British house of commons in 1920. Official censure soon became physical threat as cooperative societies in disturbed areas were attacked by British forces in retaliation for IRA attacks. Russell condemned the attacks in the *Irish Homestead*, but soon realised that the British media had to be involved if his message was to have any impact. The editor of the London *Times*, Wickham Steed, disliked the policy of reprisals. Accordingly, Russell published a letter in *The Times* on 23 August 1920 to protest against the destruction of creameries at Castleiney, Loughmore, and Killea. The consequences of denying Ireland justice were thrown into clear relief in the weeks following. As Terence MacSwiney, lord mayor of Cork, died slowly on hunger strike in prison, Russell again wrote to *The Times*, publishing his poem 'Brixton prison: August 31, 1920' on 2 September 1920. MacSwiney read the sonnet in his cell before he died on 25 October, which is shocking considering Russell's final direction: 'Farewell, Lightbringer, fly to thy heaven again.'

The violence finally resulted in the Anglo–Irish treaty that passed the dáil on 7 January 1922. Russell had spent much of 1921 defending the cooperative movement in the *Irish Homestead*, and examining, in pamphlets such as *Ireland and the empire at the court of conscience* and *The inner and the outer island*, what practical and psychological adjustments would be needed to make independence work. Russell excelled in this pragmatism, having the foresight to widen the public debate beyond the rights and wrongs of the independence struggle in an attempt to focus minds on the means by which to secure finance, employment, and security. This determination led to Russell's support for the Free State government during the civil war, by which he signalled his distance from the radical elements whose support he had courted in previous years. (Mary MacSwiney, sister of the dead lord mayor, afterwards railed against Russell for deserting the cause.) Russell tried to resolve his position in *The interpreters* (1922), a prose work which is nearly unreadable as fiction. As a commentary on his own sympathies after independence it has some interest: its central character, Heyt, is a capitalist, educated to a form of sympathy for others during his conversation with the other characters, an architect, an anarchist, a labour leader, and a poet.

The *Irish Statesman*

The interpreters sets the frame of reference for Russell's late career, when his project became the amelioration of present conditions rather than changing them entirely. Plunkett, his sponsor, encouraged this transition, in the belief that the new Ireland needed new influence. Accordingly, Plunkett raised funds in Ireland and the United States to fold the *Irish Homestead* into the *Irish Statesman* under Russell's editorship; the first issue appeared on 15 September 1923. Russell's assistant editors were Susan Mitchell and James Good, who had worked previously for the *Freeman's Journal*. Each issue of the new journal comprised a leading article, pages of 'Notes and comments' on contemporary events, original writing from emerging and established authors, book and theatre reviews, letters, and advertisements. As subscriber lists show, the journal was read throughout Ireland, in Britain, and in America.

Culture had played a fundamental part in the conception and realisation of the Irish Free State. In this context, the *Irish Statesman* acted as an international bulletin with semi-official status, and Russell, like Yeats, was recognised internationally as an authoritative voice. The *Irish Statesman*'s correspondence columns contained plenty of criticism of this perception, including mockery by Maud Gonne of Russell's anti-republican remarks. The fact remained that Russell's journal, at this particular moment of national transition, exerted an influence that no cultural journal has matched since. Ironically the situations where this influence became most visible were those in which Russell's power began to slip. The Free State government began to legislate for Ireland's cultural difference from its neighbour, with censorship of films, bans on contraception and divorce, and then legislation to protect against what was termed 'evil literature'. These repressions were partly motivated by the growing influence on the state of religiously affiliated bodies. Russell revolted at this alliance, defending Irish writers' right (within reason) to represent their perception of place and people according to their choice. Russell was never against censorship *per se*, but he felt that the mechanism of censorship as proposed by the government party would lead to manipulation and ill feeling, which it did. In the early skirmishes Russell published Yeats's opinions, interviews with key ministers under the title 'As others see us' in a register of international scrutiny, and scathing editorials, sharpened by decades of practice in support of cooperation, maintaining that censorship, if it had to be passed at all, must operate under the authority of writers alone. His campaign had some success, as elements of the Censorship Act were changed in ways responsive to his arguments.

This episode used much of his energy, and was followed in quick succession by the successful defence of a libel case against the *Irish Statesman* for one of its reviews, which nevertheless cost the journal a crippling £2,500 by November 1928. Russell wondered at this time if he might leave Ireland to teach in an American university; he had received an honorary doctorate of letters from Yale in June 1927, and TCD had honoured him with the same degree in June 1929. The *Irish Statesman* struggled on financially, saved by public subscriptions until the Wall Street crash caused its key donors to withdraw their support. This signalled the end for a journal that had been crucial to the construction of Ireland's self-imagination after the civil war. This construction was, at times, partisan in favour of the ruling party and unfairly dismissive of a temporarily defeated republicanism. Russell made connections with some of the generation of writers who had fought and lost in the civil war, notably Frank O'Connor and Sean O'Faolain, whose later joint project, *The Bell*, bore the imprint of their *Irish Statesman* experience.

Russell's final editorial in the *Irish Statesman* summarised his intentions for the journal as an open space of debate over Ireland's present reality and possible future. There is no doubt that his view of the present was eccentric, and at times reactionary, but there was no other public intellectual figure in the first decade of independence who had such broad influence. That influence worked, more often than not, for the common good, advocating a mutually supportive society, civic commitment, and—still—cooperative economics, all designed to give each citizen a stake in the community. In the eight years of the *Irish Statesman*'s publication, Russell had published articles on the river Shannon electrification scheme, on James Joyce's experimental *Work in progress*, on banking, on Jack Yeats's painting, on republicanism, on Italian fascism, on farming. If the variety of his interests was a weakness when it came to his art, it was the current of his journalism, his hyperactive imagination engaging his audience in a world beyond the Free State's narrowing borders.

Last years

On the demise of the *Irish Statesman*, Russell suffered further shocks. His son, Diarmuid, who had worked at the journal for three years in the late 1920s, emigrated to America in May 1929. Violet Russell was diagnosed as suffering from cancer, and Russell was forced to give an American lecture tour to raise money for her treatment. Before he left on 13 September 1930, Horace Plunkett, R. A. Anderson, and Father Thomas Finlay organised a reception at Plunkett House, the cooperative headquarters, and presented Russell with a gift of £800. The lecture tour, which moved from east coast to west, then south and north, lasted eight months. Returning through London, Russell met George Moore for the first time since 1916; he spent a brief time in Dublin, and then moved on to Sheep Haven in Donegal, a favourite retreat since 1904. Back in Dublin his wife's illness grew worse, a strain that emerges in the account by Patrick Kavanagh in *The green fool* (1938) of meeting a distracted Russell about this time. Violet Russell died on 3 February 1932. *Song and its fountains* was published two weeks later. This was a brief achievement before bitterness crept into Russell's public writings, prompted partly by attacks made on Yeats's Irish Academy of Letters, for which Russell wrote the rules and worked as honorary secretary. His association with Yeats remained emotionally fraught. Russell's book *The avatars* (1933) was originally dedicated to Yeats, 'my oldest friend and enemy', but that line was deleted before publication.

Russell now began preparation to leave Ireland, selling his house in July 1933, resigning from the academy in July, and arriving in London in August, where he first lived in lodgings at 41 Sussex Gardens. Unsettled, he left for America in December 1934, sailing from Southampton, to lecture on cooperative societies and rural life, subjects close to Franklin Roosevelt's hopes for the New Deal. Russell met M. L. Wilson, under-secretary of agriculture, before meeting the president himself on 5 January 1935. Russell received an invitation to speak to native American communities in Arizona and New Mexico, but he felt ill and tired, and his stomach was giving him such pain as to cause him to return to London in March. In new lodgings at 14 Tavistock Place, London, Russell was diagnosed with colitis. He travelled to Havenhurst, a Bournemouth nursing home, on 21 June, in the company of two friends, Charles Weekes and Hector Munro. He was wretchedly ill, and the diagnosis of colitis was changed to cancer in early July. After an abdominal operation at another nursing home, Stagsden, Russell died 17 July 1935, having spent his last evening with Constantine Curran, Oliver St John Gogarty, and Pamela Travers, later famous as the author of *Mary Poppins*. Seán O'Sullivan arrived the morning after to sketch his face.

Russell's body was returned to Ireland on 19 July, resting at Plunkett House as people paid their respects before the burial on the 20th at Mount Jerome cemetery; the funeral procession was more than a mile long, and the mourners included de Valera, W. T. Cosgrave, Yeats, and Frank O'Connor, who gave the oration. 'He might', O'Connor said, 'if he had devoted himself to one art only, have been amongst the very greatest figures in the world; but if he had done so, he would not have been Æ, and Ireland, and we, would have been poorer for that' (*Irish Times*, 22 July 1935). Russell was, for four decades and more, a radical intellectual engaged with the cultural, economic, social and political changes that transformed twentieth-century Ireland. A connection point between his readers and the world, Russell was a poet, painter, prose writer, and journalist, an administrator, visionary, and polemicist, whose commitment to the ideal reality of Irish independence was the signature of all his thinking.

Nicholas Allen

Sources

L. P. Byrne, *Twenty-one years of the Irish Agricultural Wholesale Society, 1897–1918* (1919); William Clyde, *Æ* (1935); John Eglinton, *A memoir of Æ: George William Russell* (1937); Patrick Kavanagh, *The green fool* (1938); C. Coates, *Some less-known chapters in the life of Æ (George Russell): being the substance of a lecture delivered at Belfast, November, 1936* (1939); H. Wallace, 'Æ: a prophet out of an ancient age', *Colby Quarterly*, iv, no. 2 (May 1955), 28–31; Alan Denson (ed.), *Letters from Æ* (1961); Darrell Figgis, *Æ (George W. Russell): a study of a man and a nation* (1970); Henry Summerfield, *That myriad-minded man: a biography of George William Russell 'Æ', 1867–1935* (1975); Patrick Bolger, *The Irish co-operative movement: its history and development* (1977); R. B. Davis, *George William Russell (Æ)* (1977); Peter Kuch, *Yeats and 'Æ': the antagonism that unites dear friends* (1986); Trevor West, *Horace Plunkett: co-operation and politics, an Irish biography* (1986); Nicholas Allen, *George Russell (Æ) and the new Ireland, 1905–30* (2003)

Sir Thomas Wallace Russell

1841–1920

Sir Thomas Wallace Russell, radical Ulster politician, was born 28 February 1841 in Cupar, Fife, Scotland, son of David Russell, stonemason, and Isabella Russell (née Wallace). Educated at the Madras Academy, Cupar, Russell settled in Ulster in 1860, aged 19, and was employed by James Brown of Donaghmore, Co. Tyrone, a soap and candle manufacturer.

Highly intelligent and possessed of enormous energy, Russell, a Presbyterian, became involved in the temperance movement as agent, organiser, and lobbyist. It was in these capacities (1863–85) that he perfected both his skills as a public speaker and knowledge of the parliamentary system. A natural liberal, Russell first sought entry to parliament, unsuccessfully, at Preston in 1885, becoming a liberal unionist after Gladstone's conversion to home rule in 1886. His selection as the unionist candidate to contest the Tyrone South seat at the general election of that year, against the formidable nationalist leader William O'Brien, was a reflection of his widely acknowledged abilities. Successful in Tyrone South, Russell, together with the less talented Thomas Lea in Londonderry South, represented the Ulster liberal unionist interest at Westminster.

For Russell it was a pivotal moment, with the path to career advancement clearly open to one with his political talents. Political ambition, however, was complicated by a combination of principle and personal idiosyncrasies. As to the latter, Timothy Healy described Russell thus: 'Devoid of the geniality and humour of his [Scots] race, he sported a bilious face and splenetic manners' (Healy, i, 261). Excitable, arrogant, and easily offended, and with an almost monomaniacal obsession with the land question, Russell, the grandson of an evicted crofter, was a loose cannon on the unionist deck, pursuing his own independent political course. Antagonising the landlord interest through constant agitation for agrarian reform, Russell was also an untypical Ulster unionist. Devoid of the crude anti-Catholic bigotry that permeated large sections of that community, he often supported nationalists and Catholics on specific issues when he thought their cause was just. At the same time, his highly effective campaigning for the unionist cause in Britain meant his services could not easily be dispensed with. In fact, Russell had made himself indispensable to Joseph Chamberlain as an authority on the Ulster problem, and exercised a significant influence on the agrarian legislation introduced for Ireland in the late nineteenth century.

Appointed under-secretary of the local government board (1895) by a unionist government anxious to silence him, Russell extracted agrarian commitments as the price of acceptance. However, he found the constraints of office unbearable, aggravated by suspicions that the landlord interest was exploiting his absence from the backbenches to cheat the tenant farmers of their rights. Accordingly, shortly after the 1900 general election Russell engineered his sacking from office and, in a context where the home rule issue seemed insignificant, embarked on a campaign in Ulster for the compulsory purchase of landed estates. Russell's initiative went together with increased cooperation with nationalist MPs on Irish issues in general. Most controversially, he was known to support the claim for a Catholic university in Ireland, and had only secured his reelection for Tyrone South in 1900 by promising his constituents that he would not raise the subject, and, in the event of a bill to effect such a university being brought forward, he would submit himself again to the constituency before voting on it. With Russell increasingly close to nationalists, the success of 'Russellite' candidates in by-elections in Down East (1902) and Fermanagh North (1903) was a worryingly divisive development for unionist leaders, though many Ulster unionist MPs in fact supported the compulsory purchase demand.

Russell's success in mobilising a significant section of tenant farmer opinion against the existing Ulster unionist hierarchy, however, was a function of the political space created by the absence of the home rule threat. When home rule was once again given currency by the devolution crisis of 1904–5, that political space narrowed sharply. Of nine Russellite candidates at the 1906 general election, only one apart from Russell himself was successful, while the recent by-election gains were lost.

Compulsory purchase was not conceded, but Russellism, nevertheless, had an influence both on the Wyndham act (1903), which effectively settled the land question, and on the setting up of the Ulster Unionist Council (1905), motivated in part by the need to prevent the emergence of factions likely to disrupt unionist unity. This period, moreover, was one of political transition for Russell. With the land question on its way to ultimate resolution and constitutional nationalism now divested of its 'revolutionary' aspects, and reunited under the leadership of the pro-imperial John Redmond, the reasons for Russell's opposition to home rule in the 1880s were gone. Accordingly, he accepted the post of vice-president of the Department of Agricultural and Technical Instruction for Ireland (1907–18) from the liberal administration of Henry Campbell-Bannerman, and became an Irish privy councillor in 1908. Losing Tyrone South at the general election of January 1910, he succeeded as liberal candidate for Tyrone North (1911–18). Awarded a baronetcy in 1917, Russell lost his only son in the Great War and died on 2 May 1920, aware that the home rule solution to the Irish question he preferred was increasingly irrelevant. A prolific author on subjects of the day, from the land issue to the Irish question in general, his most significant work was *Ireland and the empire: a review 1800–1900* (1901), part review of Anglo–Irish relations and part personal political memoir.

Russell's political career points up clearly his significant contribution to the resolution of the Irish land question; and yet the impression is also left of great political talent given rather too narrow a focus. Certainly his character flaws were a serious impediment to political advancement, but perhaps the key to his career and the limits of his achievement lie in his political apprenticeship as a temperance lobbyist. Russell began and remained an interest-group enthusiast.

He married (1865) Harriet, daughter of Thomas Agnew of Dungannon, a union that lasted twenty-nine years until her death in 1894. Russell married secondly (1896) Martha, daughter of Lieutenant-colonel Keown, 15th Hussars.

James Loughlin

Sources

T. M. Healy, *Letters and leaders of my day* (2 vols, 1928); *WWW*; Elizabeth Malcolm, *'Ireland sober, Ireland free': drink and temperance in nineteenth-century Ireland* (1986), 171–7; Alvin Jackson, 'Irish unionism and the Russellite threat 1894–1906', *Irish Historical Studies*, xxv (1986–7), 376–404; James Loughlin, 'T. W. Russell, the tenant-farmer interest, and progressive unionism in Ulster, 1886–1900', *Éire–Ireland*, xxv, no. 1 (1990), 44–63.

Edward James Saunderson

1837–1906

Edward James Saunderson, politician, was born 1 October 1837 at Castle Saunderson, Co. Cavan, the fourth of five sons (there were also two daughters) of Alexander Saunderson (d. 1857), landlord, and his wife, Sarah Juliana (née Maxwell; d. 1870), eldest daughter of the Rev. Henry Maxwell, 6th Baron Farnham. The Saundersons were a family of Scots descent who had settled in Tyrone in the reign of James I and acquired estates in counties Cavan and Monaghan during the Cromwellian and Williamite confiscations. The family intermittently represented Cavan in the Irish and Westminster parliaments from 1692; Saunderson's grandfather, Francis, opposed the act of union, and the family boasted that he had declined the offer of a peerage to vote for it. Saunderson's eldest brother died young;

the next two brothers were on bad terms with their dominant mother, who appears to have been responsible for the choice of her favourite son, Edward, as principal heir. He inherited 12,000 acres (mostly in Cavan, with just over 100 acres in Fermanagh); the rent roll was about £6,000 p.a. (The third son was left some Welsh property and the fifth son received a small estate in Cavan.)

Saunderson grew up at Nice, where his father settled in 1846 for health and financial reasons (the latter relating to non-payment of rent during the famine). He was educated privately by tutors, two of whom were Jesuits—one was dismissed for attempting to proselytise his pupils. Saunderson developed an intense evangelical Anglican faith, fervently expressed in letters to his mother and wife; he liked to preach in the estate chapel, and three of his sermons were published posthumously. After Alexander Saunderson's death the Castle Saunderson estate was run by trustees until Edward reached the age of twenty-five; he spent the intervening years in southern England, developing his lifelong passion for yachting. He also had a talent for sketching, and illustrated his correspondence with caricatures.

On his return to Cavan, Saunderson took out a captain's commission in the Cavan militia, of which his father had been colonel; he was promoted major in 1875, lieutenant-colonel in 1886, and full colonel in December 1891, and retired as commander of the corps in 1893. Hence he was generally referred to by contemporaries as 'Colonel Saunderson'. He lacked administrative skills and did not exercise close supervision over the running of the estate, but was deeply attached to the demesne and the community of neighbouring landlords—he went yachting with the Ernes of Crom castle and his cousins the Maxwells of Farnham, who became his closest political allies. He formed part of a network of large landlord families stretching across south Ulster, linked by intermarriage and evangelical activism, which provided the leadership of Irish conservatism for much of the nineteenth century. The estate was notably solvent and Saunderson a fairly generous landlord: he employed many Catholics and in 1879 the *Freeman's Journal* praised him for allowing tenants a 25 per cent rent rebate; but relations grew more tense in the later stages of his life.

Saunderson was elected liberal MP for Co. Cavan in 1865 and re-elected in 1868 (unopposed on both occasions). He was a largely silent member who made little impact. In general he can at this stage of his career be described as a conservative but not utterly intransigent Palmerstonian whig, who supported the 1870 Land Act as well as coercive legislation and displayed some sympathy for Adullamite opposition to parliamentary reform. His local popularity was considerably diminished when he voted against the disestablishment of the Church of Ireland (1869), trenchantly expressed his disbelief in transubstantiation during debates in the Church of Ireland synod (1873), and accused Bishop Thomas Nulty of conniving at murder because of the existence of Ribbonism in his Meath diocese (1871). In the 1874 general election Saunderson was defeated by two home rulers, Joseph Biggar and Charles Joseph Fay (1842–95), and thereafter home rulers monopolised the Cavan representation.

Saunderson retreated into private life for a time, but returned to politics in the early 1880s as the result of the land war. In 1882 he publicly announced his adherence to the Orange Order (which he had previously ridiculed as an organisation of people who enjoyed frightening their neighbours with big drums). He became a leading member of a group of Ulster landlords, whose figurehead was Lord Rossmore, who used the Orange Order to mount a loyalist counter-mobilisation against the National League; he was present at the Rosslea incident of December 1883, which resulted in Rossmore's dismissal from the magistracy for leading Orange demonstrators dangerously close to a nationalist meeting. In 1884 (with help from E. C. Houston, Richard Bagwell, and others) Saunderson published a pamphlet, *The two Irelands: loyalty versus treason*, aimed at presenting a loyalist view of recent events and portraying the National League as inherently criminal and seditious, through quotations from members' speeches. Although recognised as a prominent Orangeman, he preferred to take a secondary role at major demonstrations. His power was limited: he was not able to impose candidates on constituencies, and failed to gain the mid-Antrim conservative nomination against a well-entrenched sitting MP. He also encountered some residual suspicion because of his former liberalism (he occasionally described himself as a liberal unionist after 1886, and did not resign from the whig Brooks's Club until 1890 though he had joined the conservative Carlton in 1886).

The Ulster conservative mobilisation of the mid-1880s was directed not only against the nationalist threat but also against the perceived indifference of the British political establishment to Irish concerns. Saunderson frequently threatened that loyalists would undertake armed resistance if they were abandoned to their enemies; it is disputed how seriously these threats—which were repeated during the debates over the two home rule bills—should be treated. In 1885 Saunderson succeeded in obtaining the conservative nomination for North Armagh by harnessing Orange populist local support against the officially favoured contender, John Monroe.

After his return to parliament at the 1885 general election, Saunderson emerged as leader of a group of Irish unionist MPs who emphasised their autonomy in the face of what they saw as temporising tactics by the conservative leadership. He now emerged as a significant though limited parliamentary personality, making vehement presentations of the Irish loyalist case to public meetings in Britain as well as in parliament (though he took little interest in the hard labour of scrutinising legislation in committee). Saunderson liked to contrast himself with the inarticulate Ulster tory MPs he had encountered during his earlier time in parliament, and privately claimed that God had raised him up to defend the righteous cause. Initially aligned with Lord Randolph Churchill, he moved closer to Salisbury as the struggle over Gladstonian home rule developed. (In 1912 Michael McCarthy claimed that Saunderson and Churchill had been involved in a confrontation when Churchill privately threatened to embrace home rule, but this is unsupported by Saunderson's contemporary correspondence and should not be given credence.) Saunderson presented himself as a party leader and therefore (nominally at least) the equal of Salisbury or Arthur Balfour, and proved sufficiently useful for his allies to humour him: for example, they made him a British privy councillor in 1899 after he had turned down a place on the Irish privy council as insufficiently grand. His British role is symbolised by his appointment as Orange grand master of Scotland (1886–95), though to some extent this reflected not so much Saunderson's qualities as the unwillingness of Scottish grandees to identify with a plebeian organisation—Saunderson himself was dissatisfied with some aspects of Scottish Orangeism.

Although some accounts present his relations with Irish nationalist MPs as mildly affectionate, a real bitterness underlay his description of them as 'eighty-six arguments against home rule', and his comment that under an Irish parliament loyalists would indeed rise to 'the highest positions', but with a rope round their necks. Saunderson was quite prepared to act as a stage Irishman in order to reinforce his audiences' perception that the Irish as a whole were unfit for self-government, and to make provocative remarks to nationalist MPs during commons debates in the hope that their reaction would discredit their claims to responsible citizenship.

After the home rule threat receded with unionist victory at the 1895 general election, Saunderson's leadership became increasingly nominal as he reverted from spokesman of a pan-unionist coalition to landlord representative, and his political activities centred on Westminster rather than Ulster. He regarded the conciliatory policies pursued by 'constructive unionism' as unfair to loyalists in general and landlords in particular. His desire to show that landlord interests could not be neglected with impunity made him one of the few Ulster unionists to ally with nationalist MPs in campaigning against the alleged over-taxation of Ireland after the release in 1896 of the Childers report on financial relations with Britain. From 1898 Saunderson was the only Ulster unionist MP who openly opposed compulsory land purchase. He was able to retain his seat, despite challenges from liberal tenant-farmer activists, because of urban support in Lurgan and Portadown: he cultivated the handloom weavers, whose livelihood was under threat, and backed industrial protectionism long before Chamberlain's declaration in favour of tariff reform. However, the absence of an immediate nationalist threat had a disruptive effect on the cross-class unionist coalition, and his attitude contributed to the tenant-farmer revolt led by T. W. Russell, which severely disrupted Ulster unionism at the beginning of the twentieth century.

For populists such as T. H. Sloan, Saunderson came to symbolise an effete and temporising official unionism. Sloan's secession from the Orange Order was precipitated by a confrontation with Saunderson in his role as county grand master of the Belfast Orange Order (1901–3) at the Belfast celebration on 12 July 1901, when Sloan wrongly accused Saunderson of failing to support the inspection of Irish convent laundries. In truth, Saunderson's anti-sacerdotalism made him sympathetic to such causes; he was on friendly terms with the anti-Catholic polemicist Michael McCarthy and lent some support to McCarthy's unsuccessful attempt to win the unionist nomination for the marginal seat of St Stephen's Green in 1904.

Saunderson was a strong man but increasingly suffered some degree of physical frailty. In later years his health declined; he experienced repeated heart attacks and in 1905 underwent a major lung operation without anaesthetic. His convalescence led him to avoid attending the inaugural meeting of the Ulster Unionist Council, and his function as first chairman of that body was largely nominal. He died at Castle Saunderson on 21 October 1906 from pneumonia contracted while yachting on Lough Erne. On 29 May 1910 a statue was unveiled at Portadown, symbolising his famous statement that 'home rule may pass through parliament, but it will never pass the bridge at Portadown'; it became a local Orange icon and a tradition grew up of decorating it with a sash every 12 July.

Despite this local reputation Saunderson was overshadowed in unionist memory by Edward Carson and James Craig, just as the landed south Ulster unionism he represented, while maintaining some political representatives, was eclipsed by a more professional movement centred on the business classes of east Ulster. His standing was not enhanced by the official biography by Reginald Lucas, which emphasised the humorous and flamboyant elements in his personality; in a later account of his life, Alvin Jackson, while emphasising his limitations, portrayed a more capable figure (at least in the early stages of the home rule conflict), haunted by a persistent sense of embattlement and probable defeat.

On 22 June 1865 Saunderson married Helena de Moleyns (d. 1926), daughter of Thomas, 3rd Baron Ventry; they had four sons and one daughter. Their eldest son, Somerset, briefly achieved political prominence in 1916, when he led an abortive attempt to rouse Cavan and Monaghan unionist opposition to Carson's acceptance of a proposed compromise based on six-county partition; he vacated the Castle Saunderson demesne because of IRA threats in 1920 and died in England in 1927. A younger son, Edward, became an Irish local government board inspector and exercised significant official influence for a short time in 1918–20 as private secretary to the lord lieutenant and as a supporter of hardline policy. A third son, Armar, contested the marginal East Tyrone seat against Thomas Kettle in January 1910. Kettle mocked his opponent's reliance on pedigree: 'he has said so often that he is the son of Colonel Saunderson that I, for one, am inclined to believe him'. Saunderson's papers are in PRONI (Saunderson T/2996 and MIC/281).

Patrick Maume

Sources

Reginald Lucas, *Colonel Saunderson MP: a memoir* (1908); M. J. F. McCarthy, *The nonconformist treason* (1912); Elaine McFarland, *Protestants first! Orangeism in nineteenth-century Scotland* (1990); Alvin Jackson, *Colonel Edward Saunderson: land and loyalty in Victorian Ireland* (1995); *ODNB*

Thomas Sinclair

1838–1914

Thomas Sinclair, merchant and politician, was born 23 September 1838 in Belfast, son of Thomas Sinclair (1811–67), merchant and shipowner, and his wife Sarah (1800–49), daughter of William Archer of Hillsborough, Co. Down. Thomas Sinclair the elder was born and educated in Belfast. With his brother John Sinclair (1808–56), he set up a provisions and general merchant store at 5–11, Tomb Street, Belfast. John married Eliza Pirrie of a prominent ship-building family, and this may have contributed to both brothers becoming shipowners. Thomas was president of the Belfast chamber of commerce and was appointed chairman of the Belfast harbour commissioners in May 1863. He died in office at the house of his brother-in-law, Samuel Gibson, in London on 2 January 1867;

his remains were shipped to Belfast, where he was buried in the New Burial Ground. He was predeceased by his brother, his wife, and a son and daughter. Only Thomas the younger survived him, inheriting some £35,000.

The younger Thomas was educated at the Royal Belfast Academical Institution and QCB, graduating BA (1856) with a gold medal for mathematics, and MA (1859) with gold medals in logic, political economy, and English literature. On his father's death he took over the family general provisions business and further increased its prosperity by amalgamating with Kingan and Co, a large provisions concern with extensive American branches, owned by Samuel Kingan of north Co. Down, who was married to Thomas's cousin, Sarah, daughter of John Sinclair. Kingan's brother, John, established the Kingan Mission to the Deaf and Dumb in Belfast, of which Thomas Sinclair was a supporter.

Sinclair refused requests to stand for parliament, but as a wealthy and prominent Belfast citizen who was DL, JP, president of the Ulster chamber of commerce (1876, 1902), and privy councillor (1896), he played a highly influential role in the affairs of the province. Originally a supporter of W. E. Gladstone, he joined the liberal party in 1868 and supported the 1870 and 1881 land acts. The 1886 home rule bill provoked him to his first act of defiance: he convened a large meeting of liberals in the Ulster Hall on 30 April of that year and passed a resolution condemning the bill. He then formed the Ulster Liberal Unionist Association and, in his capacity as its chairman, organised the Ulster Convention, held in Belfast on 17 June 1892, which brought together 11,879 Ulster unionists of every creed, class, and party in the first mass protest against home rule. Nine months later he was appointed to the executive committee of the new unionist clubs, hastily founded throughout the province to protect the union. However, the liberal defeat of 1895 lessened the threat of home rule, the unionist clubs were temporarily suspended, and Sinclair returned to his liberal reformist activities. From 1895 he was a leading Ulster member of the recess committee originated by Horace Plunkett, and was a steady support to Plunkett, backing him in his choice in 1899 of the nationalist T. P. Gill as secretary of the Irish Agricultural Organisation Society, despite the strong protest of conservative unionists.

However, the 1904 devolution crisis saw Sinclair joining forces with those same unionists. He was one of thirty members of the standing committee of the Ulster Unionist Council on its formation in December 1904, and devoted the rest of his life to defending the union. In January 1911 he proposed that the suspended unionist clubs should reorganise, extend their membership, and take on new responsibilities. This translated to the clubs taking up arms: by April over eighty were drilling and had formed the basis for the UVF. A succinct and cogent writer, Sinclair was appointed on 25 September 1911 to a commission of five to frame a constitution for a provisional government of Ulster. The following year his was among the clearest and best argued of the contributions to the unionist party's collection of essays, *Against home rule* (1912). Identifying Ulster as the six counties, he advanced the two-nation theory in refutation of nationalist claims and warned that Ulster would certainly resist until the end. Later that year he was given the crucial task of drafting the text of the Solemn League and Covenant, which pledged signatories to defeat home rule and refuse to recognise the authority of an Irish parliament. This was signed by 471,414 people in the Belfast city hall on 28 September 1912. Sinclair did not live to see the outcome of his struggle; he died at his home, Hopefield House, Belfast, on 14 February 1914 after a prolonged illness. His funeral to the city cemetery on 18 February was headed by a procession of 200 UVF officers. Sinclair's portrait, by Frank McKelvey, is in the Ulster Museum.

Concerned with religious and educational matters, he framed the financing proposals on what became known as the commutation and sustentation funds after the withdrawal of the *regium donum* from the Presbyterian church in 1869. As chairman of the convocation of the Queen's University, he resolutely defended its non-sectarian principle and rejected denominational teaching in any form. Through his position on the recess committee, he ensured that the system of vocational and technical education administered by the new Department of Agriculture would be secular.

Sinclair married first (1876) Mary Duffin (d. 1879) of Strandtown Lodge, Belfast, who came from another family prominent in the mercantile, cultural, and public life of Belfast, and secondly (1882) Elizabeth, daughter of William Richardson of Brooklands, Belfast, niece of John Grubb Richardson, and widow of Thomas's cousin John M. Sinclair. He had four sons and three daughters, the eldest of whom, **Frances Elizabeth Crichton** (1877–1918), was educated privately, travelled in Europe, and after her marriage to W. S. Crichton (benefactor of Liverpool University) lived in Liverpool and took up writing as a recreation. *The precepts of Andy Saul, The soundless tide* (1911), and *Tinker's Hollow* (1912) are pleasant sketches of Ulster character and speech; she also wrote for children. She died in England on 23 November 1918.

Bridget Hourican

Sources

Burke, *Peerage* (1912), 2448; *WWW*; *Times*, 16 February 1914; *IBL*, x (1918), 45; T. W. Moody and J. C. Beckett, *Queen's Belfast, 1845–1949* (1959); A. T. Q. Stewart, *The Ulster crisis* (1967); S. J. Brown, *Ireland in fiction*, i (2nd ed., 1919; reprint, 1968); John F. Harbinson, *The Ulster unionist party, 1882–1973* (1973); Trevor West, *Horace Plunkett: cooperation and politics* (1986); R. S. J. Clarke and A. C. W. Merrick, *Old Belfast families and the New Burying Ground* (1991); information from Linde Lunney

Thomas Henry Sloan

1870–1941

Thomas Henry Sloan, Orange populist and independent unionist MP, was born 13 March 1870 in Belfast, the son of John Sloan, a labourer, and his wife Mary Jane (née Semple). Thomas Sloan worked as a plater, red-leader, and cementer at Harland and Wolff's shipyards; he was a Methodist lay preacher who held lunchtime prayer meetings in the platers' shed. He was a member of the National Amalgamated Union of Labourers and the Ancient Order of Foresters, and an Orangeman. In 1900 he became Worshipful Master of St Michael's Total Abstinence LOL 1890. Sloan was active in the Belfast Protestant Association (BPA), founded in 1894 by Arthur Trew. During Trew's imprisonment in 1901–2 Sloan became principal speaker at the BPA's Custom House meetings and developed a personal following.

On 12 July 1902 Sloan and some associates disrupted a speech by Edward Saunderson at the Belfast Orange demonstration, heckling him about the prohibition of an Orange parade through the predominantly Catholic village of Rostrevor, south Co. Down; Sloan accused Saunderson of voting for factory legislation exempting convent-run Magdalene laundries from inspection (Saunderson voted for the bill on second reading, intending to oppose the offending clause at committee stage). Sloan claimed he tried to raise the matter at district and county grand lodge, but was overruled by a deferential 'clique'. The death of the MP for Belfast South on 17 July was followed by dissension within the Belfast Conservative Association. The eventual candidate was an Orangeman, but lacked popular credentials; both Trew and Sloan sought BPA support for an independent candidacy. Sloan's support among working-class Orangemen (especially in the Sandy Row and Donegall Road areas) allowed him to prevail.

Several lodges endorsed Sloan, despite opposition from the County Grand Lodge. Sloan received support from Dublin unionist hard-liners and anti-ritualists, notably Lindsay Crawford. He was also supported by Belfast trades council (he advocated pro-labour policies including support for old-age pensions) and local temperance associations (he joined the Independent Order of Good Templars soon after his election). Sloan allegedly received financial support from W. J. Pirrie, who had been rejected by the Belfast Conservative Association; Sloan countercharged that Saunderson offered him £500 to stand down. (Crawford's *Irish Protestant* (9 July 1903) claimed that Sloan's campaign cost over £1,000, paid by sixpenny subscriptions from supporters, and that he refused 'lucrative appointments'.) On 18 August Sloan won by 3,795 to 2,969; he was the first unionist MP to have received only a primary education.

The campaign was followed by the suspension of Sloan and numerous supporters (including three entire lodges) from the order. Sloan appealed to the Grand Lodge of Ireland, claiming he had established friendly relations with the unionist MPs, and that his real opponents were the Belfast 'clique'; his followers contested Belfast local elections against official candidates. In June 1903, after the rejection of Sloan's appeal, his supporters formed the Independent Orange Order (IOO). Sloan became deputy Grand Chaplain (subsequently Belfast County Grand Master).

In addition to his Irish support, Sloan became a parliamentary spokesman for the wider Protestant anti-ritualist crusade in Britain (strong in Liverpool and Scotland). As chairman of such bodies as the National Protestant Electoral Federation (fatally disrupted in 1905 by personal rivalries between Sloan and the populist founder of the Liverpool Protestant Party, George Wise) and the Protestant Press Federation, Sloan called for English Protestants to form an independent Protestant party to counterbalance the pro-Catholic influence of the Irish parliamentary party. Through parliamentary questions Sloan raised such issues as the intimidation of Jews by Catholic mobs in Limerick, attacks on Protestant street-preachers in various parts of Ireland, underfunding of QCC (attributed to a conspiracy to force a pro-Catholic settlement of the university question), and alleged clerical influence over Catholic policemen; Crawford presented Sloan as champion of scattered southern Protestants, and chief bulwark against the supposed clericalist influence of Sir Antony MacDonnell. Sloan informed a Belfast crowd that the declaration which British monarchs were obliged to take at their coronation, denouncing transubstantiation and Marian devotion, should be taken by all judges and civil servants.

Lindsay Crawford, who emerged as ideologist of the Independent Order, is often presented as a far-sighted visionary, with Sloan as an unintelligent and bigoted follower. This view underestimates Crawford's own sectarianism. The Crawford–Sloan relationship resembled that between Desmond Boal and Ian Paisley in the 1960s, joining a clever, articulate, and somewhat erratic ideologue and a more provincial street-corner tribune channelling the discontents of a local audience, though Sloan's deference was tinged with jealousy. It may be less significant that Sloan eventually broke with Crawford than that he followed him to the extent he did; their differences reflect Sloan's awareness of his political base as much as his short-sightedness and bigotry.

In December 1904 Crawford organised a debate between Sloan and Shawe-Taylor on devolution and the university question. (Characteristically, Shawe-Taylor declared that the debate showed the spread of enlightened ideas among Belfast Orangemen, while Sloan claimed his speech killed Shawe-Taylor's university proposals.) In July 1905 the IOO issued the 'Magheramorne manifesto' written by Crawford and signed by the order's officers, including Sloan. Its conciliatory expressions towards the nationalist population and criticisms of Dublin Castle bureaucracy were read by some as endorsement of devolution (Crawford favoured a 'conditional nationalism', based on expectations of the wholesale conversion of Irish Catholics to Protestantism and imperialism) but could also be interpreted as offering cooperation with nationalists on matters of common concern. Sloan adopted this minimalist interpretation, declaring that while he would give nationalists a fair hearing he would never vote for home rule if he lived to the age of Methuselah, and that he had not been subjected to 'a mantle of mesmerism' by Crawford. Nevertheless, the manifesto was used against the Sloanites by the official unionist party (now distancing itself from the government, asserting a Protestant-populist standpoint, and regrouping around the newly formed Ulster Unionist Council (UUC)).

In December 1905, on the verge of a general election, Sloan denounced any portions of the manifesto misconstrued as anti-unionist and endorsed the UUC (he was an ex-officio member as MP for Belfast South); he was on the platform at an UUC rally in the Ulster Hall, Belfast, on 2 January 1906. This was denounced by Crawford as apostasy and betrayal. Sloan was too late to win acceptance from other Ulster MPs (who privately demanded that the conservative whip should be withdrawn from him after the Magheramorne manifesto) and he was opposed by Lord Arthur Hill. Sloan's victory (4,450–3,634; an almost identical margin on a higher turn-out) reflected an unofficial electoral pact; Belfast South nationalists voted for him in return for Sloanite support for Joseph Devlin in Belfast West. The unionists claimed that Sloan received financial support from Pirrie, then aligned with the liberal party; Moore called Sloan Pirrie's 'paid servant' (*Irish Weekly Independent*, 19 January 1907). Sloan was formally expelled from the UUC for standing against the UUC-endorsed Hill. He continued to sit on the conservative benches.

Sloan retained membership of the Orange Order in England until he was expelled in 1906 (at a meeting held on the Isle of Man, to make it harder for his plebeian supporters to attend). The IOO had c.500 members at its inception and at its height (July–August 1904) 1,000–1,200 Belfast members in twenty lodges. The IOO's other stronghold was rural Antrim, reflecting a well-established tradition of Presbyterian tenant-farmer radicalism. Lindsay Crawford established an Independent lodge in Dublin, and one was founded in Bryn Mawr, Pennsylvania; after the 1906 general election Independent lodges were founded in Merseyside and Scotland by Orangemen expelled from the parent order for opposing conservative candidates in favour of ultra-Protestant liberals or independent Protestant candidates.

While Sloan received the conservative whip and claimed fellowship with the official unionist MPs, their relations were chequered; William Moore later claimed he initially thought a working-class Ulster unionist member could be an asset, but found it impossible to ally with Sloan at Westminster while being attacked in the constituencies (*Irish Weekly Independent*, 19 January 1907). Like dissident Protestant conservative MPs on Merseyside, some of whom defected to the liberals around the 1906 election, Sloan supported free trade and opposed Joseph Chamberlain's tariff reform proposals (supported by most conservative MPs), saying tariffs would harm the working class. He maintained a pro-labour voting record, supporting the restoration of trade unions' legal immunities, the reversal of the Osborne judgement, and the inspection of factories, and voting for the introduction of old-age pensions; he introduced a bill for the Sunday closing of public houses, but this was talked out twice.

After 1906 Sloan's position grew precarious, as the revival of an Ulster-centric unionist party and the presence of a nationalist-influenced liberal government encouraged unionist unity, while pan-Protestant politics in Britain declined, unable to transcend conservative–liberal and anglican–nonconformist divides (many anti-Catholic and anti-ritualist liberals supported home rule after 1910). Sloan campaigned for Crawford in the 1906 Armagh North by-election, and joined him in supporting the 1907 Belfast strike led by Jim Larkin. Unlike Crawford, Sloan moderated his support for the strike after it ended, condemning attacks on blacklegs and declaring that while he stood for the rights of labour he recognised that capital also had rights. In May 1908 Crawford was expelled from the IOO for advocating home rule; Crawford complained that after expelling him from Belfast County Lodge, Sloan sat in judgement on his appeal to Grand Lodge (mirroring Sloan's complaints about his treatment by the parent order). Thereafter the Independent Order became largely a Sloan support machine relying on outspoken sectarianism. Sloan was perceived by some supporters as giving himself airs (his wearing a coat with a fur collar attracted comment), and lost temperance support by ceasing to be a total abstainer. He was defeated in the January 1910 general election by a unionist lawyer (despite continued trade union support); his final contest in December 1910 saw a further decline.

Sloan and the Independent Order were marginalised as the home rule issue revived, though they tried to maintain political relevance by accusing the unionist party of going soft on the necessity of opposing home rule for all of Ireland (not just Ulster)—once again Sloan presented himself as the voice of persecuted southern Protestants. The IOO denounced the appointment of the Catholic Lord Edmund Talbot (Edmund Howard) as conservative chief whip in 1913. Like other Protestant dissidents, the IOO was subjected to intimidation; during the Belfast riots of July 1912 Sloan's house was stoned while he lay ill. Sloan contemplated emigration to Canada (with the assistance of former temperance supporters) soon after his electoral defeat; but he stayed in Belfast and his later years were peaceful. Appointed a JP for Belfast by the liberal government, he attended Belfast petty sessions until lay JPs were excluded from the bench. The Turf Guardians Association was represented at his funeral, which suggests that he may have become a bookmaker; he left Methodism for the Church of Ireland, probably when he ceased to be a teetotaller.

Sloan died 11 October 1941 at his home (178 Tate's Avenue, south Belfast); his funeral to the city cemetery was attended by Independent Orangemen. He was predeceased by his wife Mary Anne with whom he had at least three daughters and a son. Although overshadowed by the more articulate Crawford and by optimistic labour and nationalist readings of Independent Orangeism, Sloan exemplified the Ulster Protestant populist tradition which periodically erupted in the nineteenth and twentieth centuries.

Patrick Maume

Sources

Catholic, passim; *Irish Protestant*, passim; 'Jurist', *The iron heel: or, The fight for freedom* (1903); [Lindsay Crawford], *Orangeism, its history and progress—a plea for first principles* (1904); William O'Brien, *An olive branch in Ireland* (1910); Denis Gwynn, *Life of John Redmond* (1932); *Belfast Telegraph* 13, 14 October 1941; *Belfast News Letter*, 14 October 1941, p. 4; J. W. Boyle, 'The Belfast Protestant Association and the Independent Orange Order, 1901–10', *Irish Historical Studies*, xiii (1962–3), 117–52; Henry Patterson, 'Independent Orangeism and class conflict in Edwardian Belfast: a reinterpretation', *Proceedings of the Royal Irish Academy*, lxxx C (1980), 1–27; Alvin Jackson, *The Ulster party: Irish unionists in the house of commons, 1884–1911* (1989); Austen Morgan, *Labour and partition: the Belfast working class 1905–23* (1991); Kevin Haddick-Flynn, *Orangeism: the making of a tradition* (1999); *ODNB* (on John Kensit and Walter Walsh)

Charles Stewart Vane-Tempest Stewart

1852–1915

Charles Stewart Vane-Tempest Stewart, 6th marquis of Londonderry, politician, was born 16 July 1852 in London, eldest of the six children of the 5th marquis, George Henry Robert Charles William Vane-Tempest (1821–84) and his wife Mary Cornelia, only daughter of Sir John Edwards of Garth, Montgomeryshire. Charles was educated at Eton, and matriculated at Christ Church, Oxford, but did not graduate. After two expensive and unsuccessful attempts to get into parliament, he was returned for the tories as Viscount Castlereagh at a by-election in Co. Down in 1878, after election expenses of a colossal £14,000. He held the seat until 1884, when he transferred to the lords on the death of his father; at which time he succeeded to extensive estates in Wynyard Park, Co. Durham, and Mount Stewart, Co. Down.

On 27 July 1886 Londonderry was appointed lord lieutenant of Ireland by the new prime minister, Lord Salisbury, and served three years. Relations with the more liberal-minded chief secretary Sir Michael Hicks Beach were strained; the situation improved for Londonderry when Beach was replaced with Arthur Balfour. His most significant acts in the light of his future career as a leading Ulster unionist were his befriending Edward Carson, and his conferring (13 October 1888) the charter of city on Belfast, observing that it was the first town without a bishopric to receive this honour. He resigned in August 1889, in part because of the expense of the office, which entailed personal costs of £15,000–£20,000 a year.

With the threat posed by Gladstone's second home rule bill in 1893, Londonderry threw all his energies into the defence of the union brokered by his ancestor, Lord Castlereagh. He opposed the bill in the lords and presided over the meeting in which the political alliance between conservatives and liberal unionists was formally ratified. In 1900 Londonderry entered government as postmaster-general, and in 1902 joined the cabinet as president of the board of education. In this capacity he administered with success Balfour's English education act of 1902, which gave support from local rates to religiously affiliated schools, but led the protest against the Irish university bill brought forward by the chief secretary, George Wyndham, in 1903. After the devolution scheme of September 1904, supported by the under-secretary Sir Antony MacDonnell, Londonderry followed Carson in threatening to resign from cabinet if Wyndham was retained. He was one of the ten original members of the Ulster Unionist Council (UUC) standing committee on its inception in 1905 and was appointed president. His was the second signature after Carson's to the Solemn League and Covenant in Belfast city hall on 28 September 1912, which pledged its 471,414 signatories to use all possible means to defeat home rule. He contributed an essay to the unionist party's publication *Against home rule* (1912) and argued the unionists' interest in the prosperity of Ireland as a whole as against what he perceived to be the nationalists' willingness to see an independent Ireland in rags. On 23 September 1913 he was present with 500 UUC delegates assembled in Ulster Hall to approve the setting up of an Ulster provisional government in the event of home rule, despite Carson's protestations that a man in his position had too much to lose from such a 'clandestine' association. At the meeting he personally pledged £10,000 for an indemnity guarantee fund for UVF members. He addressed a mass meeting at Hyde Park on 3 April 1914, and two months later he and Lord Lansdowne were the main opponents of the third home rule bill in the lords. The outbreak of war shelved the question and Londonderry did not live to see the outcome. He died 8 February 1915 at his estate in Wynyard Park, Co. Durham. He was a great asset to the Ulster unionists, more by reason of his fortune and family status than of his political gifts, which were of no great order. Simple and unpretentious, he was a popular and good landlord who provided land for a market in Newtownards, Co. Down (1873), gave permanent leases for industrial sites, and built a Catholic church (1876). He was survived by his son Charles Stewart Henry, who became 7th marquis of Londonderry, his daughter, and his wife (m. 2 October 1875), the former Lady Theresa Chetwynd Talbot (1856–1919), eldest daughter of the 19th earl of Shrewsbury. Theirs was a dynastic rather than a love match and Londonderry suffered through his wife's infidelities; but they were politically attuned and, in later years at least, relations were affectionate. Beautiful and dynamic, Lady Londonderry was more forceful than her husband, and her political talents were more impressive. She used her influence to effect and was the model of a great political hostess, befriending Edward Carson and Walter Long, with whom she held important correspondences, and arranging the social calendar for Andrew Bonar Law after the death of his wife in 1908. As one of the founders and its first president, she left a lasting legacy in the creation of the Ulster Women's Unionist Council. She died 16 March 1919 at home, 5 Carlton Terrace, London. Her papers and those of her husband are held in PRONI and Durham County Record Office.

Bridget Hourican

Sources

F. S. L. Lyons, 'The Irish unionist party and the devolution crisis of 1904–5', *Irish Historical Studies*, vi (March 1948), 1–22; H. Montgomery Hyde, *Carson* (1953); L. P. Curtis, *Coercion and conciliation in Ireland 1880–1892* (1963); A. T. Q. Stewart, *The Ulster crisis* (1967); H. Montgomery Hyde, *The Londonderrys* (1979); Trevor West, *Horace Plunkett: cooperation and politics* (1986); Catherine Shannon, *Arthur J. Balfour and Ireland* (1988); Alvin Jackson, *The Ulster party* (1989); Alvin Jackson, *Colonel Edward Sanderson* (1995); Jonathan Bardon, *History of Ulster* (1992); B. M. Walker, *Ulster politics, 1868–86* (1989); *ODNB*

Isabella Maria Susan Tod

1836–96

Isabella Maria Susan Tod, feminist and reformer, was born 18 May 1836 in Edinburgh, daughter of James Banks Tod, a merchant, and Maria Isabella Tod (née Waddell). There was at least one other child, a brother who became a prosperous merchant in London. Tod seems to have had no formal education but was encouraged by her mother in studies at home. Maria Tod (a native of Co. Monaghan) was related to Charles Mastertown, an influential Presbyterian minister, and to Hope Mastertown Waddell (1804–95), who was the first missionary from an Irish Presbyterian background; he worked in Jamaica for thirteen years and then with Jamaican colleagues founded the Calabar mission in west Africa in the mid 1840s. The Tod family moved to Belfast when Isabella was in her twenties, and she became involved in charity work with poor people in the city. Her strong Presbyterian religious beliefs and her experiences in Belfast prompted her to develop radical views on social issues and women's rights. She wrote anonymously in the 1860s and 1870s for the *Dublin University Magazine* and the *Banner of Ulster*, and in the early 1880s for the *Northern Whig*.

Like many of her contemporaries, she had her first experience of politics in response to the contentious provisions of the Contagious Diseases Acts of 1864, 1866, and 1869. In an effort to combat venereal diseases among soldiers, the government had proposed such stringent controls of prostitution that middle-class women recognised, in some cases for the first time, that implicit in the legislation were double standards of sexual morality and of the social constraints that adversely affected the lives of all women. Tod was active in organisations set up to demand the repeal of the acts, notably the Ladies' National Association, founded in 1869. She served on the London-based executive committee of this body until 1889.

Her work to reform the law with respect to women's education and married women's property (she was the only woman called to give evidence to the parliamentary select committee on the married women's property bill in 1868), combined with her temperance and charity work, convinced her that women were best suited to the work of reforming society, but that their success in this would depend on gaining the right to vote. It was because of this realisation that she was the main force behind the establishment of the Northern Ireland Society for Women's Suffrage in 1871, acting as secretary until the 1890s. This was the first organisation in Ireland that displayed a recognisably feminist political agenda. Tod campaigned vigorously for women's right to be considered as full members of society; she spoke at meetings throughout the country and in Britain, and was an effective lobbyist. She formed friendships with prominent suffragists in Ireland and Britain, and utilised contacts and networks assiduously in efforts to change society's attitudes. It was largely as a result of her work that Belfast women were allowed to vote in local elections in 1887, eleven years ahead of other Irish municipalities, and that in 1896, subject to property qualifications, women were permitted to become poor law guardians.

Her first public statement was a speech on women's education, delivered for her at a meeting in 1867 of the National Association for the Promotion of Social Science. She campaigned for the provision of secondary and higher education for women, and was involved with the foundation of several schools offering academic and practical education for girls—notably the Ladies' Institute in Belfast (1867). The intermediate education bill of 1878 was intended to organise examinations and to award prizes based on their results, but it referred solely to male education. Consequently, Tod and Margaret Byers organised a delegation to London to urge the inclusion of girls in the bill. Their efforts were successful, and the Intermediate Education Act gave awards to schools for all students who passed examinations, whether male or female. A year later (1879) the government introduced a new university bill, and Tod immediately formed a committee to lobby for the inclusion of women in any benefits that the bill would produce. She was the prime mover in the establishment (1880) of the Ulster Schoolmistresses' Association, intended to act as a pressure group to foster female education.

Tod was a strict teetotaller and very involved in temperance work, seeing in this an important focus for women's efforts to improve society. She was a founding member with Margaret Byers of the Belfast Women's Temperance Association (formed 1874), and acted (1877–92) as vice-president of the British Women's Temperance Association. The Belfast group set up a number of projects intended to ameliorate life in the city: temperance eating-houses, a home for alcoholic women and another for destitute girls, and classes in hygiene and cookery for working-class women. The WTA split in 1893 and Tod became vice-president of the Women's Total Abstinence Union, a position she held until her death.

Tod's career took another direction when she threw herself into opposition to Gladstone's first home rule bill of 1886. She believed that an Irish-based assembly, bereft of the mitigating influence of the large numbers and wealth of the educated classes of the United Kingdom, would inevitably fall into illiberal and divisive modes of government, and that such a government would be inimical to all the causes for which she had campaigned. In 1886 she organised a Liberal Women's Unionist Association in Belfast to formulate a policy of opposition. Tod cared so passionately about this issue that she campaigned in England as well as Ireland on behalf of the liberal unionists. The split between unionists and nationalists over home rule was mirrored within the suffrage movement, and Tod was estranged, sometimes permanently, from some of her suffragist friends who supported the bill.

In 1884 a testimonial worth £1,000 was presented to her, and she was honoured in 1886 by the presentation of a portrait. She lived, unmarried, with her mother, who died in 1877. For many years her secretary, Gertrude Andrews, was a constant companion. After years of illness, Tod died 8 December 1896 at her home at 71 Botanic Avenue, Belfast. In October 1898 a memorial portrait of her by Margaret Rothwell (1890) was unveiled in the Free Public Library of Belfast. It is now held in the Ulster Museum, Belfast. Annual scholarships of £30 are awarded at QUB in Tod's memory.

Georgina Clinton and Linde Lunney

Sources

Belfast News Letter, 10 December 1896; James Dewar (ed.), *A history of Elmwood church* (1900); Maria Luddy, 'Isabella M. S. Tod (1836–1896)', in Mary Cullen and Maria Luddy (ed.), *Women, power and consciousness in nineteenth-century Ireland* (1995), 197–230; Maria Luddy, 'Women and politics in nineteenth century Ireland', in Maryann G. Valiulis and Mary O'Dowd (ed.), *Women and Irish history* (1997), 89–108; Diane Urquhart, 'An articulate and definite cry for political freedom: the Ulster suffrage movement', *Women's History Review*, xi, no. 2 (2002), 273–92; information from Eileen Black, Ulster Museum, Belfast; Tomás O'Riordan, 'Isabella Tod', available online at: http://multitext.ucc.ie/d/Isabella_Tod (photo) (internet material downloaded July 2006)

William Copeland Trimble

1851–1941

William Copeland Trimble, newspaper editor, was born 8 November 1851, eldest son of William Trimble, newspaper proprietor, and his second wife Anne (neé Stewart). Educated at Enniskillen Royal School (Portora) in the 1850s and 1860s, he entered his apprenticeship to Alexander Thom, Dublin printer, in 1868. Though briefly considering other careers, first at the bar, and then as a concert singer (he had a fine tenor voice), he returned to Enniskillen as junior partner in the *Impartial Reporter* in 1875. His father was delighted, enthusing: 'Copeland...writes well, no better reporter exists, is a good printer and is a perfect gentleman' (W. T. to John Nevin Trimble, 3 January 1876). Though he ultimately grew more conservative in politics than his father, he was at first active in the liberal–nationalist tenant demand for legislative reform. In early 1880 he joined the Land League. After the land act of August 1881 he disassociated himself from the militant nationalism of the League, establishing the Fermanagh Tenant Right Association on 22 December 1881 and acting as county secretary for several years. From *c.*1880, for practical purposes he was in charge of the *Impartial Reporter* (though it was issued under the name of William Trimble until 1886). The paper became critical of the Parnellite demand for self-government, though continuing to advocate tenant protection and relief. In a number of instances in 1881–2 Copeland exposed great injustice and inhumanity in the treatment of smallholders on landed estates in Cavan and Fermanagh, to the wrath of the county landed interest. On one occasion in early 1882 he was attacked and badly beaten up late at night in Enniskillen, the suspicion being that hired supporters of county landlords were responsible—the culprits were never discovered.

He alienated radicals on both sides of the question: tenant association meetings under his guidance were mobbed sometimes by Land League sympathisers. His editorials lamented the polarisation of political feeling in the region as Catholics began to withdraw support from the liberal party, and Orangeism reorganised. At a major home rule meeting at Rosslea, Co. Fermanagh, in October 1883, where large numbers of Orangemen assembled in counter-demonstration, he was lucky to escape a mauling from Orange farmers who mistook him for Tim Healy, whom at the age of 30 he closely resembled. Though he desired to have the assistance of his brothers in the operation of the newspaper, he resisted shared editorial and managerial control, telling his brother Sinclair Trimble (1853–1937) that he would provide him with employment as overseer but 'could not give up my place, which while a sort of managership is virtually mastership...knowing the business as you do not and the customers' (W. C. T. to S. T., 17 November 1883). He had considerable fluency as a journalist, but his writing was more facile than that of his father.

From 1886, when the liberal party split over home rule, Copeland became a liberal unionist under the leadership of Joseph Chamberlain. In demand as a public speaker, he was frequently invited to England to present the Ulster case against home rule. He toured English constituencies on this basis, speaking for the Conservative party in the 1895 general election. When in November 1901 the family printing works in Enniskillen burned down, he exerted himself vigorously to maintain newspaper production, using works in Omagh for six months before the paper was reestablished at home in May 1902. During the second Boer war and the first world war, he collected by newspaper appeals large sums of money to make up a comfort fund for the Inniskilling regiments. He participated enthusiastically in the Ulster anti-home-rule campaign of 1912–14, raising a troop of mounted horse from Enniskillen as part of the Ulster Volunteer Force. His *History of Enniskillen* (3 vols, 1919–21) is one of the most substantial Irish local histories of the century. Some days after suffering a partial stroke, he died 24 January 1941 in Fermanagh county hospital. He is buried in Breandrum cemetery, Enniskillen.

He married first (3 October 1881) Letitia Jane (1854–92), third daughter of John Weir of Letterbreen, Co. Fermanagh; they had three sons and two daughters. He married secondly (8 May 1893) Lily (1866–1949), third daughter of Henry Reilly of Armagh; they had two sons, one of whom was killed serving with the 8th Inniskillings on the western front in April 1916. His granddaughter was the composer Joan Trimble.

Desmond McCabe

Sources

Trimble correspondence and family papers (in possession of Joan McVeigh, *Impartial Reporter*, Enniskillen); William Copeland Trimble, *Garlands from Lough Erne* (1917); William Copeland Trimble, *A history of Enniskillen* (3 vols, 1919–21); William Egbert Trimble, *Memoir of the Trimble family, with the lineage of some allied families* (privately printed, 1949) (portr.); *Impartial Reporter*: commemorative anniversary issue, 1825–75 (May 1975) (portrs of W. Trimble and W. C. Trimble); Paul Bew and Frank Wright, 'The agrarian opposition in Ulster politics, 1848–87', in Samuel Clark and James S. Donnelly, jr (ed.), *Irish peasants: violence and political unrest, 1780–1914* (1983), 192–229; Hugh Oram, *The newspaper book: a history of Irish newspapers in Ireland, 1649–1983* (1983); B. M. Walker, *Ulster politics: the formative years, 1868–86* (1989); Joan Trimble, 'A nineteenth century printer: William Trimble of Enniskillen and his newspaper, *The Impartial Reporter*', *Long Room*, no. 40 (1995), 34–40 (portr.); Seamas Mac Annaidh, *Fermanagh books, writers and newspapers of the nineteenth century* (1999)

William Walker

1871–1918

William Walker, socialist and trade unionist, was born 9 January 1871 at 35 McCluny Street, Belfast, son of Francis Walker, shipyard boilermaker and latterly trade-union official, and Sarah Walker (née McLaughlin). After attending St George's national school, he was apprenticed as a joiner in the Harland and Wolff shipyard (1885). While serving his apprenticeship he assisted in the organisation of semi-skilled platers' helpers into what became the National Amalgamated Union of Labour (1891). Briefly a member of a Belfast branch of a small Scottish-based carpenters' union, which he represented at the 1892 British Trades Union Congress (TUC), he soon joined the Belfast 9th branch of the Amalgamated Society of Carpenters and Joiners (ASCJ). Commencing a lengthy tenure (1893–1912) as the union's delegate on Belfast Trades Council (BTC), where he served on the organisation and propaganda subcommittee, throughout the 1890s he worked as a joiner with various building and textile machinery firms. Though belonging to a skilled craft union, he vigorously promoted the 'new [trade] unionism' of organising semi-skilled and unskilled workers. Involved from 1893 in organising efforts among Belfast's predominantly female linen workers, he served several months (1894–5) as temporary secretary of the newly formed Textile Operatives Society of Ireland before handing over office to a woman. Throughout his career he remained keenly interested in women's rights and the status of women workers.

Walker's socialism and organising militancy clashed with the outlook of the staid and respectable tradesmen then dominant on BTC. Key founder of a Belfast branch of the Independent Labour Party (ILP), he became its most prominent propagandist. A fluent and energetic speaker, bohemian in dress and cut of hair, he was conspicuous at ILP Sunday-afternoon public meetings amid the evangelical lay preachers on Belfast's Custom House steps. He represented BTC at the 1893 TUC held in Belfast, and at the first Irish Trade Union Congress (ITUC) (1894). Protestant in religion and pro-union in politics, he sought to forge an independent non-sectarian labour politics as a working-class alternative both to nationalist politics and to the conservative unionist establishment. During the bitter Belfast–Clyde engineers' strike (1895–6)—which shattered the comfortable Belfast consensus regarding trade unions as devices for employer–worker collaboration, and forums for conciliating industrial conflict—he sought with mixed results to propagate socialist consciousness. Amid violent clashes with Protestant action groups, notably the Belfast Protestant Association of Arthur Trew, the ILP ceased its open-air meetings at the 'steps', and Walker was placed for some time under police protection. When the Belfast ILP collapsed in the strike's aftermath, he worked to expand his influence within BTC, assisting in organisation of such semi-skilled sectors as beetling engineers, seamen, and municipal employees. Amid increasing BTC involvement in municipal politics around issues of public health and quality of housing, he was elected to the board of poor law guardians (1899). His election as BTC assistant secretary (1899–1900) and secretary (1900–01) under the presidency of John Murphy, a long-time ally, indicated a power-shift within the body toward the new trade unionism. Dismissed from his job at Clonard foundry after writing as BTC secretary to the War Office regarding the firm's non-compliance with the fair wages clause in its contract, he was blacklisted by local employers and collected trades council victimisation pay. Elected ASCJ district delegate (1901–12), a full-time paid union office, he resigned as BTC secretary, but was soon elected the body's president (1902–5, 1906–7). He was BTC delegate to the ITUC (1899–1905, 1907–11), and ASCJ delegate to the TUC (1901–5).

Now dominant within the Belfast labour movement, whose socialist element was the strongest in Ireland, Walker became the foremost Irish advocate of independent labour political representation, urging affiliation with the British-based Labour Representation Committee (LRC), which after 1906 became the Labour Party. Owing to his efforts, BTC affiliated to the LRC (1902), and an LRC Belfast branch was established (1903). As member of the ITUC parliamentary committee (1902–4), he was instrumental in securing adoption by the 1903 Newry congress of a compromise resolution recommending that Irish trade unions affiliate with the LRC as a means to promote independent labour representation in Ireland. President of the 1904 Kilkenny congress, he devoted his presidential address to passionate argument of the efficacy of labour political action. For the next several years he was the foremost figure in the Irish labour movement. At successive congresses he led Belfast delegates in pressing unsuccessfully for the ITUC to move beyond the compromise formula, and establish its own political organisation as a subordinate constituent of the LRC; he was opposed by labour supporters of the Irish parliamentary party, advocates of a separate Irish labour party, and 'pure labourists' who wished the movement to shun all political action.

Defeated in Pottinger ward in elections to Belfast city council (1902), he was elected for Duncairn ward (January 1904), and led a small labour group that sharply attacked corruption among councillors and corporation officials. He was a leading contributor to the *Belfast Labour Chronicle* (1904–6), joint organ of BTC and the Belfast LRC. As the first LRC parliamentary candidate in an Irish constituency, in the September 1905 North Belfast by-election, with LRC national secretary James Ramsay MacDonald as election agent, he opposed conservative candidate Sir Daniel Dixon, wealthy entrepreneur and sometime lord mayor. Attacking Dixon's public record, rumoured moral laxity, and flamboyant lifestyle, Walker received tacit support from dissident unionist elements represented by the idiosyncratic Independent Orange Order of Thomas Sloan and Robert Lindsay Crawford. Replying to a Protestant Association questionnaire, which Dixon deftly ignored, Walker expressed sectarian sentiments, asserting that 'Protestantism means protesting against superstition, hence true Protestantism is synonymous with labour.' The resultant alienation of vital Catholic support contributed to his defeat by 474 votes in a poll of some 8,400, and damaged his influence within Irish labour circles. Campaigning soon after in the January 1906 general election, he accused Dixon of garnering windfall profits in the sale of sloblands to the corporation; printed in the *Labour Chronicle* ('Dodger Dan's Deal'), the allegations resulted in a successful libel action against the printer, and Walker's estrangement from the journal. Defeated again, he reduced Dixon's majority to only 291 votes. However, the return to Westminster of a liberal government revived the prospect of home rule; in reaction, breaches within unionist opinion were healed, and independent Belfast labour politics rapidly declined. Standing for the Shankill ward aldermanship, Walker was defeated along with all six other labour council candidates (January 1907), followed by heavy defeat in a parliamentary by-election occasioned by the death of Dixon (April 1907).

Walker's ruthlessness in demarcation disputes involving building trades unions led to his six-month resignation as BTC president (1905–6), and was a factor in his decision after January 1907 not to seek further election to BTC office. With a revived Belfast ILP as his base, he concentrated activities within the British labour movement. After addressing the 1907 Belfast conference of the British Labour Party, he was elected for the first of four occasions to the party's executive committee. He was twice defeated in attempts to regain a Belfast city council seat (1908, 1911), and as Labour candidate in the January 1910 general election in the Scottish constituency of Leith Burghs. The rise from

1909 of James Larkin's ITGWU dented Walker's and Belfast's standing as the unrivalled vanguard of Irish socialism and labour militancy, while Larkin's nationalism challenged Walker's ideological position. His fusion of constitutional unionism with socialist labourism—variously termed 'Belfast socialism', 'Belfast internationalism', or simply 'Walkerism'—was cogently expressed in his pamphlet *The Irish question* (1908). Advocating nationalisation as the only progressive settlement of the Irish land issue in the general national interest, he argued the impossibility of its realisation by a home rule parliament, bound to be dominated by representatives of the class of peasant proprietors created by the reactionary land transfer policies of successive British governments. At the 1911 ITUC, Walker, deploring efforts to establish a 'purely local party, 'utilised the 1903 compromise formula to defeat by three votes a motion to establish an Irish labour party. He subsequently engaged in a celebrated debate over six issues of the Glasgow socialist journal *Forward* (May–July 1911) with James Connolly, Belfast organiser of the ITGWU and of the Socialist Party of Ireland, on the relationship between socialism and the national question. Accused by Connolly of a 'false internationalism' tantamount to imperialism, he retorted that nationalism was a divisive and regressive doctrine, and argued that owing to the complete identity of interest between Irish and British workers—'oppressed by the same financial power'—Irish labour should be part of the larger and more powerful movement.

Vice-chairman of the British Labour Party (1911–12), Walker withdrew his candidacy for the chairmanship and resigned his ASCJ office to accept a position in Belfast in the Irish executive of the government's newly established national insurance scheme (1912). Accordingly, he did not attend the 1912 ITUC at which an Irish Labour Party was launched. Subsequently he became inspector under the insurance act for the north-eastern district of Ireland. Although he may have intended to return to trade unionism and labour politics once the new social services—to which he was sincerely devoted—were well established, it is likely that his decision indicated demoralisation and confusion within the altered political climate, marked by armed mobilisation within Ulster unionism to resist the seeming imminence of home rule.

Through two decades of engagement in Irish workers' struggles, Walker consistently maintained that 'the progress of their class and the benefit of their country' could only be realised within the existing political union with Great Britain, while holding that the safety of that union lay in the assertion of a socially progressive and inclusive version of unionist identity. Ever committed to independent labour politics, he avoided identification as a mere left-leaning political unionist. Ultimately he failed, both in ideology and in practice, to establish the validity of a labour democracy allied with a unionist ethos that was primarily concerned with cross-class collaboration to preserve a communal ascendancy delineated by sectarian identification. His own rhetoric revealed slippage into sectarian bias, an easy equation of Protestantism with all that is progressive, and Catholicism with all that is backward. In Walker the structure of feeling identified by Raymond Williams (*The country and the city*) as long endemic among European socialists, of deep revulsion towards pre-industrial and non-urban classes, parties, and ideologies as intrinsically regressive, is compounded by sectarian inflections particular to his locale.

Walker married Margaret Adams, who survived him. His last residence was at Rathcoole, Park Avenue, Strandtown, Belfast. He died 23 November 1918 in the Royal Victoria hospital after a lengthy illness, and was buried in Newtownbreda cemetery.

Lawrence William White

Sources

Belfast Newsletter, 25 November 1918; *Irish News*, 25 November 1918; J. Dunsmore Clarkson, *Labour and nationalism in Ireland* (1925); C. Desmond Greaves, *The life and times of James Connolly* (1961); John W. Boyle (ed.), *Leaders and workers* (1966); Cork Workers Club, *The Connolly/Walker controversy* (1974); Arthur Mitchell, *Labour in Irish politics 1890–1930: the Irish labour movement in an age of revolution* (1974); Walker, i (1978); Henry Patterson, *Class conflict and sectarianism: the Protestant working class and the Belfast labour movement 1868–1920* (1980); John W. Boyle, *The Irish labour movement in the nineteenth century* (1988); Austen Morgan, *James Connolly: a political biography* (1988); Austen Morgan, *Labour and partition: the Belfast working class 1905–23* (1991); Emmet O'Connor, *A labour history of Ireland, 1824–1960* (1992); Donal Nevin (ed.), *Trade union century* (1994), 437, 445; *ODNB*

Robert Hugh Wallace

1860–1929

Robert Hugh Wallace, Orangeman, soldier and political activist, was born in English Street, Downpatrick, Co. Down, on 14 December 1860, son of William Nevin Wallace, solicitor and landowner, and his second wife, Catherine Mary (d. 1877), daughter of Francis Charles Annesley (1775–1832), naval captain and fourth son of the second Earl Annesley. He had one full brother, a captain in the King's Shropshire Light Infantry.

The Wallace family had a long connection with Downpatrick, where Robert's paternal great-grandfather James Wallace and grandfather Hugh Wallace served as seneschal. The latter founded a highly successful solicitor's firm, Hugh Wallace and Co. of Downpatrick and Belfast. His son William Nevin Wallace considerably increased the family fortunes by working as a parliamentary lawyer and by some fortunate inheritances; he also served as secretary and treasurer to Down cathedral board from disestablishment in 1870 until his death in 1895, when he was succeeded in both positions by Robert Hugh Wallace, who held them until his own death and served for a number of years on Down and Connor diocesan council.

Robert Hugh Wallace was educated at Harrow and Brasenose College, Oxford, graduating in law (1883) and MA (1886). He was called to the English bar at the Inner Temple (1886), but did not practise because of his father's desire that he should succeed him as head of the family firm of solicitors. Accordingly, Wallace was enrolled as a solicitor in the Irish courts in 1890. He also acted as a land agent and owned extensive property in Belfast and counties Down and Armagh; through a further bequest, he acquired Myra Castle near Strangford, Co. Down, which became his principal residence. Wallace's considerable wealth underpinned his extensive social, political and military activities. He was a deputy lieutenant for Co. Down (serving as high sheriff in 1908) and an active member of the county grand jury.

An active freemason, who eventually attained the 33rd degree, Wallace became grand junior warden of Ireland, and until his death was grand first principal of the Royal Arch Chapter of Down and treasurer of the Victoria Jubilee Masonic Annuity Fund for the Province of Down, increasing contributions received from the county from £70 to over £1,000. He also served on the board of general purposes of the Grand Lodge of Ireland. At the time of his death he was the third-highest-ranking mason in Ireland.

Fond of foxhunting and yachting on Strangford Lough, he was also given to antiquarian research, frequently lecturing local associations on such topics as the history of the South Down Militia and the penal laws against Catholics (which he argued had been legitimate attempts at political self-defence rather than expressions of religious bigotry (*Down Recorder*, 16 November 1912)). He published several articles on military history in the *Ulster Journal of Archaeology*. In 1899 he began a history of Orangeism, but subsequently abandoned it and made his source materials available to R. M. Sibbett. The surviving fragment of Wallace's account, notable for its use of oral tradition and for combining some critical acumen with its generally apologetic approach, was published by the education committee of the Grand Orange Lodge of Ireland in 1994. Wallace also completed a history of Downpatrick, which remained unpublished (PRONI, Wallace papers, D1889/8/4). In 1897 he helped to reconstruct the mediaeval high cross outside Down cathedral.

Wallace joined the junior branch of the Orange Order at the age of eight, and in childhood he and his brother paraded through Downpatrick during Orange festivals, wearing miniature sashes and beating drums. As an adult he was a member of Eldon LOL no. 7, a high-status lodge for the social elite. In the 1890s he was deputy grand secretary of the County Grand Orange Lodge of Down.

Under the liberal government of 1892–5, Wallace was a leading member of Downpatrick Unionist Club, an outspoken advocate of resistance to Gladstone's second home rule bill, and a delegate to the 1893 anti-home rule convention held in Belfast. In 1899 he was an unsuccessful unionist candidate in a rowdy contest for the Downpatrick division of the new Down County Council, though he was simultaneously elected to Downpatrick Urban District Council and became one of that body's two representatives on the county council. Wallace later cited expressions of anglophobia by newly formed nationalist local councils—'legalised Fenian lodges' (*Ulster Echo*, 13 July 1903)—as showing what could be expected from a home rule parliament. He also ran the Orange Order's emergency committee (1908–10), which recruited labour for landowners boycotted by nationalists. Despite his staunch unionism, Wallace's private relations with Catholics were relatively good. During the 1899 county council elections, he denounced claims that he discriminated against Catholics, pointing out that he had repeatedly used the services of the Catholic auctioneer who made the allegations, and also employed a Catholic surveyor.

Wallace had a strong family connection with the South Down Militia (5th Royal Irish Rifles (RIR)), which had a large Orange membership, and joined the regiment as a second lieutenant on 29 March 1879; after successive promotions, he became lieutenant-colonel and battalion commandant (22 January 1898) and honorary colonel (22 March 1899). He led the South Downs to service in the South African war in April 1901. The battalion guarded lines of communication in the Orange Free State against Boer guerrillas, while a section served as mounted infantry in anti-guerrilla 'sweeps', regularly suffering casualties. They returned home in July 1902; Wallace received the CB and the Queen's South Africa Medal with five clasps as well as mention in dispatches. While in South Africa, he kept a diary (PRONI, D1889/4/13) much more critical of the British military command than his public utterances.

Wallace was a regular composer of occasional verse. His best-known ballad, 'The South Down Militia' (originally called 'The terrors of the land'), a half-humorous celebration of the regiment, was composed in South Africa and is still sung, played and recorded by Orange and military musicians. He himself frequently sang it on social occasions, for his connection with the regiment was as much social as military; he regularly organised and paid for celebrations and excursions, which he saw as reinforcing the regiment's identity. In 1907 he received a five-year extension of his command, serving as commander of the RIR militia brigade in 1908 and of the RIR special reserve battalion (1909–11). He finally retired as commander of the militia on 5 January 1913.

While absent in South Africa, Wallace was nominated as official Unionist candidate in the Down East by-election of February 1902, in which his status as 'the khaki candidate' and strong local credentials were emphasised. He was narrowly defeated by James Wood, the Russellite liberal candidate (see Thomas Wallace Russell). At the 1906 general election, the Down East seat was recaptured for the unionist party by James Craig, with Wallace as chief local organiser. Craig and Wallace developed a strong personal friendship, Craig describing Wallace as 'the mainstay of East Down' (31 January 1910; PRONI, D1889/3/18). Wallace turned down subsequent parliamentary candidacies to concentrate on the Orange Order and the militia. He was an active committee member of the Irish Unionist Alliance, and in 1905 a founding member of the Ulster Unionist Council, but it is above all his Orange activities that mark him as a key member of the less patrician and more aggressively Ulster-centric, post-1899 Ulster unionist leadership, dominated by professionals and businessmen from east Ulster.

Wallace served as county grand master of Belfast (1903–21) in succession to Edward Saunderson, and led the official Orange Institution's struggle to contain the breakaway, working-class

Independent Orange Order led by T. H. Sloan by making aggressive populist calls for Protestant unity against the Catholic-nationalist threat. His duties were administrative as well as political; one of his proudest achievements was the organisation of a fund for Belfast Orange widows. He was grand secretary of the Grand Orange Lodge of Ireland (1903–10), and from 1911 grand secretary to the newly formed Provincial Grand Lodge of Ulster, established for closer liaison with Ulster resistance to the third home rule bill. He held the honorific title of grand president of the Grand Orange Council of the world (1909–12) and was deputy grand master of the Grand Black Chapter of Ireland.

Because of the age and peripheral location of the order's grand master, the fourth earl of Erne (John Henry Crichton), Wallace was the key figure in the mass mobilisation of the Orange Order behind the anti-home rule campaign of Edward Carson. He was a member of the executive committee of the nascent Ulster provisional government, of the volunteer advisory board and of the personnel board, and of the five-member committee that drafted the constitution of the provisional government. His prominence is indicated by a contemporary postcard (reproduced on the cover of English and Walker, *Unionism*) in which Wallace is one of 'four aces' held by the red hand of Ulster, the others being Carson, Craig and Bonar Law. As early as December 1910, Wallace began to organise drill training for members of the Orange Order in preparation for the revival of the home rule threat once the house of lords' veto was abolished; it was Wallace who first secured legal advice (from J. H. M. Campbell) that two magistrates could authorise drilling, and it has been argued (though not universally accepted) that large-scale drilling by the Ulster Volunteer Force (UVF) first began in east Down.

On 'Ulster Day' (28 September 1912), Wallace was present at Belfast City Hall as commander of the section of Carson's honour guard recruited from the Orange Order. He is visible in photographs of Carson signing the Ulster covenant. Later in the day, Wallace ceremonially presented Carson with a banner said to have flown over William III at the Boyne. Wallace commanded the North Belfast Regiment of the UVF (1912–14), and was generally regarded as a hawk within the Ulster unionist party leadership, actively engaging in arms smuggling and supporting the distribution of arms to the

UVF rank and file. However, health problems curbed his active involvement throughout 1913 and he resigned his UVF position in January 1914 after suffering a breakdown due to overwork.

On the outbreak of the first world war, Wallace was recalled to the colours. Placed in command of Donard training camp near Newcastle, Co. Down, on 11 September 1914, he recruited and trained first the 17th and then the 19th battalions, RIR, with considerable success until his retirement for health reasons (gout and depression) in January 1918; he was awarded the CBE for his services. During the conflicts of the early 1920s, Myra Castle was fired on by the IRA. On the formation of the Northern Ireland state, Wallace accepted nomination to the NI privy council but declined a baronetcy and membership of the senate of Northern Ireland.

Wallace married (1895) Caroline Wilhelmina Twigg, with whom he had a son and three daughters. He also privately acknowledged and supported a daughter in England by a pre-marital relationship (PRONI, D1889/1/1/2). His last years were marked by declining health, though he remained active in freemasonry and Orangeism, and worshipped in Down cathedral the day before his sudden death on 23 December 1929. He is buried in the churchyard beside Down cathedral, and commemorated by a stained-glass window (erected by the masonic Grand Lodge of Ireland and the Provincial Grand Lodge of Down) showing Hiram king of Tyre and Solomon constructing the Temple in Jerusalem.

The fact that Wallace never held a parliamentary seat and was not active in the new Northern Ireland state apparatus, the tendency of accounts of the Ulster crisis to personalise it through Carson and Craig, and the eclipse of the Wallace dynasty after his only son's death in a boating accident in 1930 and the closure of Hugh Wallace and Co. in 1945, help to explain the longstanding failure to recognise his full significance as a central organiser of early-twentieth-century Ulster unionism. His career sheds much insight into the adaptation of local Ulster elites to new political and economic circumstances during the nineteenth century, the role of the male camaraderie of lodge and mess room in socio-political life, and the way in which older gentry-led Orange and local military structures provided the steel frame around which the façade of official Edwardian unionism was constructed.

Wallace's personal War Office file is in the British National Archives in Kew (WO339/16249). There are collections of Wallace papers in the Down County Museum in Downpatrick (DB1008 2002–140) and PRONI (D1889), and letters in other PRONI collections (e.g., D627/434/6 and D1507/A/4/25).

Patrick Maume

Sources

Belfast Telegraph, 23, 24 December 1929; *Belfast Newsletter*, 24 December 1929; *Northern Whig*, 24, 28 December 1929; *Newtownards Chronicle*, 28 December 1929; 4, 11, 18 January 1930; Patrick Buckland (ed.), *Irish unionism 1885–1923: a documentary history* (1973); *Down Recorder*, June–July 1988 (series on the South Down Militia in the South African war); Education Committee of the Grand Orange Lodge of Ireland, *The formation of the Orange Order 1795–1798: the edited papers of Colonel William Blacker and Colonel Robert H. Wallace* (1994); Anthony M. Wilson, *Saint Patrick's town* (1995); David Burnett, 'The modernisation of unionism, 1892–1914?', in Richard English and Graham Walker (ed.), *Unionism in modern Ireland: new perspectives on politics and culture* (1996), 41–62; J. Frederick Rankin, *Down cathedral: the church of Saint Patrick of Down* (1997); Burke, *Peerage* (1999 ed.), 85 (under 'Annesley'); Timothy Bowman, *Carson's army* (2007); *The Ulster Volunteer Force* (n.d. [2013?]), Ulster Scots Community Network, available online at: www.ulster-scots.com/uploads/901740969819.PDF; 'Transformations: politics and protests in Co. Down, 1900–1920s', section 8: 'The road to partition', Down County Museum, available online at: www.downcountymuseum.com/Transformations/Section-8-The-Road-to-Partition (websites accessed 11 August 2015)

James Robert ('Jack') White

1879–1946

James Robert ('Jack') White, soldier and anarchist, was born in May
1879 in Broughshane, near Ballymena, Co. Antrim, only son among
five children of Field-marshal Sir George Stuart White, an Anglo-
Irish landowner and distinguished soldier, and his wife Amy,
daughter of Joseph Baly, archdeacon of Calcutta. White was educated at Summerfield, Winchester (until expelled), and Sandhurst
military academy. Gazetted to the 1st Gordon Highlanders in 1899,
he fought at Magersfontein and Doornkop in the Boer war. Despite
threatening to shoot an officer who ordered him to kill an unarmed
Boer soldier, White was awarded the DSO for bravery in 1901. The
following year he joined his father (then governor of Gibraltar) as
ADC. In 1905 he married Anna Mercedes ('Dollie') Mosley, a

Catholic Spanish society beauty with whom he had one daughter. Their marriage broke up during the first world war. In 1905 White was appointed adjutant of the territorial battalion of the Gordon Highlanders in Aberdeen. Although White found war 'rather fun', he was an unenthusiastic peacetime soldier, and the influence of Leo Tolstoy's writings and his disgust for King Edward VII influenced him to resign his commission. For several years he lived, in both senses, a bohemian existence, teaching English in Bohemia, travelling through England as a virtual tramp, and emigrating to Canada, where he worked as a lumberjack. He returned to England and became a follower of the nudist Francis Sedlak, joining his communistic free-love colony in a field near Stroud in the Cotswolds.

In 1912 White returned to Ireland during the home rule crisis and became an outspoken opponent of the Ulster unionist party. The following year he helped organise a widely publicised home rule meeting in Ballymoney at which he, Sir Roger Casement, and Alice Stopford Green spoke to a mainly Protestant attendance. White was invited to Dublin, where he spoke at the Literary and Historical Society in UCD alongside John Dillon and Tom Kettle, but was unimpressed by the social conservatism of the nationalist leadership. With his aristocratic background, dapper appearance, and flamboyant air, White became a well known figure in Dublin. During the 1913 lockout he offered his services to the transport workers' strike committee at Liberty Hall. As chairman of the Civic League, it was White who suggested the idea of drilling the workers ('to teach the police manners') and he became a central figure in the subsequent formation of the Irish Citizen Army (ICA) in November 1913. After the end of the lockout, White, now drawn to socialism, took up the cause of unemployed and victimised workers and was beaten and arrested for organising a march on the Mansion House. After several disagreements with the ICA council, particularly one caused by White's offer to subordinate a section of the ICA to the Irish Volunteers (characteristically made without the ICA council's agreement), White was replaced as chairman of the ICA army council by James Larkin in May 1914.

He returned to Ulster, where he organised the Irish Volunteers in Derry city and Omagh, Co. Tyrone, but was dismissed from both commands after political disagreements. White felt the outbreak of the Great War offered an opportunity to unite Protestants and Catholics, but the local Volunteers, whom he regarded as sectarian, viewed him as a unionist sympathiser. He left for France, where he spent two years with an Australian ambulance unit but was mistrusted due to his previous association with Casement. Disgusted by the war, he returned to Britain shortly after the Easter rising and was imprisoned for three months for organising a Welsh miners' strike to protest against the execution of James Connolly. After his release he was served with an exclusion order from Ireland by Henry Duke, chief secretary for Ireland. He remained in England, where he became friendly with the literary circle of D. H. Lawrence (who portrayed White as 'Jim Bricknell' in his novel *Aaron's rod*). In 1923, after the civil war, a Donegal republican workers' council invited White to stand for the general election. Although initially enthusiastic, White withdrew, denouncing republican physical force as 'morally and politically unsound' and advocating Christian communism. He joined James Larkin's Irish Workers' League (founded in 1923) and, along with Roddy Connolly, was a founder member of the communist Workers' Party of Ireland, established in 1926. In 1930 he published an autobiography, aptly titled *Misfit*. He was jailed the following year in Northern Ireland for his involvement in the Revolutionary Workers' Groups' unemployment protests. Served with an exclusion order from Northern Ireland by Sir Dawson Bates, minister for home affairs, in 1931 White agreed not to participate in northern politics in order to continue seeing the child of his estranged wife.

White supported the short-lived Republican Congress, established in 1934, and organised a Dublin branch composed of ex-servicemen. In the mid-1930s he became a committed anti-fascist, writing the anti-fascist tract 'Where Casement would have stood today' and travelling to republican Spain as a Red Cross worker when the Spanish civil war broke out in 1936. After reportedly falling out with the communist-led International Brigades, White converted to anarchism on witnessing anarchist collectivisation and militias in action. He supported the anarchist Confederación Nacional del Trabajo (CNT) trade union and, it is thought, trained militias in Spain. He subsequently published a pamphlet, *The meaning of anarchism*, which argued that workers must free themselves through revolution by direct action and the substitution of 'free humanity' for the state. He left Spain for London where, despite disapproving of the CNT's cooperation with the republican government, he worked alongside Emma Goldman to support the Spanish anarchists through publicity and, reportedly, gun-running. In 1937 White married Noreen Shanahan, a Catholic from Dalkey, Co. Dublin, with whom he had three sons. He died in February 1946 and is buried at Broughshane First Presbyterian Church. White's eccentricity, idiosyncratic political outlook (a mixture of Christianity, Leninism, and mysticism) and unconventional enthusiasms (including psychoanalysis, free love, and anti-clericalism) rendered him a permanent outsider among even Irish radicals. A naïve and romantic figure, White believed his life was characterised by 'involuntary yet outrageous, even indecent, revolt against discipline, established custom, and mechanical habit' (*Misfit*, 15).

Fearghal McGarry

Sources

J. R. White, *Misfit: an autobiography* (1930); PRONI, Home Affairs papers, 32/1/608; *Irish Times*, 15 September 1978; Uinseann MacEoin, *The IRA in the twilight years* (1997); Fearghal McGarry, *Irish politics and the Spanish civil war* (1999); Andrew Boyd, *Jack White (1879–1946): first commander Irish Citizen Army* (2001); James Meenan, *Centenary history of the Literary and Historical Society...1855–1955* (2005 ed.), 118

Abbreviations and bibliographic conventions

ADC	aide-de-camp
AOH	Ancient Order of Hibernians
b.	born
BA	Bachelor of Arts
Ball, *Judges*	F. E. Ball, *The judges in Ireland, 1221–1921* (2 vols, London, 1926)
Burke, IFR	*Burke's Irish Family Records* (London, 1976)
Burke, *Landed gentry*	John Burke, *A genealogical and heraldic history of the commons of Great Britain and Ireland, enjoying territorial possessions* (3 vols, London, 1833–8; reissued 1837–8 as *A genealogical and heraldic history of the landed gentry...*; variant titles in later editions)
Burke, *LGI*	Sir [John] Bernard Burke, *A genealogical and heraldic history of the landed gentry of Ireland...* (London, 1899; 4th ed. (1958) published as *Burke's genealogical and heraldic history of the landed gentry of Ireland*)
Burke, *Peerage*	J[ohn] Burke, *A general and heraldic history of the peerage and baronetage...* (London, 1826; 6th ed. (1839) published as *A genealogical and heraldic dictionary of the peerage and baronetage...*; variant titles in later editions)
c.	about (*circa*)
CB	companion of the Order of the Bath
CBE	companion of the Order of the British Empire
CBS	Christian Brothers' School
C-in-C	commander in chief
CMG	companion of the Order of St Michael and St George
d.	died
DBE	dame commander of the Order of the British Empire
DIAS	Dublin Institute for Advanced Studies

DIB	*Dictionary of Irish Biography*
DIH	D. J. Hickey and J. E. Doherty, *A dictionary of Irish history since 1800* (Dublin, 1980; paperback ed., as *A dictionary...1800–1980, 1987*; 2nd ed., 2003)
DL	deputy lieutenant
DNB	*The dictionary of national biography*, ed. Sir Leslie Stephen and Sir Sidney Lee (66 vols, London, 1885–1901; reprint with corrections, 22 vols, London, 1908–9; supplementary vols for 1901 and after)
DNB, MP	*The dictionary of national biography: missing persons*, ed. C. S. Nicholls (Oxford and New York, 1993)
DSO	(companion of the) Distinguished Service Order
ed.	edited by, edition, editor(s)
FRCSI	fellow of the Royal College of Surgeons in Ireland
GOC	general officer commanding
GPO	General Post Office
GRO	General Register Office (Dublin)
HMC	Historical Manuscripts Commission
IBL	*The Irish Book Lover* (Dublin, 1909–57, 32 vols)
ICA	Irish Citizen Army
IHS	*Irish Historical Studies: the joint journal of the Irish Historical Society and the Ulster Society for Irish Historical Studies* (Dublin, 1938–)
IMMA	Irish Museum of Modern Art
IRB	Irish Republican Brotherhood
ITGWU	Irish Transport and General Workers' Union
ITWW	*A Zircon book. Who's who, what's what and where in Ireland in association with the Irish Times* (London and Dublin, 1973)
JP	justice of the peace
KC	king's counsel
KG	knight of the Order of the Garter
KP	knight of the Order of St Patrick
LLB	Bachelor of Laws
LLD	Doctor of Laws
LOL	Loyal Orange Lodge

MA	Master of Arts
MD	Doctor of Medicine
MICE	member, Institution of Civil Engineers
MIME	member, Institution of Mining Engineers
MP	member of parliament
MRIA	member of the Royal Irish Academy
MRSAI	member of the Royal Society of Antiquaries of Ireland
NAI	National Archives of Ireland
NCO	non-commissioned officer
Newmann	Kate Newmann, *Dictionary of Ulster biography* (Belfast, 1993)
NGI	National Gallery of Ireland
NHI	*A new history of Ireland* (9 vols, Oxford, 1976–2005)
NLI	National Library of Ireland
NMI	National Museum of Ireland
NUI	National University of Ireland
O'Donoghue	D. J. O'Donoghue, *The poets of Ireland: a biographical and bibliographical dictionary of Irish writers of English verse* (Dublin and London, 1912; facsimile reprint, New York, 1970)
obit.	obituary
OC	officer commanding
ODNB	*Oxford dictionary of national biography*, ed. H. C. G. Matthew and Brian Harrison (60 vols, Oxford, 2004, and online, www.oxforddnb.com)
PRO	Public Record Office
PRONI	Public Record Office of Northern Ireland
QC	queen's counsel
QCB	Queen's College, Belfast
QCC	Queen's College, Cork
QUB	Queen's University of Belfast
QUI	Queen's University of Ireland
RBAI	Royal Belfast Academical Institution
RCSI	Royal College of Surgeons in Ireland
RIA	Royal Irish Academy
RIC	Royal Irish Constabulary
RSAI	Royal Society of Antiquaries of Ireland

RTÉ	Radio Telefís Éireann
RUC	Royal Ulster Constabulary
RUI	Royal University of Ireland
TCD	Trinity College, Dublin
TD	Teachta Dála (dáil deputy)
Thom, 1844 [etc.]	*Thom's Irish almanac and official directory for the year 1844 [etc.]* (Dublin, 1844–; subsequent changes of title)
TNA	The National Archives of the UK
TUC	Trades Union Congress
UCD	University College, Dublin
UCG	University College, Galway
Walker	Brian M. Walker, *Parliamentary election results in Ireland ...* (2 vols, Dublin, 1978, 1992)
WWW	*Who Was Who...1897–1916 [etc.]* (London, 1920–)

Bibliography

Archives

Belfast Central Library:
   Francis Joseph Bigger papers
   Local History Newscuttings Collection
British Library:
   Gladstone papers
   Royal Literary Fund, Registered Case 1511
Down County Museum:
   Wallace papers, DB1008 2002–140
GRO (Dublin)
Henry family papers
Impartial Reporter, Enniskillen:
   Trimble correspondence and family papers
   (in possession of Joan McVeigh)
King's Inns, Dublin:
   Admission papers
Mount St Mary's College archives
NAI:
   DFA 31, 200–210
   Military Archives: *Spearhead* (journal of Army 2nd Division),
   December 1944
NLI:
   Mac Neill papers
   Patrick McCartan papers
O'Connell Schools, Dublin:
   Brother Allen Library
Omagh Public Library:
   Catherine Morris research archive on Alice Milligan
PRO:
   W. E. Wylie papers: Unpublished memoir, PRO 30/89-1.
PRONI:
   Brooke papers, D3004, 998
   CAB/4/48/11
   CAB/4/79/6
   CAB/4/140/7
   CAB/6/57
   CAB/8/B/11
   CAB/9D/9/11
   Cahir Healy papers, D2991
   Carson papers, D/150/F/11/11–16, D/1507/F/11/11, D/2298/16/1

Craig papers (and papers of Lady Craigavon)
D/1792/A3/1/24; D/1792/A3/3/1
D627/434/6
D1507/A/4/25
James Henry and family members (will of), LR/141
Home Affairs papers, 32/1/608
Northern Ireland government papers
Records of Draperstown national school for boys, 1870–1903, SCH/665/1/1
Unionist Party papers
Wallace papers, D1889/8/4; Diary, D1889/4/13
Saunderson papers, T/2996 and MIC/281
Queen's University Belfast:
    Herbert M. Pim papers
    Records and senate minutes, 1912–13
TNA:
    Robert Hugh Wallace, War Office file, WO339/16249
UCD Archives:
    Aiken papers, P104
    Seán MacEntee papers P67/776 (11); P67/281; P67/734; P67/520; P67/479(13)
    MacNeill papers
    Denis McCullough papers, P120
    Desmond Ryan papers, LA10
Wilson and Simms, solicitors, Strabane:
    Holdings of correspondence between Carson and Henry

Commemorative publications

Cuimhneachán Mhuineacháin 1916–66. Monaghan: Clogher Historical Society, 1966.

Down Recorder, series on the South Down Militia in the South African war, June–July 1988.

Impartial Reporter, commemorative anniversary issue 1825–75, May 1975.

Reference

American Biography: a new cyclopedia, vol. 35. New York: American Historical Society Inc., 1928.

Annual Register. London, 1924.

Ball, F. E. *The judges in Ireland, 1221–1921*. London, 1926.

Breathnach, Diarmuid, agus Máire Ní Mhurchú. *Beathaisnéis 1882–1982*, v. Dublin, 1997.

Belfast street directory. Belfast, 1885 and subsequent years.

Burke. *Peerage*. London, 1999.

Burke. *Burke's Irish family records*. London, 1976.

Debrett. *Baronetage*. London, 1940.

Dictionary of Irish history since 1800. Dublin, 1980 and subsequent editions.

Dictionary of national biography. London, 1885–1901 and supplements.

Hansard. *Parliamentary debates*. London, 1812 and subsequent years.

Thom. *Incorporated Law Society's Calendar and Law Directory for 1920*. Dublin, 1920.

Irish Law Times and Solicitors' Journal. Dublin, 1867 and subsequent years.

Irish Law Times Reports. Dublin, 1871 and subsequent years.

Irish Trade Union Congress. *Annual Reports (1901–13)*. Dublin, 1901 and subsequent years.

Newmann, Kate. *Dictionary of Ulster biography*. Belfast, 1993.

New History of Ireland, 9 vols (vol. 6). Oxford, 1996.

O'Donoghue, D. J. *The poets of Ireland*. Dublin and London, 1912.

Oxford dictionary of national biography. Oxford, 2004, and online.

Slater's national commercial directory of Ireland. Manchester and London, 1856 and subsequent years.

Thom. *Irish almanac and official directory*. Dublin, 1844 and subsequent years.

Thom. *Irish Who's Who*. Dublin and London, 1923

Walker, Brian M. *Parliamentary election results in Ireland* (2 vols). Dublin: Royal Irish Academy, 1978, 1992.

Who's who, what's what and where in Ireland. London and Dublin: Zircon, in association with the *Irish Times*, 1973.

Who was who 1897–1916 [*etc.*]. London, 1920–.

www.election.demon.co.uk/stormont/biographies.html, accessed 4 August 2003.

Newspapers and periodicals

Banbridge Chronicle
Belfast Newsletter
Belfast Telegraph
Belfast Weekly Telegraph
Catholic
Catholic Bulletin
Clogher Record
Coleraine Chronicle
County Down Spectator
Daily Telegraph
Derry Journal
Derry Standard

Donegal Independent
Down Recorder
Fermanagh Times
Fermanagh Herald
Freeman's Journal
Frontier Sentinel
Gaelic-American
Garda Review
Glasgow Observer
Impartial Reporter
Irish Book Lover
Irish Independent

Irish News
Irish People
Irish Protestant
Irish Times
Irish Truth
Irish Weekly
Leader
Londonderry Sentinel
Newry Telegraph
Newtownards Chronicle
Northern Constitution
Northern Whig
Scotsman

Shan Van Vocht
Strabane Chronicle
Sunday News
Times
Toronto Daily Star
Tyrone Constitution
Ulster Echo
Ulster Guardian
Ulster Herald
Ulster Year Books (1926–69)
United Irishman
Vindicator

Books and articles

Allen, Gregory. *The Garda Síochána: policing independent Ireland 1922–82.* Dublin: Gill and Macmillan, 1999.

Allen, Nicholas. *George Russell (Æ) and the new Ireland, 1905–30.* Dublin: Four Courts, 2003.

Anderson, R. A. *With Plunkett in Ireland: the Co-op organiser's story.* Dublin: Irish Academic Press, 1983 (reprint of 1935 edition).

Andrews, C. S. *Dublin made me: an autobiography.* Dublin: Mercier, 1979.

Andrews, C. S. *Man of no property: an autobiography* vol. 2. Dublin, Irish Book Centre, 1982.

Anon. *In memoriam Reverend Richard Lyttle, Moneyrea.* Belfast, 1906.

Anon. Obituary notice: Francis Joseph Bigger, *Journal of the Royal Society of Antiquaries of Ireland* 6th series, xvii, 1927, 73.

Armour, William Staveley. *Armour of Ballymoney.* London: Duckworth, 1934.

Armour, William Staveley. *Facing the Irish question.* London: Duckworth, 1935.

Armour, William Staveley. *Mankind at the watershed.* London: Duckworth, 1936.

Armour, William Staveley. *Ulster, Ireland, Britain: a forgotten trust.* London: Duckworth, 1938.

Barton, Brian E. *Brookeborough: the making of a prime minister.* Belfast: Institute of Irish Studies, Queen's University, 1988.

Barton, Brian E. 'Relations between Westminster and Stormont during the Attlee premiership', *Irish Political Studies*, vii, 1992, 1–20.

Barton, Brian E. *Northern Ireland in the second world war.* Belfast: Ulster Historical Foundation, 1995.

Bardon, Jonathan. *A history of Ulster.* Belfast: Blackstaff, 1992.

Bell, Sam Hanna. *The theatre in Ulster*. Dublin: Gill and Macmillan, 1972.

Bennett, Thomas J. G. *North Antrim families*. Aberdeen: Volturna Press, 1974.

Bew, Paul and Frank Wright. 'The agrarian opposition in Ulster politics, 1848–87', in Samuel Clark and James S. Donnelly, jr (ed.), *Irish peasants: violence and political unrest, 1780–1914*, 192–229. Madison, Wisc. and Manchester: University of Wisconsin Press and Manchester University Press, 1983.

Binchy, D. A. 'Eoin MacNeill', *Dictionary of national biography 1941–1950*. London: Oxford University Press, 1959.

Blair, S. Alex. 'Just a youth of fifty-five: the story of the Young Farmers' Clubs of Ulster', *Ulster Local Studies*, ix (1984), 16–19.

Blaney, Roger. *Presbyterians and the Irish language*. Belfast, Ultach Press, 1996.

Blavatsky, H. P. *The secret doctrine: the synthesis of science, religion, and philosophy*. London: Theosophical Society, 1888.

Blythe, Ernest. *A new departure in northern policy: an appeal to the leaders of nationalist opinion*. Dublin: Basil Clancy, 1959.

Bolger, Patrick. *The Irish co-operative movement: its history and development*. Dublin: Institute of Public Administration, 1977.

Bossence, Ralph. 'Aunt Jane boiled bones' [on Pim's *Unknown immortals*], *Belfast Newsletter*, 12 October 1966.

Bossence, Ralph. 'Diary', *Belfast Newsletter*, 19 October 1966.

Bossence, Ralph. 'More about Herbert Moore Pim', *Belfast Newsletter*, 2 November 1966.

Bossence, Ralph. 'Words and a man of action', *Belfast Newsletter*, 22 November 1966.

Bowman, Timothy. *Carson's army: the Ulster Volunteer Force, 1910–22*. Manchester: Manchester University Press, 2007.

Boyd, Andrew. *Jack White (1879–1946): first commander Irish Citizen Army*. Belfast: Donaldson Archives, 2001.

Boyle, John W. 'The Belfast Protestant Association and the Independent Orange Order, 1901–10', *Irish Historical Studies*, xiii, 1962–3, 117–52.

Boyle, John W. (ed.). *Leaders and workers*. Cork: Mercier Press, 1966.

Boyle, John W. 'Robert Lindsay Crawford, 1910–1922; a Fenian Protestant in Canada', in Robert O'Driscoll and Lorna Reynolds (ed.), *The untold story: the Irish in Canada*, vol. 2, 635–46. Toronto: Celtic Arts of Canada, 1988.

Boyle, John W. *The Irish labour movement in the nineteenth century*. Washington, D.C.: Catholic University of America Press, 1988.

Bradbury, John. *Celebrated citizens of Belfast*. Belfast: Appletree Press, 2002.

Brady, Conor. *Guardians of the peace*. Dublin: Gill and Macmillan, 1974.

Breathnach, Eibhlín. 'Charting new waters: women's experience in higher education, 1879–1908', in Mary Cullen (ed.), *Girls don't do honours: Irish women in education in the 19th and 20th centuries*, 55–78. Dublin: Argus Press, 1987.

Brooke, R. F. *The brimming river*. Dublin: Allen Figgis, 1961.

Brown, William Francis. *Through windows of memory*. London: Sands, 1946.

Brown, S. J. *Ireland in fiction: a guide to Irish novels, tales, romances, and folklore*, i (2nd ed.). London: Maunsel and Company, 1919; reprint, 1968.

Buckland, Patrick. *Irish unionism, i: the Anglo-Irish and the new Ireland 1885–1922*. Dublin: Gill and Macmillan, 1972.

Buckland, Patrick (ed.). *Irish unionism 1885–1923: a documentary history*. Belfast: PRONI, 1973.

Buckland, Patrick. *Irish Unionism, ii, Ulster unionism and the origins of northern Ireland, 1886–1922*. Dublin: Gill and Macmillan, 1973.

Buckland, Patrick. *The factory of grievances: devolved government in Northern Ireland 1921–39*. Dublin: Gill and Macmillan, 1979.

Buckland, Patrick. *James Craig, Lord Craigavon*. Dublin: Gill and Macmillan, 1980.

Burls, John (ed.). *Nine generations: a history of the Andrews family, millers of Comber*. Belfast: Isaac Andrews, 1958.

Burnett, David. 'The modernisation of unionism, 1892–1914?', in Richard English and Graham Walker (ed.), *Unionism in modern Ireland: new perspectives on politics and culture*, 41–64. London: Macmillan, 1996.

Byrne, Art and Sean McMahon. *Great northerners*. Dublin: Poolbeg Press, 1991.

L. P. Byrne, *Twenty-one years of the Irish Agricultural Wholesale Society, 1897–1918*. Dublin: Irish Agricultural Wholesale Society, 1919.

Campbell, Flann. *The dissenting voice: Protestant democracy in Ulster from plantation to partition*. Belfast: Blackstaff Press, 1991.

Carbery, Ethna. *The passionate hearts*. Dublin and London: M. H. Gill and Isbister and Company, 1903.

Carbery, Ethna. *In the Celtic past*. New York: Funk and Wagnalls, 1904.

Carbery, Ethna. *The four winds of Eirinn*, ed. Seumas MacManus. Dublin: M. H. Gill, 1906.

Carbery, Ethna. *We sang for Ireland: poems of Ethna Carbery, Seumas MacManus, Alice Milligan*. Dublin: M. H. Gill, 1950.

Carroll, F. M. *American opinion and the Irish question, 1910–23: a study in opinion and policy*. Dublin: Gill and Macmillan, 1978.

Casey, J. *The Irish law officers: roles and responsibilities of the Attorney General and the Director of Public Prosecutions*. Dublin: Round Hall Sweet and Maxwell, 1996.

Clarke, Kathleen. *Revolutionary woman: Kathleen Clarke, 1878–1972, an autobiography* (edited by Helen Litton). Dublin: O'Brien Press, 1991.

Clarke, R. S. J. and A. C. W. Merrick. *Old Belfast families and the New Burying Ground* (vol. 4 of *Gravestone Inscriptions*). Belfast: Ulster Historical Foundation, 1991.

Clarkson, J. Dunsmore. *Labour and nationalism in Ireland*. Studies in History, Economics and Public Law, 120. New York: Columbia University Press, 1925.

Clyde, William. *Æ*. Edinburgh: Moray, 1935.

Coates, C. C. *Some less-known chapters in the life of Æ (George Russell): being the substance of a lecture delivered at Belfast, November, 1936*. Privately printed, 1939.

Collins, Peter. 'Mary Galway', *Labour History News*, no. 7, summer 1991, 14–15.

Collins, Stephen. *The power game: Fianna Fáil since Lemass*. Dublin: O'Brien Press, 2000.

Colvin, Ian. *The life of Lord Carson*, ii. London: Victor Gollancz, 1934.

Coogan, Tim Pat. *Michael Collins: a biography*. London: Hutchinson, 1990.

Cork Workers' Club. *The Connolly/Walker controversy*. Cork Workers' Club Historical Reprints, 9. Cork: Cork Workers' Club, 1974.

Cousins, Mel. *The birth of social welfare in Ireland, 1922–1952*. Dublin: Four Courts, 2003.

Craig, Patricia. *Brian Moore: a biography*. London: Bloomsbury, 2002.

Crawford, Fred H. *Guns for Ulster*. Belfast: Graham and Heslip, 1947 (reprinted Books Ulster, 2014).

Crawford, R. Lindsay and Richard Braithwaite. *Orangeism, its history and progress—a plea for first principles*. Belfast: Independent Grand Lodge of Ireland, 1904.

Crichton, Frances Elizabeth. *The precepts of Andy Saul*. Belfast: McCaw, Stevenson and Orr, 1908.

Crichton, Frances Elizabeth. *The soundless tide*. New York: Baker and Taylor, 1911.

Crichton, Frances Elizabeth. *Tinker's Hollow*. London: E. Arnold, 1912.

Crone, J. S. and F. C. Bigger (ed.). *In remembrance. Articles and sketches: biographical, historical, topographical by Francis Joseph Bigger M.A., M.R.I.A., F.R.S.A.I.* Dublin and Cork: Talbot Press, 1927.

Cronin, Mike. *The Blueshirts and Irish politics*. Dublin, Four Courts, 1997.

Cronin, Sean. *The McGarrity papers*. Dublin: Anvil Books, 1972.

Crossland, Bernard and John S. Moore. *The lives of great engineers of Ulster*, i. Belfast: NE Consultancy and QUB, 2003.

Curtis, jr, L. P. *Coercion and conciliation in Ireland, 1880–82: a study in conservative unionism*. Princeton, NJ: Princeton University Press, 1963.

Daly, Mary E. *Industrial development and Irish national identity, 1922–1939*. New York, Syracuse University Press, 1992.

Daly, Mary E. *The first department: a history of the Department of Agriculture*. Dublin: Institute of Public Administration, 2002.

Davis, R. B. *George William Russell (Æ)*. London: George Prior Publishers and Boston: Twayne Ltd, 1977.

Davison, John Biggs- and George Chowdharay-Best. *The cross of St Patrick: the Catholic unionist tradition in Ireland.* Bourne End: Kensal Press, 1984.

de Blaghd, Earnán. *Briseadh na teorann.* Dublin: Sáirséal agus Dill, 1955.

de Blaghd, Earnán. *Trasna na Bóinne.* Dublin: Sáirséal agus Dill, 1957.

de Blaghd, Earnán. *Slán le hUltaibh.* Dublin: Sáirséal agus Dill, 1970.

de Blaghd, Earnán. *Gaeil Á Múscailt.* Dublin: Sáirséal agus Dill, 1973.

Denson, Alan (ed.). *Letters from Æ.* London: Abelard-Shuman, 1961.

Dewar, James (ed.). *A history of Elmwood Presbyterian church, with biographical sketches of its pastors and founders, 1859–1899.* Belfast, 1900.

Dillon, Charles and Henry A. Jeffries (ed.). *Tyrone, history and society.* Dublin: Geography Publications, 2000.

Dixon, Roger. 'Francis Bigger, Ulster's Don Quixote', *Ulster Folklife*, xliii, 1997, 40–7.

Down County Museum. 'Transformations: politics and protests in Co. Down, 1900–1920s', section 8: 'The road to partition', available online at: www.downcountymuseum.com/Transformations/Section-8-The-Road-to-Partition (accessed 11 August 2015).

Dudgeon, Jeffrey. *Roger Casement: the black diaries: with a study of his background, sexuality and Irish political life.* Belfast: Belfast Press, 2002.

Dunraven, Earl of. *Past times and pastimes*, ii. London: Stodder and Houghton, 1922.

Edwards, Ruth Dudley. *Patrick Pearse: the triumph of failure.* Dublin: Irish Academic Press, 1977.

Eglinton, John. *A memoir of Æ: George William Russell.* London: Coracle Press, 1937.

Ervine, St John. *Craigavon: Ulsterman.* London: Allen and Unwin, 1949.

Fanning, Ronan. *The Irish Department of Finance 1922–58.* Dublin: Institute of Public Administration, 1978.

Fanning, Ronan. 'Playing it cool: the response of the British and Irish governments to the crisis in Northern Ireland, 1968–69', *Irish Studies in International Affairs*, xii, 2001, 57–85.

Fanning, Ronan. *Fatal path: British government and Irish revolution, 1910-1922.* London: Faber and Faber, 2013.

Fanning, Ronan, *et al.* (ed.). *Documents on Irish foreign policy*, i, *1919–1922.* Dublin: Royal Irish Academy, 1998.

Fanning, Ronan, *et al.* (ed.). *Documents in Irish foreign policy*, ii, *1923–1926.* Dublin: Royal Irish Academy, 2000.

Faulkner, Pádraig. *As I saw it: reviewing over 30 years of Fianna Fáil and Irish politics.* Dublin: Wolfhound Press, 2005.

Farrell, Brian. *Seán Lemass.* Dublin: Gill and Macmillan, 1991 (originally published 1983).

Farrell, Michael. *Arming the Protestants: the formation of the Ulster Special Constabulary and the Royal Ulster Constabulary 1920–7.* London: Pluto Press, 1983.

Figgis, Darrell. *Æ (George W. Russell): a study of a man and a nation*. Dublin: History Press, 1975 (originally published Dublin and London: Maunsel and Co., 1916).

Fisk, Robert. *In time of war: Ireland, Ulster and the price of neutrality 1939–45*. Philadelphia: University of Pennsylvania Press, 1983.

Fitz-Simon, Christopher. *The Abbey Theatre: Ireland's national theatre—the first 100 years*. London: Thames and Hudson, 2003.

Flackes, W. D. *The enduring premier*. Belfast: 1962 (collection of interviews; also published in *Belfast Telegraph*).

Flint, John. *Cecil Rhodes*. London: Hutchinson, 1976.

Flynn, Kevin Haddick-. *Orangeism: the making of a tradition*. Dublin: Wolfhound Press, 1999.

Follis, Bryan. *A state under siege: the establishment of Northern Ireland, 1920–1925*. Oxford: Clarendon Press, 1995.

Foster, John Wilson. *The age of Titanic: cross-currents of Anglo-American culture*. Dublin: Merlin Press, 2002.

Foy, Michael, and Brian Barton. *The Easter rising*. Stroud: History Press, 1999.

Frame, Hugh. *A short history of the Lyttle Memorial School, Moneyrea*. 1932.

Gailey, Andrew. *Ireland and the death of kindness: the experience of constructive unionism, 1890–1905*. Cork: Cork University Press, 1987.

Galway, Mary. 'The linen industry in the north and the betterment of working conditions', in William G. Fitzgerald (ed.), *The voice of Ireland: a survey of the race and nation from all angles*. Dublin and London: Virtue and Company, 1924.

Gardiner, A. G. *The life of Sir William Harcourt*, ii. London: Constable and Robinson, 1923.

Gardner, Robin, and Dan van der Vat. *The riddle of the Titanic*. London: Weidenfeld, 1995.

Garvin, Tom, *et al.* (ed.). *Dissecting Irish politics: essays in honour of Brian Farrell*. Dublin: UCD Press, 2004.

Gaughan, J. A. (ed.). *The memoirs of Senator Joseph Connolly (1885–1961): a maker of modern Ireland*. Dublin: Irish Academic Press, 1996.

Grand Orange Lodge of Ireland. *The formation of the Orange Order 1795–1798: the edited papers of Colonel William Blacker and Colonel Robert H. Wallace*. Belfast: Education Committee of the Grand Orange Lodge of Ireland, 1994.

Greaves, C. Desmond. *The life and times of James Connolly*. London: Lawrence and Wishart, 1961.

Greaves, C. Desmond. *The Irish Transport and General Workers Union: the formative years 1909–23*. Dublin: Gill and Macmillan, 1982.

Greene, David. 'The Irish language movement', in Michael Hurley (ed.), *Irish anglicanism 1869–1969*, 110–19. Dublin: Figgis, 1970.

Gwynn, Denis. *Life of John Redmond*. Bombay and Sydney: George G. Harap and Co., 1932.

Gwynn, Stephen. *John Redmond's last years*. London: Edward Arnold, 1919.

Haines, Keith. *Fred Crawford: Carson's gunrunner*. Donaghadee: Cottage Publications, 2009.

Harbinson, John Fitzsimons. 'A history of the Northern Ireland Labour Party 1891–1949'. Unpublished MSc thesis, QUB, 1966.

Harbinson, John F. *The Ulster Unionist party, 1882–1973: its development and organisation*. Belfast: Blackstaff Press, 1973.

Harris, Rosemary. *Prejudice and tolerance in Ulster: a study of neighbours and 'strangers' in a border community*. Manchester: Manchester University Press, 1972.

Hay, Marnie. 'Bulmer Hobson: the rise and fall of an Irish nationalist'. Unpublished PhD thesis, UCD, 2004.

Healy, Cahir. *The mutilation of a nation*. Derry: Derry Journal, 1945.

Healy, Cahir, and Cathal O'Byrne. *The lane of the thrushes: some Ulster love-songs*. Dublin: Sealy, Bryers and Walker, 1905.

Healy, Maurice. *The old Munster circuit*. London: Michael Joseph, 1935.

Healy, T. M. *Letters and leaders of my day* (2 vols). New York: Frederick A. Stokes, 1928.

Hegarty, Peter. *Peadar O'Donnell*. Cork: Mercier Press, 1999.

Hennessey, Thomas. *A history of Northern Ireland, 1920–1996*. Dublin: Gill and Macmillan, 1997.

Hennessy, Thomas. *Dividing Ireland: World War I and partition*. London: Routledge, 1998.

Hepburn, A. C. *A past apart: studies in the history of Catholic Belfast, 1850–1950*. Belfast: Ulster Historical Foundation, 1996.

Hezlet, Arthur. *The B Specials: a history of the Ulster Special Constabulary*. London: Pan Books, 1972.

Hinkson, Pamela (ed.). *Seventy years young: memories of Elizabeth, countess of Fingall*. London: Collins, 1937.

Hobson, Bulmer. *Ireland yesterday and tomorrow*. Dublin: Anvil Books, 1968.

Hogan, Robert (ed.). *The Macmillan dictionary of Irish literature*. London: Macmillan, 1979.

Holloway, Penny, and Terry Craden. 'The Irish Trade Union Congress and working women, 1894–1914', *Saothar*, xxiii, 1998, 47–59.

Hopkinson, Michael. *Green against green: the Irish civil war*. Dublin: Gill and Macmillan, 1988.

Hopkinson, Michael (ed.). *The last days of Dublin Castle: the diaries of Mark Sturgis*. Dublin: Irish Academic Press, 1999.

Hopkinson, Michael. *The Irish war of independence*. Dublin: Gill and Macmillan, 2002.

Horgan, John. *Seán Lemass: the enigmatic patriot*. Dublin: Gill and Macmillan, 1997.

Hostettler, John. *Sir Edward Carson: a dream too far.* Chichester: Barry Rose Law Publishers, 1997.

Hyde, H. Montgomery. *The life of Sir Edward Carson, Lord Carson of Duncairn.* New York: Octagon Books, 1953.

Hyde, H. Montgomery. *The Londonderrys: a family portrait.* London: Hamish Hamilton, 1979.

Jackson, Alvin. 'Irish unionism and the Russellite threat, 1894–1906', *Irish Historical Studies,* xxv, 1987, 376–404.

Jackson, Alvin. *The Ulster party: Irish unionists in the house of commons, 1884–1911.* Oxford: Clarendon Press, 1989.

Jackson, Alvin. *Sir Edward Carson.* Dublin: Historical Association of Ireland: Dundalgan Press, 1993.

Jackson, Alvin. *Colonel Edward Saunderson: land and loyalty in Victorian Ireland.* Oxford: Clarendon Press, 1995.

Johnson, David. 'Sir George Smith Clark', in D. J. Jeremy (ed.), *Dictionary of business biography.* London: Butterworths, 1984.

Johnston, Sheila Turner. *Alice: a life of Alice Milligan.* Omagh: Colourpoint Press, 1994.

Jones, Mark Bence-. *Twilight of the ascendancy.* London: Constable, 1988.

Jordan, Alison. *Margaret Byers: pioneer of women's education and founder of Victoria College, Belfast.* Belfast: QUB Institute of Irish Studies, 1987.

'Jurist' (Lindsay Crawford). *The iron heel: or, The fight for freedom.* Belfast, 1903.

Kavanagh, Patrick. *The green fool.* London: Michael Joseph, 1938.

Keatinge, Patrick. *A place among the nations: issues of Irish foreign policy.* Dublin: Institute of Public Administration, 1978.

Keightley, Samuel R. *A king's daughter and other poems.* Belfast: McCaw, Stevenson and Orr, 1878.

Keightley, Samuel R. *The crimson sign.* London: Hutchinson and Company, 1894.

Keightley, Samuel R. *The cavaliers.* London: Hutchinson and Company, 1895.

Keightley, Samuel R. *The last recruit of Clare's.* New York: Harper, 1897.

Keightley, Samuel R. *The silver cross.* New York: Dodd, Mead, 1898.

Keightley, Samuel R. *Heronford.* New York: Dodd, Mead, 1899.

Keightley, Samuel R. *A man of millions.* New York: Dodd, Mead, 1901.

Keightley, Samuel R. *The pikemen: a romance of the Ards of Down.* London: Hutchinson, 1903.

Keightley, Samuel R. *Barnaby's bridal.* London: John Long, 1906.

Keightley, Samuel R. *A beggar on horseback.* London: John Long, 1906.

Kendle, John. *Walter Long, Ireland, and the Union, 1905–20.* Montreal: McGill-Queen's University Press, 1992.

Kennedy, Michael. *Division and consensus: the politics of cross-border relations in Ireland, 1925–69.* Dublin: Institute of Public Administration, 2000.

Kennedy, Michael, and Deirdre McMahon (ed.). *Obligations and responsibilities: Ireland and the United Nations 1955–2005. Essays marking fifty years of Ireland's United Nations membership.* Dublin: Institute of Public Administration, 2005.

Kerr, Rosalie. 'Songs from an Ulster valley: the unconventional career of Herbert Moore Pim', *New Ulster,* spring 1994, 11–15.

Kotsonouris, Mary. *Retreat from revolution: the dáil courts, 1920–24.* Dublin: Irish Academic Press, 1994.

Kuch, Peter. *Yeats and 'Æ': the antagonism that unites dear friends.* Gerrards Cross: Colin Smythe, 1986.

Laffan, Michael. *The resurrection of Ireland: the Sinn Féin party 1916–1923.* Cambridge: Cambridge University Press, 1999.

Lee, J. J. *Ireland 1912–1985.* Cambridge: Cambridge University Press, 1989.

Leslie, Shane. *The Irish tangle for English readers.* London: MacDonald, 1946.

Levenson, Samuel. *James Connolly: a biography.* London: Martin, Brian and O'Keefe, 1973.

Levitas, Ben. *The theatre of nation: Irish drama and cultural nationalism, 1890–1916.* Oxford: Oxford University Press, 2002.

Lewis, Geoffrey. *Carson: the man who divided Ireland.* London and New York: Hambledon and London, 2005.

Lindsay, Patrick. *Memories.* Dublin: Blackwater Press, 1992.

Livingstone, Peadar. *The Monaghan story: a documented history of the County Monaghan from the earliest times to 1976.* Monaghan: Clogher Historical Society, 1980.

Loeber, Rolf, and Magda Loeber. *A guide to Irish fiction 1650–1900.* Dublin: Four Courts, 2006.

Long, Patrick. 'Organisation and development of the pro-treaty forces, 1922–1924', *Irish Sword,* xx, no. 82, winter 1997, 308–30.

Loughlin, James. *Gladstone, home rule and the Ulster question, 1882–93.* Dublin: Gill and Macmillan, 1986.

Loughlin, James. 'T. W. Russell, the tenant-farmer interest, and progressive unionism in Ulster, 1886–1900', *Éire–Ireland,* xxv, no. 1, 1990, 44–63.

Lucas, Reginald. *Colonel Saunderson MP: a memoir.* London: John Murray, 1908.

Luddy, Maria. *Women and philanthropy in nineteenth-century Ireland.* Cambridge: Cambridge University Press, 1995.

Luddy, Maria. 'Isabella M. S. Tod (1836–1896)', in Mary Cullen and Maria Luddy (ed.), *Women, power and consciousness in nineteenth-century Ireland,* 197–230. Dublin: Attic Press, 1995.

Luddy, Maria. 'Women and politics in nineteenth century Ireland', in Maryann G. Valiulis and Mary O'Dowd (eds), *Women and Irish history,* 89–108. Dublin: Wolfhound Press, 1997.

Lynch, Diarmuid. *The I.R.B. and the 1916 insurrection* (edited by Florence O'Donoghue). Cork: Mercier Press, 1957.

Lynch, John P. (ed.). *Forgotten shipbuilders of Belfast: Workman, Clark 1880–1935*. Belfast: Friar's Bush Press, 2004 (reprint, with introduction, of 1903 and 1933 promotional volumes).

Lynch, John P. *An unlikely success story: the Belfast shipbuilding industry, 1880–1935*. Belfast: Belfast Society, 2001.

Lyons, F. S. L. 'The Irish unionist party and the devolution crisis of 1904–5', *Irish Historical Studies*, vi, March 1948, 1–22.

Lyttle, Richard. *The origin of the fight with the Boers* (5th ed., with additional material). London: William Brown and Sons, 1900.

Mac Annaidh, Seamas. *Fermanagh books, writers and newspapers of the nineteenth century*. Enniskillen: Marmara Denizi, 1999.

MacAtasney, Gerard. *Seán MacDiarmada: the mind of the revolution*. Leitrim: Drumlin, 2004.

McBride, Lawrence W. *The greening of Dublin Castle: the transformation of bureaucraic and judicial personnel in Ireland, 1882–1922*. Washington, DC: Catholic University of America Press, 1991.

McBrinn, Joseph. 'The peasant and folk art revival in Ireland, 1890–1920: with special reference to Ulster', *Ulster Folklife*, xlviii, 2002, 14–69.

McCartan, Patrick. *With de Valera in America*. Dublin: Fitzpatrick, 1932.

McCartan, Patrick. 'Extracts from the papers of the late Dr Patrick McCartan', *Clogher Record*, v, 1963–4, 30–45, 184–212.

McCarthy, M. J. F. *The nonconformist treason*. Edinburgh and London: Blackwood, 1912.

McCoole, Sinéad. *No ordinary women: Irish female activists in the revolutionary years 1900–1923*. Dublin: O'Brien Press, 2003.

McCormack, W. J. *Roger Casement in death; or, Haunting the Free State*. Dublin: UCD Press, 2002.

McCrea, Daniel F. *History and album of the Irish Race Convention which met in Dublin the first three days of September 1896...With memoirs, list of delegates, proceedings &c.* Dublin: Sealy, Bryers and Walker, 1897.

McCullagh, David. *A makeshift majority: the first Interparty Government, 1948–51*. Dublin: Institute of Public Administration, 1998.

McDowell, R. B. *The Irish Convention, 1917–18*. London: Routledge and Kegan Paul, 1970.

MacEoin, Uinseann. *The IRA in the twilight years*. Dublin: Argenta Publications, 1997.

MacEntee, Seán. *The poems of John Francis MacEntee* (edited by Padric Gregory). Dublin: Talbot Press, 1917.

MacEntee, Sean. *Episode at Easter*. Dublin: Gill and Son, 1966.

MacEntee, Sean. 'Sean Lemass', *Irish Press*, 12 May 1971.

McFarland, Elaine W. *Protestants first! Orangeism in nineteenth-century Scotland*. Edinburgh: Edinburgh University Press, 1990.

McFarland, Elaine W. *John Ferguson, 1836–1906: Irish issues in Scottish politics*. East Linton: Tuckwell Press, 2003.

McGarry, Fearghal. *Irish politics and the Spanish civil war*. Cork: Cork University Press, 1999.

McGarry, Fearghal. *Eoin O'Duffy: a self-made hero*. Oxford: Oxford University Press, 2005.

McInerney, Michael. 'Sean MacEntee', *Irish Times*, 22–5 July 1974.

MacKnight, Thomas. *The Right Honourable Benjamin Disraeli M.P.: a literary and political biography*. London: Richard Bentley, 1854.

MacKnight, Thomas. *Thirty years of foreign policy: a history of the secretaryships of the Earl of Aberdeen and Viscount Palmerston*. London: Longman, Brown, Green and Longman, 1855.

MacKnight, Thomas. *History of the life and times of Edmund Burke* (3 vols). London: Chapman and Hall, 1858–60.

MacKnight, Thomas. *The life of Henry St John, Viscount Bolingbroke*. London: Chapman and Hall, 1863.

MacKnight, Thomas. *Ulster as it is, or, Twenty-eight years' experience as an Irish editor* (2 vols). London: Macmillan and Son, 1896.

MacKnight, Thomas. *Political progress in the nineteenth century* revised and completed by C. C. Osborne. London, Toronto and Philadelphia: Linscott Publishing Company and Chambers, 1902.

McMillan, William. *A history of the Moneyreagh congregation 1719–1969*. Moneyreagh: Moneyreagh Church Committee, 1969.

McMinn, J. R. B. *Against the tide: a calendar of the papers of Rev. J. B. Armour, Irish Presbyterian minister and home ruler 1869–1914*. Belfast: PRONI, 1985.

MacNeill, Eoin. *Irish in the National University: a plea for Irish education*. Dublin: An Cló-Cumann Ltd, 1909.

MacNeill, Eoin. 'The North began', *An Claideamh Soluis*, 1 November 1913.

MacNeill, Eoin. *Shall Ireland be divided?* Dublin: Irish Volunteers Headquarters, 1915.

MacNeill, Eoin. *Phases of Irish history*. Dublin: Gill and Son, 1919.

MacNeill, Eoin. *Celtic Ireland*. Dublin: Martin Lester, 1921.

McNeill, Ronald. *Ulster's stand for union*. London: John Murray, 1922.

McNiffe, Liam. *A history of the Garda Síochána: a social history of the force 1922–52, with an overview of the years 1952–97*. Dublin: Wolfhound Press, 1997.

Mhic Sheain, Brighid. 'Glimpses of Erin. Alice Milligan: poet, protestant, patriot', supplement to *Fortnight*, no. 362, April 1994. Belfast: Fortnight Educational Trust, 1994.

Malcolm, Elizabeth. *'Ireland sober, Ireland free': drink and temperance in nineteenth-century Ireland*. Dublin: Gill and Macmillan, 1986.

Maloney, W. J. *The forged Casement diaries*. Dublin: Talbot Press, 1937.

Mangan, Henry. 'Introduction', *Poems by Alice Milligan*. Dublin: M.H. Gill, 1954.

Manning, Maurice. *The Blueshirts*. Dublin: Gill and Macmillan, 1970 (2nd ed. 1987; reprint 1988).

Marjoribanks, Edward, and Ian Colvin. *Life of Lord Carson* (3 vols). London: Victor Gollancz, 1932–6.

Martin, F. X. *The Irish Volunteers, 1913–1915: recollections and documents.* Dublin: J. Duffy, 1963.

Martin, F. X. *The Howth gunrunning and the Kilcoole gunrunning 1914.* Dublin: Browne and Nolan, 1964.

Martin, F. X. (ed.) 'The McCartan documents, 1916', *Clogher Record*, vi, 1966, 5–65.

Martin, F. X. and F. J. Byrne (ed.). *The scholar revolutionary: Eoin MacNeill, 1867–1945, and the making of the new Ireland.* Shannon: Irish University Press, 1973.

Maume, Patrick. *The long gestation: Irish nationalist life 1891–1918.* Dublin: Gill and Macmillan, 1999.

Maume, Patrick. 'Anti-Machiavel; three Ulster nationalists in the age of de Valera', *Irish Political Studies* 14, 1999, 43–63.

Maume, Patrick. 'Burke in Belfast: Thomas MacKnight, Gladstone and liberal unionism', in D. G. Boyce and Alan O'Day (ed.), *Gladstone and Ireland: politics, religion and nationality in the Victorian age*, 162–85. London: Palgrave Macmillan, 2010.

Meenan, James. *Centenary history of the Literary and Historical Society of University College Dublin 1855–1955.* Dublin: A & A Farmar, 2005 (revised edition, ed. Frank Callanan; originally published 1955).

Messenger, Betty. *Picking up the linen threads; a study in industrial folklore.* Austin: University of Texas Press, 1978.

Milligan, Alice. *A royal democrat.* London: Simpkin Marshall, 1890.

Milligan, Alice. *Life of Theobald Wolfe Tone.* Belfast: J. W. Boyd, 1898.

Milligan, Alice. *Poems*, edited by Henry Mangan. Dublin: M. H. Gill, 1954.

Milligan, Seaton, and Alice Milligan. *Glimpses of Erin.* London: Marcus Ward and Co., 1888.

Mitchell, Arthur. *Revolutionary government in Ireland: Dáil Éireann 1919–22.* Dublin: Gill and Macmillan, 1995.

Mitchell, Billy. 'Hobson's choice', *Fourthwrite* no. 2, summer 2000.

Moody, T. W. *Davitt and Irish revolution.* Oxford: Clarendon Press, 1981.

Moody T. W., and J. C. Beckett. *Queen's Belfast, 1845–1949: the history of a university* (2 vols; vol. i). London: Faber and Faber, 1959.

Morgan, Austen. *James Connolly: a political biography.* Manchester: Manchester University Press, 1988.

Morgan, Austen. *Labour and partition: the Belfast working class 1905–23.* London: Pluto Press, 1991.

Morris, Catherine. 'In the enemy's camp: Alice Milligan and *fin de siècle* Belfast', in Nicholas Allen and Aaron Kelly (ed.), *Cities of Belfast*, 62–73. Dublin: Four Courts, 2003.

Morris, Catherine. 'Becoming Irish? Alice Milligan and the revival', *Irish University Review* xxxiii, no. 1, 2003, 79–98.

Morris, Catherine. 'Alice Milligan: republican tableaux and the revival', *Field Day Review* vi, 2010, 132–65.

Morris, Catherine. *Alice Milligan and the Irish cultural revival*. Dublin: NLI, 2010.

Morris, Catherine. *Alice Milligan and the Irish cultural revival*. Dublin: Four Courts, 2012.

Mulcahy, Risteárd. *Richard Mulcahy (1886–1971); a family memoir*. Dublin: Aurelian Press, 1999.

Mullin, J. E., and T. H. Mullin. *Roots in Ulster soil*. Belfast: B. N. L. Printing, 1967.

Murphy, Desmond. *Derry, Donegal and modern Ulster, 1790–1921*. Derry: Aileach Press, 1981.

Newby, A. G. '"Scotia major and Scotia minor": Ireland and the birth of the Scottish land agitation, 1878–82', *Irish Economic and Social History* xxxi, 2004, 23–40

Nevin, Donal (ed.). *Trade union century*. Cork: Mercier Press, 1994.

Nixon, K. 'Interviews with Brookeborough', *Sunday News*, January–February 1968.

Ó Braonáin, Cathal, G. O'Neill, Peter McBrien and Arthur Clery. *Poets of the insurrection*. Dublin and London: Maunsel and Company, 1918 (originally published as a four-part series in *Studies*).

O'Brien, Máire Cruise. *The same age as the state*. Dublin: O'Brien Press, 2003.

O'Brien, William. *An olive branch in Ireland, and its history*. Dublin: Macmillan, 1910.

Ó Broin, León. *Revolutionary underground: the story of the Irish Republican Brotherhood 1858–1924*. Totowa, NJ: Rowman and Littlefield, 1976.

Ó Broin, León. *No man's man: a biographical memoir of Joseph Brennan, civil servant and first governor of the Central Bank*. Dublin: Institute of Public Administration, 1982.

Ó Broin, León. *Protestant nationalists in revolutionary Ireland: the Stopford connection*. Dublin: Gill and Macmillan, 1985.

O'Byrne, Cathal. *As I roved out: in Belfast and district*. Belfast: E. P. Publishing, 1946 (reprinted 1970).

O'Connor, Anne V. 'The revolution in girls' secondary education in Ireland, 1860–1910', in Mary Cullen (ed.), *Girls don't do honours: Irish women in education in the 19th and 20th centuries*, 31–54. Dublin: Women's Education Bureau, 1987.

O'Connor, Emmet. *A labour history of Ireland, 1824–1960*. Dublin: Gill and Macmillan, 1992.

O'Donnell, Peadar. *Storm: a story of the Irish war*. Dublin: Talbot Press, 1925.

O'Donnell, Peadar. *Islanders*. London: Jonathan Cape, 1927.

O'Donnell, Peadar. *Adrigoole*. London: Jonathan Cape, 1929.

O'Donnell, Peadar. *The knife*. Dublin: Irish Humanities Centre, and London: Jonathan Cape, 1930.

O'Donnell, Peadar. *The gates flew open*. London: Jonathan Cape, 1932.

O'Donnell, Peadar. *On the edge of the stream*. London: Jonathan Cape, 1934.

O'Donnell, Peadar. *Salud! An Irishman in Spain*. London: Methuen, 1937.

O'Donnell, Peadar. *The big windows*. London: Jonathan Cape, 1955.

O'Donnell, Peadar. *There will be another day*. Dublin: Dolmen Press, 1963.

O'Duffy, Eoin. *Crusade in Spain*. Dublin: Browne and Nolan, 1938.

O'Flaherty, Eamon. 'Aiken: gunman and statesman', *History Ireland* xv, no. 1, January–February 2007, 54–5.

Ó Gadhra, Nollaig. 'Earnán de Blaghd, 1889–1975', *Éire–Ireland* xi, no. 3, 1976, 93–105.

Ó Gráda, Cormac. *Ireland: a new economic history 1780–1939*. Oxford: Clarendon Press, 1994.

O'Halpin, Eunan. *Defending Ireland: the Irish state and its enemies since 1922*. Oxford: Oxford University Press, 1999.

O'Kelly, Denis J. *Salute to the Gardai: a story of struggle and achievement, 1922–1958*. Dublin: Parkside Press, 1958.

O'Leary, Philip. *Gaelic prose in the Irish Free State, 1922–1939*. University Park, PA and Dublin: University of Pennsylvania Press and UCD Press, 2004.

O'Neill, Terence. *The autobiography of Terence O'Neill*. London: Rupert Hart-Davis, 1972.

O'Riordan, Michael (ed.). *James Connolly: collected works* (2 vols, vol. i). Dublin: New Books Publications, 1987.

O'Shannon, Cathal. 'Winifred Carney—a link with Easter week', *Torch* (Dublin), 27 November, 4 December 1943.

O'Shannon, Cathal. 'Herbert Moore Pim—an appreciation', *Irish Times*, 15 May 1950.

O'Shiel, Kevin. *The making of a republic*. Dublin: Talbot Press, 1920.

O'Shiel, Kevin. 'Memories of my lifetime', *Irish Times*, 11–22 November 1966.

O'Shiel, Kevin. 'The times that were in it'. Unpublished memoir.

O'Shiel, Kevin, and T. O'Brien. *The land problem in Ireland and its settlement*. Presented at the Congress on Agrarian Law, Florence, 1954.

Ó Snodaigh, Pádraig. *Two godfathers of revisionism: 1916 in the revisionist canon*. Dublin: Fulcrum Press, 1991.

Oram, Hugh. *The newspaper book: a history of newspapers in Ireland 1649–1983*. Dublin: MO Books, 1983.

Patterson, Henry. 'Independent Orangeism and class conflict in Edwardian Belfast: a reinterpretation', *Proceedings of the Royal Irish Academy* 80C, 1980, 1–27.

Patterson, Henry. *Class conflict and sectarianism: the Protestant working class and the Belfast labour movement 1868–1920*. Belfast: Blackstaff Press, 1980.

Phoenix, Eamonn. 'Introduction and calendar of the Cahir Healy papers'. Unpublished MA dissertation, QUB, 1978.

Phoenix, Eamonn. 'Nationalist father figure', *Irish Times*, 9 June 1982.

Phoenix, Eamonn. *Northern nationalism: nationalist politics, partition and the Catholic minority in Northern Ireland 1890–1940*. Belfast: Ulster Historical Foundation, 1994.

Phoenix, Eamonn (ed.). *A century of northern life: the* Irish News *and one hundred years of Ulster history 1890s–1990s*. Belfast: Ulster Historical Foundation, 1995.

Phoenix, Eamonn. 'Cahir Healy (1877–1970) northern nationalist leader', *Clogher Record* xviii, no. 1, 2003, 32–52.

Pim, Herbert. ('H. M. P.'), *A vampire of souls*. London: A. Gardner, 1905.

Pim, Herbert. ('Herbert Pym'), *The man with thirty lives*. London: Everett and Company, 1909.

Pim, Herbert. *The pessimist: a confession*. London: David Nutt, 1914.

Pim, Herbert. *Selected poems*. Dublin: Candle Press, 1917.

Pim, Herbert. *Unknown immortals in the northern city of success*. Dublin and London: Talbot Press and T. Fisher Unwin, 1917.

Pim, Herbert. *Unconquerable Ulster*. Belfast: Carswell, 1919.

Pim, Herbert. *A short history of Celtic philosophy*. Dundalk and London: W. Tempest/Dundalgan Press and T. N. Foulis, 1920.

Pim, Herbert. 'Adventures in the land of Sinn Féin', memoir, serialised in *Plain English*, 10 July–25 September 1920.

Pim, Herbert. *Songs from an Ulster valley*. London: Grant Richards, 1920.

Pim, Herbert. *New poems and a preface*. London: Burnes, Oates and Washbourne, 1927.

Pim, Herbert. *French love*. London: 1927.

Rafter, Kevin. *The Clann: the story of Clann na Poblachta*. Cork: Mercier Press, 1996.

Rankin, J. Frederick. *Down cathedral: the church of Saint Patrick of Down*. Belfast: Ulster Historical Foundation, 1997.

Rankin, Kathleen. *The linen houses of the Lagan valley*. Belfast: Ulster Historical Foundation, 2002.

Reade, Charles A. *The cabinet of Irish literature. Selections from the works of the chief poets, orators, and prose writers of Ireland: with biographical sketches and literary notices* (vol. i). London: Blackie and Son, 1880.

Regan, John M. *The Irish counter-revolution 1921–1936: treatyite politics and settlement in independent Ireland*. Dublin: Gill and Macmillan, 1999.

Richardson, David. 'The career of John Miller Andrews 1871–1956'. Unpublished PhD thesis, QUB, 1998.

Rosenbaum, Simon (ed.). *Against home rule: the case for the union*. London: Frederick Warne, 1912.

Rosenberg, J. L. 'The 1941 mission of Frank Aiken to the United States: an American perspective', *Irish Historical Studies* xxii, 1980–81, 162–77.

Ross, John. *The years of my pilgrimage: random reminiscences*. London: Edward Arnold, 1924.

Ross, John. *Pilgrim scrip: more random reminiscences*. London: H. Jenkins, 1927.

Ross, John. *Essays and addresses*. London: Edward Arnold, 1930.

Russell, George ('Æ'). *Homeward: songs by the way* (3rd ed.). London: Joseph Lane, 1901 (originally published 1894).

Russell, George ('Æ'). *The divine vision and other poems*. London and New York: Macmillan, 1904.

Russell, George ('Æ'). *The mask of Apollo and other stories*. Dublin and London: Whaley and Company and Macmillan, 1905.

Russell, George ('Æ'). *The earth breath and other poems* (2nd ed.). London: Joseph Lane, 1906 (originally published 1897).

Russell, George ('Æ'). *Deirdre*. London: Maunsel, 1907.

Russell, George ('Æ'). *Co-operation and nationality: a guide for rural reformers from this to the next generation*. London: Maunsel, 1912.

Russell, George ('Æ'). *The national being: some thoughts on an Irish polity*. London: Maunsel, 1916.

Russell, George ('Æ'). *The candle of vision*. London: Macmillan, 1918.

Russell, George ('Æ'). *The interpreters*. London: Macmillan, 1922.

Russell, George ('Æ'). *Song and its fountains*. London: Macmillan, 1932.

Russell, George ('Æ'). *The avatars: a futurist fantasy*. London: Macmillan, 1933.

Russell, Thomas W. *Ireland and the empire: a review 1800–1900*. London: G. Richards, 1901.

Ryan, Desmond. *The rising: the complete story of Easter week*. Dublin: Golden Eagle Books, 1949.

Savage, D. C. 'The origins of the Ulster Unionist Party, 1885–6', *Irish Historical Studies* xii, March 1961, 189.

Shannon, Catherine. *Arthur J. Balfour and Ireland: 1874–1922*. Washington, DC: Catholic University of America Press, 1988.

Shearman, Hugh. *Not an inch: a study of Northern Ireland and Lord Craigavon*. London: Faber and Faber, 1942.

Skelly, J. M. *Irish diplomacy at the United Nations, 1945–1965: national interests and the international order*. Dublin: Irish Academic Press, 1997.

Skinner, Liam C. *Politicians by accident*. Dublin: Metropolitan Publishing Company, 1946.

Smith, George Hill-. *The north-east Bar. A sketch, historical and reminiscent*. Belfast: Belfast Newsletter, 1910.

Smith, George Hill-. *Sketch of 'The supreme court of judicature of Northern Ireland', from its establishment under the Imperial Act of 1920 down to the present day*. Belfast: Northern Whig, 1926.

Snodgrass, Len. *Armour's meeting house: the first hundred years, 1885–1985*. Ballymoney: Trinity Presbyterian Church, 1985.

Solden, Norbert C. *Women in the British Trade Union 1874–1976*. Dublin: Gill and Macmillan, 1978.

Staunton, Enda. *The nationalists of Northern Ireland 1918–1973*. Dublin: Columba Press, 2001.

Stewart, A. T. Q. *The Ulster crisis: resistance to home rule, 1912–14*. London: Faber and Faber, 1967.

Stewart, A. T. Q. *Edward Carson*. Dublin: Gill and Macmillan, 1981.

Stradling, Robert. *The Irish and the Spanish civil war 1936–39: crusades in conflict*. Manchester: Mandolin (Manchester University Press), 1999.

Sullivan, A. M. *New Ireland: political sketches and personal reminiscences of thirty years of Irish public life* (2 vols). Glasgow and London: Sampson, Low and Company, 1877.

Summerfield, Henry. *That myriad-minded man: a biography of George William Russell 'Æ', 1867–1935*. Gerrards Cross and Totowa, NJ: Colin Smythe and Rowman and Littlefield, 1975.

Townshend, Charles. *Political violence in Ireland: government and resistance since 1848*. Oxford: Clarendon Press, 1983.

Thompson, Hugh C. *A history of Moneyrea*. Belfast: Hugh C. Thompson, 1985.

Thompson, Hugh C. 'Rev. Richard Lyttle: a home rule Protestant', *Familia* ii, no. 2, 1986, 95–100.

Thornley, David. *Isaac Butt and home rule*. London: Macgibbon and Kee, 1964.

Tierney, Michael. *Eoin MacNeill: scholar and man of action, 1867–1945*, edited by F. X. Martin. Oxford: Clarendon Press, 1980.

Trimble, Joan. 'A nineteenth century printer: William Trimble of Enniskillen and his newspaper, *The Impartial Reporter*', *Long Room* no. 40, 1995, 34–40.

Trimble, William Copeland. *Garlands from Lough Erne*. Enniskillen: Impartial Reporter, 1917.

Trimble, William Copeland. *The history of Enniskillen with reference to some manors in Co. Fermanagh, and other local subjects* (3 vols). Enniskillen: William Trimble, 1919–21.

Trimble, William Egbert. *Memoir of the Trimble family, with the lineage of some allied families*. Enniskillen: Published privately, 1949.

Ulster Scots Community Network, *The Ulster Volunteer Force* (n.d. [2013?]), www.ulster-scots.com/uploads/901740969819.PDF; accessed 11 August 2015.

Unterecker, John (ed.). *Yeats and Patrick McCartan: a Fenian friendship*. Dublin: Dolmen Press, 1967.

Urquhart, Diane. *Women in Ulster politics, 1890–1940: a history not yet told*. Dublin: Irish Academic Press, 2000.

Urquhart, Diane. 'An articulate and definite cry for political freedom: the Ulster suffrage movement', *Women's History Review* xi, no. 2, 2002, 273–92.

Valiulis, Maryann Gialanella. *Portrait of a revolutionary: General Richard Mulcahy and the founding of the Irish Free State.* Lexington: University Press of Kentucky, 1992.

Walker, Brian M. *Ulster politics: the formative years, 1868–86.* Belfast: Ulster Historical Foundation, 1989.

Wallace, Henry. 'Æ: a prophet out of an ancient age', *Colby Quarterly* iv, no. 2, May 1955, 28–31.

Walsh, Liam. 'General Eoin O'Duffy—his life and battles'. Unpublished MS, NLI, n.d.

Ward, Margaret. *Unmanageable revolutionaries: women and Irish nationalism.* London: Pluto Press, 1983.

Welch, Robert. *The Abbey Theatre 1899–1999: form and pressure.* Oxford: Oxford University Press, 2003 (originally published 1999).

West, Trevor. *Horace Plunkett: co-operation and politics, an Irish biography.* Gerrards Cross: Colin Smythe, 1986.

White, J. R. *Misfit: an autobiography.* London: Jonathan Cape, 1930.

Whitford, F. J. 'Joseph Devlin, Ulsterman and Irishman'. Unpublished MA thesis, University of London, 1959.

Williams, T. D. 'Irish foreign policy, 1949–69', in J. J. Lee (ed.), *Ireland 1945–70),* 136–51. Dublin: Gill and Macmillan, 1979.

Williams, Raymond. *The country and the city.* New York: Oxford University Press, 1973.

Wilson, Anthony M. *Saint Patrick's town: a history of Downpatrick and the barony of Lecale.* Belfast: Isabella Press, 1995.

Woggon, Helga. *Silent radical, Winifred Carney 1887–1943: a reconstruction of her biography.* Studies in Irish Labour History 6. Dublin: Irish Labour History Society and SIPTU, 2000.

Workman, Clark (1928) Ltd. *Shipbuilding at Belfast 1880–1933.* London: Cheltenham, 1935.

Young, Robert M. *Belfast and the province of Ulster in the 20th century: contemporary biographies.* Brighton: W. T. Pike and Company, 1909.

Picture credits

163   Bulmer Hobson; photograph *c.* 1914–16; Hobson Papers, NLI Ms 13,174(7), © National Library of Ireland.

172   Samuel Keightley; photograph *c.* 1912; courtesy of Charles Rosenfield.

176   Richard Lyttle; photograph, reproduced in *History and album of the Irish Race Convention...Dublin September 1896* (Sealy, Bryers and Walker, 1897).

180   Sean MacEntee; detail from photograph, June 1938, Irish Cabinet; UCDA P150/2534, © UCD School of History and Archives.

190   Thomas MacKnight; photograph, reproduced as frontispiece to *Political Progress in the Nineteenth Century* by Thomas MacKnight, revised and completed by C.C. Osborne (Linscott Publishing Company, 1902); courtesy of Patrick Maume.

199   Eoin MacNeill; photograph by Keogh Brothers Ltd, *c.* 1914–23; Keogh Collection NLI KE77, © National Library of Ireland.

211   Patrick McCartan; detail from photograph *c.* 1919–20, taken in USA; Republican Photographs Collection, NLI NPA RPH6, © National Library of Ireland.

215   Timothy McCarthy; photograph in *Irish News*, 2 January 1929; NLI 9A 6323, © National Library of Ireland.

219   Denis McCullough; photograph from passport issued in 1922; UCDA P120/72, © UCD School of History and Archives.

222   Alice Milligan; detail from photograph by Seumas McManus *c.* 1896.

226   Right Hon. Thomas Moles P.C., M.P; black and white photograph; ARMCM.82.2012.512, © Armagh County Museum Collection; reproduced with permission.

230   Hugh de Fellenberg Montgomery; photograph; courtesy of the Lowry family, Blessingbourne Estate, Co. Tyrone.

234   Peadar O'Donnell; photograph; GGra4, Civil War Collection, © Mercier Press Photographic Archive.

238   Eoin O'Duffy, photograph by Lafayette Ltd, 1934; UCDA, LA30/PH/412, Tierney/MacNeill Photographs Collection, © UCD School of History and Archives.

244   Kevin O'Shiel; photograph *c.* mid 1950s; courtesy of Eda Sagarra, MRIA.

247   Herbert Pim; photograph *c.* 1910–20; Irish Personalities Photographic Collection, NLI NPA PERS67, © National Library of Ireland.

251   William Pirrie; photograph, 1911; Science and Society Picture Library, 90764604, © Getty Images.

255   John Ross; portrait photograph from *The years of my pilgrimage* by Sir John Ross (Edward Arnold & Co., 1924); courtesy of the Royal Irish Academy.

258   George Russell ('Æ'); photograph by Zlata Llamas, *c.* 1925–30; Photography Collections, 31.993, gift of Ananda K. Coomaraswamy, © Boston Museum of Fine Arts.

270   Thomas Russell; photograph by (John) Benjamin Stone, 1900; Photographs Collection, NPG 44945, © National Portrait Gallery, London.

274   Edward Saunderson; photograph by James Russell and Sons, 1891; Photographs Collection, NPG 22349, © National Portrait Gallery, London.

281   Thomas Sinclair; portrait by Henrietta Rae, courtesy of the Naughton Gallery, Collection of Queen's University Belfast.

285   Thomas Sloan; photograph by (John) Benjamin Stone, 1903; Photographs Collection, NPG 74792, © National Portrait Gallery, London.

292   Charles Vane-Tempest Stewart; bromide print by (Mary) Olive Edis, *c.* 1910s; Photographs Collection, NPG 15466, © National Portrait Gallery, London.

295   Isabella Tod; photograph; Collection Ulster Museum, © National Museums Northern Ireland.

299   William Copeland Trimble; photograph, *c.*1912; courtesy of Joanna McVey.

302   William Walker; photograph; Walker Papers, © Linen Hall Library; reproduced with permission.

308   Robert Wallace; Photographic postcard *c.* 1912; Collection Ulster Museum, BELUM.W2011.1280, © National Museums Northern Ireland.

315   Jack White; photograph, reproduced as frontispiece to *Misfit: an autobiography* (Jonathan Cape, 1930).

Index

Irish Decorative Art Association 51
Irish Ecclesiastical Record 201
Irish Folk Song Society 51
Irish Free State 55, 59, 130, 153, 245
Irish Freedom 55, 167, 212, 262
Irish Historical Studies 209
Irish Homestead 260, 261-5
Irish Independent 200
Irish Industries Association 223
Irish Landowners Convention (ILC) 148,
    149-50, 232
Irish language 66-8, 200-2, 205, 206-7
Irish Loyal and Patriotic Union (ILPU) 147, 232
Irish Manuscripts Commission 205
Irish Nation League 20, 245
Irish Nation and the Peasant 166
Irish National Federation 133
Irish National Land League 140-1
Irish National League 133
Irish National Theatre Society 260
Irish News 132, 133, 178, 197, 216, 217, 218
Irish Parliamentary Party (IPP) 12, 216, 217
Irish Peasant Home Industries 51
Irish People 216
Irish Press 70
Irish Protestant 128, 129, 130, 286
Irish Republican Army (IRA) 21, 80
    Aiken and 28-9, 30
    Craig and 118, 119
    O'Donnell and 235, 236-7
    O'Duffy and 5, 239-40
Irish Republican Brotherhood (IRB) 9, 54-5, 153
    Hobson and 165-7
    McCartan and 13, 212
    McCullough and 219-20
    MacNeill and 202, 203-4
    Volunteers and 55-6
Irish Republican Prisoners' Dependants Fund 92
Irish Review 262
Irish Rosary 237
Irish Statesman 265-7
Irish Textile Workers' Union 91, 144
Irish Times 70, 232
Irish Trade Union Congress (ITUC) 143, 144,
    303, 304, 306
Irish Transport and General Workers' Union
    (ITGWU) 91, 92, 136, 235, 262, 306
Irish Volunteer (newspaper) 203, 248
Irish Volunteers 18, 28, 55-6, 181, 201
    McCartan and 212
    McCullough and 220
    MacNeill and 201, 202-3
    O'Duffy and 239
    White and 316-17
Irish Women's Association 70, 178, 223
Irish Women's Temperance Union 85
Irish Workers' League 317
Irish-American Alliance 134
Irishman 248, 249
Isaacs, Sir Rufus 98

Johnson, Thomas 204
Johnston, Anna *see* Carbery, Ethna
Johnston, Charles 259
Johnston, Robert 87, 88
Johnston, William 6, 8, 84, 193, 259
Joyce, James 260-1

Keating, Geoffrey 207
Keatley, Samuel and Catherine 172
Keightley, Sir Samuel Robert 172-4
Kettle, Thomas 280, 316
Kingan, John 282
Kingan, Samuel 282
Kirwan, Martin Waters 140
Knox, E. F. Vesey 256

Labour Representation Committee (LRC)
    304, 305
Ladies' Collegiate School, Belfast 84
Ladies' National Association 296
Ladies' Temperance Union 85
Lalor, James Fintan 166
Land Act (1870) 193, 195
Land Act (1881) 10, 149, 196, 231, 300
Land Act (1903) 256
Land Act (1904) 256
Land Act amendments 148
land agitation 10, 245, 256-7
Land Commission 246
land courts 245
Land League 10, 300
land reform 14, 140-1, 149, 300, 306
    compulsory purchase 173, 178, 271-2
Larkin, James 9, 143, 160, 262, 289, 306, 317
    Irish Citizen Army and 316
Lavery, Sir John 138
Law, Andrew Bonar 3, 16, 102, 110, 294
Lawless, John 9
League Against Poverty 169
League of Nations 33
League for Social Justice 169
Lemass, Seán 32, 33, 35, 69, 183
    MacEntee and 185-6, 187-8
Leslie, T. E. Cliffe 139
liberalism 7-9
Lloyd George, David 102, 103, 105, 118, 136,
    217, 232-3
Loans Guarantee Acts (1922-36) 121
Londonderry, Charles Stewart Vane-Tempest
    Stewart, 6th Marquis of 292-4
Londonderry, George Henry Robert Charles
    William Vane-Tempest, 5th Marquis
    of 292
Londonderry, Theresa Vane-Tempest Stewart,
    Marchioness of 294
Long, Walter 99, 115, 117, 294
Lucas, Reginald 279
Lynch, Jack 35-6, 188
Lynch, Liam 29
Lynn, Kathleen 56
Lyttle Memorial School 178